Advance praise for

THE PROGRESSIVE LEGACY

"This is no nostalgic journey into the abstractions and high rhetoric of the past. This book portrays and honors the vision of a school and of a movement that are powerfully alive in the present and reach powerfully into the future...."

David Mallery, Director of Professional Development,
National Association of Independent Schools

"This superb book shows that over the last century Francis W. Parker has been more than just another fine private school. It represents the flowering of one of the most important social movements in American history.... The richness of the Parker experiment is vividly conveyed here by one of the school's all-time greatest teachers in a story of theory, practice, and people that will be of interest to anyone who cares about education."

Jonathan Alter '75, Newsweek Magazine columnist;
Contributing Correspondent for NBC News

"In an historical moment when educators once again discuss academic standards, moral character, the nature of learning, and the fundamental function and mission of the public school, comes this magnificent narrative of one of America's boldest educational experiments. Marie Kirchner Stone's chronicle... ought to be read by anyone who even occasionally reflects on the nature and purpose of education and what it takes to construct a truly fine school."

Thomas J. Cottle '55, Professor of Education, Boston University

"Francis W. Parker, in the early '60s, had the finest teachers I have ever encountered. It is a great school."

David Mamet '65, Playwright and Author

THE PROGRESSIVE LEGACY

HISTORY OF
SCHOOLS &
SCHOOLING

Alan R. Sadovnik and Susan F. Semel
General Editors

Vol. 1

PETER LANG
New York • Washington, D.C./Baltimore • Bern
Frankfurt am Main • Berlin • Brussels • Vienna • Oxford

Marie Kirchner Stone

THE PROGRESSIVE LEGACY

Chicago's Francis W. Parker School
(1901-2001)

PETER LANG
New York • Washington, D.C./Baltimore • Bern
Frankfurt am Main • Berlin • Brussels • Vienna • Oxford

LIBRARY OF CONGRESS CATALOGING-IN-PUBLICATION DATA

Stone, Marie Kirchner.
The progressive legacy: Chicago's Francis W. Parker
School (1901-2001) / Marie Kirchner Stone.
p. cm. —— (History of schools and schooling; v. 1)
Includes bibliographical references (p.   ) and index.
1. Francis W. Parker School (Chicago, Ill.). 2. Progressive education——
Illinois——Chicago——Case studies. 1. Title. 11. Series.
LD7501.C426 S86   373.773'11——dc20   96-042960
ISBN 0-8204-3396-9
ISSN 1089-0678

DIE DEUTSCHE BIBLIOTHEK-CIP-EINHEITSAUFNAHME

Stone, Marie Kirchner:
The progressive legacy: Chicago's Francis W. Parker
School (1901-2001) / Marie Kirchner Stone.
—New York; Washington, D.C./Baltimore; Bern;
Frankfurt am Main; Berlin; Brussels; Vienna; Oxford: Lang.
(History of schools and schooling; Vol. 1)
ISBN 0-8204-3396-9

Cover design by Lisa Dillon
Cover layout and cover photo by Roger Gleason

The paper in this book meets the guidelines for permanence and durability
of the Committee on Production Guidelines for Book Longevity
of the Council of Library Resources.

Printed in the United States of America

To the memory of my mother,
who always thought I didn't do enough

To my colleagues, who always thought I did too much

And to my advisees and students from 1966 to 1998,
whom I pushed to do more

Table of Contents

Preface

Chicago's Francis W. Parker School was conceived from an educator's struggle with the public sector of education. Francis Parker, the school's founding president, devoted his entire career to implementing education experiments that would transform public schools. To achieve this education revolution, he waged battle after battle against public school officials but with little success. Believing he could not triumph in the public sector, he finally accepted the offer of the farsighted, straight-shooting, controversial heiress of the McCormick fortune. For several years, Anita McCormick Blaine had invited Parker to design a private school for Chicago's North Side, suggesting that a private school could teach students and train teachers to carry forth Parker's education revolution as well as a public school. The centerpiece of Parker and Blaine's experiment was a private school that enrolled all creeds, races, nationalities, and economic groups as in the public sector. To this enterprise, Anita McCormick Blaine contributed millions of dollars in financial aid for a diverse student body and for the construction of a school on the city block she purchased near Lincoln Park.

From the onset, Chicago's Francis W. Parker School became one of America's premier experiments in new education, a showcase for curious educators worldwide. Throughout the school's hundred-year history, these observers, the returning alumni, the vintage teachers, and the current students rarely, if ever, asked the question, "Is the Parker School a good school?" The answer was taken for granted. The question was always, "Has the Parker School remained a progressive school?" This question haunted the halls like Anita McCormick Blaine's ghost and provided the framework for this centennial history, which is organized into four historic eras from 1901 to 2001. Each era is judged by those progressive principles identified and defined by Francis Parker and John Dewey.

I wrote the history for two audiences, alumni and educators, and therefore divided it into two sections: theory and practice. Unsure that the alumni would be interested in the theory underpinning their school, I thought they would begin by reading *Part Two: The School's Practice* and that educators might wish to begin with *Part One: The School's Theory*.

Part One: The School's Theory focuses on the era before the Parker School was built. Chapter 1, "The Evolution of Progressive Education," defines progressive education and traces its evolution. The chapter explains the sources of the theory of progressive education and describes the changes.

Chapter 2, "Pedagogue, Philanthropist, and Philosopher," presents a biographical sketch of Francis Wayland Parker, the Father of Progressive Education, upon whose philosophy and principles the school is founded. The chapter continues with a portrait of the philanthropist, Anita McCormick Blaine, who founded and financed the school and devised a structure to ensure that progressive principles would prevail. A third profile features John Dewey, the Philosopher of Progressive Education. Unlike Francis Parker, the practitioner, Dewey was a world-renowned theoretician who defined progressive education in his prolific writings on the subject.

Chapter 3, "The European Intellectual Genealogy of Francis Parker," traces Parker's educational philosophy and principles, which were not original but instead were a synthesis of his life's experiences and the ideas of the European pedagogues and philosophers he studied during his travels in Germany.

Chapter 4, "Francis Parker Introduces New Education in American Schools," tells how Francis Parker broke the lock step of traditional education in America as superintendent in Quincy, Massachusetts, where he introduced new content and new methods, and at the Cook County Normal School in Englewood, Illinois, where he developed his doctrine of concentration and correlation. In Quincy, Parker earned national recognition, and at the Cook County Normal School, he gained international prominence. Parker then left the public sector and became president of the new private Chicago Institute Academic and Pedagogic, the forerunner of the School of Education at the University of Chicago, where Francis Parker and John Dewey collaborated as colleagues until Parker's death, and of the Francis W. Parker School. Blaine helped to found and finance all three schools. Section One ends with Chapter 5, "The Parker School Heritage: Second-Generation Schools," which describes the seven schools fashioned in the image of Chicago's Francis W. Parker School by Parker alumni or former teachers.

Part Two: The Practice covers one hundred years of progressive education at the Francis W. Parker School and includes Chapter 6, "The Pioneering Years (1901-1935)," Chapter 7, "The Stabilizing Years (1935-1965)," Chapter 8, "Challenges to Progressive Education (1965-1995)," and Chapter 9, "Toward the New Millennium (1995-2001)." In Chapter 9, Principal Donald Monroe describes the school during his five years as principal and projects the school's plans for the future. Each of these chapters opens with a historical perspective of the era to show how "the needs of society" changed the nature of the school; continues with the governance of the school by the Boards of Trustees, the Educational Council, and the principals; and concludes with a spotlight on the school's central concerns: the curriculum, the faculty, and the students.

During my thirty years at the school, I was a teacher, Chairman of the English Department, Dean of Students, College Counselor, Curriculum Coordinator, an advisor to high school students, a nonvoting member of the Board of Trustees for more than a decade, and several times a member of the Education Council. Deeply steeped in the Parker School's progressive legacy, I edited *Between Home and Community* (1976) to commemorate the school's seventy-fifth anniversary. To prepare this centennial history, I researched documents in the Parker archives, the Chicago Historical Society, and the Wisconsin Historical Society. I also interviewed students, teachers, alumni, principals, and trustees.

I relied on help from a community of alumni, colleagues, students, and friends. I especially want to thank my advisee, Barbara Goodman Manilow '78, for arranging a Crown Foundation grant for the preparation of the manuscript and David Heller '49 for his essential financial support. When organizing and editing, I was expertly assisted by editor and writer Anne Basye and writer Bill Mahin.

Principals Jack Ellison, William Drennan Geer Jr., and Donald Monroe gave their perspectives on those eras when they governed the school, and Professor Gerald Gutek, who taught educational foundations at Loyola University, gave advice on Francis Parker's intellectual genealogy. Colleagues Bernard Markwell, Maryanne Kalin-Miller, and Catherine Chambers Haskins offered their interpretations, memories, and advice. My colleague Roger Gleason took the photograph for the cover, and Andrew Kaplan searched the Parker archives for photos for the book.

A former student, Lorraine Anderson, read every Parker School newspaper and yearbook in preparation for the three profiles of the student body, and researcher Paula Perkins examined and organized the minutes of the Board of Trustees according to issues. All but one of the living board chairpersons completed a survey and wrote an interpretation of the period when they served. The faculty who taught at Parker for more than twenty years completed a questionnaire about their careers. Several students in my 1996 Non-Fiction Writing class also interviewed and wrote biographies of vintage teachers. Gilbert Harrison's *A Timeless Affair* was a substantial source of inspiration on the life of Anita McCormick Blaine.

Without the able assistance of school librarian Anne Duncan and secretaries Laurel Carlson and Cokey Evans, many questions would have remained unanswered. The help of Henrietta Adarna in the management of materials was an invaluable contribution to the production of this history. I take great pleasure in sharing the school's story, which I had the privilege of living from 1966 to 1998.

Part One

The School's Theory

Chapter 1

The Evolution of Progressive Education

Francis W. Parker School: An Experiment in Progressive Education

At the turn of the century, the opening of Chicago's Francis W. Parker School, a coeducational day school, represented a momentous occasion for education but was not celebrated in Chicago. The school was an isolated institution without support in the city. It had neither a religious affiliation, like the growing number of Chicago's Catholic schools, nor was it a feeder school to a university, like many of the nation's independent schools. Parker School did not cater to an elite population who could afford private schools like the Boys' or Girls' Chicago Latin Schools, established thirteen years earlier and within walking distance from the Parker School. The vision for this twentieth century elementary and secondary school was different from traditional schools. Its purposes were to educate a citizenry for a democracy in a rising industrial city with an increasingly diverse immigrant population and to attempt to develop a science of education.

On October 7, 1901, the progressive experiment of the Francis W. Parker School began when 144 students from different economic levels, nationalities, and religions; a corps of thirteen experienced teachers and Principal Flora Cooke, all trained at the Cook County Normal School under Francis Parker; a generous benefactor, Anita McCormick Blaine; and the educational visionary Francis Wayland Parker walked through the door of the new two-story building, designed by architect James Gamble Rogers. The children, ages six to eighteen, filed into classrooms on Monday morning at 8:45, carrying with them, according to age level, paint clothes and paint boxes, paste cups, brushes, and general supplies. The school furnished glazes, woods, and writing, drawing, painting, and coloring paper. The Opening Notice informed families that parents would be involved in school activities and encouraged them to schedule every Friday in the fall, weather permitting, for a day excursion, joined by teacher trainees from the School of Education at the University of Chicago, which was staffed by Professors Parker and Dewey. The first excursion was a boat trip on the Chicago Harbor.

Chicago's Francis W. Parker School was among the earliest and the longest-sustained progressive school experiments in America. A diverse student body, emphasis on the pupil, "learning by doing," instruction based on experience, activity-centered learning, expression used for instruction, a place for the arts in the course of study, well-trained teachers, and parental involvement—these were some of the hallmarks of this new progressive school. No wonder Parker students were excited as they entered classes. At that very moment, their public school counterparts were beginning another humdrum day confined to the classroom, where they would read, memorize, and recite lessons little suited to their interests and needs. Francis Parker sarcastically remarked that the traditional education of their counterparts was measured "by the yard and weighed . . . by the pound."[1]

The Francis W. Parker School was part of a larger revolution in American education led by the Father of Progressive Education, Francis Parker, and the Philosopher of Progressive Education, John Dewey. In 1875, it was Francis Parker who waged the first battle of the revolution against traditional education in the schools of Quincy, Massachusetts, and he continued the war as principal of the Cook County Normal School in Englewood, Illinois. The fighting subsided somewhat when Parker transferred the experiment from the public sector to the private Chicago Institute Academic and Pedagogic in 1898, the new School of Education for teachers at the University of Chicago in 1900, and the Francis W. Parker School in 1901. While Francis Parker insisted that there was no "Parker method," the Francis W. Parker School was founded on a different set of educational principles: (1) a new definition of the child, (2) a broader definition of the school, (3) transformed school goals and purposes, (4) an integrated course of study, and (5) innovative instructional methods based on the new psychology and sociology.

Sources and Definition of Progressive Education

The authoritative historian of progressive education Lawrence Cremin placed the theoretical origins of progressive education in the 1890s, a decade he called "the great watershed in American history," when most fields of study, including education, came under the influence of the scientific revolution. Cremin credited two books on education—Francis Parker's *Talks on Pedagogics* (1894) and John Dewey's *The School and Society* (1899)—and two on psychology—Edward Thorndike's *Animal Intelligence* (1898) and William James's *Talks to Teachers on Psychology* (1899)—with revolutionizing educational thought.[2] Two other books by Dewey also defined progressive education: *My Pedagogical Creed* (1897) and *Democracy and Education* (1916). These books focused on two dominant progressive themes: (1) the goal of progressive schools is to create citizens for a democracy and (2) progressive education is a science enhanced by psychology and sociology. The texts also reformulated the nature of a school, the definition of curriculum and teaching, and the role of the student and learning.

In *Talks on Pedagogics* (1894), Parker was the first to formulate the foundations for a new education. In the first chapter, Parker placed the emphasis on "the child," stating that "the organism itself determines the external conditions of development" and should be studied as "we study all phenomena." As he explained, "In the past of education, attention has been directed too much to dead forms of thought . . . the sciences are a modern creation of man and have not yet reached the child."[3] He declared that the starting point of progressive education is the child, unlike traditional education, where the starting point is subject matter. Progressive educators were to create a new curriculum.

In the second chapter, "The Central Subjects of Study," Parker presented his only original doctrine of curriculum, the doctrine of concentration and correlation, which called for the unification of educative subjects into what he named central subjects. Parker did not believe that subjects should be taught as fragments or in isolation from each other but believed subjects should be unified based on Froebel's theory of unity and Herbart's theory of concentration (see Chapter 3). Parker defined the central subjects of study as "but the main branches of one subject, and that subject is creation." The most central of all subjects he called geography, but other central subjects included meteorology, geology, mineralogy, physics, and chemistry. Parker integrated all other subjects—literature, history, and art—into the central subject and organized them into units.[4] Traditional education, in

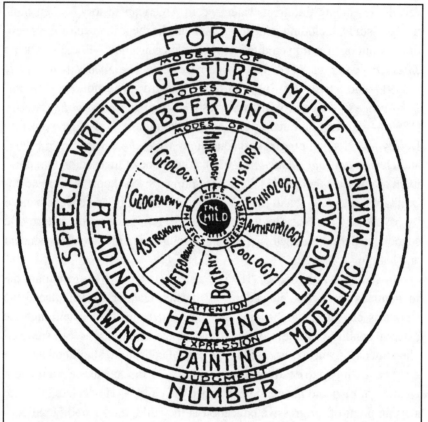

Figure 1.1
Original Diagram of Parker's Doctrine of Concentration and Correlation as Illustrated in *Talks on Pedagogics (1894)*
Parker's interpretation of the doctrine of concentration shows the relationship of a child's life to the school learning process. At the center is the child in his tripartite nature—mind, body, and spirit. The second circle, the environment in which the child lives naturally, is surrounded by ten central subjects of "creation." The third circle identifies the modes of attention which the child possesses and the school trains; the fourth circle identifies eight modes of expression, which are natural and learned behaviors. The outer circle identifies the modes of judgment, form and number, which permeate the child's life.

contrast, presented subjects in isolation and excluded the new disciplines. Parker drew his theory in a diagram of concentric circles to show the inter-relationship of life and learning (see Figure 1.1).

Parker also called for a new kind of instruction named quality teaching, which he equated with selection of the appropriate materials and the search for truth or the scientific method. He objected to quantity teaching, which he defined as "the textbook method, page learning, and percent examina-tions," which kept the students from "anything like the search for truth" and forced them to "go over," "go through," and "finish" the material. Traditional schools used the quantity teaching method, while progressive schools introduced quality teaching.

Several chapters of Parker's book explained new learning theories. Parker identified five revolutionary theories that were influenced by European pedagogues: (1) children learn through experience or by doing; (2) the whole child in his triple nature—body, mind, and spirit—must be educated; (3) expression is an essential element in the learning process; (4) learning numbers, language, and reading require a holistic process; and (5) children learn through attention and observation. Parker reasoned that the experience of the whole child provided the rationale for an activity-centered school. He therefore incorporated linguistic, dramatic, musical, manual, and physical expression as part of instruction. Children painted, sculpted, molded, sewed, and carved; they sang, wrote stories, acted in plays, danced, and played sports. These activities were integral to the learning process and became the handmaidens to learning abstract principles. For example, molding the Greek shoreline and forming mountains in clay taught pupils the geography of Greece. The performance of an activity increased the stu-dent's comprehension of the concept. Unlike progressive schools, tradi-tional schools omitted learning by doing and expression as part of the course of study and relied almost solely on reading and rote.

Parker transformed the child's learning to read from a fragmentary exercise to a holistic process. Instead of teaching children to read a letter, then a word, then a sentence, Parker went directly to the story. He made reading "subsidiary and auxiliary to the study of central subjects." Parker rejected the old hypothesis, which asserted that forms must be learned by themselves for use thereafter, in favor of the new hypothesis, which stated that each step in the development of reading-power must be taken under the immediate impulse of intrinsic thought.[5] Traditional schools dedicated a major percentage of the day to teaching reading in the fragmentary manner, and progressive schools used the holistic approach.

Historian Lawrence Cremin called *Talks on Pedagogics* (1894) a "watershed work within the field of education" because the book introduced the parameters of a new education that differentiated it from traditional education. The text originated as a series of presentations given at a Teacher's Retreat at Chautauqua Assembly in New York in 1891 and was repeated at the New York Teachers' Training College, the University of Minnesota, and the Cook County Normal School.

In many respects, John Dewey's *My Pedagogical Creed* (1897) was in agreement with Francis Parker's theoretical assumptions. In Dewey's first text on education, he asserted eighty pedagogical beliefs about education, school, the subject-matter of education, the nature of method, and the school and social progress. Dewey's main belief was that "education proceeds by the participation of the individual in the social consciousness of the race." He envisioned the school as a social institution and education as a social process. The subject matter of education, he thought to be "the social life of the child" and the goal of education, "the reconstruction of experience." Instructional method, he believed, should be active rather than passive. He concluded his creed by calling education "the fundamental method of social progress" (see Figure 1.2).[6]

Democratic Purpose for American Education

The attempt to create an education system to serve a democracy posed a challenge of great magnitude. Parker first introduced his philosophy of democracy in the last chapter of *Talks on Pedagogics* (1894), and Dewey amplified the theory in *The School and Society* (1899) and later developed it extensively in *Democracy and Education* (1916).

In the final two chapters of *Talks on Pedagogics*, "School Government and Moral Training," and "Democracy and Education," Parker ascribed to the school a moral and social function, a larger role than merely the teaching of the three R's. At the core of his definition of education was morality, because "education is the outworking of God's design into character"; "there is no separation of intellectual and moral training"; and "education consists wholly and entirely in the cultivation of the altruistic motive."[7] He

Figure 1.2
Major Points from Dewey's *My Pedagogical Creed* (1897)

Education

I believe that all education proceeds by the participation of the individual in the social consciousness of the race . . . [and] that this educational process has two sides—psychological and sociological.

School

I believe that the school is primarily a social institution. Education being a social process, the school is . . . that form of community life in which all those agencies are concentrated that will be most effective in bringing the child to share in the inherited resources of the race, and to use his own powers for social ends . . . [and] that the school must represent present life—life as real and vital to the child as that which he carries on in the home, in the neighborhood, or on the playground . . . . Much of present education fails because it neglects this fundamental principle of the school as a form of community life . . . [and] conceives the school as a place where certain information is to be given, certain lessons are to be learned, or certain habits are to be formed.

Subject-Matter

I believe that the social life of the child is the basis of concentration, or correlation, in all his training or growth . . . that the only way to make the child conscious of his social heritage is to enable him to perform those fundamental types of activity which make civilization what it is . . . [and] that education must be conceived as a continuing reconstruction of experience; that the process and the goal of education are one and the same thing.

Method

I believe that method is ultimately reducible to the order of development of the child's powers and interests. The law for presenting and treating material is the law implicit within the child's own nature . . . that the active side precedes the passive. . . ; that expression comes before conscious impression; that the muscular development precedes the sensory; that movements come before conscious sensations; . . . that consciousness is essentially motor or impulsive; that conscious states tend to project themselves in action . . . [and] that interests are the signs and symptoms of growing power . . . [and] represent dawning capacities.

Social Progress

I believe that education is the fundamental method of social progress and reform.[8]

also defined the school socially. "A school is a community; community life is indispensable to mental and moral growth. If the act of an individual in any way hinders the best work of the community, he is in the wrong. The highest duty of the individual is to contribute all in his power to the best good of all." A school should be "a model home, a complete community and an embryonic democracy." School life should be similar to real life, and it is the social, intellectual, and moral training ground for democracy. Parker captured his fundamental rule of order in this motto, "Everything to help and nothing to hinder."

In these chapters, Parker underscored the major purposes of progressive education—to develop character and to create an ideal citizenry. He interrelated morality and democracy, which was another reason he considered activity-centered learning. As Parker explained, "a child is born a worker and activity is the law of nature"; therefore, "the foundation of education consists in training a child to work, to love work, to put the energy of his entire being into work; to do that work which best develops his body, mind, and soul; to do that work most needed for the education of mankind." Parker concluded, "Education is self-effort in the direction of educative work."9

To Francis Parker, the school was an instrument for the reconstruction of society and the preservation of the American democracy. Parker believed, "The school is the central means to preserve and perpetuate true democracy." He stated his belief system:

> I believe four things, as I believe in God—that democracy is the one hope of the world; that democracy without efficient common schools is impossible; that every school in the land should be made a home and a heaven for children; fourth, that when the ideal of the public school is realized, 'the blood shed by the blessed martyrs for freedom will not have been shed in vain.'10

Believing that society can rule itself, Parker indicted the aristocratic ideal, "the rule of many by the few," which he thought to be motivated by selfishness, enforced by power—physical force and standing armies—and by the division of people into classes through different kinds of education. He defined the democratic ideal as the responsibility of "each for all, and all for each," which he based on the "central principle of democracy—mutual responsibility." The democratic ideal was motivated, he believed, by altruism and was implemented through the common school by "true education . . . the presentation of the conditions necessary for the evolution of personality into freedom."[11]

Parker defined democracy as "the shortest line of resistance to human development," adding that the goal of humanity is freedom and that "the means of acquiring freedom may be summed up in one word—education." Parker perceived the common school as the ideal school for democracy because

> Children of all classes, nationalities, sects, rich and poor and boys and girls alike, work together under the highest and best conditions in one community for eight to twelve years . . . before prejudice . . . and mistrust [have] become a habit.

Parker called this living together "the social and the greatest factor in education: it stands higher than subjects of learning, than methods of teaching, than the teachers." "This mingling and blending gives personal power and makes the school a tremendous force for the upbuilding of democracy." Parker saw the principal mission of the common school, "to dissolve the prejudices that have been inculcated under the method of oppression."[12]

Dewey's *The School and Society* (1899), the second book Cremin credited for the early theoretical origins of progressive education, was divided into six chapters. Each chapter was based on a lecture presented at the home of Anita McCormick Blaine, to whom he dedicated the book. Like Parker, he defined the social aspects of the school and explained the necessary readjustments that had to be made to render the school effective in the present social conditions. Dewey presented a remarkably similar vision to Parker on the role of the school in the democracy, calling it "a miniature community, an embryonic society," constantly widening its own understanding of itself. He went beyond Parker in describing the school as an institution in relation to society and its own members, connecting new education with the general march of events in society, and called for a broader and a social view of education that made the school the agent of social progress. Dewey called for the transformation of the narrower individual goals of the school into, "what the best and wisest parent wants for his own child, that must the community want for all of its children. Any other ideal for our schools is narrow and unlovely; acted upon, it destroys our democracy."[13]

In his magnum opus, *Democracy and Education* (1916), Dewey presented his theory of the conception of education. He called education a social process based on a particular American social ideal of equality of intellectual and moral development and opportunity of all individuals. Dewey elaborated on this point:

> A society which makes provision for participation in the good of all its members on equal terms and which secures flexible readjustment of its institutions through interaction of the different forms of associated life is in so far democratic. Such a society must have a type of education which gives individuals a personal interest in social relationships and control, and the habits of mind which secure social changes without introducing disorder.[14]

Dewey also defined democracy as a social organization aimed to promote cooperation among its members and cooperation with other groups on the basis of mutual recognition of interests. Dewey, however, believed that not all distinctions between classes could be removed through education. "The school cannot immediately escape the ideals set by prior social conditions but it should contribute through the type of intellectual and emotional disposition which it forms to the improvement of those conditions." In other words, economic conditions might cause pupils to be unable to use all of their potential, but the school should be able to help students use more potential. He concluded that the importance of education in a democracy was the development of the potential that existed in its citizens. Education is the freeing of individual capacity in a progressive growth direct to social aims.[15] Dewey believed that "democracy had to be born anew every generation and education was the midwife."[16]

Parker's chapter, "Democracy and Education," and Dewey's books, *The School and Society* (1899) and *Democracy and Education* (1916), provided the first complete statement about the interrelationship between democracy and education. American education had to be different from education in other countries if democracy was to succeed. Cremin described the relationship between democracy and education as "part of a vast humanitarian effort to apply the promise of American life—the ideal of government by, of, and for the people—to the puzzling new urban-industrial civilization that began during the latter half of the nineteenth century."[17] Progressive education from 1890 until World War I was "a many-sided effort to use the schools to improve the lives of individuals." During the first quarter of the twentieth century, the progressive movement was "closely related to the broader currents of social and political progressivism," and progressive education included four major purposes:

> First, it meant broadening the program and function of the school to include direct concern for health, vocation, and the quality of family and community life. Second, it meant applying in the classroom the pedagogical principles derived from new scientific research in psychology and the social sciences. Third, it meant tailoring instruction more and more to the different kinds and classes of children who were being brought within the purview of the school . . . . Finally, Progressivism implied the radical faith that culture could be democratized without being vulgarized, the faith that everyone could share not only in the benefits of the new sciences but in the pursuit of the arts as well.[18]

Before Parker and Dewey, American education had not been democratic. The approach that began in Greece with Plato pervaded western education and served hierarchical societies; American elementary and secondary schools, like their ancestors, conformed to that tradition. Greek and European education subscribed to a dual system that divided education by establishing one set of goals for the leisure class and the other for practical life. Devotion to intellectual and aesthetic values was a leisure time affair and a mark of distinction; practical affairs and manual labor were the business of commoners. It was thought that the appropriate education for the leisure class was the classics; knowledge for its own sake was education's purpose. In contrast, the appropriate education for common man was information handed down by authority and practical knowledge about the things common man needed to know—mainly the cultivation of farm products, getting along with people, curing a cold, and a variety of other useful topics. For common man, usefulness of knowledge was measured by a simple test: knowledge is sound if things work out according to expectations.

Separated from the world of practical affairs, the leisure class was compelled to contrive some other meaning or function for education. The older traditional form of education, based on Plato's concept of "absolute truths," continued to be a mark of distinction for leisure class education even when transplanted on American soil. The weight of tradition seemed to be on the side of the system of education that met the goals of the leisure class. For a democratic society, educators faced the dilemma of how to serve two educational ends, the demand for the practical necessities and the pursuit of truth. Fundamentally, progressive education was an attempt to change a 5,000-year-old education tradition designed for socially stratified nondemocratic societies into a method suitable for educating all of the American citizenry for a democracy.

The early history of American education had not been hopeful for common man or the democracy. Education was a matter of direct participation in the life of the community. The chief purpose of the rural school was to reinforce the way of life practiced in the community and to produce individuals with sufficient skills and information needed for that way of life. The home was at the center of society and in many ways fulfilled these educational purposes, making the school a peripheral institution. Colonial leaders were concerned but inactive in addressing the issue of education. In analyzing the relationship between democracy and education in early America, Parker stated, "Not the dimmest outline of a common school system was in the minds of the founders of America . . . . The idea of the responsibility of communities for each child was repugnant to the people."[19]

In post-Revolutionary War America, schooling continued to be a limited commodity. Only the financially well-off living in cities or adjacent small towns attended academies, which mainly served the leisure class. Rural youth, if they had time away from chores, attended the country schools. When Thomas Jefferson introduced the first measure to establish free public education for the state of Virginia, it was considered a radical measure and the legislators defeated the bill.[20] Although intellectual, religious, and governmental leaders judged education to be "the primal necessity of social existence" because "a community without a conscience would extinguish itself," education was neither a priority nor was the aim of education clear.[21] American schools rose only as the requirements of an increasingly complex society demanded.

In the early nineteenth century, "when the proposition was under way that society should rule itself, thoughtful men made up their minds that society must be intelligent, and that the state must furnish the means of intelligence."[22] By 1830, Horace Mann (1796-1859) universalized education for pupils in the first eight grades through the invention of America's common school. Mann's Twelfth Annual Report to the state of Massachusetts iterated the importance of education. "Without undervaluing any other human agency, it may be safely affirmed that the common school, improved and energized as it can be, may become the most effective and benignant of all the forces of a civilization."[23]

The Industrial Revolution, stimulated by the Civil War, caused a shift toward a more inclusive democratic order that transformed the social organization of the nation and created a new social ideal. The nation was expanding as new territories were added, and the population was growing as more immigrants poured into the urban centers. Innovative technology advanced the manner of farming, reducing the need for farm labor, and industrialization created urban complexes transformed by the use of railroad transportation. Forces for change like the unions and the settlement houses organized and assisted the common laborer. These social and economic changes conflicted with traditional ways of family living and challenged political institutions, causing upheaval in the nation's social and cultural institutions—the home, the school, the church, and the community. Andrew Jackson's "common man" held fast to Jefferson's truth, "All men are created equal with the right to life, liberty, and the pursuit of happiness." The democratic upheaval that took shape in the nation was a demand not only for political equality but was "a more profound aspiration towards an equality of intellectual and moral opportunity and development."[24] It was the expectation of the common man that education was to provide this new "opportunity and development" and open doors to their American dreams.

The challenge for twentieth-century America was "to detect the ideas implied in a democratic society and to apply them to the enterprise of education." It was certain that a democratic government that rested on popular suffrage needed educated citizens, but on a deeper level a democracy was more than a form of government; "it is primarily a mode of associated living, of conjoint communicated experience."[25] "A democratic program of education must necessarily rest on the perception that democracy is a challenge to all forms of absolutism, that it has its own standards, ideals, and values, and that these must pervade the entire program." "If progressive education is to fulfill its promise, it must become consciously representative of a distinctive way of life. In other words, a progressive school must be a place where children attend to carry on a democratic way of life."26

The new democratic ideal required a new vision of education that met the democratic, social, intellectual, scientific, and industrial needs of society. Parker and Dewey articulated that vision.

A Science of Education

Progressive education not only faced the challenge of developing an education that was democratic but also making education a science. The publication of Charles Darwin's *The Origin of Species* (1859) resulted in changes in philosophical theory which reshaped thought in the second half of the nineteenth century. Plato's coherent theory of philosophy placed truth in the dominion of absolutes, but as science emerged it divorced truth from absolutes and treated them as operational or relative truths. Plato's coherent theory tended toward standards or ideals derived from a fourth dimension, the world of ideas. Twentieth-century science and the philosophical pragmatists like Charles Peirce, William James, and John Dewey tended toward the conclusion that investigations fell within the three-dimensional world of space, time, and material, and that truths were constructed as man proceeded in life. Truth was neither handed to man nor embedded in the structure of things to be discovered; it must be created and recreated out of the raw material of man's experience. Similar to other sciences, a science of education meant a body of verified facts and tested principles that could provide intellectual guidance to a school as a way to proceed practically. Unlike some sciences, however, a science of education was not based on one truth, but it entertained different points of view, different hypotheses, and different theories; it presented no fixed or closed orthodoxy. When applied to education, the word science was used "humbly and modestly."

Both Parker and Dewey placed great weight on the influence of psychology on the creation of a science of education. Parker related his writing to the early nineteenth-century views of Froebel and Herbart, which influenced him during his travel in Germany (see Chapter 3). Parker was at the end of his career when Thorndike's *Animal Intelligence* (1898) and James's *Talks to Teachers on Psychology* (1899) were published. When Parker wrote

Talks on Pedagogics (1894) four years earlier, however, he credited his theoretical formulation to psychology in general, which he called "a guide in the direction of the work," to Froebel's "sublime idea . . . the unity of creation and the Creator," to Herbart's theory of concentration, and to "the study of education as a science."[27]

Parker interpreted the science of education to mean "the science that comprehended all sciences." He called science "the organized knowledge of the law" and posited "to deny a science of education is to deny that the development of human beings is governed by law."[28] He confined the science of education to psychology, which he defined as "the science of the soul of the laws of development of the child," and to pedagogy. As explained earlier, Parker called scientific pedagogy the "quality method" of teaching. Quality teaching was a scientific process because it placed the student in contact with nature, where every step of personal development was through original influence and practical application.

Unlike Parker, Dewey was a trained psychologist. In *The Sources of a Science of Education* (1929), Dewey called education "an art that incorporates more and more science into itself."[29] He described how science takes out the guesswork and uses an intellectual technique by which discovery and organization of material go on cumulatively and by means of which one inquirer can repeat the researches of another, confirm or discredit them, and add to the capital stock of knowledge. At the end of the 1920s, Dewey believed that progressive schools possessed enough common elements worth scientific investigation. He named six elements that distinguished progressive from traditional schools: (1) "respect for individual capacities, interests, and experience"; (2) "enough external freedom and informality. . . to enable teachers to become acquainted with children as they really are"; (3) "respect for self-initiated and self-conducted learning"; (4) "respect for activity as the stimulus and center of learning"; (5) "belief in social contact, communication, and cooperation as the all-enveloping social medium"; and (6) "the intellectual organization and the body of facts."[30] These elements constituted a departure and a starting point for the contribution that progressive schools might make to the theory or science of education.

To that end, Dewey posed three questions: (1) Is there a science of education? (2) Can there be a science of education? (3) Are there procedures and aims that can be reduced to anything called a science? He called these divisive questions between traditional and progressive educators. To the first question, Dewey answered that as yet, there is not a science of education because it takes a long time to produce one. The transition from an empirical to a scientific status is "recent and imperfect."[31] According to Dewey, the empirical factors of education, those that can be measured, are limiting and their study incapable of yet producing progress in the education field.

To the second question, "Can there be a science of education?" Dewey responded, "A science emerges when the various findings of education are linked together to form a relatively coherent system that reciprocally confirms and illuminates the findings of the parts." A science of education needs "the existence of systematic methods of inquiry, which when brought to bear on a range of facts enables one to understand them better and to control them more intelligently, less haphazardly and with less routine." In order to develop a science of education, Dewey suggested this question as the scientific model:

> What are the ways by means of which the function of education in all its branches and phases—selection of material for the curriculum, methods of instruction and discipline, organization and administration of schools—can be conducted with systematic increase of intelligent control and understanding?[32]

To answer his third question—"Are there procedures and aims of education such that it is possible to reduce them to anything properly called a science?"—Dewey explained that education was not an independent science and had to interface with other sciences, namely psychology and sociology. He likened the science of education to the science of medicine. "In medicine the primary source of the inquiry is the medical problem of the patient. In education the primary source of inquiry is the concrete educational experience of the student. The educational experience sets the problem and tests, modifies, confirms or refutes the conclusions of intellectual investigation."[33] Unlike engineering's interface with mathematics and physics, which are precise sciences, education was in a difficult position because like medicine, education needed to interface with the imprecise human sciences to advance—mainly psychology and sociology, both in their infancy at the onset of the twentieth century.

Dewey believed that in education the psychological and sociological questions were intertwined. Psychology helped answer the question of the *means* of education by investigating how pupils learn; sociology tackled the questions of the *ends* of education, or what pupils need to learn to thrive in society.[34] Not only Parker and Dewey, but according to Cremin, Thorndike's *Animal Intelligence* (1898) and James's *Talks to Teachers on Psychology* (1899) helped transform progressive education into a science through psychology.

Edward Thorndike (1874-1949) was called the "father of American learning psychology." His "law of effect" defined the basic principle governing some of learning, although it could not account for all learning. He began his career by observing many kinds of animals in what he called "puzzle box" problems. An animal was placed in a box from which it would attempt to escape by experimenting with a variety of behaviors such as sniffing, scratching, and climbing until it caught the designated string in its claws to open the door. Eventually, the animal would pull the string and escape. Thorndike named these trials random or "chance" operations. "Learning was a matter of trial and error, a chance success." When a trial was successful, it led to an outcome characterized as "rewarding or satisfying." Thorndike named the basic operations in learning a gradual strengthening of some "stimulus-response" connection that at first occurred by chance and happened to be successful. Thorndike's laws have all "been criticized or found wanting by one critic or another." To Thorndike, however, goes the credit for putting what was to become experimental psychology of animal learning on a sound laboratory and theoretical footing.[35]

Thorndike earned bachelor's degrees from Wesleyan and Harvard and completed his graduate work at Columbia University, where he spent his academic career. Three other of his noteworthy books also greatly influenced education—*The Psychology of Learning* (1914), *The Measurement of Intelligence* (1926), and *Fundamentals of Learning* (1932)—but it was *Animal Intelligence* (1898) that first described the application of psychology to education and became known as "educational psychology."

William James (1842-1910) strongly endorsed Thorndike's work. It was Thorndike's first book and James's second book on psychology that Cremin called "watershed works" that shaped progressive education from outside of the field. James's two major books on psychology, *Principles of Psychology*

(1890) and *Talks to Teachers on Psychology* (1899), were purported to have been read by 90 percent of all teachers at that time. *Talks to Teachers on Psychology* (1899), a collection of lectures which James gave at Harvard, made the first "serious inroads" that overturned the popular scholastic faculty psychology, which theorized that each mental faculty was developed independently and therefore students should enroll in difficult courses to improve their intellectual capacity. James was also the first to "bring modern psychology into the school room and apply it to the everyday problems . . . of education."[36] As James explained, "The child is a behaving organism, whose mind is given to aid him in adapting to this world's life; that interests must be awakened and broadened as the natural starting points of instruction; that will must be trained to sustain proper attention for productive thought and ethical action, that the right sorts of habits must be inculcated early to free the child for his role as an intelligent being, and that a child's ideas must be put to the practical test whenever possible." To James, "the purpose of education is to organize the child's powers of conduct to fit him for his social and physical milieu." The function of the teacher is to turn the "sensitive, impulsive, associative, and reactive organism" into a purposeful thinking adult who will use his talents to the fullest in the struggle for a better life.[37]

James applied Darwin's doctrine of evolution to psychology, explaining that the mind is molded by the environment, but the mind also acts upon the environment. James's theory of the mind differed from the determinists' "survival of the fittest" interpretation. To James, volunteerism, defined as the mind acting upon the environment in a creative way, is the main factor in the mind. Therefore, the central task of education is the early inculcation of as many good and useful habits as possible. James argued that life itself rather than any formal notions of mind or soul is the starting point of psychology. His concept of consciousness makes the knower the actor, whose acts of knowing help transform the world. James's viewpoint, which strongly influenced Dewey, ascribed to schools a powerful role in shaping the child's life for a democratic society.

At Harvard University, James studied chemistry under Charles Eliot, earned a degree in medicine in 1869, and held faculty appointments in physiology in 1872, psychology in 1889, and philosophy in 1890. Beginning in 1875, James led the effort at Harvard University to establish psychology as a scientific discipline, and when the noted psychologist G.

Stanley Hall was a doctoral student at Harvard in 1878, James introduced him to the scientific method.

Sociology, another new science at the turn of the century, also contributed to making education a science. As Dewey stated, psychology related more to the means of education and sociology to the ends of education. At this point in the history of education, sociologists translated Darwin's biological theory of evolution into a sociological theory that affected how educators perceived the purpose of the school. As Darwin explained, certain forces in the environment act as agents of natural selection on succeeding generations of organisms in which heritable changes occur. If a species "vary in any manner profitable to itself, it will have a better chance of survival" and thus be naturally selected. According to Darwin, the species evolve slowly and gradually and adjust and adapt to the environment in order to survive. Those species which succeed in surviving do so because they possess favorable characteristics that enable them to adjust satisfactorily to environmental changes. The transmission of these favorable characteristics to their offspring guarantees the continuation of particular species.[38]

Two opposing sociological viewpoints shaped educators' perspectives on the school's purpose. The Social Darwinists applied the survival of the fittest theory of biological natural selection to society, postulating that education could not be an important factor in social progress. Social Darwinists like English philosopher Herbert Spencer (1820-1902) and Yale sociologist William Graham Sumner (1840-1910) saw only a narrow purpose for the school. They saw man as a species locked into a fiercely competitive struggle that led intelligent and competitive individuals who adjusted more readily to environments to advance to positions of social, economic, intellectual, and political leadership, and those less intelligent and less competitive in their behavior to survive less well. Since only the fittest would survive, schools could make little if any difference.

Spencer was well known to American educators through his popular text, *Education: Intellectual, Moral, and Physical* (1860), which stressed adaptation and progress proceeding according to the laws of evolution. Spencer defined his ideal of education as a complete preparation for the activities that constituted human life, which he classified into activities of preserving self, securing necessities of life, rearing and disciplining offspring, maintaining proper social and political relations, and gratifying tastes and feelings.[39] He believed education to be private and individualistic, a preparation for the life of the individual. In Spencer's system, education played a passive and indirect role in social evolution. Spencer also believed that education was valuable but could never be an important factor in social progress because the mind followed an evolutionary process.[40]

Like Spencer, William Sumner showed resistance to social reform in general, placing his faith in the processes of nature and arguing that scientific progress of society could evolve through natural workings of the evolutionary process. A *laissez-faire* individualist, he reasoned that those who held power gained it because they were the "fittest." His classic works included *Folkways* (1906) and a group of essays, *What Social Classes Owe to Each Other* (1883). In the main, progressive educators opposed Spencer and Sumner's Social Darwinist brand of sociology that preached the status quo and resignation to the laws of nature but embraced the Reform Darwinists Lester Frank Ward and Albion Small, who envisioned the school as an essential institution for progress.

Lester Frank Ward (1841-1913) was a self-educated man who later in life earned degrees in law and medicine and became the chairman of the Sociology Department at Brown University. Ward considered education the most important activity of man. In Ward's system of sociology, he emphasized active adaptation, that is, social improvement was dependent only indirectly on the inheritance of acquired characteristics and on natural selection. It was opportunity and the social environment that affected change in the individual. From Ward's perspective, similar to Dewey's and Parker's stances, education played a direct and dynamic role in life, and its purpose was social. Education was the chief method for the improvement of society and it was the first duty and prime object of society to provide universal education.[41] In *Dynamic Sociology* (1883), Ward explained, "Education that was scientific, popular, and universal could be the 'mainspring of progress,' 'the piston of civilization,' and the 'embodiment of all that is progressive.'"[42] He envisioned "popular scientific education as the first element of a truly progressive system." As he explained, "The diffusion of knowledge among the masses of mankind is the only hope we have of securing any greater social progress than that which nature itself vouchsafes through its own process of selection."[43]

Like Ward, Albion Small (1854-1926) placed great faith in education. Albion Small became the chairman of the first Department of Sociology in the United States in 1892 at the University of Chicago, where John Dewey joined him on the faculty two years later as chairman of the Department of Philosophy, Psychology, and Pedagogy. A publication combining Albion Small's *The Demands of Sociology on Pedagogy* (1896) with Dewey's *My Pedagogical Creed* (1897) defined, established, and formalized the interrelationship of sociology and pedagogy for the first time. Dewey's pedagogical creed explained how the school should bring the child to share in the inherited resources of the race and how discipline and method should be influenced to this end. Small's statement was "a trenchant exposition of the principle that education should direct its attention to sociology and learn what the work of reality demands of the teachers." He argued that education should be broadened by sociology because "the processes of education have come to be recognized as fundamental and vital in any attempt to improve human conditions and elevate society"; therefore, the isolation of the teacher is a thing of the past.[44]

Small rebutted the "pre-sociological view of the world" that established the goal of education as the "training" of intelligence or the strengthening of perception, reasoning, and judgment accomplished through isolated subjects. From his sociological perspective, training intelligence alone through the analytical separation of subjects made learning unreal. The proper education is the whole reality, not conventionalized abstractions from reality, because the world of experience is one, not many, experiences. Small explained that the school is a social institution and the aims, management, disciplines, and method of instruction should be dominated by this idea. "The life task for each individual is to accommodate himself to prevailing conditions in such a manner that he may both accomplish and enjoy a maximum share of the development which his stage in social evolution is empowered to accomplish, and the life task of man sets the pedagogical task of teachers." To Albion Small, education meant the evolution of the whole personality and required a conception of the whole reality with each subject in the curriculum a part of that reality. Small identified the new goal of education as "first, the completion of the individual and second, the adaptation of the individual to the society to create conditions favorable to the development of a more perfect type of individual."[45]

When Dewey accepted the position of honorary president of the Progressive Education Association in 1928, he used the occasion to speak about what contribution progressive education might make to the development of a science of education. He suggested two procedures that progressive schools should emphasize: the examination of the development of subject matter and the study of conditions favorable to learning. Dewey informed the members of the Association that qualitative methods of measurement might be used because "all subjects pass through a qualitative stage before they arrive at a quantitative one," adding that teachers "cannot sit down and wait until there are methods by which quality may be reduced to quantity." He admonished teachers to begin.[46]

After three decades of progressive education, little had been accomplished toward the advancement of a science of education. Progressive education had been shaped by its own new theories and by the disciplines of psychology and sociology, but it failed to create a science of education to the extent that Dewey had anticipated. "Dewey's doubts and warnings had little effect upon those who called themselves his followers." The fundamental question was did "the ambiguities of Dewey's own philosophy encourage the oversimplifications and exaggerations, which he condemned."[47]

Changes in Progressive Education

The concept of progressive education evolved and as it did, the name changed four times. In the 1870s, Francis Parker used the phrase "new education" to describe his initial "departure" from the traditional older teaching methods and course of study. The American public school was a twelve-grade scheme of classifying children from ages six to eighteen into eight elementary and four secondary grades. Uniform textbooks—morphological and encyclopedic compendiums of facts—provided curriculum material. Teachers were untrained because teaching was not thought to be a profession. In 1892, the National Education Association's Committee of Ten, comprised of college presidents, established the goals of the secondary school curriculum and recommended that all secondary students be liberally educated in English, foreign languages, mathematics, history, and science, whether they intended to go to college or not.[48] Only a small percentage of the population attended schools, and more than half left school on or before the completion of the fifth year. Five percent attended high school, and less than one percent enrolled in higher education. The two main curriculum questions in the late 1800s were: "Should the emphasis be placed on cultural education for the leisure class or on practical education for a vocation?" and "Should education be based on societal needs or on individual needs and interests?" The individual had either to be fitted to become a cog in the social mechanism or had to be educated according to some notion of how this mechanism should be changed.[49]

Building on the changing methods and content of new education, the second phase of the education revolution from 1890 to 1914 was called progressive education, mainly because it affiliated with the broader social and political currents of the Progressive Reform Movement. In the Progressive Era, "the democratic upheaval took shape not merely in a demand for political equality, but in a more profound aspiration towards an equality of intellectual and moral opportunity and development." As the social order in the nation was shifting to the new democratic ideal—"the equality of intellectual and moral opportunity and development of all citizens"—it became necessary to devise a new system of education in the direction of that social ideal.[50] The Deweyan and Parker progressives defined the school as an instrument of democracy, an agency of social reconstruction, and an "effort to cast the school as a fundamental lever of social and political regeneration.[51]

World War I, called "the great divide in the history of education," diverted national energy from education and when progressive education separated from a dwindling Progressive Reform Movement, it began to manifest itself in a remarkable diversity of pedagogical protest and innovation. The War led progressive schools to abandon their role as agents of social reform and instead emphasize "individual impulses." "Pedagogical progressivism came to be identified with the child-centered school; with a pretentious scientism; with social efficiency and social utility rather than social reform; and with a vigorous suspicion of 'bookish' learning."[52] The movement became professionalized and institutionalized, and educators capitalized on the innovations of university professors from the new and growing number of university departments of education.

Several new strands of progressive education were introduced, which caused confusion in the definition: social efficiency, multiple life-centered objectives, the project method, and child-centered schools. Overlap among these occurred in method and content, but each started from a different vantage point. The major social reconstructionists had been Francis Parker and John Dewey, whose purpose for the school was to reform society. Parker's sole disciple was Flora Cooke. Dewey's main followers were William Wirt and William Heard Kilpatrick, but neither continued Dewey's social reconstructionism.

Social efficiency or scientific management, an unpopular strand of progressive education, was patterned on the work of Frederick Winslow Taylor (1856-1915), who designed a task system for industry which educators applied to schools. Dewey's disciple William Wirt applied scientific management in the Gary, Indiana, school system when he became superintendent. At first Wirt earned high praise and social efficiency was imitated in a number of schools, but later he received robust criticism from both educators and politicians. William Heard Kilpatrick introduced another strand of progressive education called the Project Method. In his book, *The Curriculum* (1918), Franklin Bobbitt, a professor of education at the University of Chicago, rejected traditional subjects—English, history, science—for a completely different set of "numerous, definite, and particularized" objectives based on human life. Bobbitt identified 821 objectives for curriculum-making, directed to language, health, leisure, parental, vocational, and other "life activities." In 1918, the Commission on the Reorganization of Secondary Education, overturned the school goals established in 1892 by the Committee of Ten and introduced seven new *Cardinal Principles of Secondary Education*: "(1) Health. (2) Command of fundamental processes. (3) Worthy home-membership. (4) Vocation. (5) Citizenship. (6) Worthy use of leisure. (7) Ethical character." The Commission's report concluded that the "schools should derive their goals from the life activities of adults in society."[53] These goals were in keeping with the progressive trend in education.

Progressive schools experienced a great shift in emphasis after World War I. Progressive education became more experimental and child centered, giving significance to a child's creativity. In this decade, the most popular strand of progressive education was the child-centered school. Harold Rugg and Ann Schumaker in *The Child-Centered School* (1925) described it as an institution that worked out in practice "something which Rousseau perceived and only vaguely described to his contemporaries; which Pestalozzi comprehended only in the personal love and goodness of his heart; toward which Froebel strove through obscure mysticism; and which Dewey partially phrased and could not entirely exemplify" (see Chapter 3). The practices of the child-centered schools focused on child freedom, direct experience with the world and its activities, the use of the senses in training pupils in observation and judgment, and cooperation between the school and home and between parents and teachers. Rugg and Schumaker identified the marks of the child-centered school as "freedom, activity, creative expression, and a place of self-expression and maximum child growth."[54] Several historians and education critics labeled Francis Parker's philosophy child centered. It was true that Parker's definition of the child placed the child as central, but the school was emphatically shaped by its social reconstructionist ideals and it did not label itself child centered.

Among the most influential proponents of child-centered progressive education was William Heard Kilpatrick, a Dewey disciple who advocated "'the project method' as the best way to educate children through their own experiences, rather than through what he called 'subject matter fixed-in-advance.'" Kilpatrick advanced the idea that "a good teacher brings in subject matter only when needed as part of a student's experiences, and that learning activities may be judged by their contribution to future growth."[55] Kilpatrick defined his "project method" as a pedagogical principle that emphasized purposeful activity consonant with the child's own goals. He located this activity in a social environment that he believed could facilitate certain ethical outcomes.[56] Kilpatrick was a popular professor at Teachers College, Columbia University, who taught some 35,000 students in his long career, which provided a built-in audience for his ideas. The "project method" gave Kilpatrick national and international recognition.

Sensing the existence of a progressive movement that they wanted to articulate and propagate, several teachers organized a Progressive Education Association in 1919. The Association did not intend to speak for all progressives; it was not to be a mouthpiece but a clearinghouse for the increasing number of progressive schools being developed in the nation. The Association embraced all strands of progressive education, and the result was the dilution of a clear definition.

As progressive education became diluted by the proliferation of non-theoretical experiments, many disciples and most critics began to misunderstand its basic theoretical foundations. Even John Dewey, the movement's major architect, became its main critic. Dewey voiced his doubts about what people were labeling progressive education and what direction the movement was taking. He criticized educators for what he called the "extremist or romantic oversimplifications of the movement." He sharply warned against the aimlessness and dangerous permissiveness of the notion of "the child-centered school," with its mixture of postwar bohemianism, undisciplined expression in the name of individual creativity, and Freudian solicitude for avoiding inhibitions. Dewey complained about what he considered evasions of educational responsibility in many so-called progressive schools. He thought that subject matter, for example, too often had been eliminated or minimized, when the truly progressive approach called for recreating the curriculum to develop new subject matter. The idea of adjustment and free expression too had been exaggerated and even perverted wherever the schools did not promote an actively critical attitude toward society. Dewey outlined the need for rigor and clarity and for consideration of "the intellectual contribution which [progressive education] may make to the art of education."[57]

During the Great Depression, liberal voices called for education to revisit the idea of the school as a "lever of political and social change." Progressive education returned to a societal orientation and sometimes a Marxian viewpoint, which George Counts, author of *Dare the Schools Build a New Social Order?* (1932), explained:

> If Progressive Education is to be genuinely progressive, it must emancipate itself from the influence of this class, face squarely and courageously every social issue, come to grips with life in all its stark reality, establish an organic relationship with the community, develop a realistic and comprehensive theory of welfare, fashion a compelling and challenging vision of human destiny, and become less frightened than it is today at the bogies of imposition and indoctrination.[58]

Reconstructionists like Harold Rugg, a renowned educator of the time, opposed Counts's Marxian analysis of American society, arguing that American society did not consist of two warring classes but existed through the interplay of many small special-interest groups.[59] William Kilpatrick flatly rejected 'class struggle,' 'the workers' dictatorship,' 'indoctrination of teachers,' 'teacher class consciousness,' 'class war morality,' and other tenets of what he called "High Marxism."[60] Dewey also questioned the usefulness of class struggle and suggested that it conflicted with democratic tradition and methods.[61]

Between the two world wars, progressive education was no longer an exclusive term that defined the movement in all of its variation, but it became a popular and inclusive term. By 1950, "the ideals and tenets of progressive education became the dominant pedagogy." In tracing what she called the "perilous career" of progressive education, historian Diane Ravitch, who favors traditional education, noted:

> Both its admirers and detractors acknowledged that progressive ideas had transformed the American public school during the first half of the 20th century. Progressive concepts proved to be particularly appropriate in easing the transition to a mass secondary education. At the opening of the century, about a half million students (about 10 percent of the age group) attended high schools, when the curriculum was strongly academic; though only a minority graduated or went on to college; by mid-century, high school enrollment was over five million (65 percent of the age-group), and secondary curriculum was remarkably diverse. Progressive education offered a rationale to include vocational and other nonacademic studies . . . and to fulfill what the education profession believed was its special role in a democratic society.[62]

Despite the existence of fifty years of progressive education, Carleton Washburne recognized the continuing confusion and the need to answer *What Is Progressive Education?* (1952). Washburne's book reiterated the three dominant themes of early progressive education: (1) the interrelationship of science and education. (2) the interrelationship of democracy and education for responsible citizenry, and (3) the emphasis on the development of the whole child. In the 1950s, he defined progressive education as "education that attempts to apply on the education of children the findings of sciences, whether these confirm some old ways or point to better and more effective ones for helping boys and girls develop their potentialities as individuals and as contributing and responsible members of society." Different sciences—medical science, physiology, psychology, psychiatry—could enlighten different educational problems. Although Washburne validated Dewey's projection that education would interface with psychology and sociology, he concluded that fifty years later, "Much of education is unscientific, proceeding by tradition and pious hopes, with little regard for what science can contribute."[63]

Washburne added little that was new to the definition of progressive education, but he summarized important theories about democratic education. Paraphrasing Dewey and Parker, he reiterated three main tenets: (1) "thinking, planning, and acting together is at the heart of democratic living"; (2) "democracy is not just a system of government," but consists of respect for individual human beings, of coordinating the activities of widely differing people toward the achievement of goals they hold in common; and (3) "full freedom to individuals and minorities except where abuse of that freedom will reduce the freedom of others."[64]

Washburne also underscored the differences in curriculum, method of instruction, the approach to discipline, and the use of community life to develop character and an ideal citizenry. From Washburne's critical viewpoint, neither "the science of education" nor "the needs and demands of society" changed the progressive school radically; only psychology made a significant impact.

A product of progressive education, Washburne was well qualified to clarify the ambiguities. He knew the progressive movement and most of the important contributors well. His early schooling was under Francis Parker at the Chicago Institute Academic and Pedagogic, he was John Dewey's friend, and a cofounder with Flora Cooke and Perry Dunlap Smith of the Graduate Teachers College of Winnetka, Illinois. Washburne was the Superintendent of Winnetka Schools when he introduced the Winnetka Plan, a design for the individualizing of instruction.

First called new education, then progressive education, in its third phase the name became simply "modern education" because its tenets pervaded most of Amerca's schools. Modern education generally emphasized:

Active learning (experiences and projects) rather than passive learning (reading); cooperative planning among pupils of classroom activities by teacher and pupils; cooperation among pupils on group projects instead of competition for grades; the recognition of individual differences in students' abilities and interests; justifying the curriculum by its utility to the student and by the way it met identifiable needs and interests of the students; the goal of effective living rather than acquisition of knowledge; the value of relating the program of the school to the life of the community around it; the merging of traditional subjects into core curricula or functional problem areas related to family life, community problems, or student interests; the use of books, facts, or traditional learning only where needed as part of the students' activities and expression.

Both Washburne and Ravitch called progressive education "democracy in action" because it substituted teacher-pupil cooperation for authoritarianism, stressed socialization to the group instead of individualism, and championed an educational program that was for all children in the here and now rather than for the minority that was college bound.[65] Originally, new and old education held opposite positions on almost all variables of education, but as the century unfolded, traditional education assumed characteristics of progressive education and vice versa, as Figure 1.3 shows.

Figure 1.3
Carleton Washburne's Comparison of Traditional and Progressive Education

Traditional Education

1. School designed for a socially stratified society, which the school often reinforces

2. Education is based on Plato's theory of absolute truth

3. Pedagogical principles based on that which is incorporated in books and in the minds of elders

4. Aim of education—the transmission of the cultural heritage to the next generation

5. Purpose of school—the acquisition of knowledge, the development of skills to acquire that knowledge, and conformity to standards of conduct

Progressive Education

1. Schools designed for a democratically organized society for which it tries to create a citizenry

2. Education is based on Charles Peirce's theory of pragmatism or relative truth

3. Pedagogical principles based on scientific truths

4. Aim of education—to educate for character as well as the acquisition of knowledge. Moral training at least as important as mental training.

5. Purpose of school—the education of the whole child—intellect, body, emotions, and soul

Figure 1.3 *continued*

6. Nature of school—an institution sharply marked off from any other form of social organization and based on a pattern of organization unique to staff—time-schedules, schemes of classification, of examination and promotion, and rules order

6. Nature of school—school is a "social institution," "education is a social process," "school is a community"; through community life moral education results, lessons are learned, and habits formed

7. Content of curriculum—body of knowledge from the past organized by discipline

7. Content of curriculum—"subject matter is the child's own social activities organized in a variety of different ways—" "central subjects," "occupations," "project method"

8. Method of instruction— "quantity method" "books and textbooks are the chief representation of the lore and history of the past"

8. Method of instruction—"quality method," "learning by doing"

9. Theory of learning—reading and theory of experience

9. Theory of learning—writing

10. Teacher—"scheme of imposition from above and outside"; "imposes adult standards; authoritarianism"

10. Teacher—co-participant in learning process

11. School is preparation for future life

11. School is a process of living

12. Discipline—teacher dominated; attitudes of pupil—"docility, receptivity, and obedience"

12. Discipline—self-discipline centered on community life. [66]

For the evolution of the Parker and Dewey social reconstructionist strand of progressive education, Parker established four goals that gave the school a social and moral purpose. With these goals, excerpted from *Talks on Pedagogics* (1894), Parker shaped the democratic foundation upon which the school was built, and the faculty reiterated them as epigrams in the Francis W. Parker School Catalogue and Course of Study from 1901 to 1929 (see Figure 6.1). In those eras when the Parker School affirmed these measures, it was developing as a progressive institution.

Chapter 2

Pedagogue, Philanthropist, and Philosopher

In Chicago at the turn of the century, the progressive revolution in American grammar schools began to flourish when Francis Wayland Parker, John Dewey, and Anita McCormick Blaine, respectively the father, philosopher, and philanthropist of progressive education, joined forces in a valiant effort to provide a better form of schooling for the children of this country.

The relationship among the three began when Mrs. Blaine and Mr. Dewey enrolled their children in the Cook County Normal School in Englewood on Chicago's South Side, where Parker was principal. The relationship between Parker and Dewey continued when Parker invited Dewey to present his first book on education, *My Pedagogical Creed* (1897), to the faculty and the teachers in training at the Normal School. The relationship grew when Dewey introduced his experimental Laboratory School at the University of Chicago, where Francis Parker and Mrs. Blaine observed classes and Blaine later invited the school's parents to a series of lectures Dewey presented at her home. Blaine subsidized their publication under the title, *The School and Society* (1899), which Dewey dedicated to her. Parker purchased twenty-five copies for the teachers of the Chicago Institute Academic and Pedagogic, which Blaine founded for him in 1899.

When Blaine met Parker at the Cook County Normal School in 1895, she was thrilled with his approach to education and tried to persuade him to become president of a new Chicago Institute Academic and Pedagogic, which she planned to have built on Chicago's North Side. Blaine expanded her educational philanthropy in 1901 and appointed Parker the president of the Francis W. Parker School. That same year, Blaine invited Parker to become the director of the new School of Education at the University of Chicago, which she was helping to finance. Dewey was then the chairman of the Department of Philosophy, Psychology, and Pedagogy and head of his new experimental Laboratory School. Blaine's total contribution for these three interrelated schools—the Chicago Institute, the School of Education, and the Francis W. Parker School—exceeded four million dollars. Parker, Dewey, and Blaine became friends, confidants, and collaborators, and Parker and Dewey became colleagues at the University of Chicago.

For one moment in history, these three reformers possessed all of the ingredients to transform America's traditional education into a science of education. When this triumvirate collaborated at the University of Chicago, the potential for pre-college education in America grew exponentially. Dewey had developed a body of educational theory, Parker possessed the practical genius and charismatic leadership to implement the theory into practice, and Blaine had the money to finance the vision.

The moment, however, was lost. Parker died, Dewey left the university in a huff, and Blaine ultimately funded only the Francis W. Parker School. What remained of their collective efforts were the Francis W. Parker School of Chicago, and the education building called Emmons Blaine Hall on the University of Chicago campus. Later a number of second-generation schools built in the Parker image were developed throughout the country. Dewey's Laboratory School at the University of Chicago continued but did not remain a progressive school. The School of Education of the University of Chicago plans to close its doors on June 30, 2001. What was learned is that to change elementary and secondary schools is an enormous undertaking.

Francis Wayland Parker (1837-1902): Father of Progressive Education

Called a genius by his admirers and a crank by his foes, Francis Wayland Parker was driven by a missionary zeal to improve the quality of education for the children of America. An iconoclast, he abandoned most of the sacred cows of traditional education—the use of textbooks, the overemphasis on subject matter and rote learning, and silence in the classroom. During Parker's era, education was authoritarian, numbing, and dismal. When Parker was a young student and later a country schoolmaster, the only sound that could be heard in classrooms across the country was the drone of untrained teachers demanding that intimidated children read from dull textbooks, memorize the lesson, recite by rote, and write the answers to examinations. Parker reacted to this stultifying misuse of a child's time by envisioning classrooms as vital learning centers for developing the potential of the individual child.

Facing unrelenting opposition throughout most of his career, Parker traveled ever westward in pursuit of the grail of free and effective public education for all children, so that they might participate in the American dream of the new democracy. Adventurous and uncompromising, Parker frequently sacrificed his reputation as well as his peace of mind for the new education. Parker single-handedly and radically altered elementary education, changed the child's role in the classroom, and advanced teaching as a profession. He eventually became known as the "Children's Crusader" and the "Teacher of Teachers."

Parker was born on October 9, 1837, in the village of Piscatauquog, New Hampshire, to Robert Parker, a cabinet maker of modest means, and Millie Rand, a teacher. About his mother, Parker wrote in an autobiographical sketch, "She never taught as anyone else did . . . she had ways of her own."[1] The youngest of four children, he was proud of his family and his ancestors, which included five strands of ministers, two strands of teachers, several soldiers of the Revolutionary War, and a Harvard University librarian.

The earliest challenge of Frank Parker, as he was then called, was to obtain a formal education. He attended an old-fashioned village school in Piscatauquog, but he begged his family to enroll him in a nearby academy for boys three years his senior because he felt he was as capable as the academy students. His father's premature death put an end to Frank's dream, and when he was seven years old, his uncle bound him out to a farmer. For the next five years, Parker worked on the farm and was able to attend school for only two winter months a year. Not only was the time in classes short, but the school was far from excellent. He remembered, "The schools were very poor indeed, and I do not know as I learned anything in them."[2]

Young Parker learned by doing while on the farm. His biographer Ida Cassa Heffron wrote that eventually, "He knew every tree on the old farm, the grasses, flowers, and berries . . . He knew the animals. He studied in a spontaneous way the butterflies and insects: learned about the rocks by building them into a wall; studied physics by logging in the woods, and in ploughing."[3] Parker later said, "If any teacher had told me in school that that was real true education that I was getting on the farm . . . how it would have lit up the whole farm in a blaze of glory for me."[4] His experience on the farm eventually provided both method and content for his educational philosophy—animals on the school campus, a garden adjacent to the city school, geography as the central subject, and field trips to learn the flora and fauna of the surrounding environment. These were the remnants of an education that worked for him, and they became an important dimension of his educational philosophy.

Despite the experience and knowledge he acquired on the farm, Parker had completed only four years of schooling by age thirteen. He left the farm without fulfilling his contract to attend the Mount Vernon Academy in New Hampshire, where his sisters were enrolled. He paid his way "by sawing wood, varnishing boxes, and doing chores . . . He loved to saw wood, for he could think as he worked."[5]

Lacking the funds to continue his formal schooling beyond the academy, Parker made reading the mainstay of his education. He read the Bible at an early age, as well as John Bunyan's *Pilgrim's Progress* and Wayland's *Life of Judson*. He developed a love of poetry, especially Wordsworth, Tennyson, and Browning, often quoting them aloud. The essays of Goethe and Emerson inspired him. At the time of his death, his library contained more than 12,000 titles. His love of literature carried over into his pedagogy; Parker insisted that a library be built for each school he directed, and he made reading an essential part of the course of study.

Parker became a country schoolmaster at age sixteen, saying, "I cannot remember the time when I had not made up my mind to be a school teacher."[6] In nineteenth-century America, credentials were not a requirement for schoolmasters or principals. After teaching at several rural schools, Parker earned his first principalship at a school in Corson Hills, New Hampshire, when he was twenty-two years old. In nineteenth-century rural America, the school was the center of community life. Parker's years in rural schools became the basis for his later insistence that the school was not only tied to its community but was a community in itself. The concept of school as a community became a third significant ingredient of his educational philosophy.

In his late twenties, Parker was still without teaching credentials and without money to earn them, but in 1855, a friend submitted his name for the principalship at a small country school in Carrollton, Illinois, a frontier town sufficiently violent that two of Parker's predecessors had literally been driven from the school. In what was to be another formative decision, Parker decided to eschew "the common practice of using coercion [on his students]. He laid down no rules and made no threats."[7] Instead, "he surprised his pupils into good behavior by turning them all out of doors to dig weeds, mend and whitewash the fence, and sow seeds, in order that they and he might have a better place in which to play. He believed, even then, in play as well as work."[8]

After a short tenure in the Carrollton school, Parker left Carrollton to join the Union Army, fighting in Civil War battles from Cape Hatteras to Virginia. When his regimental commander fell in battle, Parker succeeded to command. At the Battle of Deep Bottom on August 16, 1864, "Captain Parker did the work that made him Colonel Parker." Wounded in the neck, he received a promotion while he was convalescing. After returning to active duty, he was captured by rebel forces, eventually repatriated, and promoted to colonel. "He loved to be called by this name better than any other because it stood for four years of hard, self-sacrificing service to his country."[9] He had entered the Civil War a stern disciplinarian but left it with a considerably greater understanding of leadership, democracy, and cooperation, which constituted another dimension of his educational philosophy. Biographer Jack Campbell observed that throughout the war Parker was concerned about how "humanity could be saved from such 'barbarism' and from another 'fratricidal war.'" Parker concluded "'The hope of the world' and even 'perpetuating the Republic' depended on the schools."[10]

For Parker the years after the war were the most rewarding personally and the least troubling professionally. While convalescing from his war wound, Parker married Josephine Hall, a reserved woman and a schoolmistress about whom little is known. When the governor of New Hampshire recommended Parker for a school position in Dayton, Ohio, calling him "one of the best educators in New England," Parker accepted, and the couple and their baby daughter, Annie, moved west.[11]

The Dayton schools were in the vanguard of education when Parker accepted the principalship in September 1868. After two years, the School Board appointed him director of Dayton's first Normal School, and he was in a position to influence the entire Dayton educational system with its 4,000 students and hundreds of teachers.[12] He introduced effective, though minor educational innovations, such as emphasizing the child's learning and deemphasizing the subjects learned. He did not, however, take advantage of the greater opportunity to apply his philosophy which called for integrating minority children into the school community.

While "Parker may have been convinced that education was the only salvation for the Negro people . . . it is unlikely that the Colonel took any stand on the racial integration of schools."[13] Student diversity in the school constituted a sixth essential ingredient of his educational philosophy, but, at least in this instance, not of his practice.

Parker only remained in Dayton for a short period before he resigned his position for personal and professional reasons. His wife died in 1871 and his widowed mother died the following year. His daughter Annie had to move to live with relatives in the East. Annie received surprisingly little attention from her father until her illness from tuberculosis at age twenty. Professional criticism also caused him to submit his resignation. Although recognized as "the Father of the Normal School," he was constantly criticized by colleagues for "his poor educational background," suggesting that he was an "illiterate man." Textbook producers had become Parker's bitter enemies because his educational approach reduced the use and therefore the sales of textbooks. In Parker's words, "The papers poured out the vials of their wrath against me, and a great book house by its agents did its best to kill me . . . . In fact, there was very little they did not accuse me of."[14]

Having received a small inheritance from an aunt, Parker left the Dayton schools and went abroad in 1872 to study education under the tutelage of a private instructor, as Horace Mann had done previously. During two years abroad, Parker attended lectures at the University of Berlin, was inspired by the Herbartians and what he observed in the German kindergartens, and read Hegel and other philosophers. He closely examined the works of John Amos Comenius, Jean Jacques Rousseau, Johann Pestalozzi, Friedrich Froebel, and Johann Friedrich Herbart (see Chapter 3). He came in contact with the most fertile minds when he traveled through Germany, Holland, Switzerland, Italy, and France, observing the European pedagogical innovations of the day. Having hewn his educational philosophy from his own life experiences for three decades without the aid of formal training, he found these German philosophers and pedagogues a powerful influence on his thinking about education. Parker concluded, "My observations, and what I had learned in Europe, had convinced me that the philosophers and thinkers of the ages were right . . . that reading and writing and numbers could be taught in a better way than the old fashioned way."[15]

Parker returned to New Hampshire in the winter of 1874 and confidently accepted his first major position as superintendent of schools in Quincy, Massachusetts. Here he introduced his first large-scale and significant educational reform, a synthesis of what he learned on the farm, through reading, from the community, and in the Civil War, all validated by the philosophers and pedagogues in Germany. In Quincy, Parker overturned the old and launched new education. Educators called Quincy "epoch-making" because it was the first departure from the traditional approach to education, which America inherited from Europe. During its first 200 years, America had not found a way to educate its citizens for a democracy. That was Parker's quest (see Chapter 4).

After five years in Quincy, Parker, now a recognized and effective educational innovator, submitted his resignation, but for a different set of reasons than in Carrollton or Dayton. His novel approach to education alone was enough to condemn him, but ugly rumors circulated that he was profiting from selling coal and transporting pupils to and from school. It was never certain that he could remain peaceably as superintendent in Quincy, and he himself was fearful of the conservative forces that were beginning to dominate the School Committee.

The catalyst for his resignation seemed to have been a single episode with a School Committee member, Edwin Marsh, a conservative politically and a traditionalist educationally who was "after Parker." Marsh reputedly unearthed some information which led him to call Parker a libertine. What Marsh discovered remained unknown, except that the issue of the allegation was not educational but moral. Charles Adams, who was usually on an informal and friendly basis with Parker—they dined, sailed, and spent evenings in conversation about education and the Civil War—set an official meeting with Parker to discuss his character. Whether Marsh's accusation was truth or fabrication, the Adams brothers decided to stand by their superintendent and to suppress rather than investigate the allegation. Reportedly, had it been true, it would have destroyed Parker's career as an educator in Quincy.[16] Parker's achievements at Quincy profoundly changed American primary and grammar school education, but Quincy's new education deteriorated after his departure. That a system could sustain the educational changes in his absence was far from certain.

Parker's educational philosophy and personal beliefs seemed to have meshed at Quincy. He was a Christian but was not bound by a specific religion. He held a nonsectarian view of religion and retained the spirit of the Puritan tradition, if only in his commitment to study the Bible. To him, education and salvation were synonymous. Parker's annual reading of I Corinthians 12:12-27 at school exercises—which asserted that each part of the body was important to the whole—expressed his belief in the unity of mankind. More important, it was the teachings of Christ, especially the "Sermon on the Mount," that symbolized for Parker the ultimate educational objective, "making one's own life and character of the greatest possible benefit to mankind."[17] Parker called this "the social motive of education."[18] The biblical message of love—God's love for mankind and man's love for his neighbor—constituted a world view that motivated his love for children, a humanitarian outlook, a reformer posture, a passionate zeal for teaching, and an ardent and deep-seated belief in democracy.

In his educational philosophy, he combined his religious view with the transcendentalism of the "philosopher of democracy," Ralph Waldo Emerson, whose writings he quoted abundantly. Like Emerson, Parker believed, "Study the mind of the past, study nature, and above all, express yourself in action." Parker found great appeal in Emerson's denunciation of dogmatism in religion, and he espoused his realism in philosophy and his "faith in the potentialities of child growth."[19] Transcendental philosophy and "the link between education and nonsectarian Christianity . . . [became] as firmly fixed in his thinking as the link between education and the preservation of the democratic ideal."[20] He emphasized other transcendental values—love, loyalty, freedom, cooperativeness, tolerance, humility, justice, and unselfishness. He defined happiness as "the product of doing the greatest amount for humanity" and felt that it should become a reality with each individual.[21] Both books Parker wrote revealed his Emersonian viewpoint.

After Parker resigned from Quincy in 1880, he accepted a position as supervisor of Boston's forty-two primary schools, which he considered to be among the best schools in the civilized world. During the summers of 1881 and 1882, Parker also offered classes to teachers on Martha's

Vineyard, where he wrote *Talks on Teaching* (1883), a compilation of the "talks" he presented in these summer sessions. *Talks on Teaching* focused on his philosophy of education and the new methods he discovered and implemented at Quincy. The book sold more copies than any other book on education of its time.[22]

While supervisor of Boston schools for two years, Parker married Mrs. Frances Stuart, a teacher in the Boston School of Oratory, whom Parker first met professionally, as she attempted to soften his rough voice, which was the lasting result of his Civil War injury to the throat. An accomplished teacher, Mrs. Stuart attended Parker's summer sessions at Martha's Vineyard and after they were married, she enrolled in the Professional Training Class at the Cook County Normal School in Chicago. Mrs. Parker provided valuable professional assistance and advice to her husband and became a close friend of Anita McCormick Blaine. It was she who encouraged her husband to leave the public sector and to accept Mrs. Blaine's offer to endow a private school for him. It was said of Mrs. Parker that "few women have been privileged to be of so much service to the cause of education, directly or indirectly, as was Mrs. Parker . . . . She was greatly admired for what she was, and she added materially to the efficiency of her husband in all his public and professional life."[23]

After Boston, Parker settled permanently in the Midwest—this time in Chicago—where he became principal of the Cook County Normal School in 1883. Before he arrived, Parker was warned about "the battles he might expect with the board of education."[24] His appointment worsened these problems because he led the school in even more radical ways. Parker was often declared a heretic and a charlatan by the public and by many education critics of the period prior to 1900. In spite of the controversy, Parker's greatest work was accomplished at the Cook County Normal School. During his sixteen-year tenure, his major achievements included: (1) the evolution of his curriculum doctrine of concentration and correlation, (2) the training of teachers in a professional school with emphasis on a new technique called "illustrative teaching," (3) the definition of a school as an embryonic democracy, and (4) the introduction of the first parent association. It wasn't, however, only what was changed but also the scientific manner in which the changes were undertaken that was significant. Parker began to differentiate between the art of teaching and the science of teaching and reflected on the more encompassing concept of the science of education. Just as he wrote about his educational findings in Quincy in his first book, he defined his educational philosophy as it evolved at the Normal School in his second book, *Talks on Pedagogics* (1894). Parker had gained a national reputation in Quincy; he became recognized internationally at the Normal School (see Chapter 4).

Coparticipants in the Normal School saw Parker as a study in contrasts. With the parents he was patient and attentive, when he engaged them in the school process; with teachers he was "no easy task-master," known to yell and holler and strike terror into some.[25] "His criticism, while merciless, was always impersonal and constructive."[26] Conversely, he was quiet and reflective, even reticent when he observed teaching. It was with little children, however, that his humanity, love, and joy were overflowing. The children flocked to know their Pied Piper.

Parker's belief in democracy and his insight into psychology "caused him to make each individual under his care feel himself to be an important and potentially useful member of the community." He made no distinctions between "superior" and "inferior" groups and assured that everyone "was made to feel that his own particular strength was something to use and develop and that his special weakness or limitation, whether of character or ability, was something the school existed to help him strengthen or overcome."[27] The entire undertaking was on an absolutely democratic basis with principal, teachers, and pupils working together for a common end.

This "teacher of teachers" trained more than 1,000 teachers, from which he developed a corps who became his spokespersons and traveled to most states and several countries to introduce the new education. More than any other educator of the nineteenth century, he elevated the classroom teacher to a higher status by emphasizing teacher selection, higher salaries, and significant positions in the educational process. "My fellow teachers," he stated, "the day has now fully come when high-grade professional training schools and colleges are an absolute necessity . . . steps should be taken to see that no college or university graduate is ever allowed to take upon himself the sacred office of teacher without at least two years of professional training in a school or college fully equipped for that purpose."[28]

The educational process at the Normal School was flourishing, but Parker engaged in continuous political battles with the Chicago Board of

Education and a full-scale war broke out in 1894, when the county commissioners drastically cut Parker's school budget. One outspoken commissioner, Charles Thornton, a vociferous critic of Parker's lack of academic credentials, called the Normal School "Parker's Fad Factory."[29] Parker, however, seemed to thrive on such agitation and made a fearless stand for what he believed, often proceeding on his own authority. Insolent in words and actions, no one could oppose him without an open fight. "This man of vision, with his controlling love for mankind, had no fears of the issues." He felt that he had been "called," and there could be "no side-stepping, no compromise."[30] With those who opposed him, he was a "noisy, bold, aggressive figure," who made few mistakes, proceeded confidently and "impetuously," and was "impatient of obstacles."[31]

Parker's days were not all contentious. He took great joy in his work and included "vacation days when he reveled in close contact with Nature—days when friends and co-workers had wonderful companionship, both with him and Mrs. Parker in their home and in their trips across the country."[32] He loved to fish and take rides along country roads. He also liked to read the Bible aloud and recite nature poetry. Recreation in nature, comradeship with colleagues, and pleasure in the relationship with his wife gave him peace. Out of friendship, Mr. and Mrs. Parker made their two-story home at 6640 Honore in Englewood a social center for the teachers, who were invited for an informal evening every Sunday night. It was also the center for planning educational strategy.[33] The wainscoted library that dominated the first floor held several thousand books, including all the works of Horace Mann, a supposedly original volume by Rousseau, and books of Pestalozzi, Froebel, Herbart, and other educators.

Not all criticism of Parker's Normal School was negative. It was counterbalanced by supporting voices of national prominence, such as William James of Harvard University, Nicholas Murray Butler of Columbia University, William Rainey Harper and John Dewey of the University of Chicago, and Jane Addams of Hull House. Germans, Jews, Catholics, unions, and many prominent families also supported his reforms. Nonetheless, the intensity of the battles between Parker and the Chicago School Board grew increasingly fierce.

Anita Blaine, whose friendship and early offers to fund a school for Parker began when she enrolled her son in the Normal School, questioned the waste of Parker's energy caused by these political battles. Why not establish a private training school for teachers? However, Parker's "whole idea throughout his life work had been to do the thing as he saw it for *all* the children of the country. The public schools were the high road he saw for this public good."[34] Having rejected Mrs. Blaine's previous offers, finally, in December 1898 Parker's wife persuaded him to accept. Conceding that a private school could have a long-lasting effect on the public schools, Parker sent Blaine a letter describing his ideal school:

> Lately I have allowed myself to dream of what we would do! . . . I long to prove what a tremendous waste of energy there is in ordinary preparation for college. Students will come from all over the country; parents from a distance will send their children to the Elementary School—A good boarding house...On the farm there could be a model rural school. The school itself . . . might be made an Effective Social Center.[35]

Accepting the presidency of Blaine's school called the Chicago Institute Academic and Pedagogic added greatly to Parker's prestige and reputation. However, some of the fight had gone out of the warrior, now in his early sixties, who had been battling the opponents of the new education since the Civil War. "With his striking personality, his radiant mental energy, his love for humanity as a whole, his aggressive fight for educational freedom for the child, and his zeal in awakening teachers to a true conception of their high calling," Parker had not given up, but tried a new way.[36]

Parker and Blaine began to discuss the plans for the Chicago Institute at the end of 1898, continued to try to advance them throughout the following year, and opened the Institute in 1900. Ultimately, their vision—a private school for the instruction of children and the training of teachers—was too grand, and Blaine's $1,000,000 funding was inadequate for this large educational adventure. With Parker acting like "a splendid big boy and a wise man in one skin" and continually battling with her trustees over plans for the Institute, Blaine turned to President William Rainey Harper of the University of Chicago, who had been courting Blaine's favor and Parker's employment for some time. Blaine merged the pedagogic goals of the Institute with the University to form its School of Education. No longer the solitary hero working on the cutting edge of new education, Parker was now affiliated with a prestigious university, and America's greatest educational philosopher, John Dewey, was his coleader. The two were in basic agreement philosophically, but practical differences between them over Parker's model elementary school and Dewey's Laboratory School, turf wars, and personnel issues smothered their similarities. Parker's venture into the private sector was brief but again riddled with battles. His presidency of the Chicago Institute lasted but one year; his directorship of the School of Education at the University of Chicago for eight months; and his presidency of the Francis W. Parker School from October 1901 to March 1902, was foreshortened by his death (see Chapter 4).

"A born teacher, a non-conformist by nature, a leader of vision and force," Francis Wayland Parker pioneered a revolution in American education that irrevocably transformed primary and elementary schools and teacher training. Dubbed "The Father of Progressive Education" by John Dewey, Parker stirred and influenced the intellectual and emotional life of American education" for more than forty years.[37]

Anita McCormick Blaine (1866-1954): Philanthropist of Progressive Education

Seldom in history has there been a confluence of factors such that one individual could change the course of history. Anita McCormick Blaine was such an exception, when, at the close of the nineteenth century, she was in a position to enable an education revolution. A major philanthropist, Blaine had sufficient funds to underwrite a new educational undertaking and obtain the cooperation of educational theoretician John Dewey and pedagogue Francis Parker to implement the new education.[38]

Speaking at a ceremony held to honor Blaine's philanthropic contributions, Katharine Taylor '06, a former faculty member of Chicago's Francis W. Parker School, captured the essence of Blaine's giving. Taylor identified Blaine's typically decisive and far-sighted responses to a problem, her singular generosity in meeting an immediate need, and her ability to recognize and lead others to the larger issues involved.[39] From the time she was a young woman, Anita McCormick Blaine gave vast sums of money to an array of causes, ranging from summer camps for poor children to President Wilson's League of Nations. In her early thirties, Blaine became a pivotal force in advancing the progressive education revolution emanating from Chicago. She contributed to a new College for Teachers and helped to finance the School of Education at the University of Chicago, underwrote the Chicago Institute Academic and Pedagogic, and later funded the Francis W. Parker School. Her philanthropies proved costly and exceeded $100,000 a year. For example, in 1900, her personal expenditures totaled $154,108, of which $105,261 was given to the Chicago Institute. Her extreme generosity was unsurpassed, but she gave more than money. A pragmatist and visionary, she provided a keen intelligence that guided and governed her largesse. She not only funded these institutions, but she also used the McCormick name to battle the clamorous political opposition to the new education.

Donating to religious rather than education causes would have seemed more predictable because of the integral role her Presbyterian training played in shaping her life. Each Sunday, the Sabbath began before service with morning prayers in the library of her home, followed by services at the Fourth Presbyterian Church with her family and Sunday School classes. Sundays ended with an after-supper evening service. The family home was regarded as a port of call by seminarians, ministers, and missionaries from foreign lands. Dwight Moody, the evangelist and leader of the Young Men's Christian Association, frequently invigorated evening conversations on the topic of religion. By the time Anita McCormick was fourteen, she was attending missionary meetings, teaching Bible lessons at Sunday School, and venturing into philanthropy for the needy.

Anita McCormick was a difficult person to deal with as a philanthropist. Her parents' opposing traits were reflected in her personality. Her father was regarded as a "great power" and an "unyielding foe of whatever was opposed to him." Tenacity, competitiveness, and relentless attention to detail," qualities that made him successful, did not engender love. In contrast, her mother "preferred indirection and evasion to confrontation." The daughter could be unyielding and tenacious at times but indecisive at others. Ultimately, Mrs. Blaine developed a style and a code for her giving which balanced the rights of giver and recipient. She believed the giver should not dominate the receiver's rights, and the receiver should give due respect to the principles and wishes of the giver. As a philanthropist, it was said, "Her heart was with the poet, not with the experts . . . . hers was the politics of frankness and full disclosure, however improbable victory." Some thought that she "dallied inordinately with the relatively unimportant, and progressed slowly, painfully and often with digressions from the promised goal."

Anita McCormick was the middle child in a family headed by Nancy "Nettie" Fowler and Cyrus Hall McCormick, inventor of the McCormick Reaper, a revolutionary labor-saving device that made it possible to harvest wheat mechanically instead of manually. The family was originally from Virginia but moved to New York and then to Chicago, where Cyrus increased his fortune by investments in real estate. Anita had four siblings—Cyrus, Jr., who became president of the McCormick Reaper Company upon his father's death; Harold, who married Edith Rockefeller and became the company's vice president; Virginia, who lived "in the shadow of mental illness"; and Stanley, who after graduating *cum laude* from Princeton suffered from what was diagnosed later in his life as *dementia praecox*. Theirs was a life of privilege—a luxurious mansion on Rush Street on Chicago's North Side, summers in the country, residences from the East to the West Coast, private schools, extravagant travel, and access to the accomplished and world famous.

Typical for women of the times, Anita McCormick's educational background was limited. She attended Misses Grant's Seminary half-days and otherwise adhered to a strict timetable drawn up by her mother: rise at 7:00, dress by 7:30, practice piano for the next half-hour, then breakfast, followed by another hour of piano practice and, until lunch, study in her room. Classes alternated between the afternoon and the morning, as did her schedule. Before the evening meal, she would go for a walk or drive and retire for the night by 9:00 p.m.

In 1878, at age twelve, Miss McCormick traveled to Paris, where her father exhibited the reaper. Prohibited by her mother from attending regular French schools, she was tutored by an English woman in Neuilly, and when she returned to Chicago, Miss McCormick continued her education at the Misses Kirkland's Academy. There she found geometry "perfectly fascinating," natural philosophy "nice but growing much harder," and Latin, "the stupidest thing on earth." She reportedly thought the school routine "a regular treadmill" and questioned the expectation of her teachers that she "defer to their superior judgment, never encouraging her to argue a point, since that would be 'unbecoming.'" She wrote a theme during her last year at the school which closed with the following call to arms:

School-girls! What we want is redress of grievances! But to whom shall we turn to get it! To teachers? No! To mothers? No!! Shall we take the reins of government in our own hands and break loose from all restraint? I think we will have to do that, and overthrow the present system of education![40]

Although it might be dismissed as such, this was not some fit of childish pique on Anita McCormick's part; much of what was to become her lifelong commitment to improving the quality of education in this country was in direct reaction to her own negative schooling experience. The Misses Kirkland's Academy was Miss McCormick's last opportunity to obtain a formal education. Her education was truncated because of her gender. At the end of the nineteenth century, even daughters from wealthy families did not attend college or pursue a career. They were also deemed incompetent in the management of their own finances.

Anita McCormick's fortune was considerable, and after her father's death in 1884, it increased even more. A loan of $4.5 million from John D. Rockefeller, the father-in-law of Harold McCormick, enabled the McCormicks to gain control of the Deering Harvester Company and form the International Harvester Company. Although control of her fortune was turned over to her brother and her uncle, Anita McCormick would be allowed to determine the disposition of the income from her property. As her mother wrote, her daughters *"ought* to have considerable to say about their own property," adding prophetically, "they might want to do good with some of their money."

By age eighteen, Miss McCormick had already received several marriage proposals, although she was more socially conscious than sociable, and her acquaintances more likely to be social reformers than socialites. She met her future husband Emmons Blaine at her coming-out party, when she was twenty-one. The Democratic McCormicks had enormous wealth; the Republican Blaines possessed social status and fame. Emmons Blaine's father had been a Republican nominee for the presidency, the senator from Maine, and was to serve as Secretary of State under presidents Garfield and Harrison. "The uniting of one of America's richest families and one of its best known" on September 26, 1889, "was national news."

Birth and death shaped Mrs. Blaine's young married life. An idyll that began with the birth of their son, Emmons Jr., on August 29, 1890, ended in June 1892 with her husband's premature death, caused by "ptomaine intoxication with uraemia as a fatal complication." Because "Em" was fatherless, Mrs. Blaine was determined to educate him well. Her fervent desire that Em obtain a better education than she had received initially motivated her compelling interest in education. Not long after her husband's death, Mrs. Blaine began to investigate schools that might be appropriate for her son. She had heard of the accomplishments of Francis Parker at the Cook County Normal School through a friend, who took her to observe classes and introduced her to Parker. She also observed John Dewey's Laboratory School at the University of Chicago. She enrolled Em in the Normal School, but because the travel distance from the North to the South Side of Chicago presented a problem for young Em, Mrs. Blaine persuaded Parker to establish a North Side branch. Parker consented and sent a good teacher, Miss Hattie Bradley, who taught regular classes for a small group of neighborhood children.

Within a year of Em's enrollment, Mrs. Blaine invited Francis Parker to her North Side mansion to present a series of lectures on primary instruction to her wealthy friends. It was during this time, in 1897, that she directly discussed endowing a school for Francis Parker, where he might implement his vision for the education of children without the onslaught of opposing forces that had plagued him throughout his tenure at the Cook County Normal School. Because of his fervent belief in the value of public over private schools, Parker initially refused her offer. Expanding her interests in education, two years later, Blaine invited John Dewey to present six lectures at her mansion for the parents of children in his Laboratory School.

With her son enrolled in school, Mrs. Blaine's interest in financing education deepened. Her first gift was an 1898 pledge to contribute $5,000 annually over a five-year period to help fund a College for Teachers at the University of Chicago. In 1899, she increased the figure to a $12,000 annual contribution for seven years. That same year, Francis Parker accepted her offer to endow a private school, and Blaine applied for the incorporation of the Chicago Institute Academic and Pedagogic, a name she chose to illustrate her two goals. Initially, she endowed the Chicago Institute with $400,000 for land, building, and equipment and guaranteed $95,000 each year for the next seven years. Ultimately, Blaine contributed $1.5 million to the Chicago Institute before squabbling between Parker and the trustees forced her to turn to William Rainey Harper, President of the University of Chicago, who wanted to make the Chicago Institute the cornerstone of the School of Education at the University of Chicago.

Blaine's final educational philanthropy established the Francis W. Parker School on the city block she had purchased for the Chicago Institute and had deeded to the University of Chicago in the trustees' negotiations between the two institutions. Blaine allowed the Parker School to be built on the land, which she ultimately gave to the school. In total, Blaine contributed more than three million dollars to the Parker School. She also served on its Board of Trustees and introduced an Education Council to ensure the school would remain constant to the progressive vision she shared with Parker.

Blaine's philanthropy in education achieved its chief purpose—Em did not suffer from the same "miseducation" as did his mother. Although a sickly boy, prone to attacks of nausea and fever, he was able to attend several schools directed by Francis Parker—the Cook County Normal School, a special North Side neighborhood school, the Chicago Institute Academic and Pedagogic, and the Francis W. Parker School. After he graduated from the Francis W. Parker School at age sixteen, he enrolled at Harvard College and studied engineering. He was rejected for military service in World War I due to his medical record, but at Harvard he met and married a Vassar girl, Eleanor Gooding, in 1917. After additional study in engineering at the Boston School of Technology, Em applied to the American Shipbuilding Company in Philadelphia and moved there to help in the war effort. When turned down at the shipbuilding company, he joined a railroad crew. His wife Eleanor became pregnant just at the time the influenza epidemic was transforming Philadelphia into a plague city. Eleanor remained healthy, but Em got a cold, became delirious, and after a short bout of pneumonia, died on October 9, 1918. Upon his death, Eleanor Blaine moved to live with her mother-in-law in Chicago, where she gave birth prematurely to twins—the boy was stillborn, and the girl weighed only four pounds but lived.

Upon her son's death, Mrs. Blaine expanded her philanthropy beyond education. A fan and friend of Woodrow Wilson, she was a strong moral and financial backer of the League of Nations. She supported the work of spiritualist Sir Oliver Lodge and, beginning in the 1940s, pledged campaign funds for Henry Agard Wallace, vice president to Franklin Delano Roosevelt, because "she discerned the uplifting imperative of the social gospel." In the end, Blaine arranged for two-thirds of her estate to be invested in her New World Foundation, whose primary objective was "the right education of children." Driven by her liberal philosophy in giving, these gifts followed her belief that a full life "begins with the realization of other people's needs and woes."

There were many views of Blaine's generosity. According to her biographer Gilbert A. Harrison, her critics charged that she had "abnormal standards of perfection and conscience," which her friends thought to be liabilities and not assets, because they believed she "lacked the zest for maneuver and manipulation." A member of her family thought her to be a perfectionist, and "it mattered little to her whether or not her generosity was expected or even needed." "From a cynic's angle, it could be said that Anita gave up nothing by her generosity, and that the satisfaction of helping others more than compensated for the incidental financial loss." Called eccentric, unconventional, and radical, Blaine was a respected woman with a flair for fun and "a compelling grace and goodness."

Born on the Fourth of July in 1866, Anita McCormick Blaine died on Lincoln's birthday in 1954. Her granddaughter Nancy Blaine Harrison spoke at the memorial service. She brought her grandmother's life full circle, back to her overriding religious beliefs, commenting:

> It has probably occurred to you before now, that the person I am describing sounds very much like the ideal of Christian behavior that is frequently held up to us as children to try and emulate. To a child, this ideal seems remote, impossible of achievement and even rather dreary. And yet my grandmother was none of these things. Her sense of humor, her capacity for enjoyment of mundane things like good food, movies, theatre, music, was wonderful. . . . . As long as there are children that attend the Parker School, as long as there are people who care about others, as long as there are people who experience the invincible courage, gaiety and vitality which she brought to life, my grandmother will be with us.[41]

John Dewey (1859-1952):
Philosopher of Progressive Education

At the beginning of the twentieth century, John Dewey became the "leading figure in American psychological and philosophical circles" and by mid-century, Dewey had developed theories of philosophy, psychology, education, democracy, ethics, and other areas of the social sciences that advanced progressive education for the nation.[42]

It is true that Francis Parker was the main force who moved American education away from traditional school practices, but it was John Dewey who provided the philosophical and theoretical bases for the new education. Parker's educational philosophy formed the bedrock of Chicago's Francis W. Parker School, and Dewey's theories of psychology, education, and democracy, articulated in his writings between 1897 and 1916, shaped the Parker School's direction after Parker's death in 1902. The original corps of teachers, many of whom served the Parker School for the next thirty years, heard Dewey present his *Pedagogical Creed* (1897) when they taught at the Cook County Normal School. The teachers applied the "Creed" and also utilized Dewey's *The School and Society* (1899) as a basis for a democratic school when they transferred to the Chicago Institute Academic and Pedagogic. The Parker School's philosophic foundation was a hybrid, the cross-fertilization of Parker's principles of curriculum and pedagogy and Dewey's philosophic, psychological, and pedagogic theories.

Many of Parker's and Dewey's educational principles were similar, but Dewey's intellectual interests covered a much broader range of subjects. Both placed experience at the heart of the educational process. Parker's approach was "learning by doing," and Dewey's belief was that "all genuine education comes about through experience."[43] Dewey called education "the continuous reconstruction of experience . . . trying and undergoing the consequences of activity [that] provides the organism with intelligent foresight and is fundamental in the education process." Similarly, both educators envisioned education as moral. Parker set the formation of character as the prime goal for education; Dewey agreed, asserting that, "I believe that the moral education centers upon the conception of the school as a mode of social life, that the best and deepest moral training is precisely that which one gets through having to enter into proper relations with others in a unity of work and thought."[44] Dewey insisted that "it is . . . useless to give abstract and didactic moral teaching . . . it should be shown by examples . . . the practical problem is . . . the cultivation of feelings and disposition which may be relied upon to impact the pupil to right action."[45] Both educators also explained the importance and the function of the community in moral education. Dewey called the school a "miniature democracy"; Parker defined a school as "a model home, a complete community, and an embryonic democracy."[46] Democracy and education were prime concerns of both; Parker wrote the last chapter of his 1894 book on the subject, and Dewey theorized about democracy and education in *The School and Society* (1899) and *Democracy and Education* (1916).

Dewey and Parker were products of rural backgrounds. Both were New Englanders: Parker was born in New Hampshire, where he worked on a farm, and Dewey was born in Burlington, Vermont, where he was able to attend grammar and high school. The son of a merchant, Dewey spent a share of his youth on his grandfather's farm, and it was a rural rather than an urban culture that molded his early years. "A democratic neighborliness and a sort of nonconformist individualism modified the social conservatism of the Vermont community in which he lived."[47] The memories of these early years on the farm remained with both educators but affected their educational philosophies differently. Parker retained an enduring love of nature and a deep respect for the education nature could provide, which led him to use nature as the basis for his course of study. Dewey, on the other hand, remembered the social activities and occupations that farm life provided, causing him to use social patterns and different occupations as the basis for his course of study. Parker retained a strong commitment to democracy; but Dewey was a radical in his beliefs about democracy, insisting not only on intellectual and social but also economic democracy.

Their contrasting academic and pedagogical backgrounds produced different kinds of careers. Both began teaching in rural schools, after which Dewey became a high school teacher of science and mathematics for two years, the sum of his precollege teaching experience before he introduced the Laboratory School.[48] Parker, on the other hand, taught grammar school pupils and trained teachers for almost four decades. Unlike Parker, Dewey was able to earn an undergraduate degree from the University of Vermont and to pursue advanced formal education. It was Parker's lack of college credentials that compelled him to travel and to study in Germany later in his life. The absence of formal training undermined Parker's accomplishments throughout his career, and more than once Parker was heard to comment on Dewey's superior grasp of educational philosophy and psychology. Mrs.

Blaine was heard to repeat that "the Colonel himself said that Dewey was a better spokesman for his ideas."[49]

Parker's life was his laboratory, and his educational principles had to be derived through life experiences. For Dewey, educational and pedagogical theories had their origins on his grandfather's farm but were more strongly influenced by his formal training and scholarship. After Dewey completed his degree at the University of Vermont, he earned his doctorate degree in philosophy at Johns Hopkins University under the tutelage of three world-renowned professors—George Morris, an ardent neo-Hegelian philosopher, Charles Peirce, the founder of pragmatism, and G. Stanley Hall, the father of the Child Study Movement.

In his early intellectual pursuits at Johns Hopkins, it was Professor George Morris (1840-1889) who awakened Dewey's interest in the German idealist, Hegel. Morris was a philosophy professor at the University of Michigan and a lecturer in the Philosophy Department at Johns Hopkins when Dewey attended. In *Hegel's Philosophy of the State and History* (1889), Morris championed the idealistic movement initiated by Emanuel Kant and advanced by Hegel.

The Hegelianism in which Dewey was immersed set the frame of reference for his initial outlook on three educational concepts: the definition of man as a social rather than a private being, the necessity of participation in the activities of life, and the importance of communication with others in the learning process. "The concepts of activity, process, organism, and continuity" provided the foundation for the structure of Dewey's thought and became central to his philosophical inquiry.[50] Another premise for Dewey's educational philosophy was the dictum, "Human beings think in order to live." Dewey's philosophy of knowledge was predicated on the belief that "the mind and intelligence have evolved in a purely natural way . . . therefore, nature is inherently neutral, being neither rational nor irrational." Dewey explained that thinking "is an instrumentality used by man in adjusting himself to the practical situations of life . . . . Knowledge is experience and true experiences are functional. Action has always preceded knowledge." For Dewey, "All knowledge has been the result of man's activities in his endeavor to obtain food, shelter, and clothing."[51] "Although the next fifteen years marked a gradual drifting away from Hegel, Dewey himself admitted that his acquaintanceship with this absolute idealist left a permanent mark on his thinking."[52]

Professor Charles Peirce (1839-1914), regarded as the most original thinker and logician of his times, introduced Dewey to another theory of truth that was to put its stamp on Dewey's philosophy. Peirce, who trained at Harvard under William James, was the founder of pragmatism, which was later developed by James and often credited to him. "Pragmatism or radical empiricism . . . contends that there is no such thing as Truth or Reality . . . human beings act and produce results rather than understand and contemplate."[53] By a process of trial and error and perhaps intelligence, called the experimental method, individuals interact with the environment and hit upon some hypothesis which works. Dewey used the experimental method throughout his career.

Another Hopkins professor, G. Stanley Hall (1844-1924), also influenced Dewey's theories of psychology. Hall, a student of William James but predisposed to Wilhelm Wundt's German School of Psychology, did much to make psychology a discipline. He established the American Psychologic Association, edited the first *American Journal of Psychology*, and when he became President of Clark University, invited Sigmund Freud to deliver the only lectures he was to give in the United States. Hall's greatest significance was in his scientific validation of the new definition of the child. Hall's seminal work, *The Contents of Children's Minds* (1893) and a two-volume study on *Adolescence* (1904) explained the findings that children were distinct creatures and not merely miniature adults. Hall was instrumental in establishing the Child Study Movement, which Dewey joined in Illinois, when he moved to the University of Chicago.

In Dewey's book, *Psychology* (1886), he joined the individual theory of the mind and the biological theory of society, and he modified both in a new synthesis. "He recognized the need of reconstructing the static theory of the mind, which isolated it from the actual contents of life. He admitted impulse, emotion, and intellect into the biological theory of society . . . thus recognizing that mind is conditioned by social institutions."[54] In other words, Dewey believed that man was a product of evolution but that the individual mind and social institutions shaped man's life. Although psychology began to absorb Dewey's interests, his initial university appointments were to philosophy departments; the distinction between the two disciplines was as yet vague.

Four years after completing his doctorate degree in philosophy at age twenty-four, Dewey became professor of philosophy at the University of

Minnesota, where he remained for one year before transferring to become a professor and later the chairman of the Philosophy Department at the University of Michigan, where it was George Herbert Mead (1863-1931) who influenced Dewey's view of psychology. Mead was the author of two books published posthumously, *Mind, Self, and Society* (1934) and *The Philosophy of the Act* (1938). Dewey's association with Mead was meaningful to both. The two professors enjoyed a close relationship at the University of Michigan that continued when they became colleagues and neighbors at the University of Chicago.

Among Mead's seminal ideas were evolutionary naturalism, "the belief that the mind and the self have their origin in the interaction of the human organism with its environment" and the psychology of the act, "the emphasis on the continuing interplay between stimulus and response in every human action." "These two theories imply the necessity of man's development in and through his continual contact with other members of society and the inescapable need for active experience through which he acquires and builds his intelligence and controls his behavior and surroundings." In other words, man becomes educated through active experience in the society. "For Mead, the only adequate means for learning to know one's environment, for learning to 'think' about it, or for learning to cope adequately with it is the scientific and experimental method."[55] Dewey's *My Pedagogical Creed* (1897) reflected Mead's theories on "development through social contact" and "active experience." The experimental method was also Dewey's method.

Although Mead's contributions to Dewey's theoretical formulations were considerable, it was the intellectual influence of William James on Dewey's psychological theories that others recognized. Perhaps it was because James was the better known of the two scholars. Mead, however, indicated that, "it would be an error to ascribe to James's *Principles of Psychology* (1890) the starting point of Dewey's independent thought."[56] Mead believed that Dewey's ideas were original and not attributable to James or himself.

After the University of Michigan, Dewey was invited to become chairman of the Department of Philosophy, Psychology, and Pedagogy at the University of Chicago in 1894. In the organizational structure of the University of Chicago, this Department was united under a single head trained in philosophy and psychology. Dewey combined the three disciplines and became a nationally recognized pedagogical theoretician. In the fall of 1895, Dewey began to put his pedagogical beliefs into practice when the University appropriated $1,000 for the establishment of the University Elementary School. At the founding of what came to be called the Laboratory School, its faculty formulated four questions for the school to address: (1) In what manner can the home-school gap be bridged? (2) How can history, science, and art be introduced so that they will be of positive value and have real significance in the child's own present experience? (3) How can instruction in the formal symbolic branches of learning be gained out of these studies? and (4) How should teachers follow the needs of the child that required individual attention?[57] These four questions were asked and answered similarly by both Dewey and Parker, but they were translated into different courses of study.

Dewey "started from the concept of the child living in the world of humans. Mother and father, brothers and sisters, home, family, neighbors, food and shelter, communication and participation . . . Dewey experimented with a course of study centering on social studies and developing a process of reasoning that was to lead the child to an acquaintance with the structure, materials, and operations of the human community."[58] Dewey's central subjects were occupations, defined as activities common to the evolution of all people in the civilization. Dewey based his selection of occupations as the basis for curriculum on the fact that mankind evolved occupations in the struggle to modify a natural environment to his ends. The sources of the occupations examined were domestic, such as cooking, sewing, and weaving, and industrial, like farming, lumbering, and mining. Students passed, according to age group, from one occupation to another. For example, a second grader might learn all about the weaving trade, while a seventh grader would focus on lumbering. Dewey placed emphasis on the social patterns of participation and communication in the various occupations because individuals participate differently when sewing a quilt than when cooking a meal, and they communicate in one way when talking about planting seeds and in another when discussing the War of 1812.

Conversely, Parker's starting point was the concept of the child living in the world of nature. "Rocks, seeds, birds, flowers, leaves, insects, seasons—such natural phenomena as these provide the subjects and objects of thought . . . . Thus, Parker evolved a course of study centering on science and teaching a process of reasoning that was to bring the child to the discovery of the laws of the universe acting through matter."[59] However, Dewey's approach was considered superior because the social studies could incorporate the sciences in the curriculum more readily than the reverse, but both Parker and Dewey used an experience-based foundation for their courses of study.

The Laboratory School was central to Dewey's goals for the Department of Pedagogy, and it divided his ten-year career at the University of Chicago into three periods according to a critic's analysis of Dewey's chairmanship. Dewey's first period extended from his arrival in Chicago in July 1894 to the announcement of the union of the Blaine-Parker Chicago Institute with the School of Education at the University in February 1901. The second period began in March 1901 with Dewey's effort to prevent the consolidation of his Laboratory School with what was now called Parker's University Elementary School and ended with the death of Francis Parker in March 1902. The third period extended from Dewey's appointment to succeed Parker as director of the School of Education in April 1902 to Dewey's angry departure from the University in June 1904.[60]

Between 1894 and 1901, Dewey built the university coursework in philosophy, psychology, and pedagogy substantially. Before Dewey arrived, the Department of Philosophy listed fourteen philosophy courses, three psychology courses, and one pedagogy course. By school year 1899-1900, the Department listed thirty-two philosophy courses, twelve psychology courses, and twenty-three pedagogy courses. In this period Dewey introduced the elementary school, which served as a laboratory for educational experimentation and demonstration and became a source of great interest to President William Rainey Harper. In 1896, Harper proclaimed, "It is our desire to do for the work of the Department of Pedagogy what has not been undertaken in any other institution." Harper commended Dewey on the Laboratory School, but at the same time he neglected to provide finances. Arguing for the necessity of funds for the Laboratory School, Dewey asserted, "the mere profession of principles in a department of pedagogy 'without their practical exhibition and testing will not engage the respect of the educational profession. Without it, moreover, the theoretical work partakes of the nature of a farce and imposture—it is like professing to give thorough training in a science and then neglecting to provide a laboratory for faculty and students to work in.'"[61]

Dewey's first seven years at the University of Chicago were marked by high achievement, national recognition, and unquestioned support. But the conflict over funds for the Laboratory School ushered in a more contentious period. Between March 1901 and March 1902, Dewey's Laboratory School, lacking adequate funds for development, faced stiff competition for resources from a new source, the new Blaine-Parker school, which became the elementary school and the practice school for training teachers. The Blaine-Parker school became part of the School of Education after the University matched Anita McCormick Blaine's $750,000 contribution dollar for dollar. Blaine designated the money solely to Parker as the director of the School of Education.

Harper was not persuaded about the substantive differences between Parker's University Elementary School and Dewey's Laboratory School. He was fearful that the Laboratory School would incur debt for the university, and debt was inexcusable to John D. Rockefeller, the university's major funder. Harper insisted that the Dewey School be self-supporting and that Dewey persuade some generous donors to come forward and endow it. To accommodate Harper, Dewey contacted donors and raised the tuition, but he would not increase enrollment as Harper had suggested. Like Dewey, Harper also wrote to wealthy Chicagoans requesting donations. In his letter to patrons Harper reiterated his earlier sentiments and his praise: "I am confident that nothing is being done today from which greater good may be expected for the public school system not only of Chicago and Illinois, but of the entire country, than the work of the Elementary School, which is, after all, a pedagogical laboratory."[62] A group of well-to-do parents would not let the Laboratory School die, and Dewey went on to appoint his wife, Alice Chipman Dewey, as the principal.

The third period of Dewey's career at the University of Chicago began with Parker's death in March 1902 and concluded with Dewey's resignation from the University. After Parker's death, the trustees of the Chicago Institute appointed Dewey as successor to Francis Parker at the School of Education. Dewey faced an almost impossible task—coordinate the Department of Philosophy, Pedagogy, and Psychology; merge the faculties of the two elementary schools; supervise several high schools which the university had acquired; train teachers; and direct a graduate school. Dewey was eminently qualified but did not resolve the problems. The large, integrated educational enterprise that held the promise of revolution-izing education on a grand scale, collapsed.

When he resigned, his career was at its height. The Department of Philosophy, Psychology, and Pedagogy was flourishing, the pupil enrollment in the Dewey School was growing, and the experiments in education were being observed with great attention. In the Laboratory School, Dewey suc-cessfully solved three major educational problems: (1) he brought the school into closer relationship with the community; (2) he related the studies of the school with real life; and (3) he introduced subject matter in history, litera-ture, science, and other subjects that had positive value and real significance in the child's own life. At the University of Chicago, Dewey introduced "the most important experiment in education that has ever been attempted in this country," one that was "in some respects unique in the history of education."[63]

Parker was a self-taught nineteenth-century idealist, who was born twenty-two years before Dewey and died as the century ended. Dewey was a twentieth century scholar born the year Charles Darwin's *On the Origin of Species* (1859) ushered in the scientific revolution. Those twenty-two years created a chasm between the two scholars, and their experiences gave them very different world views. A social, intellectual, and industrial revo-lution changed the face of America, and Parker's pioneering pedagogy and Dewey's new education theory changed the face of American education, and Mrs. Blaine's educational philanthropy for pre-college education was unsurpassed at this time. "Between the two great educators of Chicago there was a very genuine friendship," but their collective vision went unre-alized in their lifetimes.[64] Nonetheless, these three visionaries made it pos-sible for the progressive legacy to be transferred to the twentieth century, although there was no young leadership to advance their theories.

Chapter 3

The European Intellectual Genealogy
of Francis Parker

Francis Parker was an unschooled schoolmaster until his studies in Europe from 1872 to 1874, at age thirty-five, helped to solidify his educational philosophy and principles. The European pedagogues' views refined his five educational principles about (1) the child and learning, (2) teaching methods, (3) the content of curriculum, (4) the definition of a school, and (5) the nature of the science of education. When Parker returned to American shores two years later, he confidently introduced a "departure" in education based on these principles.

Although a literate, knowledgeable, and highly intelligent person, Francis Parker seemed to remain a naive scholar. For example, he borrowed generously from numerous education heroes, paraphrased them elaborately in his writings, and synthesized their different and sometimes contradictory viewpoints. His newly articulated educational principles were crudely theoretical although he subscribed to a science of education. He developed only one principle, the doctrine or theory of concentration and correlation. Most of his principles were not original except the use of the community as part of the educational process, a concept to which Dewey later subscribed. Derived by trial and error, his philosophy was eclectic, synthetic, and revolutionary. Parker credited his education principles to "all the great teachers of the past," but identified that they were "mainly stolen from Aristotle, Pestalozzi, Spencer," and anyone who had a good idea. He recommended that other educators should also steal because "there was not half enough for the famished minds of children."[1] Parker successfully introduced the revolution in education in classrooms from Massachusetts to Illinois by training teachers in the ideas of the great pedagogues and philosophers of Europe.

Parker's European intellectual genealogy revealed his debt to Comenius for validating what Parker saw as the purpose of education; to Rousseau for his romantic view of the child; to Pestalozzi for his quality teaching method; to Froebel for learning theory; and to Herbart for pedagogy, psychology, and the science of education. Most of the thoughts of these philosophers and pedagogues overlapped, making it difficult to trace or isolate who influenced Francis Parker on what principles.

The American Comenius

The Pansophist philosophy of Comenius deepened Parker's vision of the purpose of education. Born centuries before Parker, John Amos Comenius (1592-1670) was a Czech philosopher of education and a member of the Moravian Brethren persecuted during the Thirty Years War for his religious beliefs. Comenius studied Protestant theology at the Universities of Herborn and Heidelberg and became a pastor before being made a bishop. The most recognized theologian and educator of the seventeenth century, Comenius was noted for unifying his Christian beliefs with the principles of education and for dedicating his life to the advancement of humanity through religious learning. He expressed hope for the regeneration of mankind through education. Comenius believed "the ultimate aim of education was eternal happiness with God."[2] Parker, a Christian, also equated education and salvation.

Comenius's classic, *The Great Didactic* (1638), perhaps the most important educational treatise of its era, was translated from Czech into Latin and published in Amsterdam in 1657. *The Great Didactic* explained the concept of the regeneration of mankind. The six chapters of the book combined religious with educational goals. The final chapters asserted that the ends of learning, virtue, and religion are naturally implanted in mankind and that if man is to be productive, "it is necessary that he be formed by education."[3] Comenius also believed that children could be taught quickly, pleasantly, and certainly the sum of all knowledge and at the same time develop character.

The Czech theologian stated six principles of nature that influenced his view of learning, curriculum, and teaching. He characterized learning as natural, in these ways: Nature provides suitable time for being, does not rush life, proceeds in order, does not take leaps but develops from within, completes all acts, and avoids obstacles. Comenius's main goal was to make the logical interconnections between the child and the subjects learned in the curriculum, which was one of the origins of the child-centered curriculum.

Comenius's goal was based on the principles of the child's mental growth. Psychological principles were to replace the formal logical structure of subject matter as the organizing principle of curriculum. In Comenius's conception, the psychological principles of child development and the logical principles of subject matter or disciplines stemmed from the single arching principle of organic unity, which simply defined meant that the entire universe was unified under the creator. The unity of knowledge, he believed, derived from sensory precepts, which were integrated into a series of concepts at levels of increasing abstraction and complexity. In other words, the child sees, hears, and feels the whole of things with his whole being. Parker, ever in search of a theory of unity, integrated Comenius's concept in his doctrine of curriculum, as he explained it in *Talks on Pedagogics* (1894).

The parallels between Comenius's and Parker's philosophy of life and education were significant and plentiful. For both pedagogues, the formation of character was the goal for the child being educated. Parker also espoused Comenius's doctrine that education was the development of the whole man, restating his precept, "Permanent happiness is the result of continuous, persistent, self-effort in the normal, all-sided development of the body, mind, and soul."[4] Parker also applied psychological principles of the child in preference to the logical principles of the disciplines to organize his course of study. But the parallels did not end there.

In his earliest book, *Talks on Teaching* (1883), Parker paraphrased several principles attributable to Comenius: (1) "schools should become workshops humming with work," (2) "actual objects and things should be studied first, before language," and (3) "pleasantness and interest should replace force and drudgery." He iterated still more of Comenius's principles later in *Talks on Pedagogics* (1894) and other sources: (4) "education should be according to nature," (5) school training is necessary for all classes of children, (6) education should be adapted to the pupil's age and stage of development, and (7) the school system should be adapted to the child and not the child to the school system.[5]

In seventeenth-century Europe, Comenius criticized the schools of the day as being "slaughter houses of the mind," where children's senses and sensibilities were dulled by rote, mindless routine, and psychological and physical punishment. Parker criticized American schools of his era for the identical problems. Both were optimistic and believed that the prevalent ignorance among the lower classes could be eradicated through education.[6] Comenius solidified Parker's thinking by asserting, "We learn to do by doing it," but to Comenius and Parker "doing" or "action" alone were insufficient; the critical and speculative capacities of a student had to be cultivated as well.[7] It was not surprising that some educators called Parker "the American Comenius."

Rousseau's Child-Centered Philosophy

Francis Parker's understanding of the child to be educated reflected Rousseau's romantic definition of the child. Writing in an age of intellectual ferment, Rousseau expounded a theory of education that accorded with the trends of Enlightenment thought. Education was not only integral to Rousseau's philosophical construction for social reform, it was a prior and necessary condition.[8]

Born of humble origins in France, Jean Jacques Rousseau (1712-1778) received scant formal education. His personal life was less than exemplary; he alienated family and friends and intentionally provoked authorities, which necessitated his leaving France for Prussia, then Switzerland, and later England. Rousseau's writings concentrated on a single theme, the utopian desire to reconstruct society by means of a new theory of natural order. He stated his fundamental concept of education in the opening line of his seminal work, *Émile* (1762), "Everything is good as it comes from the hands of the Maker of Things: everything degenerates in the hands of man." In Rousseau's construction, man through wrong institutions and artificial practices deformed his own nature and therefore his society and failed in genuine fulfillment. Rousseau's solution was a careful study of nature and its process in order to bring mankind to achieve appropriate ends in life. Since the formation of life derived from three sources—nature, man, and things—Rousseau argued, the proper end of man is the completion of nature's own goal, the harmonious blending in correct sequence of these three formative influences.[9]

In *Émile*, Rousseau reasoned that, since the child was naturally good, learning was most effective when it followed the child's interests and needs. Natural development meant that the child was not a miniature adult, and education should proceed along natural lines without coercion. Rousseau argued, "Nature wants children to be children before being men." Rousseau introduced the concept of stages of development of the human being: infancy, childhood, preadolescence, young adult, and maturity, and indicated that each stage had appropriate learning activities, which education should follow. "Childhood has its own way of seeing, thinking, feeling," and since the child cannot deal with abstractions, education must come through contact with things. The activities of the child acquainted the child with the world and with the uses and limits of its own powers. Because physical and mental activities reinforced each other, Rousseau reasoned that to learn to think, the child must exercise his limbs, senses, and body organs, which Rousseau identified as the tools of the intellect. Rousseau saw the senses as part of the child's apparatus of action by which the child adjusted to the environment.

Parker was influenced by Rousseau, but he was critical of Rousseau's advocacy of "wild growth." Parker thought Rousseau meant to leave the child alone until "a wise purpose could apply the proper conditions." Growth for Parker was subject to divine and natural laws, and he believed that the teacher should guide and interfere when necessary. "The teacher must know the immediate needs of life at every stage and supply the external condition to change the internal conditions of the child."[10]

Unlike Rousseau and many of the child-centered educators who advocated "wild growth," Parker qualified the freedom and spontaneity of the child, concentrating rather on the child's needs and interests. Parker's child-centered Rousseauean philosophy was strongly molded by and competed with his community-centered definition of the school, which called for disciplining the child through the school community, where responsibility and altruism replaced freedom and narcissism. Parker's course of study was planned, organized, deliberate, and he was not prone to permitting the child "wild growth."

Some authorities called Francis Parker "more Rousseauean than anything else" because of the emphasis he placed on "the spontaneous tendencies of the child."[11] It is true that Rousseau's and Parker's world views were congruent in several respects: (1) education was an *a priori* condition to improve life, (2) the child needed freedom, (3) learning was natural, (4) the growth of the child was inward, (5) a child's life differed from an adult's life and education should provide learning activities that are stage appropriate, and (6) the happiness of the individual was a cardinal principle. In both philosophers' minds, education was summarized in the goal, "The end of all education should be to promote man's happiness." Rousseau's ideal of emancipating childhood from the restrictions of discipline, authority, and regimentation was inspired by his desire to lay the foundations of a happy life for every child. Parker's emphasis on self-discipline, character development, and community responsibility ruptured his compatibility with Rousseau's romantic philosophy, and this factor more than any other differentiates the Parker School from most child-centered schools. Parker's school was community centered more than child centered.

Pestalozzi's Quality Teaching Method

Swiss educator Johann Heinrich Pestalozzi's pedagogical method was the prevailing method in German elementary schools when Parker observed them. It was also the dominant pedagogy in the few normal schools that were training teachers at that time in America. Francis Parker attributed to Pestalozzi the American reform of teaching from quantity or book teaching to quality teaching or the natural method based on experience.

Johann Heinrich Pestalozzi (1724-1827), a native of Zurich, Switzerland, and a disciple of Rousseau, named his child Jean Jacques and tried to raise him according to the principles of *Émile* (1762). Pestalozzi wrote no single exposition of his philosophy, but he upheld the major principle, education should follow nature, in voluminous writings in different genre. His first major work, *Evening Hours of a Hermit* (1780), stated his dominant principle of natural education, which was explored further in his didactic novel, *Leinhard and Gertrude* (1781). The protagonist, Gertrude, showed how the good mother can make the home into the "foundation of pure and natural education of mankind."[12]

Pestalozzi viewed man less romantically than Rousseau. He did not glorify the state of nature and did not accept that discipline was a negative. Rather, he asserted that the child must also be acted upon. In his view, man had a primitive impulse, was a social being, and had ethical yearnings. His aim for education was an ethical society, and the process was one whereby ethics triumphed over primitive impulses in the child. Pestalozzi believed that the ethical life of man was primary and that all education was moral. He too asserted that education was "the outworking of the design of God into highest character." He also believed that the intellectual and psychomotor activities were subordinate. The supreme task of education, Pestalozzi asserted, was to get man in harmony with other men and God. He advocated that the atmosphere of the schools should imitate a good Christian home, characterized by sympathy and love. A humanitarian, Pestalozzi's message was essentially a love message in an environment of compassion, understanding, and security. Like others in the Era of Enlightenment, Pestalozzi made "the child the center of the educational process, upholding an organic rather than a mechanical conception of the child's nature, emphasizing that the child's growth should be 'a natural, symmetric, and harmonious development' of his physical, vocational, intellectual, and moral life."[13]

Like Comenius, Pestalozzi's method incorporated "learning by doing" with learning extended to training of the head, hand, and heart. The Pestalozzian object lesson became popular in the United States in the second half of the nineteenth century. Children examined and explored objects and then determined their shape and quality before naming them. In *Talks on Teaching* (1883), Parker wrote several chapters to explain "number, form, and sound lessons," which moved instruction away from the highly verbal recitation to a child's interaction with actual objects.

To Pestalozzi and Parker, natural education replaced formal method and the education of all of the domains of the child and not solely the intellectual domain were key. Teaching the child in an atmosphere of love rather than authority, and teaching morals and not solely subject matter were other mutual goals. Both pedagogues emphasized the interrelationship of mental and moral education and addressed the moral, the ethical, and the development of character. Both also found in geography the perfect content and method for instruction.

Parker acknowledged indebtedness to Pestalozzi's quality method in both of his books; some chapters are almost direct translations of Pestalozzian principles. Parker wrote, "In Prussia the . . . discussions in philosophy . . . came with awakening force; but a still greater influence came from the Republic of Switzerland . . . when . . . Pestalozzi translated his fundamental precept, 'Education is the generation of power' into action."[14] In other words, a child is empowered by knowledge to action. The more the pupil can do, the more the pupil will do. Action begets more action, a reaction, and an interaction. Through this empowerment, the latent potential of the individual is realized.

Froebel's Learning Theory

Friedrich Froebel was the most significant educator in the Activity Movement and the Kindergarten Movement. Froebel founded the first kindergarten in Blankenburg, Germany, and according to Parker's observations, the nineteenth-century Prussian kindergarten was advanced in pedagogy and "possessed a zeal for true methods, and . . . contempt for mere book-cramming."[15] Froebel's kindergarten was based on a unity theory, placing man in nature as both a part and a whole, a member of the universe and a complete being.

Friedrich Froebel (1782-1852) was born in Oberweissbach, Prussia, and studied at the University of Jena and later Gottingen and Berlin. Like Rousseau and Pestalozzi, Froebel saw most problems in education arising from interference with the natural processes of learning. In 1805, when in his early twenties, Froebel traveled to Yverdon to study Pestalozzi's methods, became converted, and for a time, worked with Pestalozzi at his school. Froebel was determined to develop a systematic exposition of the subjects of instruction. His major aim of education was developing the latent power of the individual.

In his masterpiece, *Education of Man* (1826), Froebel wrote, "Education consists in leading man, as a thinking, intelligent being, growing into self-consciousness, to a pure and unsullied, conscious and free representation of the inner law of divine unity and in teaching him ways and the means thereto." To Froebel, education was a continuation of the world's unceasing evolution on the level of consciousness with child's play the first sign of life's urge toward consciousness or purposeful activity. His educational theory and practice were determined by his conviction of the ultimate oneness of life, nature, and spirit, and the latent powers of the individual. Froebel argued for productive activity and play as education, reasoning that since every person forms his own world for himself, and play is the chief means by which the child constructs an interpretation of reality, then play or active engagement with the environment is productive activity, and productive activity is both the content of the curriculum and the means of implementing it.[16]

Froebel's philosophy of the unity of the curriculum and his unity of the body, mind, and soul of the child formed one of Parker's major ideals, the use of all modes of expression. Parker explained how "expression," according to Froebel, "acts to develop motive; it makes the highest demand for thought power, and requires the most healthful exercise of the body."[17]

In at least three significant ways Froebel's and Parker's educational principles were congruent. In Froebel as in Herbart, Parker found a unity of purpose and method in curriculum, which provided a basis for his doctrine of concentration and correlation. Second, Parker organized the subjects of the curriculum organically and in harmony with the natural inner development of the child. Third, Parker emphasized the education of the whole child and his major teaching method, like Froebel's, was based on principles of play, activity, and expression. In his two books, Parker quoted Froebel's aim of education—"the harmonious growth of the whole being." Parker's philosophy echoed Froebel's principle of unity— "We get the sublime idea of the unity of the human spirit; the unity of creation and the Creator: all life for one life, and each for all."[18] Like Froebel, Parker added a kindergarten class at the Cook County Normal School when he became a principal.

Froebel also influenced Parker's interpretation of education as a science. Froebel's *The Education of Man* (1826) was the first expression in the educational record to state that education was capable of becoming a science and pedagogy becoming scientific. "Educational theory," Froebel wrote, "consists in the principles derived from such insight, which enable intelligent beings to become aware of their calling and achieve the purpose for which they are created."[19] Froebel saw that the art of education lies in the free application of this knowledge and insight to the development and training of men so that they are enabled to achieve their purpose as rational beings. In Froebel's view, the educator's function was to organize the instructional process in a way that the subjects to be taught supported the learner's inner development, and the entire program of study was to help the student realize the reflection of the unity of life in the unity of knowledge.

Froebel was also a major influence on Dewey's educational principles. In fact, Dewey called his Laboratory School of the University of Chicago "an exponent of Froebel's educational philosophy." The Laboratory School carried into effect principles, which "Froebel was perhaps the first consciously to set forth." The three major Froebel principles that Dewey underscored overlapped with several Parker principles: (1) "the primary business of the school is to train the children in cooperative and mutually helpful living," (2) "the primary root of all educative activity is in the instinctive, impulsive attitudes and activities of the child," and (3) play is a "mental attitude."[20] Dewey named one chapter in *School and Society* (1899), "Froebel's Educational Principles"; however, in *Democracy and Education* (1916), Dewey praised but also criticized Froebel.

Herbart's Psychology, Pedagogy, and Science of Education

Several key postulates articulated by Johann Herbart (1776-1841) concerning the unity of creation, the education of the whole child, and the science of education shaped Francis Parker's educational posture significantly. Born in Oldenburg, Prussia, Herbart attended the University of Jena, completing his degree in Göttingen, where he became a lecturer in philosophy. Between 1809-1831, Herbart held the Konigsberg philosophy chair at what was one of the two major universities in Prussia, where it was hoped that new education ideas could be introduced. In 1810, however, the Prussian Minister founded a third Prussian university in Berlin to which he appointed the preeminent philosophy chair to Hegel, who served until his death in 1831. Herbart, the heir-apparent, failed to receive the appointment because of the shift in Prussia toward more conservative views. Nonetheless, Herbart's philosophy influenced the pedagogy, psychology, and the science of education in Europe and in America. Herbart was receptive to the converging Enlightenment traditions of philosophy and science. In his view, the world was an organized coherent whole, sustained by moral purpose. Education was an intervention in the normal course of events in order to restructure the child's experience in the direction of morality.[21]

Rousseau and Pestalozzi stressed the importance of the individual over the society, but Herbart theorized a balance between freedom and authority in education. Herbart believed in the need for individual freedom through personal effort, which Parker conceptualized as "movement ahead" and what he called eternal becoming. Both Parker and Dewey, however, criticized Herbart because he placed too little weight on freedom and too much on authority.

Herbart's major work, *General Pedagogy Deduced from the Aim of Education*, was translated into four English titles, *The Science of Education* (1806), *Textbook in Psychology* (1816), *Psychology as a Science Based on Experience* (1824), and *The Application of Psychology to the Science of Education* (1831). These four books were Herbart's attempt to place teaching on a scientific footing.

Herbart defined pedagogics as the process in which the teacher deliberately intervened. To intervene effectively, he explained, the teacher must study each child carefully since educability is limited by individuality. This scrutiny must encompass the whole child so the teacher must make observations both of the child's thought masses and physical nature.[22] The function of the teacher is to arouse the many-sided interests in the cultivation of the child's mind. Pedagogy to Herbart was essentially intellectual in its emphasis. His taxonomic approach to pedagogy was felt to be the scientific method of inductive inquiry.

Herbart constructed a pedagogy based on a taxonomy of objectives with two categories, which classified six disciplines. The first category focused on those conditions providing social experiences for the purpose of learning sympathy for mankind and society. These included the four disciplines of language, literature, religion, and history. The second category emphasized those conditions which provided object experiences for the purpose of learning knowledge of the external world of laws and aesthetic relationships, including mathematics, natural sciences, and handicraft. Herbart's term "concentration" "involved an organic unity of subjects, while correlation was a mechanical unity of five parallel but not intersecting studies."[23] Parker credited his curriculum theory of concentration and correlation to Herbart. To Parker, "the psychology of Herbart, and the doctrine of concentration enunciated and applied by his disciples Ziller, Stoy, and Rein, have been a source of inspiration and a guide in the general direction of the work."[24]

Herbart made a number of distinct pedagogical advances over existing theory. He designed a four-step formal lesson plan in which a teacher: (1) arranges the formal curriculum between social and object experiences, (2) age grades the curriculum to the intellectual level of the child, (3) designs the lesson plan, and (4) sequences the instruction. This lesson plan provided the best explanation to that date of how children learn. According to Herbart, to sequence instruction, teachers must use four additional steps: Step 1—the preparation or clarification of the lesson, Step 2—the association of the new lesson with the previous lesson, Step 3—the broadening and deepening of the association, and Step 4—the summarization of the lesson in broad principles.[25] Parker adapted Herbart's pedagogical taxonomy and trained teachers to create lesson plans through what he called "Illustrative Teaching."

Herbart not only influenced Parker's view of pedagogy but also his view on psychology. In Herbart's three books on psychology, he attempted to make psychology an autonomous science, divorced from philosophy and metaphysics. He focused on the relationship between latent and innate ideas in the mind, or on what was known as "the plasticity or educability of the pupil." The process of molding the child was to be achieved by working with two psychological processes: reflection and concentration.

Herbart's influence was also apparent in Parker's definition of the science of education. Although Parker did not join the Herbart Club for the Scientific Study of Education when it was introduced in the United States in 1892, he did, however, accept an invitation to speak at a meeting. Soon thereafter Herbartianism became the ultimate expression of the scientific movement of education.

Francis Parker solidified the educational principles formulated during the first thirty-five years of his life through the examination of the German pedagogical tradition, which closely followed utopian lines and scientific principles. The European pedagogues' collective influence aided Parker in the transformation of the traditional American subject-centered school to a Rousseauean-influenced child-centered school, rote learning into Comenius' "learning by doing," quantity or subject-centered teaching to Pestalozzi's quality or experience-centered method, and the passive role of the child into Froebel's activity and expression learning. Herbart added to the American educator's modest understanding of the science of education. Parker applied the European philosophy and pedagogy for the first time in Quincy, Massachusetts, when he returned from Germany.

Chapter 4

Francis Parker Introduces
New Education in American Schools

Until the nineteenth century, education in America was not a national priority, nor did a consensus exist about its aims and goals. At the birth of the nation, there was little recognition of the importance of an educated citizenry to create a democracy. Two centuries passed before Americans began to realize that education was "the primal necessity of social existence" because "a community without a conscience would extinguish itself."[1] In the 1800s, two educators, Horace Mann and Francis Parker, were the first to acknowledge the importance of the free public school to the new democratic society.

Horace Mann (1796-1859), the first Secretary of the Massachusetts Board of Education, became known as "the father of public education" in 1837 because he created the American common school—so called because its aim was to educate the common man for the common good.[2] Mann also revolutionized public school organization and teaching and established the first normal school in the United States.

By the last quarter of the nineteenth century, routine student work, the grading of tests and assignments, and the mechanics of teaching had become such absorbing tasks in American schools that the individuality of the child had practically dropped out of the reckoning. As Americans were organizing their schools like "mechanical education machines," modeled on the cotton mill, the railroads, and the state prisons, voters, through their local school boards, were demanding that even less money be devoted to education than the inadequate amounts originally allocated.[3] The Economic Depression of 1873 caused the public call for further educational efficiencies. Henry Adams summarized education in nineteenth-century America in these words: "The generation that lived from 1840 to 1870 could do very well with the old forms of education; that which had its work to do between 1870 and 1900 needed something quite new."[4] That "something quite new" would be brought about in 1875 by Francis Parker when he initiated the first large-scale pedagogical transformation of the common schools in Quincy, Massachusetts.

The Quincy Experiment (1875-1880)

"As a suburb of Boston, Quincy was losing its rural character and separate identity . . . . The business leaders still ruled, although there was competition developing among the Irish stone cutters who had established their own subcommunity." While the Quincy leadership was interested in education, the Economic Depression of 1873 prompted the Quincy School Committee, like so many school boards in America, to call for reduced spending. Unlike most boards, however, the Quincy School Committee included reformers, notably, John Quincy Adams II, the grandson of President John Adams; his younger brother, Charles Francis Adams, Jr., who had been influenced by the writing of Horace Mann; and James Slade, a Quincy businessman. Their goal was not only educational efficiency but also educational excellence, especially when the School Committee discovered, after administering a set of final examinations, that Quincy students did not understand the content of their studies, the thought processes involved, or the application of knowledge. Pupils merely memorized definitions and rules and acquired disconnected facts. This teaching by rote did not result in learning.[5]

Charles Adams summarized this deplorable condition, saying: "After eight years, children could neither write with facility nor read fluently; nor could they speak or spell their own language very perfectly. The whole existing system was wrong—a system from which the life had gone out. The school year had become one long period of diffusion and cram, and smatter had become the order of the day." The School Committee reported, "The ever-present object in the teacher's mind was to have students pass a creditable examination," and to ensure this objective the teachers unconsciously turned their students into parrots, making education a meaningless farce.[6]

Determined to bring about educational reform, the School Committee decided to hire a superintendent. Because the position of superintendent was as yet unrecognized, candidates were unlikely to be trained. Charles Adams wrote, "The ordinary superintendent is apt to be a grammar school teacher, some retired clergyman, or a local politician out of a job." He added that, "It was a noticeable fact that as large and costly as the common school system of this country is and greatly as it stands in need of intelligent direction, not a single step has yet been taken towards giving it such a direction through an educated superintendency."[7]

Early in 1875, the School Committee asked the citizens of Quincy to support the new position of superintendent and "to put the working out of a new system of education in his hands." The Committee's charge for the new position was, "Education was to recur to first principles. Not much was to be attempted; but whatever was attempted was to be thoroughly done, and to be tested by its practical results, and not by its theoretical importance." Assigning a mandate of "economy and excellence," the new superintendent was "to secure, if possible, a thorough going, good common school education at a not unreasonable cost, keeping in view the fact that neither was to be subordinated to the other."[8]

The Committee entrusted the challenge of finding a superintendent to James Slade, who advertised the position in a Boston newspaper. Francis Parker, who had recently returned from Germany to Manchester, New Hampshire, saw the advertisement and applied. The Committee explained its eventual selection of Francis Parker in these words—"We chanced across one who had not only taught himself but in teaching had become possessed with the idea that it was a science and that he did not understand it," and so he "went abroad to master German theories of common school education." Adams explained Parker to the citizens of Quincy as "a self-educated and a self-made man with all the defects as well as the virtues of men of that class." In April 1875, Francis Parker signed a one-year contract but remained in the position for five years. Parker received "unhampered support" from the Committee and was alone "held accountable for results," despite opposition from a number of detractors.[9]

Practical results, rather than educational theory, guided Parker's work. His goals at Quincy were ostensibly simple—to "help to free child and youth from the bonds of ancient pedagogical formalism, and the dulling routine of textbook learning." Parker asserted that he was "introducing nothing new, no new principles or methods; he was simply seeking to find something better for children" and to carry out the recommendations of great educators of the past. His approach, he argued, did not consist of methods for teaching certain fixed details but rather presented teaching as the greatest art in the world, which demands: "(1) an honest, earnest investigation of the truth as found in the learning mind and the subjects taught and (2) the courageous application of truth when found." "'What he trusted in—was man's creative soul'—rather than methods, routine, and compulsory drudgery."[10]

Francis Parker added little new to the organization and administration of the Quincy school system, although an article in the *New York Tribune* credited his success to administration. Parker's idea of administration was being an effective head teacher and engaging in the educational rather than in the administrative processes of the schools. He saw the superintendent as a teacher of teachers, who organized the principals into a supervising body to assist the superintendent in training teachers. As superintendent, Parker developed a common, continuous, and systematic plan of work for six elementary schools, one secondary school, 1,600 students, forty-two teachers, and several principals. The system's hierarchy descended from the School Committee to the superintendent, who was solely accountable for results; from the superintendent to the principals, who were to help in the observation and supervision of teachers; and from the superintendent working with the teachers to help them advance. Education and not administration was central to the schools.

More autocratic than authoritarian, Parker delegated new responsibilities to the principals and the teachers, advancing their status and giving teachers the freedom to experiment, to study, and to learn. He established a new school schedule, reducing nine grades to eight and a forty-three-week school year to forty weeks. He organized office hours on Monday and Saturday mornings for parent meetings, and he canceled Monday afternoon classes so teachers might meet to develop new courses.[11] He added a library and made it an integral part of the approach to reading. Children and adults made free use of the library for research, and students showed an increasing interest in reading. The school proper was made more attractive— chairs were placed in circles around tables, and the shades were pulled up to let in the sunshine.

Lelia Patridge's *The Quincy Method* (1889) provided the most extensive account of the new education Parker developed at Quincy. Patridge, a graduate of a Massachusetts normal school, had attended Parker's summer classes at Martha's Vineyard and spent six months observing the Quincy schools first-hand. In her book, she identified twenty-four of Parker's approaches to learning, teaching, the course of study, and the school as a democracy.[12]

Within the Quincy classrooms, Parker reversed the process of traditional education. Instead of starting with definitions and rules, the new education began with the observation of objects or participation in experiences and concluded with definitions and rules. Natural learning, which was based on life experiences, often occurred outside of the classroom, perhaps in the fields or at the water's edge, and replaced formal classroom learning. Parker's goal for the first year was to make school a "pleasant, cheerful home," as Pestalozzi recommended. Students were "taught to read, write, spell, and think all at the same time."[13] Language exercises were learned by doing. For example, teachers used four different writing exercises—"talking with a pencil," which led students to answer questions by writing an original account; a "story lesson" that asked students to view an object and write a narrative; an "action lesson" that taught pupils to study thought through expression; and a "picture lesson" that trained students in observation. Teachers used what was called the "Object Method," or "Mother's Method," showing the object, or a picture of the object, before naming it.[14]

Patridge named eight qualities inherent in the Quincy method: (1) the carefully varied programs of the teachers; (2) a thoughtfully mixed program for the students; (3) an economy, naturalness, and practicability of teaching devices; (4) the substitution of the expression of original thought for traditional memory recitation; (5) the constant use of drawing as a means of expression; (6) a skillful use of a great amount and variety of "busy work;" (7) the marked attention paid to the so-called dull pupils; and (8) the evident growth in the moral power of the pupils. Parker referred to this kind of instruction as unified, holistic, and natural. Because Parker grouped pupils according to mental achievement rather than by chronological age, classes were smaller, allowing teachers to observe pupils more closely and give special attention to dull students, and allowing pupils to work together better with less friction.[15]

The "new departures" from the older form of education in Quincy were "experiments continuously tried and results from time to time noted." The goal in the Quincy schools was to have the children "seek unity without uniformity." "Children were to learn to read and write and cypher as they learned to swim, skate, or to throw a ball," said Charles Adams. "The study under the new method becomes full of life and interest; while under the old it was tedious."[16]

To transfer the new learning process, Parker trained the teachers through a variety of techniques—visiting classrooms to teach a little or to identify the weaknesses and strengths of the teachers, organizing weekly faculty meetings and extending blocks of time for planning new courses, and presenting demonstration lectures complete with model lessons and corollary readings to provide theory to support what he was doing. He supplemented training sessions with teacher study groups that examined the works of Comenius, Pestalozzi, and Froebel.

Patridge named four distinguishing features of the teachers trained in Quincy: "(1) the remarkable skill of the teachers evidencing their comprehension of underlying principles; (2) the originality and individuality of the teachers—none being imitators and the devices used changing from day to day; (3) the high ideal set before the teachers by the superintendent and their hearty cooperation with him in striving to attain it; and (4) the absence of machinery and the absolute freedom from any fixed or prescribed mode of work with each teacher being encouraged to invent and try any device not violating fundamental laws."[17]

Although the Quincy teachers became actively engaged under Parker's new pedagogical approach, and some became his disciples, low salaries caused many to resign in order to take better paying positions. The high turnover caused Parker to comment to the School Committee that "Quincy paid for the training of teachers and other towns reaped the rewards." Indeed, Parker, "A Teacher of Teachers," trained his teachers so extensively and effectively that the School Committee authorized him to establish a training school for the preparation of teachers. Although Parker resigned before the training school materialized, the teachers did begin to develop a new course of study.

For the first time in American education, Parker discarded the subject-centered course of study as teachers attempted to make the experience of the child central. As Patridge observed, "The making of the child is the objective point and not the course of study, examinations, or promotions." Subject matter was learned but the starting point and the aim were different. "In the old days," Patridge wrote, "it was taken for granted that children knew nothing when they entered the schoolroom, had no power of gaining facts until they were taught how, and the first thing that they should learn was to read." In the new course of study, the teacher regarded pupils as "bundles of possibilities," observing the children and then beginning with the "thought of the generation of power," adding to what the children already knew and "following closely the methods they have already pursued under nature's teaching."[18]

Parker injected life into the older more formal approach to schooling in several ways. "Old forms were courageously set aside; routine was broken; the textbook as formerly used was discarded, also the copybook."[19] Reading was learned naturally through the "word method," which meant abolishing the study of the formal alphabet and learning the meaning of the full word, rather than learning a word a letter at a time. Spelling, grammar, and writing were taught through exercises or through learning by doing. Textbooks were supplemented with books from the library.

With respect to arithmetic, Parker and the Quincy faculty found that meaningless numbers and rules did not teach pupils to solve mathematical problems. Arithmetic should be taught "by teaching one definite thing at a time, and teaching 'things' with figures as their representatives."[20] The study of geography became the most marked departure from traditional teaching. Pupils were taught how to mold a "heap of moistened clay into a well shaped continent with its mountains, rivers, depressions, coastal indentations, and all geographic peculiarities."[21] The faculty learned how to reverse the process of instruction, by naming, defining, and then giving the rules. In the primary grades, Quincy teachers presented the reality of things and taught principles and rules later in the grammar school.

The goal of the course of study shifted and was no longer the gaining of skill and knowledge, but the new ideal was the ideal of growth in an atmosphere of enthusiastic but normal activity of self-poised and self-controlled and happy pupils."[22] The new course of study was distinguished by lessons in subjects not usually taught—drawing, modeling, form, color, and natural history, supplementary reading, and examinations that tested the children's power to do rather than to memorize. Parker's biographer Ida Cassa Heffron, a teacher who worked with him after the Quincy experiment, explained the course of study in these words: "What Parker did was apply methods of quality teaching, reduced the number of subjects in the curriculum, set old forms aside, and broke routines."[23] The course of study, a "new departure" from the old education, became the template for new education.

Philosophically, his starting point was his extended search for an organic unity in the educational process. He discovered three kinds of unities: the unity within the child or the "harmonious development of the whole being"; the unity of schoolwork; and the unity of the course of study wherein "each lesson should be a lesson in language, a lesson in attention, and a lesson in morals."[24] Parker had not yet worked out how courses were to be unified.

Although Parker had yet to define the relationship of the school to the larger democratic society, he had reconceptualized life within the school as "a miniature and a model democracy." To this end, he called for the transformation of authoritarian discipline based on the dictum that children "be seen and not heard" to a democratic discipline based on self-control and student participation in self-government. He wanted to create an informal atmosphere in which learning was motivated not by fear but by interest.[25] Of the twenty-four distinguishing features of the Quincy system, Patridge ascribed one-fourth to the nature of school discipline and atmosphere within the school: (1) the joyous life of the schools and the comradeship of the teacher and pupils; (2) the atmosphere of happy work; (3) the confidence, courtesy, and respect of pupils to teachers and of teacher to pupils; (4) disorder not worrying the teacher and wasting her time; (5) the absence of scolding, snubbing, or spying; and (6) the dignity, self-possession, and lack of self-consciousness of pupils.[26]

Parker discovered that democracy called for a moral citizenry and education implied moral training. He already realized that it was a fatal error for teachers "to believe that mental training was a thing apart from moral training, and that therefore the teacher had no responsibility in the latter direction." Rather, he insisted, "Every exercise in the classroom . . . involves on the part of the child one or more of the three divisions of a moral action—comprehending, choosing, and doing—and is therefore generating power." A child's power could be developed either morally or immorally. In his view, the teacher was under at least the same obligation "to train the pupil to love the good and do the right" as she was to teaching him to "think clearly and work well." He believed that the intellect of the pupil must be developed so the pupil can "see his duty plainly" and exercise the will until he "can do it cheerfully and unhesitatingly." This meant "persistent training in self-reliance and self-control and an education in all the virtues by means of unremitting exercise. In this . . . the child can only learn to do by doing, and all reform must be a matter of growth."

At this point in his career, Parker characterized education as "the unceasing training in good habits, and the unremitting exercise of the better nature and the noblest impulses of the children."[27] The status of moral training and the creation of a democratic school were in the planning stage more than the implementation stage, as was the definition of education as a science.

At Quincy, Parker began to shape his interpretation of what education as science meant to him. Basically, he equated the science of education with psychology and pedagogy, but he also equated it with the training of teachers. Scientific to him meant inductive research should replace *a priori* knowledge.[28] It also meant encouraging teachers to undertake experiments with caution. Experiments, he warned, "followed zigzag routes of . . . failures and successes." Teaching was exhilarating "work filled with errors and doubts, crude, uninformed, experimental, but withal progressive."[29] He thought, "no teacher is properly equipped who is not an eager student of the significant trends of his age . . . No subject of inquiry, study, or investigation is comparable to the Science of the soul of man and the laws of its development. This is the Science of Education, the Science that comprehends all sciences."[30]

Quincy Outcomes

Parker was less than satisfied with the immediate results of the Quincy experiment. Although the Norfolk County Report on the pupils' examinations in 1879 showed that the Quincy pupils distinguished themselves by the highest percentage scores in all subjects except mental arithmetic, Parker termed the results in the primary grades "fairly a success"; in the grammar school years "by no means a failure"; and in the high school years "a compromise between the natural methods and book cramming." Parker judged the best effect of his work in Quincy to be "the more humane treatment of little folks."[31]

The School Committee believed the "great work" of Parker's tenure was the "emancipation from arbitrary rule" and said "he breathed life, growth and happiness into our schoolrooms."[32] In *The New Departure in the Common Schools of Quincy* (1879), Charles Adams reported, "For five years the town had the benefit of Parker's faithful, intelligent, and enthusiastic services. In those years he transformed our public schools. He found them machines and left them living organisms; drill gave way to growth, and the weary prison became a pleasure-house. His dominant intelligence as a master and his pervasive magnetism as a man informed his school work. The results are plain, solid, substantial, unmistakable. So daring an experiment was tested by its practical results—of 500 grammar school children, not less than 400 showed excellent or satisfactory results on their exams." Adams added that the most notable changes were in the primaries, where the children learned to read and write as they learned to speak, not by rule and rote or by piecemeal, but altogether and by practice.[33]

Scholar Edward Dangler and biographer Ida Cassa Heffron critiqued Parker's five-year experiment at Quincy as "epoch-making."[34] Nothing since the time of Horace Mann created such a sensation. European and American journalists both condemned and praised the schools. Most of the negative press provided only a spare description of the schools and denounced them as nothing new. The remarks in the *New England Journal of Education*, for example, were unflattering and reported that the schools in the middle and western states had long been working on these ideas. On the other hand, the *School Journal* called the Quincy schools "magnificent work," and the *New York Tribune* called them "the starting point in the reorganization of the deplorable American system."[35] Overall, the 30,000 visitors to the schools from America and abroad told a positive story.

Following his five years in Quincy, Parker developed four other school experiments, each an evolution of the Quincy experiment, which he designed to answer five questions about education that absorbed him throughout his lifetime: (1) What was the nature of the child and how was the child to be taught? (2) How should the teacher be trained? (3) What subject matter should the child learn and how should it be organized? (4) What were the nature and purpose of the school in a democratic society? and (5) How could educators develop a science of education?

The Cook County Normal School Experiment (1883-1898)

Parker made his final move to the Midwest when he accepted the position as principal of the Cook County Normal School in January 1883. On his first journey west, he served as a country school teacher in Carrollton, Illinois; then he became principal of the Dayton School System; and now his destination was Chicago, "storm centre of American civilization." In his words, he accepted the position because, "There is one great inducement for me to take a Normal School, and that is to work out my ideal face to face with my own pupils."[36]

The Cook County Normal School was born in travail. Bitter fighting and struggle ensued from its beginning. Often confronted by political enemies and a hostile press, ignored by the Chicago School Board, and hampered by inadequate financing, its building was dilapidated and its facilities were meager—no library, laboratories, or gymnasium existed for the students, and the dormitory that housed the teachers in training was dilapidated. Founded by school commissioner John Eberhart in 1860 as a Teachers Institute to prepare the many rural school teachers without credentials, the Institute became a provisional Normal School in 1867. The term "normal school" was an unfamiliar phrase and out of the question for the Cook County Board of Supervisors until Eberhart persuaded them of its necessity. The cornerstone for the Normal School was laid on a twenty-acre campus in the village of Englewood in the County of Cook, seven or eight miles from downtown Chicago, in June 1869.

The survival of the Cook County Normal School was credited to Principal Daniel Wentworth, a farsighted advocate of the new education, whom Parker believed to be in "a direct line from Horace Mann." Under Wentworth, the Normal School consisted of a Professional Training Class, an elementary school of eight grades, and a high school of four grades. Desperately needed funds were often denied, and Wentworth used his personal funds to keep the school together. The Normal School graduated fewer than forty students in any one year during Wentworth's tenure. After thirteen years of struggle, Wentworth's failing health brought the school to a standstill in 1882.

Parker's appointment in 1883 inflamed the ceaseless opposition to the Normal School. His new ideas of the freedom of the child and the emancipation of the teacher "brought him into conflict with the Board of Education, the political machine men, and the whole fraternity of axe-grinding time-servers," reported Wilbur Jackman, one of his teachers. Parker responded with "eagle vision and lion-hearted courage and met them with relentless opposition."[37] For his belief in the child and democracy, he often enraged others and was sneered at by opponents. The faculty of the Normal School thought he possessed "a fearlessness of view and impetuous ardor," and that the results he had achieved in Quincy made him a famous and a worthy opponent.[38]

A man with a growing vision of the role of the common school in America, the function of education in a democratic society, and a belief in the science of education, Francis Parker at the Cook County Normal School advanced the five pedagogical tenets he experimented with in the Quincy school system.

In 1889, Parker's sixth year as principal, the City of Chicago annexed the Normal School, and Parker changed it to a Professional Training Class with eight elementary grades and a kindergarten and dropped the four high school grades. For admission, teacher candidates were required to earn a ninety percent average in four years of high school or have three years of teaching experience. Parker divided the training class into three divisions, depending on the knowledge and progress of the student teacher. Nonresidents paid a seventy-five dollar fee, but Cook County residents attended free of charge. Parker attracted student teachers from throughout the country, but few Chicago trainees enrolled because the city gave no credit to city teachers for their training there. The professional training course only lasted for forty weeks, but elective courses were offered in kindergarten training, physical education, elocution, history, geography, literature, science, manual training, mathematics, art, modeling, printing, drawing, music, and hygiene. Extension courses were available at the University of Chicago and other colleges, and most devoted students chose to remain longer than the required year. Graduates of the Normal School were judged on their professional attitude, skills, ability to govern a class, ability to teach a class, and their courage to fight for the ideals of the new education. During the Parker years the average graduating class increased to sixty-eight students. The enrollment included 600 pupils and practice teachers.

Again Principal Parker led as a coworker, more involved in the educational process than in administrative leadership. Some teachers thought him patriarchal, and others believed him to be a tyrant. He taught classes to practice teachers in psychology and education and frequently taught geography, his favorite subject, to pupils. His major problems when principal were insufficient finances to run the school; the lack of support by the Chicago Board of Education to whom he was accountable; and inadequate funds to hire good teachers. Often the board specified a given salary, but Parker would hire the teacher for a greater amount. In one case, he wanted to hire a science teacher from Harvard and paid a salary greater than the board allocated. When challenged by the board about how the difference was to be met, he responded that he hired the teachers, and it was their responsibility to obtain the money. It was criticism from parents, educators, and politicians that presented the greatest challenge. Parker explained that "the supreme task is to convince parents and the people that the old plan is utterly wrong."[39]

Parker advanced his Quincy approach to learning and teaching at the Normal School, where he reorganized the course of study, added new subjects, and formulated his doctrine of concentration and correlation (see Chapter 1, Figure 1.1). His new doctrine placed the child at the center of the learning experience and combined separate disciplines into central subjects. "Since geography, geology, mineralogy, physics, chemistry, botany, zoology, anthropology, ethnology, history and physiology constituted the child's environment, these may be considered the central subjects of study."[40] Parker defined his new doctrine of concentration and correlation as the uniting of all knowledge and activity for one purpose and using all thought and energy to build character and citizenship. "Correlation means the breaking down of the barriers of classification" of subjects. The argument for correlation was that "the strength of a thought lies in its relations" and not in the isolation of subjects, which he called "a fundamental error in education." "Expression will grow with thought, and thought will grow with expression . . . . The correlation of thought with all modes of expression is a great pedagogical truth."[41]

The doctrine of concentration and correlation followed several rules: First, "these subjects are not to be taught separately. Activities in observation, investigation, constructing, problem-solving, and experimentation covering all of these central subjects should precede any logical consideration of study by itself." Second, "all modes of expression are to be used throughout the elementary grades to develop intrinsic physical, mental, and moral action." Third, "the activities pursued in the curriculum should lead to the highest ethical behavior. Education is essentially moral in character." Fourth, "as far as it is possible there should be correlation, yes, even a unification of subject areas." Fifth, "unity of the body, mind, and soul through the educative agencies of action, expression, and thought is the aim of the Theory of Concentration."[42]

The new doctrine changed the approach to curriculum drastically not only by making the child central but in integrating all subjects and adding new ones, especially the sciences and the arts. When courses were integrated, time was spent more efficiently allowing for additional subjects. Correlation also resulted naturally in experience-based learning and in a new approach to teaching.

Parker's concept of a school as a community also matured. His definition of the school as "a model home, a complete community and embryonic democracy" meant that what the child learned at home, he learned at school in a more organized and formal way. The school was the institution linking the home to the larger society. Also, the school was to function as a community: "A school is a community; community life is indispensable to mental and moral growth. If the act of an individual in any way hinders the best work of the community, he is in the wrong . . . Every rule of a school, in order that it may be of educative influence and be felt to be right by each pupil, consists in carrying out this motto—'Everything to help and nothing to hinder.'"[43] It was this principle that guided the discipline in the school. He further explained the school as "a unit made up of groups, each group thoroughly interested in different lines of work, unified by one aim—the good of the whole." Parker discovered that, while working as a citizen in a community, "the feeling of responsibility, the dignity of belonging to a community, the desire to be personally of some use and of real importance were profound and controlling stimuli for all grades of children." The stimuli provided by this perception "increased in power as duties came or insight was gained, as higher, less self-centered motive developed."[44]

Parker also envisioned that "the social factor in the school is the greatest factor of all; it stands higher than subjects of learning, than methods of teaching, than the teacher himself." He believed "that which the children learn from each other in play or work, though the work be drudgery, is the highest that is ever learned . . . . This mingling, fusing, blending give personal power, and make the public school a tremendous force for the upbuilding of democracy."[45]

Parker reorganized the school to function as "an ideal community" to achieve the development of character, which he called the true test of the school. Character meant that students were to grow strong and skillful in body, helpful in habit, and thoughtful in help, and was equated with trustworthiness, refinement in taste, and refinement in moral power. At the Normal School, Parker transformed the aims of education from knowledge per se to citizenship, community life, and complete living. "The history of the school," Parker confessed, would be "an account of the disruption of the ideal that the acquisition of knowledge is an end in itself," and of the "beginnings of the new ideal of education: citizenship, community life, or complete living."[46] One teacher explained the manner in which the community was to function specifically to develop character. "The primal condition of right community life is that it should afford opportunity for, and encouragement of, voluntary individual service. The second is that the service performed shall be such as to react upon the individual offering the service to his best growth."[47] Because great emphasis was placed on the development of character, knowledge was considered to be not an end in itself, but a means to an end and by no means secondary.

Parker transformed the method of discipline to that end, replacing rigid imposed order with controlled freedom. Self-discipline on the part of students replaced corporal punishment, and cooperation replaced competition. Parker "abolished the whole system of rewards" and replaced authoritarian discipline with the development of "character as the goal."[48] This democratic approach to discipline was the most controversial change in the eyes of the parents and the public. To the casual observer, discipline in the Normal School might seem lacking, but "nothing was allowed which bordered on license, nothing intimating an impertinence to an adult or child— no 'uncalled-for-liberties' taken." In the community life "there was preparation for wider fields of usefulness—for service, not only for our own country, but for the cause of civilization everywhere."[49]

At the Normal School, Parker introduced a Morning Assembly as the laboratory for implementing his new ideas about community. The twenty-minute daily Morning Assembly was the common meeting ground for all students and faculty to share their observations from fieldwork and class studies. Some assemblies were carefully prepared and others were spontaneous. No applause was permitted because it aroused self-consciousness.

The Morning Assembly acted as a Parker metaphor that captured the interrelationship of the school to community, character, and knowledge. It was Parker's abbreviated answer to his wish for education, which was: "government-school boats bearing students and instructors on trips around the world; to places of natural interest in our own and in foreign lands; to great educational centers; to centers of Art and Music; to a study of the great architectural wonders of the world—both ancient and modern—thus gaining knowledge at first hand."[50] Pupils of all nationalities would study together and gain knowledge first hand and verify or correct ideas that others gained.

The Cook County Normal School provided Parker's first opportunity to train teachers formally. In the Professional Training Classes, he demonstrated how to apply psychological principles to teaching. With the shift in emphasis from knowledge to the child, the teachers undertook child study. Parker's contention was that "all real reforms in education in the past have sprung from child-study . . . . Froebel, Comenius, and Pestalozzi were students of children; hence their epoch-making reforms." Parker believed that insofar as teachers understood the nature of the child, the stages and laws of a child's growth, their individual differences, the interdependence of the body and the mind, and which actions should be aroused and which should be inhibited, they could create a pedagogical environment that would move pupils toward an ideal. Child-study developed a perception of the child as a social and a spiritual being, and from that premise education became the making of a life.[51]

The reform of the Normal School was accomplished slowly through teachers using an experimental scientific method that proceeded from a principle, began with an investigation and trial, and continued through observation and criticism by colleagues. Parker's constant exhortation was to work from principle and to have the courage to be crude. Parker understood that even if the ideal is right, "the way of attainment is long and arduous."[52] Methods varied from teacher to teacher and from day to day, but all teachers were in constant communication with each other.

Parker ascribed grave responsibility to the teacher. The function of the teacher was "to make life, society, the state, the nation, what they should be; and the function of the Normal School was to train men and women for these duties."[53] Parker argued for the necessity of the practice school, where teachers were brought face to face with the problems of teaching.

"Each member of the Professional Training Class studied with a special departmental teacher as well as with a 'critic' teacher at the grade level assignment. 'Practice' teachers spent at least one hour a day throughout the year observing the critic teacher at work and in teaching the class themselves. In addition to observation and practice at various grade levels, the student teachers were given intensive instruction by departmental teachers in the various subject-matter disciplines." The technique to be mastered was "illustrative teaching," which relied on the use of pictures, models, field trips, examples, and specimens to illustrate the lesson. The entire faculty, the department, and the critic teachers cooperated with practice teachers in preparing outlines of subject matter and "illustrative" methods and devices to make the assignments more alive to the children.[54]

Parker's success in transforming traditional education depended strongly on his "tightly knit, disciplined group of teachers." Many of the "old guard" teachers at the Cook County Normal School were graduates of the Oswego Normal School, called "the pioneer of the science of education in the United States." Parker searched for and interviewed new teachers carefully. He appointed Lelia Patridge, who had observed and written the definitive text about the Quincy School System; Dr. Collin Scott from G. Stanley Hall's psychology laboratory at Clark University; Zonia Baber, a former trainee, a principal in an Ohio school, and a master geography teacher; Ida Cassa Heffron, a distinguished art teacher; Flora Cooke, who became the principal of his next school, and other distinguished scholars and teachers. His wife was a trainee but not a faculty member. The kind of teaching Parker insisted upon required "an understanding of children," knowledge of the subject matter, an understanding "of the things to be learned," and "the nature of learning."

Cook County Normal School Experiment Outcomes

Six major initiatives at the Cook County Normal School had lasting implications for new education. Although many critics decried Parker's course of study because they said it avoided fundamentals, Parker presented a holistic approach rather than a fragmented piecemeal organization. He emphasized the correlation of subjects because it was reflective of the way children naturally experience their universe and the manner in which they learn. Integration or correlation of subjects, now called interdisciplinary education, has been long lasting and is utilized at all levels of education.

The second initiative was Parker's approach to the training of teachers. Now called practice teaching, it is one of the major strategies in schools of education for training teachers. Although the present approach to practice teaching is less elaborate, it continues to involve a practice teacher, a master teacher, and a critic teacher.

The third major initiative, the development of a faculty as a team or a corps working together, exists in too few schools today largely because of the manner in which the school day is organized. In *Basic Principles of Curriculum and Instruction* (1949), curricularist Ralph Tyler validated the reasons that teachers need to work as a collective body when he discussed the need for horizontal and vertical organization of curriculum. He posited that when teachers fail to collaborate, the students have to try to transfer training from one subject to another and from one grade to another. Students often do not see the connection. Tyler explained:

> Important changes to human behavior are not produced overnight. No single learning experience has a very profound influence upon the learner. Changes in ways of thinking, in fundamental habits, in major operating concepts, in attitudes, in abiding interests and the like, develop slowly. It is only after months and years that we are able to see major educational objectives taking marked concrete shape . . . by the cumulation of educational experiences profound changes are brought about in the learner.[55]

Parker's fourth innovation engaged the home with the school. Parker was credited with creating the first successful Parent-Teacher Association, the forerunner of today's nationwide organization. Parker "felt the need of direct contact with the parents, that he might make clear to them his educational aims and methods . . . ." He believed that "the welfare of the pupils demanded the fullest measure of cooperation between the home and school."[56] The parents, whom he engaged to the fullest, were a potent force in the school. Two other initiatives Parker considered among his major accomplishments: a permanent kindergarten and the establishment of a two- instead of a one-year teacher training program.

In 1883, the Normal School was meagerly furnished, but when Parker resigned after sixteen years of labor in 1899, the school had "excellent all-around equipment: thirteen thousand carefully selected volumes in the library . . . the largest school collection of pictures in the world"; newspaper collections, mineralogy and anthropological collections, a printing press, and duplicating equipment.[57] The head of the Child Movement in the United States, G. Stanley Hall, then president of Clark University, explained that he came each year "to set my educational clock." The school "had become so notable an institution, with its ample school grounds and splendid record, that a group of outstanding citizens of Chicago demanded its acceptance by the Chicago Board of Education. It was transferred to the city on January 1, 1896, and became the Chicago Normal School." As in Quincy, "his school in Chicago was visited by people from all quarters of the globe. They came in great numbers . . . Students came, not only from nearly every State of the Union, but from Canada, England, Norway, Denmark, Germany, and South America; even from distant Japan, Australia, Iceland, and South Africa."[58]

Many publications resulted from the experiments at the Normal School. At the peak of his career, Parker outlined his doctrine of concentration and correlation in his book, *Talks on Pedagogics* (1894). In 1895, the Normal School published its first course of study. The "Chicago Normal School Envelope" contains the leaflets and records of work written by the approximately fifty teachers who were at the Normal School during the last five years of Parker's principalship. The year Parker left, he wrote a twenty-page monograph giving "An Account of the Work of Cook County Normal School." In 1934, Ida Cassa Heffron allocated the major part of her interpretive biography on Colonel Parker to his experience at the Normal School, and Jack Campbell's *Colonel Francis W. Parker: The Children's Crusader* (1967) included a chapter on the Normal School.

The Cook County Normal School was the embodiment of Parker's reform ideals for American education. At the Normal School, Parker practiced and further developed his educational philosophy, which can best be captured in four statements—a synthesis of Comenius's philosophy of how people learn, "Let things that have to be done be learned by doing them"; Pestalozzi's one grand principle, "Education is the generation of power"; Froebel's end or aim of education, "the harmonious growth of the whole being"; and Herbart's concept of concentration and correlation.

The New Education at the Private Chicago Institute
Academic and Pedagogic (1899-1901)

Francis Parker's fervent belief in the common school was professed in these words: "The highest outcome . . . of all the ages of human progress is the common school . . . . I believe that democracy is the one hope of the world; [and] that democracy without efficient common schools is impossible."[59] It therefore seemed unlikely that Parker would abandon public for private education, even when Anita McCormick Blaine offered to endow his own school, where he could experiment with educational ideas without interference. At first, Parker resisted her offers, but after sixteen grueling years of unceasing battle with school boards, trustees, and bureaucrats at the Cook County Normal School, his resolve had weakened. In December 1898, his dying wife finally persuaded him to accept Blaine's offer. Shortly thereafter, Parker wrote Blaine, describing his vision of the ideal school they might create, a place "in which all good things come together. Health, helpfulness—trustworthiness—taste, citizenship, the highest type of community life; a place to train the body, the mind, the soul as a unit."[60]

Parker finalized his move from the public to the private sector in May 1899, and he and Blaine announced their plans for what was to become known as the Chicago Institute Academic and Pedagogic. Their grandiose vision included a teacher training school and an accompanying practice school; a junior college; a separate school in a tenement district to "show what education may do for poor children"; a manual training center; a kindergarten and playground; a library; a gymnasium and an assembly hall; a printing press, as well as a boarding school, so that children from throughout the country might attend. "It was not planned to open the doors of the school for a full year."[61]

Despite their shared vision and previous assurances, Blaine did not give Parker *carte blanche* for what was supposed to be the culmination of his life's work. Realizing that she was "inexperienced in benefactions of this magnitude," she appointed a board of trustees "to help administer her contributions and to advise Parker and the faculty." She selected four trustees: her brother, Stanley McCormick; an attorney and friend of her late husband, Owen Aldis; the family's legal advisor, Cyrus Bentley; and long-time friend and family physician, Dr. Henry Favill. "Bringing outsiders into the project could endanger 'vital principles,' she acknowledged, but she did not want to be the sole monitor of expenditures."[62]

At least in retrospect, conflict between Parker and the trustees seemed inevitable. Parker was shaping a new school unique in the nation. "Even though it was designed as a model to proclaim the superiority of the new education, there was no blueprint for the remodeling of the American school system."[63] When Parker presented his first blueprint, "'Won't that be lovely,' Anita said. Dr. Favill agreed, but they were a minority of two. Stanley McCormick and Cyrus Bentley were apprehensive; Aldis was appalled."[64]

The trustees were faced with considerable cost overruns from the onset. The actual cost of the land for the school, which was to be located in "the best residential district of Chicago," was $425,000; Blaine originally estimated $250,000. The cost of the buildings and facilities was expected to be $282,000; but the initial bids for construction were over a half million dollars.[65] The trustees noted that, "No matter how often estimates were juggled, they went up." Parker and the trustees argued "over architectural designs, land prices, and their different ideas of educational theory." The trustees grew increasingly exasperated by Parker's "nonchalance about finances." When the trustees confronted Parker about costs, he responded that "figures were not his province." Parker would not economize, and he often ignored the trustees' suggestions. In the spring of 1900, one trustee rejected Parker's plans totally in "favor of a new plan for a compact, plain, substantial, durable, well-ventilated, heated and lighted building, to cost not more than $300,000."[66] Parker's plans "were beginning to make millionaires stop to count the cost."

Although the trustees agreed to the purchase of land for the school, they rejected three components of Parker's original plan, deeming the slum school, the boarding school, and the junior college excessive. This omission was the beginning of a struggle that would remain unresolved. Parker's subsequent revised plan for the Institute made some concessions, but he argued against others, claiming that, for example, the proposed assembly hall was now too small to bring together the student body and the faculty for Morning Exercises. Adequate space for these daily meetings was crucial to his vision—to Parker, the assembly hall was "the crucible out of which community life was fused."[67] When Parker revised his plan, he added an enormous library, four laboratories, three museums, two assembly halls, a fully equipped stage, a swimming pool, an observatory, and gardens. Plans for the Institute were now at an impasse, with the trustees demanding economies and Parker expanding his vision in new ways. With no resolution in sight, Parker and the trustees agreed to secure temporary space in order that the Chicago Institute Academic and Pedagogic might open in October 1900.

In its single year of operation, the Chicago Institute existed in a struggle to be born. Blaine and the trustees rented the Turngemeinde Building and the adjoining store on Wells Street as classrooms for student instruction. As a stopgap measure, the trustees accepted the McCormick Theological Seminary's offer of space for the scheduled teachers' summer session. In spite of the confusion and changes, the Chicago Institute, which allowed for an enrollment of 600 students, opened with 150 kindergarten through twelfth grade students and two divisions of thirty-four student teachers in the Professional Training Class.[68]

In the planning phase of the Chicago Institute, Blaine and the trustees focused on the construction of an appropriate building, reducing Parker's plan by 20,000 square feet and eliminating key elements. President Parker was assisted in his planning efforts by a small administrative staff of three—Wilbur Jackman, the dean; Flora Cooke, the principal of the elementary school; and Emanuel Boyer, the director, who was able to "manage everything up to the mark,"[69] according to Parker. When Boyer suddenly died, Parker missed his presence, and more decisions fell into the hands of the trustees.

Parker invited fourteen teachers from the Cook County Normal School to the Chicago Institute and from an anticipated million-dollar endowment, he granted all of his faculty full salaries for a year of sabbatical leave. Some enrolled at colleges—Columbia, Harvard, and the University of Chicago; others studied abroad—children's literature in Norway, the Delsarte system in Paris, and science and physical education in Germany—while they waited for classes to begin.[70]

The faculty continued to work on the course of study as it had at the Normal School and the Institute's "Preliminary Announcement" of 1899 identified the six basic educational doctrines of the Chicago Institute: (1) "the power of attention is an essential factor and must be stimulated and strengthened"; (2) "mental concentration may be enhanced by a correlated study of related subjects, as geography and history, science and mathematics"; (3) "knowledge and skill induced by the study of one subject are reinforced by the study of other subjects in relation"; (4) "self expression in all its modes reacts upon the mind in developing thought-power"; (5) "training to habits of attention and self-expression tends to physical, intellectual, and moral growth"; and (6) "the final aim of education is the highest development of individual ability and character."[71]

The course of study for the Chicago Institute was more flexible than at the Normal School. Parker believed that because "the demands of society are constantly changing and . . . the nature of the child is subject to perpetual study . . . there could never be a fixed course of study." "Under the managing editorship of Marion Foster Washburne, *The Course of Study* was published monthly as an exposition of the curriculum developments at the Institute." Compiled as a periodical rather than a table of laws, "it was intended as a basis for further curriculum development, a guide for methodology, and as a textbook for students in pedagogical courses . . . *The Course of Study* also served to keep the faculty continually in touch with everything being done in the school."[72]

Chicago Institute Academic and Pedagogic Outcomes

Only the reports from students attending the Institute were glowing. Of considerable significance was the fact that Anita McCormick Blaine's son Em liked being there. "That's a great school!" he told his mother. "It's fun to be up there." But even that compliment could not change the course of events. Parker dedicated two years of his life to making and breaking educational plans for the Chicago Institute, but in the end, he did not succeed. Parker had been embroiled in conflict throughout his career but never on so large a scale. By comparison, previous battles had been minor skirmishes—over a teacher's salary or new equipment, a building repair or even a new addition—and he had won them all. But now he was fighting with lawyers and men of money. Parker was overly idealistic in his plans, which had not been analyzed until he made the move to the private sector. He was naive about money and overestimated what it could purchase. He was nonchalant with the trustees and did not explain his goals. It seemed that of the five trustees, only Blaine perceived what Parker was attempting to accomplish with his plan for an ideal school. Blaine's ambivalence about money permitted President William Rainey Harper of the University of Chicago to appear as the rescuer, and in 1901 the trustees deeded the block of land that Blaine had purchased to the University of Chicago. Blaine's early fear that bringing outsiders into the project "could endanger 'vital principles'" had materialized.[73]

Undermined by his ignorance of "the province of numbers," blocked by the trustees' lack of knowledge of the new education, and outmaneuvered by President Harper of the University of Chicago, the Chicago Institute Academic and Pedagogic, Parker's ideal school and temple of new education, closed after one year. Blaine explained, "The school will be closely affiliated with the School of Education of the University of Chicago—the future name of the Chicago Institute."[74]

The School of Education of the University of Chicago (1901-1904)

It was unclear who first suggested a merger between the fledgling Chicago Institute and the University of Chicago—Mrs. Blaine, President William Rainey Harper, the trustees, or the faculty of the Institute—but it was thought to be President Harper who believed that the transfer would provide "the resources of a great university, with its fuller advantages and equipment, for the scholastic training of the student-teachers."[75] President Harper proposed to Mrs. Blaine that she donate her million dollar endowment to the Board of Trustees of the University of Chicago, and in turn the Chicago Institute would become the School of Education of the University of Chicago and its staff members university faculty.[76] Blaine, Harper, and the trustees concluded that "the Institute could draw on the academic wealth of the university; the university in turn could benefit from the practical pedagogical skills of Parker's faculty and Parker's reputation, as well as . . . from the considerable sums Anita had pledged to the Institute." The trustees assumed that Dewey and Parker held similar educational theories and ideals, and that they would translate their educational principles compatibly at the university. Only Cyrus Bentley expressed concern, arguing that the ultimate goal of Parker's pedagogy was character development, whereas the aim of the university was scholarship.[77]

At the onset, Parker and Dewey, like Bentley, had grave misgivings about the affiliation, and neither was strongly supportive of it. In fact, "at a meeting of the Institute trustees in January 1901 both Dewey and Parker stated categorically that neither would give up the headship of his school for the sake of merger." Parker additionally argued that "the university system of distinct academic departments was contrary to his theory of 'correlation,' and that Dewey was dominated by this 'departmental influence.'" Parker affirmed, "I would prefer to teach in a country school with all the conditions right than have charge of the largest institution with restrictions that could not easily be overcome."[78] Parker also had serious reservations about the efficiency and the possibility of using personnel across grade levels rather than maintaining separate teachers for each grade. He thought the quality of his work would suffer from the merger, and he would no longer have complete control.

Parker's frustration increased because the university bureaucracy seemed contrary to the single purpose of the Chicago Institute. "The Chicago Institute had been founded for a single purpose—to dramatize the ideals of the new education. Such a purpose required a tight organization. The university could not guarantee such unity. In addition, the dramatic impact of the new school on community living might be lost amid the numerous undertakings of the university."[79]

"Concerned about the organization and administration of the merger, Parker confided in Dewey that even though the proposed plans promised a great opportunity to enhance the progress of education, he could not consent to the arrangement without an absolute assurance of 'all-around efficiency.' Parker made it clear that he did not want to invade 'Dr. Dewey's zone of authority'" and did not fear that the philosophy of Dewey would conflict with his own. "He had already told the Board of Trustees that he considered Dewey the real philosopher of the new education."[80]

Dewey too was leery about the affiliation, but for different reasons. Parker's sixteen fractious years at the Cook County Normal School were marked by great battles between opponents and loyal supporters and staff. Parker had powerful supporters—public figures like Jane Addams, clergy and rabbis, union leaders—whose influence might be detrimental to Dewey's goals at the university. He also had powerful detractors—politicians, the School Board, critical educators—who might stir up controversy that would harm Dewey's fundraising efforts. Also, the university had already been criticized for expanding by incorporating surrounding schools. Adding yet another school would surely fuel that criticism. Dewey's greatest concern was about his new experimental Laboratory School, whose existence he felt was threatened.

Parker's and Dewey's resistance went unheeded by the trustees and President Harper. No one investigated the differences between the two educators, in which lay the seeds of destruction of the entire plan. Disregarding Bentley's, Parker's, and Dewey's reservations, Blaine informed President Harper on January 16, 1901, that she was willing to turn over to the university "her pledged future investment" in the Chicago Institute, estimated at $750,000, if the university would match the sum and devote the total to Parker's work. As part of this exchange, Blaine gave the University of Chicago the land on the North Side originally purchased for the Institute.[81] Parker changed his mind several times, but he ultimately deferred to his faculty, who voted thirteen to one in favor of the merger. Like a good soldier, Parker conceded and said he would support Blaine's decision.

Parker and the Dean of the Chicago Institute, Wilbur Jackman, signed an agreement with President Harper and Professor John Dewey for an affiliation in February 1901. President Harper informed the trustees one month later that the university had raised the funds to match Blaine's $750,000 and in April 1901 the trustees of both institutions signed and notarized the merger, officially establishing the School of Education of the University of Chicago in June 1901 with Parker as the Director.

On the tenth anniversary of the University of Chicago, "in an impressive ceremony Colonel Parker broke ground for the permanent building, which would one day house his theories and practices. Mrs. Blaine shared a carriage with President Harper and Mr. and Mrs. John D. Rockefeller."[82] President William Rainey Harper, the trustees, and John Dewey spoke for the University of Chicago.

The School of Education of the University of Chicago rested upon a complex bureaucracy unfamiliar to Parker. At its head were two distinct boards of trustees. The board of the University of Chicago was responsible for the finances of the entire university. The Institute trustees were responsible for the finances and management of the School of Education, which included appointing the director of the Parker elementary school. Harper, second in command as president of the university, was the policymaker and set the priorities; Blaine's endowment and her relationship with Parker and his teachers placed her third in command. Parker was fourth in line; and John Dewey followed at the bottom of the hierarchy of decision makers. It should also be recognized that Blaine deferred to the Institute trustees in financial matters but also conferred with John D. Rockefeller, with whom she had a close affiliation. Because Rockefeller would not finance debt, President Harper needed Dewey to arrange for his own financing of the Laboratory School. Throughout the Blaine-Parker project, President Harper and Dewey were engaged in ongoing struggle about the costs of Dewey's School.

A new kind of problem arose in the School of Education when Parker was appointed the Director of the University Elementary School. In this agreement, two elementary schools operated under the aegis of the university, Parker's demonstration school and Dewey's Laboratory School. The University Elementary School, the name Dewey had used until sometime after 1900, was now assigned to Parker's school, which caused confusion for parents applying their children for one or the other school.[83] Dewey blamed Parker for trying to enroll his Laboratory School students in Parker's University Elementary School. The reason Harper used the name was not sinister, as Dewey thought; Harper originally was planning on only one elementary school, and he assigned the name of the existing school to Parker. Although Dewey's experimental Laboratory School and Parker's University Elementary School existed simultaneously for a short period, Parker and Dewey were not engaged in the same kind of work. Parker's University School was "a model or practice school for use in training teachers; Dewey's was intended as a laboratory for testing educational principles and hypotheses."[84]

Although Harper tried to be conciliatory to Dewey, Harper did not want two elementary schools in the university. Harper misunderstood the differences as had the trustees of the Institute. "Harper's errors were indecision and inability or unwillingness to communicate with precision. He should either have made the Dewey school an organic part of the university . . . or he should have severed its ties and let it go free."[85] Instead, Harper wanted Dewey to find his own financing for the Laboratory School.

For the administration of the School of Education, President Harper planned two coordinate and distinct pedagogical organizations within the University. "Parker's sphere of influence, well separated from Dewey's, was still largely on paper. It was to consist of a Pedagogic School for the training of teachers, a kindergarten, and an elementary school."[86] Dewey would remain as chairman of the Department of Philosophy, Psychology, and Pedagogy and supervise the two secondary schools affiliated with the university for use by practice teachers: the South Side Academy and the Chicago Manual Training School. The plan seemed to work on paper, but in reality it was hazardous.

School of Education Outcomes

After eight months as Director of the School of Education, Parker died in March 1902, and with his death the old problems continued to fester and new problems emerged. "The Trustees of the Chicago Institute nominated John Dewey as successor to Francis Wayland Parker in the office of Director of the School of Education at the University of Chicago."[87] The Institute trustees specified several reasons for accepting Dewey's nomination: Parker and Dewey were assumed to have held similar educational theories and ideals; the School of Education faculty had heard Dewey lecture, taken courses from him, and was acquainted with him personally; Dewey could integrate the two operations so that conflicts of the kind that had been experienced would occur no more; and a coordinated approach to the tasks of teacher training and the problems of pedagogical theory could be undertaken.

But under Dewey's leadership the conflict was prolonged. The controversy centered on the fate of Francis Parker's educational philosophy, which Parker's teachers feared would be vulnerable under his wife, Alice Chipman Dewey, who Dewey had appointed principal of the Laboratory School. Parker's teachers also feared that Dewey himself would maneuver the resignation of the Parker-trained faculty from the school. Reportedly, Dewey was unsympathetic and neglectful of their needs, did not attend faculty or parent meetings, and made plans for the school without consulting with the teachers. Mrs. Blaine spoke with Dewey twice about the conflict but to no avail. "The situation called for a Parker, with his immense vitality and impressive personality and his talent for dramatizing educational issues and the process of educational reform. Dewey, with as much inner strength and a far superior mind, did not have the physical and temperamental attributes of leadership that Parker possessed to such a large degree."[88]

In the meantime, the educational work proceeded in both schools and members of the Chicago Institute began to transfer their work to the new Emmons Blaine Hall at the University of Chicago, which was completed in 1903. The Parker faculty's problems with Mrs. Dewey's principalship of the Laboratory School continued until May 1904, when she was asked to resign. As she was doing so, John Dewey was inquiring about a position from President Nicholas Murray Butler of Columbia University. Dewey accepted an appointment in the philosophy department, and the Dewey family moved to New York.

All of the components for an effective enterprise were available in Chicago—the philosopher, the practitioner, the endowment, and the desire to advance progressive education. What was absent was a trusting and supportive environment in which colleagues could work supportively with each other to produce new experiments. The two educational innovators were now gone. With them went Parker's and Blaine's dreams for the national prominence of progressive education in Chicago with a university showcase for Parker's adventurous innovations, Dewey's scientific expertise, and Blaine's endowment. The death of Francis Parker and the premature departure of John Dewey ended one of the greatest experiments in progressive education in America.

In many respects, the Blaine-Parker project was headed for failure from the beginning. Parker had confidence in his vision, but he refused to modify his grandiose plans, which caused the conservative fiscally responsible trustees to assume more and more control of the decision making, placing Parker in an environment where he could not fulfill his mission of teaching teachers, which he had successfully undertaken throughout his career. President Harper, like Parker, desired to use Blaine's endowment for educational purposes, but unlike Parker, lacked an educational vision for the School of Education at the University of Chicago. Mrs. Blaine's decisions were also deleterious to the Blaine-Parker goals. Blaine interposed trustees whose mission it was to protect her investment rather than her vision. Her resolve to proceed was weakened by a lack of confidence in her ability to manage such a large investment without trustees. Blaine, "who had wanted to liberate children from learning by rote and to give her son the best possible schooling, had been witness to and partly responsible for the clouding of Parker's dream in his last years and the angry departure of John Dewey from the Midwest."[89]

Powerful people—Blaine, Parker, Dewey, Harper, and Rockefeller—killed a powerful idea that would have begun to develop education as a science. The Laboratory School continued but ultimately did not remain a progressive school. The School of Education prevailed until the end of the twentieth century. Progressive education no longer had central leadership, except for the short existence of the Progressive Education Association.

Chapter 5

The Parker School Heritage:
Second-Generation Schools

Several dedicated alumni, teachers, parents, and associates spread Francis Parker's vision beyond Chicago by founding schools that were direct descendants of the flagship school. The seven second-generation schools, scattered from the East to the West Coast, were located in cities, suburbs, and the country. Five descendent schools were K-12 schools, one was an elementary school, and another was a graduate teacher's college.

Ethel Sturges Dummer, a Parker parent, carried both the heritage and the name of the Francis Parker School to San Diego, California, in 1912; Katharine Taylor '06, a former Parker School faculty member, transferred the heritage to the Shady Hill School in Cambridge, Massachusetts, in 1915; Perry Dunlap Smith '06, also a former Parker teacher, became the founding headmaster of the progressive North Shore Country Day School in Winnetka, Illinois, in 1919; Edward Yeomans, a Parker parent and friend of principal Flora Cooke, extended the progressive vision to the Ojai Valley School in Ojai, California, in 1923. Elizabeth Moos, a Parker alumna and former teacher, became principal of the now-defunct experimental Hessian Hills School in Croton-on-Hudson, New York, in 1924. More recently, in the 1970s, Christopher Holabird '44 was appointed principal of the Oakwood Elementary School in North Hollywood, California, and in 1980 he became the founding director of its descendant school, Los Encinos School in Encino, California. A college perpetuated one of Francis Parker's paramount objectives, the training of teachers. Parker School principal Flora Cooke, North Shore Country Day School principal Perry Dunlap Smith '06, and Carleton Washburne, one of Parker's pupils at the Normal School, the Chicago Institute, and the Chicago Parker School, founded the Graduate Teachers College of

Winnetka, Illinois, in 1932 to train teachers for positions in progressive schools.

At their founding, these second-generation schools reflected the essence of Parker's philosophy and pedagogy. All were faithful to the overarching Parker principle that the ultimate end of education is the development of character. These descendant schools also espoused specific precepts of a Parker education: (1) to create ideal citizens; (2) to develop the whole child—body, mind, and soul; (3) to establish consideration for all members of the community; (4) to utilize the community for moral education and service; and (5) to embrace diversity. Instruction was predicated on Parker's tenet "learning by doing" and teaching students to become critical thinkers. Their courses of study were more inclusive than the traditional schools and frequently organized through the correlation of subjects, based on Parker's doctrine of central subjects. Over the decades, three of these precollege schools relinquished major components of the progressive philosophy and became more traditional; three remained progressive; and one closed.

The Francis Parker School
San Diego, California

The Francis Parker School of San Diego, California, is the oldest and largest independent, nondenominational school in San Diego, enrolling students from kindergarten through the senior year. Established in 1912 by Mr. and Mrs. William Templeton Johnson, the school attained early prominence through its identification with the educational philosophies of its namesake. Influential in the Johnsons' decision to found the school was Mrs. Johnson's sister, Ethel Sturges Dummer, whose four daughters had attended Chicago's Francis W. Parker School. The Johnson family supported the ideals of the school, transferred them to San Diego, and served the San Diego School for several decades. Mrs. Johnson, like Mrs. Blaine, underwrote the school's deficit each year for more than a decade. The Johnsons' original plan was to discontinue the school at such time that the public schools had absorbed the lessons of progressive education, but when that did not materialize, Mrs. Johnson ensured the school's survival by selling the property and the buildings to the Francis Parker Parent Association in 1941.[1]

The school's first principal, Adele Outcalt, who served from 1915 to 1920, established a progressive legacy which she described in these words:

The object of the founders originally was to found a school which, by its environment, its methods, its opportunities, would develop the young for participation in citizenship . . . . The school . . . would point the way to the public school system into which it should be absorbed, where the public school would be doing the same or better work. We adopted the Dewey principle that the school is not a preparation, but is life itself—that the school must not be divorced from life, but participate.

In 1922, the Johnsons appointed their twenty-seven-year-old niece Ethel Sturges Dummer as principal. After graduating from the Francis W. Parker School in Chicago and the University of Wisconsin, Ethel Sturges Dummer taught physical education and drama at the San Diego Parker School. There she married Murney Mintzer and remained principal until 1929 and director until 1938. Under her leadership, Mrs. Mintzer continued the progressive legacy and established a "number of aims" for the school:

It tried to develop in its students the ability to think and reason clearly and logically rather than to make education simply a memory cramming process . . . it offered . . . the privilege of working to satisfy an interest in a subject rather than a required grade. It has endeavored to bring out rather than crush out individual differences . . . students should be given the opportunity . . . to learn to take responsibility for themselves rather than [be] dependent on discipline imposed by others.

Both Outcalt and Mintzer engaged the students in active learning and in the community to train for citizenship. The manner in which the community was involved and the course of study was organized was reminiscent of the flagship school. They involved students in helping with planning and budgeting for the cafeteria; purchasing playground and sports equipment; and raising flowers, vegetables, and honey bees in order to earn money for the school. Domestic sciences, manual training classes, multiple forms of expression, practical experiences, and sports and health classes expanded the narrower traditional school curriculum.

Vestiges of progressive education remain today in the curriculum. A recent curriculum guide states, "The plan of Francis Parker School is to educate children to citizenship and character." At all levels, students participate in community service. Middle schoolers and their teachers engage in four- or five-day outdoor programs that emphasize environmental studies and team building. For the high school, graduation requires ten hours of service to the community. Instruction emphasizes education of the whole child—body, mind, and spirit—which is reflected in the inclusive athletic and rigorous arts programs. The sports program includes individual and team sports. The arts program includes art, music, and sometimes woodworking for all grades, and in the high school, art electives incorporate photography, video production, and instrumental music.

Upholding its commitment to another of Francis Parker's "guiding principles," "the mingling of all races and creeds," the school currently offers international education opportunities such as exchange programs with schools in France and New Zealand, a Spanish language program in Spain, and a language immersion program for eighth graders at the Institute of Culture and Languages in Ensenada.[2] The study of foreign language begins in pre-kindergarten with Spanish, and the school also offers bilingual courses to fulfill its commitment to diversity. The school provided tuition aid for 156 of the 1,140 students in 1998.

Today, these progressive principles—the education of the whole child for character, citizenship, and service to the community—are balanced with a strong traditional course of study, focused on the teaching of traditional subjects of English, foreign language, mathematics, science, and social studies. The school has become college preparatory, emphasizing advanced placement, honors courses, and examination scores; its orientation, especially in the high school, is more subject centered than child centered. The Francis Parker School of San Diego presently reflects the differences more than the similarities with Colonel Parker's philosophy.

Shady Hill School
Cambridge, Massachusetts

Founded in 1915 by Mrs. Agnes and Dr. William Ernest Hocking, the Shady Hill School of Cambridge, Massachusetts, built an identity on the guiding principles of Francis Parker through a direct connection, Katharine Taylor '06. An early graduate of Chicago's Francis W. Parker School, Miss Taylor attended Vassar College and taught in its English Department. Subsequently she returned to teach and became Chairman of the English Department at Chicago's Parker School.[3]

Taylor directed the K-8 Shady Hill School for almost three decades, from 1921 until 1949. An ardent Parker disciple, Miss Taylor supported Parker's original aims: "to keep childhood alive to an open-mindedness and a love of learning; to develop the individual within the circle of the school community; [and] to teach by contact with actual material rather than by information about it." Taylor's administration was noted for its emphasis on the development of character and the crucial interrelationship in effective education among children, faculty, and parents. Taylor also extended Parker's concept of instruction through central subjects focused on different cultures. Edward Yeomans Jr., a member of the Shady Hill faculty, described this "year-long experience with people of another culture" as a "total immersion" that became "all-absorbing." For example, the central subject for fifth-graders was the age of discovery. In accordance with Parker's belief in the centrality of geography in the course of study, the pupils studied:

> The Vikings in Greenland and North America and the journeys of Marco Polo, the study took up the voyages of the Portuguese, Spanish, French, Dutch and English explorers to Africa, Asia and America, and finally some of the modern expeditions to the arctic and antarctic regions. The children read widely: history books, journals, biographies, technical works on map-making and navigation. They wrote and illustrated detailed articles on various explorers, chosen by individuals or by small groups to study. They made their own notebook covers in the book-binding room . . . and kept copies of each other's contributions so that each notebook became a complete record of the year's work, suitably indexed.

Taylor upheld Parker's philosophy in many other ways during her administration: a belief in public education; the conscientious training of new teachers; an emphasis on the arts—music, dance, art, shop—and, at least in some instances, on play as an integral part of the school day. "Learning by doing" dominated instruction. For example, the study of science emphasized fieldwork and practical experience. The science teacher's rationale was:

> If children have spent many hours out-of-doors, exploring under the direction and stimulation of people who themselves enjoy such exploring, if they have handled laboratory equipment, cared for it, helped to make it, if they have had time to realize something of the painstaking labor, the

patience, the imagination, and the satisfaction which are involved in gaining such knowledge, an appreciation of scientific thinking is inevitable. They have not merely taken science, but science has taken them by pleasant ways, out into a wider world.

Edward Yeomans Jr., who succeeded Taylor as director, wrote, "At the time of Katharine Taylor's retirement in 1949, Shady Hill . . . had taken important steps in the direction of becoming a national institution." In what might serve as a testimonial to the value of a progressive education in general, Langdon Warner, a school parent and a professor of fine arts at Harvard University, wrote in an April 1947 article in the *Shady Hill News*, ". . . It appears that we have developed in Cambridge a public service in the shape of an independent school dedicated to something other than an examination system set up to test individuals for further examinations . . . Thus, when they come to the universities a surprising number refuse to be swamped by a glut of mere facts . . . A great many of them are entirely fit to take advantage of the wider opportunities and deeper research that the colleges offer." Shady Hill remains a progressive school.

North Shore Country Day School
Winnetka, Illinois

The descendant schools were built from a broad spectrum of Francis Parker's philosophy, but North Shore Country Day School most closely resembles the Francis W. Parker School of Chicago. In 1919, a group of forward-looking businessmen formed the North Shore Country Day School in Winnetka, Illinois, a beautiful tree-lined suburb eighteen miles north of Chicago, and invited Perry Dunlap Smith '06 to be the founding headmaster, "an invitation he relished as an opportunity . . . to expand on what he had learned at the Francis W. Parker School as student and later as teacher."[4] Smith attended Harvard University before becoming a mathematics teacher at Chicago's Parker School from 1912 to 1916. He was also a director and teacher in the Summer Institute held by the Progressive Education Association at Vassar in 1930, and he served on many Parker committees during and after his years at North Shore.[5]

Smith implemented many principles and practices of his alma mater, but the idea of community was the most basic point of his philosophy. He often quoted Parker's belief, "A school is a community. Community life is indispensable to mental and moral growth," which he extended through the school's motto, "Live and Serve." Teachers, pupils, and parents participated in annual community outreach programs. The school was regarded as a model for parent involvement because parents were truly "partners and co-workers" who created and financed the school and served on many committees. The Parents Association sponsored activities, undertook projects, and was actively involved in cooperative volunteer programs with the pupils.

Smith was a social activist committed to "education for democracy." He believed "the primary gift of God to man is choice—and education should be the presentation of conditions for choice." Like the Parker School, North Shore Country Day School met daily for a Morning Exercise program to share ideas, to learn to communicate, and to learn the kind of inner discipline that placed the group's goals above the individual's interests. Smith added periodic town meetings to teach the basic form of democratic government, calling Morning Exercise "the Headmaster's class." North Shore also replicated the Parker Toy Shop, collecting and rebuilding toys for children less well off, and other traditions like May Day and the Santa Claus party to enhance the understanding of cooperative effort and the responsibility of the individual to the group.

Another philosophic precept upheld by Smith was his belief in the importance of the arts, which he called a way for keeping "all avenues to the soul open and in use," and the necessity of athletics. The stage was central to the life of the school and was large enough for a cast of eighty-five actors and actresses when students performed Gilbert and Sullivan operettas. Drama, music, and the visual arts interwove with each other in numerous theatrical productions. Smith held a high regard for aesthetic, social, moral, and physical development. As in the arts, so in athletics. Smith was sure teams weren't for the purpose of creating stars. The emphasis was on working with and for the group.

When the school's founders were troubled about "whether or not it was possible to meet the formal entrance requirements for college and still maintain . . . progressive principles in teaching," Smith explained:

> We decided to stick to our principles. We believed that a student who was
> truly interested in what he was doing, who understood its relationship to
> his whole life, who had had ample opportunity to practice making con-

sidered decisions affecting his own interests and, above all, who had achieved a well-rounded and happily integrated personality would be far better equipped to do well in college to further his educational progress.

This philosophy is still practiced. Presently, North Shore's rigorous academic program offers traditional subjects, advanced placement courses, and electives in drama, computer science, contemporary global issues, and other subjects. Technology is integrated into the curriculum across all grade levels. Languages include Spanish for all lower school students with French beginning in Grade 6 and Mandarin Chinese beginning in Grade 9. The school encourages independent study for Grades 11-12 by offering an annual week-long off-campus experience for Grades 9-12.[6]

Educators from North Shore Country Day School became part of an unofficial progressive network. For example, Carleton Washburne, one of the founders of the Graduate Teachers College of Winnetka, sat next to Perry Dunlap Smith when they were seventh graders at Chicago's Parker School. Cleveland Thomas, a dean at North Shore, later became principal of the Francis W. Parker School. Charles Haas, a North Shore graduate, founded the Oakwood School in California, and hired Perry Dunlap Smith's son, Ham Smith, as its first principal.

Ojai Valley School
Ojai, California

The Bristol School became the Ojai Valley School in 1923, when Edward Yeomans purchased the land to establish a school that reflected Francis Parker's principles and rejected characteristics of his own abysmal and stultifying early education. "Schools, as far as I was concerned," Yeomans wrote, "were paid to destroy the only important endowments I had: zest for living, friendliness, appreciation of beauty and the mystery and romance in human nature."[7]

A Princeton University graduate and a businessman, Edward Yeomans spent eight years working with Jane Addams at Hull House. He subsequently became a member of the Winnetka School Board and was instrumental in the appointment of Carleton Washburne. His children Andrew and Edward Jr. attended the Francis Parker School in Chicago. Edward Jr. went on to become headmaster of the Shady Hill School. At the Parker School, Mr. Yeomans Sr. met third-grade teacher Mrs. Gudrun Thorne-Thomsen, who had trained and been a teacher at Parker's Cook County Normal School and taught in the teacher training program at the School of Education of University of Chicago. At Yeomans's invitation, Mrs. Thorne-Thomsen moved to Ojai Valley in 1923 to become principal of his new school. That she brought much of Parker's progressive vision to the school is clear from a sixty-page brochure she and Yeomans published after the third year of the school's existence:

> Subjects are not taught primarily in order to enable the child to pass examinations, but for their significance as the tools of learning and for their by-products as interpreters and illuminators of life. That is, we are not thinking so much of the matter of preparation for the next grade or the next school. We are thinking more of the child before us, his emotions as well as his mind.

Another telling example of their progressive vision appears in a description that could easily have come from Chicago's Francis W. Parker School:

> The youngest in the school . . . [have an] active informal [daily life]. They sing, dance, work in a garden, take care of pets, build houses, churn, weave, draw, paint and model in clay, read and write. They listen to stories, learn poems, dramatize and make up their own . . . . They keep a store, buy and sell the necessary school materials. These children come to school with many experiences and interests. The school utilizes these, organizes them and builds further on them.

Although the Ojai Valley School frequently tottered on the brink of financial collapse, it was able to maintain its progressive vision during the Great Depression and World War II. In many instances, however, survival depended upon the faculty, who often worked at reduced salaries, assumed additional duties, and made other sacrifices. In 1943, the school was a financial disaster. Wallace Burr, headmaster from 1943 to 1975, saved the school, bringing "what the school needed so much . . . . experience in building up enrollment and financing a school. It was the breeze that fanned the spark [and] the school came to life." Survival, however, meant sacrificing Parker's progressive legacy, even though, as Burr wrote, "We tried to maintain the important elements of progressive education."

A major transformation came in response to a changing parental constituency in the 1950s. A teacher explained, "As the clientele changed and the Second World War overturned a way of life, you had parents who wanted practical, visible, immediate results—never mind dancing around with bare feet." Tough businessmen, ambitious Hollywood actors, directors, and screen writers, and some down-to-earth ranchers, wanted their children "to have their multiplication tables down cold."

Another critical event in the school's history came with the 1960s, when Burr noted, "There seemed to be a wall between faculty and students. Where we'd been a family before, the trust seemed to have broken down."

However, in the mid-1970s, the school reorganized by creating the position of board chairman, appointing a president as chief executive officer, and hiring admissions, development, and business office directors to develop "aggressive programs for the urgent demands of a new economic environment and age."

The Ojai Valley School exists today, more traditional than at its inception, but still espousing progressive principles. The school's promotional materials state: "Our students flourish . . . and benefit from a curriculum that places as much emphasis on character development as it does on academic achievement," and "Ojai Valley School students learn to think critically, to act with integrity, and to welcome the opportunity to achieve their best."

Oakwood School
North Hollywood, California

From the beginning, the Oakwood School of North Hollywood, California, was intended to contribute to the heritage of the progressive schools. This urban day school for Grades K-12 was founded in 1951 by Charles Haas, now trustee emeritus, whose roots can be traced to Chicago. Trustee Haas wrote:

> Whatever part I played in setting the goals and character of Oakwood was motivated by a desire for my children to have the joyful and creative experience I had from K-12 at the North Shore Country Day School in Winnetka, Illinois, a school modeled largely on Francis Parker School in Chicago.[8]

The affiliations with the Parker legacy are strong. The first principal of the Oakwood Secondary School was Ham Smith, the son of Perry Dunlap Smith and a graduate of North Shore Country Day School. Chicago Parker School alumnus Christopher Holabird '44 taught at Oakwood Elementary for eleven years before becoming principal. Holabird, who had earned a master's degree in biology at Harvard University, a master's degree in zoology from the University of Chicago, and a master's degree in teaching from the Graduate Teachers College of Winnetka, was recommended for the position by Herbert Smith, then the principal of Chicago's Parker School. When Holabird taught in the elementary school, the course of study replicated his alma mater. The central subject was the organizing principle for each lower grade level: the topic for the third grade was the Hopi Indians; fourth grade, the Vikings; fifth grade, medieval times; and sixth grade alternated between the study of China or Greece. Social studies dominated the course of study and the arts played a major role. The course of study was experience- based for about forty percent of the time in all disciplines except mathematics. The humanities were taught as interdisciplinary subjects for Grades 7 and 8, but other subjects were taught separately. Holabird introduced the Gillingham Reading Method, an approach passed from Anna Gillingham, the founder, to Mary Davis, Mr. Holabird's fourth grade teacher at the Chicago Parker School, to his students at Oakwood Elementary School. The Oakwood Elementary School also continued the legacy of Colonel Parker's Morning Exercise and focused on community life.[9]

Today, the Oakwood School is divided into two campuses—a lower school campus and high school campus. Each is adjacent to a large city park, which the schools utilize for "learning by doing." The traditional high school curriculum combines a rigorous academic program with a broad exposure to the fine and performing arts as well as electives, special studies, field trips, and extracurricular activities. Holabird describes the curriculum as "highly academic with the image of emphasis on the arts and the humanities." Faithful to the "education of the whole child," a math-science center and a music-dance-athletic center were built on the secondary school campus.

In the 1980s, Christopher Holabird resigned as principal and founded another progressive school, Los Encinos Elementary School."

Los Encinos Elementary School
Encino, California

Los Encinos Elementary School in Encino, California, is a co-ed day school for Grades K-5. Mr. Holabird, who directed the school for seventeen years, described it as:

> A small school with a large commitment to every child. We provide a structured but warm, caring environment where children are encouraged to develop confidence, independence, and pleasure in learning . . . We believe in success as a child's best motivation and provide an educational experience that is well balanced between the academic skills and the creative arts, between the needs of the individual and the child's responsibility to the group.[10]

Built in the Parker image, the school consistently followed progressive principles. Its student body is diverse and a large percentage of the minority students enrolled are provided financial aid. The community plays a vital role in the education of the child. The course of study replicates the program of the Oakwood Elementary School, teaching a central subject by correlating English, history, and the arts. Most instruction is "learning by doing." The school's purpose is education for character and citizenry in a democratic society, and its mission is to cater to the individual differences of a diverse student body.

Graduate Teachers College of Winnetka, Illinois

Francis Parker was convinced that the common school in America could not prevail without the training of teachers. "The people must demand the artist teacher—the teacher trained and skilled in the science of education." In his lifetime, Parker noted that "the vast majority of teachers have not the slightest professional training." Parker argued that "every other business in the world requires experts but the care of immortal souls!" "An effective school," he asserted, "means an educated, cultured, trained, devoted teacher."[11]

Thirty years after his death, three of Parker's disciples transmitted his legacy to a new kind of teacher training at the innovative Graduate Teachers College of Winnetka, which flourished from 1932 until 1954. Sometime in 1930, returning by train from a meeting of the Progressive Education Association, principals Flora Cooke and Perry Dunlap Smith and Superintendent Carleton Washburne talked far into the night about the possibilities of a new kind of teacher education. "The result of this spirited and idealistic conversation was the creation of The Graduate Teachers College."[12] The college was conceived in the spirit of the Progressive Education Movement and to fulfill the need for teachers who understood the movement.

These three founding directors and the schools they led—the Winnetka Public Schools, the North Shore Country Day School, and the Francis W. Parker School—had established reputations among progressive schools and were prepared to share their faculty. They also provided a cross section of first-hand experiences for student teachers. The Winnetka Public Schools, a large suburban system headed by national educational innovator Carleton Washburne, included elementary schools and a junior and a senior high school. Smith's North Shore Country Day School was a small, suburban independent day school for Grades K-12, and the Francis W. Parker School was a middle-sized, independent, urban day school enrolling Grades K-12.

Each instructor at the Graduate Teachers College was a full-time member of the faculty or administration of one of the three founding schools. Parker teacher Hazel Cornell taught the methods course in Secondary School Social Studies; the psychologist from the Winnetka Schools offered a course in tests and measurements; and the psychiatrist from the Winnetka Schools taught a seminar on child development. Philosophy of Education was the course entrusted to the heads of the three schools. Supervising teachers and seminar leaders donated their services; the only person who drew a modest salary was Dean Frances Murray, "an outstanding teacher in the Junior High School in Winnetka." Murray was "the heart" of the Graduate Teachers College from its founding to its closing.[13]

The program had four parts: teaching under supervision in the cooperating schools; attending seminar conference courses on such topics as philosophy, child development, and social studies; directed reading, "planned to meet each student's individual needs and interests"; and specialized fieldwork. The student teachers learned by observation and participation during the school day, and methods and theory classes were presented at the college in the late afternoon. "The program was tailored to fit each individual student . . . there were no term papers, examinations, or grades."[14] Student teachers could elect to be trained for teaching, supervision, or administrative work.

"The students had a variety of placements over the school year. They might begin with a fifth grade in a Winnetka School for the first third of the year, an eleventh grade social studies class for the second part of the year at the Parker School, and a twelfth grade English class at North Shore Country Day School for the final third. It was an important feature of the program that most of the students had teaching experiences at different grade levels to help determine the teaching level and to provide direct experiences with students at a variety of grades."[15]

The Graduate Teachers College attempted "to put into practice at the graduate level the principles of progressive education."[16] The classes were always small, ranging from a low of six in the Class of '32 to a high of twenty student teachers. The college attracted liberal arts graduates from a wide spectrum of American universities and quickly attracted international recognition. Students from Austria, Germany, China, India, and Canada attended. These future teachers came for a year of intensive professional training, stayed in private homes, and graduated with a Master's degree in Education. Graduates who became Parker faculty were psychologist and psychiatrist Alfred Adler; English teacher, author, and Melville scholar Merlin Bowen; art teacher Ruth Byrnes; teacher and principal Jack Ellison; science teacher Eggert Meyer; mathematics teacher Barr McCutcheon; and teacher and Oakwood and Los Encinos Elementary School principal Christopher Holabird, among others.[17] All distinguished themselves in their respective fields.

Because the college was "never a mainstream educational institution" and was not recognized by accrediting bodies, it joined several other teacher training programs in organizing its own association, the National Association for Intern Teacher Education. The college folded in 1954, primarily because the three visionaries, Cooke, Smith, and Washburne, had retired or moved on and "were no longer available to attract students and guide its destiny." The program led to the establishment of similar master's degree programs in education at large universities across the United States. "The teaching staffs of the three founding schools continued to be enriched by its graduates into the early 1990s."[18]

Even when progressive education was at its peak, there were few progressive schools in the nation. Thirty progressive high schools were identified for the Eight-Year Study, including the Little School in the Woods, Greenwich, Connecticut; the Phoebe Thorn School of Bryn Mawr, Pennsylvania; the Marietta Johnson Organic School in Fairhope, Alabama; the Chevy Chase Country Day School in Maryland; and the public schools of Gary, Indiana. Seven precollege schools built on the image of Chicago's Francis W. Parker School attested to the value "Parkerites" placed on progressive education at the flagship school, but Parker's greatest legacy stemmed from his ongoing concern for the teaching of teachers. It was through the countless educators trained at the Chicago Normal School, the School of Education at the University of Chicago, and the Graduate Teachers College that his contribution to progressive education continued to survive.

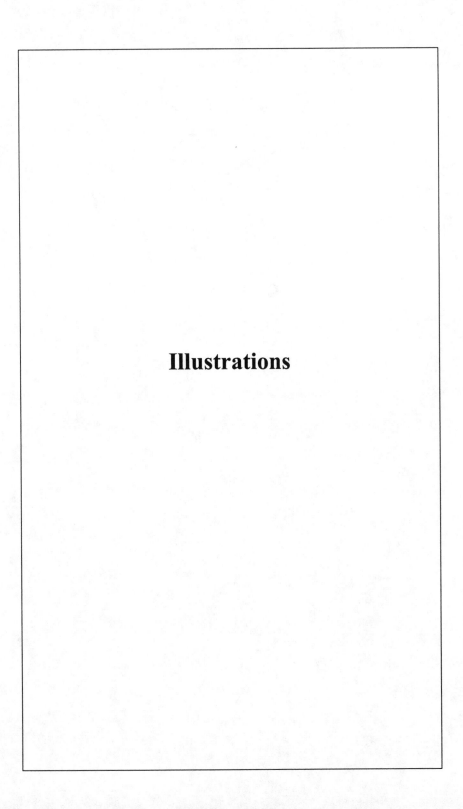

Illustrations

The Old Building of Yesterday

The original building opened in 1901.

Four Founding Visionaries Collaborate

Francis Wayland Parker,
Founding Pedagogue

Flora Cooke, First Principal

Anita McCormick Blaine,
Founder and Philanthropist

John Dewey, Philosopher

Four Progressive Principals Lead School

Herbert W. Smith
(1938–1956)

Cleveland A. Thomas
(1956–1967)

Jack L. Ellison
(1967–1972)

William D. Geer Jr.
(1973–1986)

Time-Honored School Traditions

Parker School Toy Shop rebuilt toys for Hull House.

May Day is the only tradition that did not last.

Bagpipers lead students on Class Day.

"The history of a school is the history of its teachers."

–Francis Parker

Mary Davis
Lower School

Lynn Martin
Lower School

Hazel Cornell
Eight-Year Study

Barney Negronida
Foreign Language

Sarah Greenebaum
Eighth Grade

George Barr McCutcheon
Mathematics

Herman Lukens
Fifth Grade

Delafield Griffith
Middle School

Bernard Kent Markwell
History

Marie Kirchner Stone
Upper School

Andrew Kaplan
English

Maryanne Kalin-Miller
Middle School

JoNell Bailey
Lower School

Bart Wolgamot
Music

Harriett Cholden
Fifth Grade

Lil Lowry Manning
Dean of Students

Cherished Curriculum of the Past

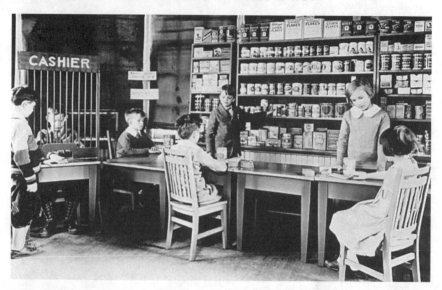

The students learned math in their grocery store.

Mr. Lukens taught geography on the linoleum classroom floor.

Parker Is an Activity-Centered School

The first cheerleaders in their new uniforms.

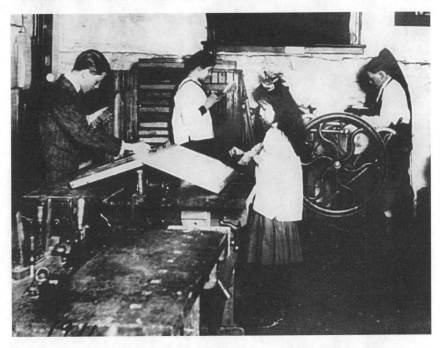

The school printing press published Parker School books.

The Arts Are Pivotal to the Curriculum

The students wrote and published *An Experiment Reports on Itself.*

Students chose their own project to build in shop.

Drama tech students worked behind the scenes of a production.

Painting and Music Teach Science and History

Science applied art to the human body.

Medieval History integrated music.

The New Buildings of Today

The 1962 building is the center of today's campus.

An addition was constructed in 1998.

Part Two

The School's Practice

Chapter 6

The Pioneering Years
(1901-1935)

Historical Perspective: Progressive Values Transform Education

The Pioneering Years began with an industrial and social revolution and concluded with a financial collapse. "Chicago, that filthy Indian village on the shores of Lake Michigan, had grown within a generation to be the second largest city in America, and even New Yorkers, bored to the point of bad digestion by Chicago's brag, were secretly admitting that the future—railroads, the produce of the Great Plains, the business of buying the world's foodstuffs—belonged to Chicago."[1] When President Harrison granted six million dollars to the city to host the World's Columbian Exposition in commemoration of the four hundredth anniversary of the discovery of America, he did not see Chicago as the harbinger of the twentieth century but as the pinnacle of the nineteenth. The 1893 Exposition did not feature Chicago's past, but it borrowed from the European heritage and gave only a glimpse of Chicago's future.

At the Exposition, Architect Louis Sullivan's Transportation Building struck the one discordant note against the backdrop of "uninteresting imitations of the ruins of the Old World." Sullivan lost the battle for architectural influence in the nineteenth century, but twentieth-century architecture evolved from his ideas and Chicago emerged as the city of the new skyscraper, the first major twentieth-century city. Just as Sullivan changed architectural forms, poet Edwin Arlington Robinson, novelists Frank Norris, Stephen Crane, Kate Chopin, and a group of daring women writers "were waiting in the wings to displace the 'graybeards'—James Russell Lowell, Oliver Wendell Holmes, and John Greenleaf Whittier."[2] As in architecture and literature, so too in education, where Francis Wayland Parker and John Dewey struck another kind of discordant chord in Chicago, a chord that would influence twentieth-century education.

Until the 1890s, traditional education dominated the American scene. At that time, Francis Parker and John Dewey began making inroads to meet the needs of a changing society, which historian Henry Commager captured in this salient description:

> On the one side lies an America predominately agricultural; concerned with domestic problems; conforming, intellectually at least, to the political, economic, and moral principles inherited from the seventeenth and eighteenth centuries—an America . . . self-confident, self-contained, and self-reliant, and conscious of its unique character and its unique destiny. On the other side lies the modern America, predominately urban and industrial . . . , experiencing profound changes in population, social institutions, economy, technology, and trying to accommodate its traditional institutions and habits of thought to conditions new and in part alien.[3]

This dramatic transformation of society resulted in a Progressive Era of Reform, which spanned from the 1890s to World War I, when the problems confronting Americans were social, cultural, economic, and industrial. The social order was shifting to a new and more democratic ideal, the intellectual world was being revolutionized by the sciences, as a result of the influence of Charles Darwin's *On the Origin of Species* (1859), and economics and culture were being restructured by the Industrial Revolution. The progressive movement in education closely related to these broader social and political issues.

America faced the dawn of the twentieth century with confidence. Unity and prosperity descended upon the nation after the Civil War and the winning of the West, and cities and industries were flourishing due to plentiful, cheap immigrant labor. Average farm income was increasing, wages for industrial labor were rising, and big business was growing fast—perhaps too fast. The tone was "set by a cheerful, though not complacent, middle class . . . often motivated by personal ambition and moral indignation."[4]

Philosophically, educated Americans of the nineteenth century were essentially defenders of the *laissez faire* doctrine. They believed that "rewards went to those who worked hard and deserved them, and poverty was the punishment for vice and laziness."[5] Americans were also individualists by tradition and therefore reformers, who believed that bad conditions could and should be changed. Even for those who thought poverty was the fault of the poor, it was impossible to ignore the epidemics that periodically spread from the slums to their neighborhoods or the fires that began in jerry-built tenements and wiped out entire business blocks.

At the turn of the century, many middle class Americans began to replace "laissez faire" theories with a more liberal viewpoint. At the root of progressive ideology was an antimonopoly sentiment from which most reforms stemmed. Settlement workers discovered urban poverty, and ministers preached social reform. Reform groups accepted the challenge of solving problems—labor organized, farmers joined the Populist Movement, and settlement houses addressed the problems of the slums. The government instigated a considerable list of societal reforms at all levels—child labor laws, conservation acts, antitrust laws, the Pure Food and Drug Act, legislation controlling industries, and others. The Progressive Reform, however, did not solve social problems or produce a new social system. "It made only the barest beginning toward the redistribution of wealth . . . the problem of Negro equality remained almost untouched . . . [and] progressive enactments were . . . emasculated and abandoned in the postwar decade."[6]

It was expected or at least hoped that new education would play a vital role in the reform of the nation. Upholding the sentiments and values of the Progressive Reformers, new education from 1890 to 1920 identified itself also as progressive education because it was based on using the school as a lever of social reform. World War I, however, transformed progressive education and shifted the national social consciousness and values from a liberal reform philosophy back to a more conservative and individualistic viewpoint. The war caused the diminution of the Progressive Reforms, and progressive education became an isolated movement, no longer part of a broader social context of social reform. When America became a world power after the war, citizens craved political isolation. The war produced intense national confusion and ambivalence and the desire to eliminate many freedoms. Progressive education in the country became a potpourri of innovations, but the Parker School stayed the course of social reconstruction.

After the war, Americans were determined to return to their cherished and familiar ways, but the Roaring Twenties, also known as the Jazz Age, ushered in changes in lifestyle. In the arts, there was a revolt of the high-brows against middle class morality. Authors like Ernest Hemingway, Gertrude Stein, F. Scott Fitzgerald, and T. S. Eliot, artists, painters, and musicians became disillusioned with America and expatriated to Europe. F. Scott Fitzgerald captured their despair when he wrote in *This Side of Paradise* (1920), "All Gods dead, all wars fought, all faiths in man shaken."[7] Historian Frederick Lewis Allen called the 1920s "a revolution in manners and morals," emphasizing changes in behaviors—small and large—in clothing, cosmetics, sports, automobiles, and in family life and sexual activity. Freud's ideas infiltrated daily life, the arts, and education, infusing them with greater freedom and prompting some to call the popular new automobile "a whorehouse on wheels."[8] During the period, progressive education was dominated by this new freedom, which popularized the child-centered school. The Parker School did place the child as central, but the school was emphatically shaped by its social reconstructionist ideals and did not refer to itself as child centered.

The era of flappers and flivvers ended dramatically on October 28, 1929, when the stock market crash prompted a severe and prolonged depression. The collapse of the market caused profound change in the economic, political, and educational milieu. Traditional values were in crisis, radical activists joined the Communist Party, and liberal voices called for education to revisit the idea of the school as a "lever of social reform." In the 1930s, progressive education returned to a societal orientation and sometimes a Marxian viewpoint.

From the Progressive Era of Reform, during World War I, throughout the 1920s, to the beginning of the Great Depression, the Parker School developed a new twentieth-century form of education that attempted to shape a school as a "social lever" to improve the lives of children and to create a science of education.

Five Trustees Oversee Blaine's Philanthropy

When Anita McCormick Blaine founded the Francis W. Parker School on April 23, 1901, under a trust agreement, she vested its management in a Board of Trustees: Chairman Cyrus Bentley, Owen Aldis, Henry Favill, Stanley McCormick, and herself (see Chapter 4). When the trustees merged the Chicago Institute with the School of Education of the

University of Chicago on the South Side, the North Side parents now without a school asked Mrs. Blaine to develop her original plan for a school on the city block she had purchased across from Lincoln Park. Blaine was amenable but this time conceived of a more limited undertaking for the new school, which she named after Francis Wayland Parker. Blaine contributed all of the seed money for the school as well as a guaranteed annual fund. Two trustees donated $5,000 each, and the McCormicks donated $15,000 at the opening of the school (see Chapter 2).[9]

Blaine's property was bordered on the south by the residential Webster Avenue, on the west by the commercial Clark Street, on the north by Grant Place, and on the east by Lincoln Park. Although Blaine deeded the land to the University of Chicago as part of the merger between the Institute and the School of Education, the University gave Blaine free use of that portion under the Parker School building at 330 Webster Avenue. The adjoining real estate on the west, north, and east sides of the building was personally owned by Mrs. Blaine, who permitted the Parker School to use the property almost as its own and to erect buildings on it.

Mrs. Blaine hired architect James Gamble Rogers to design a two-story building whose focal point was an entrance hall dominated by a large fireplace. The building included spacious halls, large playrooms, a gymnasium, laboratories, a print shop, clay modeling rooms, and an assembly hall. Between 1901 and the twenty-fifth anniversary of the school, Blaine and the trustees added several buildings. In 1907, Blaine rented a store on Clark Street to use as a lunchroom and a library and purchased a plot of land for $250 for a garden adjacent to the school. In 1909, the trustees arranged for the construction of a barn, and the eighth grade boys built a shed behind the main building facing Grant Place. In 1916, Blaine purchased a building to house an auditorium and a gymnasium. Following World War I, the trustees obtained a two-year permit, which they illegally extended to twenty years, to construct "portables," pre-fabricated World War I huts, for classrooms.

Most financial issues to which the trustees gave their time and expertise were generic school issues: low teacher salaries, the absence of a pension plan, inadequate training facilities, and an overcrowded building. Financial issues unique to Parker also plagued the trustees: the lack of donations by parents and alumni, the low cost of tuition combined with the high cost of scholarships, and the disparity between the annual deficit and the amount of the Blaine endowment. To supplement Blaine's $10,000 annual guarantee, the trustees organized a Parents Committee to raise $3,500 annually, but the parents fell short of the goal. The trustees organized a second Parents Committee to provide scholarship aid "so that Parker would not be a rich child's school."[10] This fundraising effort was equally ineffective. The annual deficit rose from a predicted $4,560 to $15,000 in 1902, soared to $60,000 in 1920, and exceeded $120,000 at the end of the era, causing Miss Cooke to warn, "The lack of permanency overshadows all the virtues which the school possesses."

The school usually had a waiting list, and enrollment grew from 144 pupils to 418 by 1932. Although the trustees had gradually increased the tuition, a senior at the Parker School in 1924 paid $200 less than a senior at Chicago Latin. In 1924, Miss Cooke presented a new proposal: (1) full tuition students who paid tuition for another student, (2) full tuition students, and (3) scholarship students.[11] When the trustees accepted Cooke's tuition proposal, the school became solvent for the 1925-1926 school year.

Another major trustee concern focused on the Blaine endowment. Blaine continued to cover the skyrocketing deficit, and in 1933 she designated funds for a faculty pension, set up an annual guarantee for ten years, established a reserve fund, paid trustee expenses, and gave an additional $100,000 to the general fund. But instead of providing the school with financial security, Blaine's pattern of giving interfered with efforts to establish a permanent endowment to which others would contribute. Some participants in the school incorrectly believed that Mrs. Blaine's funds were inexhaustible and that the school would be the beneficiary of her will. Others worried that the school would have to close its doors.

In 1930, grave new concerns erupted for the trustees. The building, now thirty years old, was plagued with heating, lighting, plumbing, and ventilation problems. City inspectors examined the building for fire and safety, causing maintenance and repair costs to mount. Impatient about the new construction, Principal Cooke gave the trustees a set of criteria for "a model, modern city school" that met the needs of "the children's all-round growth."[12] The "crude draft" was a plan for 550 students and sixty faculty. In the plan, the elementary school required a laboratory for natural sciences, a kitchen for cooking, and a rooftop conservatory for the study of plant life. The design included art studios, two shops for wood projects, two music rooms, a restroom with bunks like in English schools, and a tinker shop for small group projects. To meet the school's obligation to general education, a permanent nursery for children of apprentice teachers in training was added, a forward-thinking idea in the 1930s.

The trustees postponed a decision on Cooke's proposal for a number of reasons, including the viability of the present site of the school and the possibility that the school might not survive the financial hardships it was experiencing. In July, 1930, Cooke, however, mailed her proposal for the "Building Program for a Modern City School" to Blaine, who was visiting California, and to Architect John Augur Holabird, who made a blueprint. Cooke's plan indicated, "Any Francis Parker School should serve as an educational community and should be composed . . . to meet the needs of . . . children, a teacher training group, parents, and adults." Cooke explained that groups of adults as well as teachers should be able to use the school for lectures, clubs, dramatics, art projects, and other activities during the evenings. In her design, she described two long buildings, "one facing Lincoln Park West with a series of art shops on the ground floor to be rented as art studios for textile weaving, metal work, water color, and oil painting with pleasant apartments for rent by people interested in living near the school like teachers and artists." Cooke envisioned the companion building facing Clark Street with a ground floor rented for wholesome stores—a bakery, a green-grocer, dry goods stores, florist shops, and a second floor for offices for physicians, lawyers, and dentists. "The children of the school could use these community activities for observation and stimulation, which would educate them naturally to understand in some real measure the interdependence of people."[13] The board tabled Cooke's plan for six years, although in 1935 a building and grounds committee called the school building "totally inadequate" and deplorable in contrast to the progressive designs of the schools developed in Germany, Holland, and France. The decision to build was postponed until the next era.

The first chairman of the board, Cyrus Bentley, was profoundly engaged in the educational aspects of the school. With Mrs. Blaine, Bentley attended weekly curriculum meetings as well as all faculty meetings, and he dedicated one week a year to visit and critique the different departments. Although often an outspoken critic, Bentley was greatly respected by the faculty and Principal Cooke. Bentley possessed "scrupulous integrity and unswerving faithfulness to what he considered right . . . He had a stern and serious exterior—but an understanding of human frailty."[14] Miss Cooke hinted that someone like him ought to be made principal of the school.[15]

Bentley was an organized chairman, specific in his charges and in the delegation of responsibilities. In 1906, he and Blaine set forth an "Outline of Administration of the School," which divided responsibilities among trustees, the principal, and the teachers. The principal and trustees selected and dismissed teachers and decided their salaries. The principal was in charge of the organization of the teaching force, and the faculty was responsible for the organization of children for educational purposes. Coordination of the home and school was jointly delegated to the principal and the faculty and educational publicity was the responsibility of all.[16] Although the school required fundraising, no group was assigned responsibility for fundraising, and trustees were not invited to make donations. Few did.

Bentley established the board precedent of concentrating on education issues to the detriment of the school's financial health. The agenda for trustee meetings rarely included financial issues, fundraising, or trustee donations, focusing instead on school matters such as "ways to extend the usefulness of the school" through "summer school or summer camp, as a social center, or sharing the school with the neighborhood, the less privileged, and settlement houses."

Board membership, or lack of it, added to the school's problems. Stanley McCormick had resigned shortly after the school opened because of health problems. Henry Favill submitted his resignation in 1917, just after World War I ended, and Owen Aldis resigned in 1920. Cyrus Bentley remained until his death in 1930, leaving Blaine the sole remaining trustee.

Cyrus Bentley was an active Chicago citizen. He was chairman of the Young Men's Christian Association, which assisted new Chicago residents in adapting to life in the city. It was at the YMCA that Bentley became acquainted with Francis Parker, one of the managers for the organization. Bentley also offered *pro bono* advice to groups such as the City Homes Association, which "had been set up to investigate and clean up rat-infested tenement houses where most of Chicago's immigrant population lived."[17] As a lawyer, Bentley played several roles in the lives of Anita Blaine and the McCormick family. He assisted with the merger that created the McCormick-owned International Harvester and served as the company's first general counsel.

Known for his good judgment and astute legal mind, he advised Blaine on her investments and often investigated people and causes she was inclined to support philanthropically. Bentley was also the father of Margaret and Richard '11, who entered the Parker School the day it opened. At the time of his death, two grandchildren were enrolled in the school.

In 1932, Mrs. Blaine, the sole surviving trustee, transferred the trust agreement to a nonprofit Illinois corporation. She appointed a new Board of Trustees and established in the new Charter for the Corporation an Educational Council whose purpose was to safeguard the school's progressive principles:

> Its purpose was to act apart from the financial and practical management of the school—to counsel and advise the principal, the teachers, and the trustees on educational policies in harmony with Colonel Parker's ideas . . . This Council is tied in with the Board of Trustees sufficiently to keep both sides in touch with one another, yet allowing the Educational Council to function independently . . . . provision was made in the charter that the Principal should be chosen only from among such persons as are nominated by the Educational Council. . . . In the new organization flexibility of amendment of both charter and by-laws was provided for, but with restrictions to assure that whatever the future development of the corporation might be, it should not eliminate or in any way curtail the power of the Educational Council.[18]

The Educational Council was to function independently but to act as a medium for the interchange of views between the trustees and the faculty. An alumna, Lois Healy '22, a parent, Clay Judson, and trustees were the representatives to the original Council, whose first duty was to search for, interview, and recommend a candidate for school principal who supported a progressive philosophy. The Council established a procedure for hiring a new principal and recommended Raymond Osborne, Cooke's assistant. Other issues discussed during the Council's early years were the school philosophy, student life and activities, and the faculty's recommendation to join a union.

In this era the trustees kept the Parker School doors open, but they did not bring financial health to the institution.

Flora Cooke Serves as the First Principal (1901-1934)

During her thirty-three years as principal, Miss Cooke fashioned the school according to Francis Parker's ideals and shaped it according to the advances of psychology, sociology, and education research. When Parker invited Cooke to lead the Francis W. Parker School in 1901, he explained to her, "You won't be duplicating our experiments; you will be on your own."[19] Cooke, however, mainly duplicated his experiments and evolved few of her own. She built the school's educational foundation on three main Parker principles: (1) a school climate founded on love for children and respect for hard work, (2) a democratic school organization based on the belief in the innate worth and freedom of the individual, and (3) intellectual rigor in the classroom.[20]

Cooke translated the first principle about school climate into her dictum, a child's play is a child's work. To demonstrate that a school was a place where students should want to be and not a place of drudgery, she created an activity-centered place of learning dominated by children's projects. A Parker classroom was a grocery store filled with produce from the school garden on one day and a home economics kitchen or a humanities seminar room on another day. The students moved from the science laboratory to the art and music studios and from manual training to physical training classrooms. These classrooms did not feature uniform desks neatly filed in rows and nailed to the floor. Instead, she arranged a pleasant environment with round tables and sets of chairs. Learning paraphernalia filled the classrooms—hammers and saws, typewriters and printing press, scissors and paste, trumpets and phonograph players, and stacks of books and writing paper piled on overladen shelves. For Cooke, the happiness of the child was an important measure of an effective school.

Like Parker, Cooke possessed deep faith in democracy, which was the basis for developing a democratic approach to education. Her goal was to make the children active participants in their own education rather than obedient citizens. "Good citizenship," she said, "demands the highest degree of knowledge, power, skill and service."[21] The ideal was not given mere lip service. During World War I, when a Parker student wrote an editorial for the school newspaper promoting pacifism, a perturbed parent body wanted the boy expelled. Aware that her decision and the remarks she would make to a special parent assembly might lose her a job and close the school forever, Cooke defended the child's right to freedom of speech and refused to expel the boy. Cooke addressed the Parent Association with these words:

The United States has always stood for free speech . . . No child can
have faith in a school that preaches a theory and then denies it the first
time it is put to a test . . . Parker teachers are deeply concerned with
the problem of educating youth for good citizenship in war as in peace.
We may make mistakes . . . but we must be free to do what we think
is just and right.[22]

Cooke's assertion firmly established the curriculum not as the domain of
the parents but as "the domain of the faculty", a phrase often repeated by
teachers, parents, and trustees. Not easily intimidated, Miss Cooke and
Mrs. Blaine wrote to no lesser authority than President Woodrow Wilson
to resolve the conflict. Naturally, President Wilson's response supported
the Cooke-Blaine position.[23]

Cooke's definition of democracy included active student participation
in the community and creative but appropriate consequences for infractions
of school laws. For example, one fall day the sixth grade teacher dismissed
class early. Instead of leaving campus as directed, several girls accessed the
"off limits" basement of the old main building to play piano and to dance.
Miss Cooke insisted that if the girls wanted to dance and play piano, the
miscreants could remain after school daily to plan and create a grand spec-
tacle for the student body. When they made progress, Miss Cooke hired an
expert to assist the girls as they wrote scripts, made costumes, converted a
garden into a miniature village, and presented an outdoor pageant. The
pageant redeemed the students, but more importantly the penalty was a positive reminder to follow rules. The pageantry expert was invited to teach
after-school classes for the remainder of the year.[24]

Many students saw character as Miss Cooke's main message.
"Character was seldom dislocated from the deed . . . for both . . . were
constantly exposed to Miss Cooke's insights," reported Parker alumna
Katharine Taylor '06, later the Headmistress of Shady Hill School in
Cambridge. Taylor revealed that children felt a "nakedness of spirit, when
after committing some craven or naughty act, they encountered Miss
Cooke." Their only refuge was in "her crime-defying love, her embracing
humor, and her staunch faith in the power of good." Students felt no accusation or personal attack in their disciplinary encounters. The erring student and Miss Cooke wrestled with the action like two adults and in the end
made decisions and acted on them with strength. Cooke was an important

presence in the children's lives, "ready to listen, to interpret, and to help when help was needed."[25]

Following Parker's third principle, Cooke subscribed to intellectual rigor in the classroom and advocated strong teachers. Cooke believed, "The purpose of the American school is not merely to teach arithmetic and literature and science as unrelated subjects . . . [but] through these . . . to teach the art of living intelligently, so that the young [can] learn to take an active share in the experience and decisions of a democratic society."[26] Therefore, she demanded that teachers be familiar with psychology and child development, conversant with learning and teaching theory, and knowledgeable in their content areas in order to select and adapt the subject matter to the child's experience. Like her mentor, she sought teachers who were "educated, cultured, and trained," and possessed strong character, good scholarship, a love of children, and the ability to cooperate and to work hard. A teacher was also to establish an effective relationship with students and to help students create positive relationships with each other and with the community.

The training of effective teachers became part of her legacy. She was integrally engaged in hiring and training of teachers and familiarizing them with the theory and history of progressive education. As a first grade teacher, she established a model for other teachers to follow. Additionally, she met with the faculty one evening a week to insure that the school course of study was unified around a single goal. Cooke made the Parker School an intellectual center for progressive education by encouraging faculty publications and public speaking engagements. Cooke and her original corps of thirteen teachers created a child- and community-centered, democratic, and intellectually rigorous school in Parker's image.

Engaging the teacher centrally in the governance of the school became Cooke's imprimatur. Her greatest contribution was to define the principal as the headmaster or educational leader rather than as an administrator. Cooke's successor, Assistant Principal Raymond W. Osborne, and several subsequent principals followed her example by making educational leadership their priority.

During the Pioneering Years, Cooke led the teachers in the development and publication of twenty-nine *Catalogues and Course of Study* between 1901 and 1930 to inform the home, the school, and the nation's educators about the Parker School's educational scope, policy, principles, and purpose. Following Dewey's caveat that young sciences began with qualitative data when quantitative data were unavailable, Cooke, between 1912 and 1934, also guided the teachers in the preparation of ten *Studies in Education,* which described six pedagogical principles that teachers confirmed through classroom experimentation. Cooke supervised the selection of the principles and the practices that she believed the teachers had developed successfully and wrote the introduction for each of the *Studies.*

The educational and democratic leadership provided by Cooke advanced the progressive education legacy and earned her a national reputation. Cooke was acclaimed by educators throughout the world, who consulted and visited with her at school and during her retirement. Yet her early years of leadership were criticized by the trustees. Her tendency to emphasize education over management created an atmosphere that was tinged with disorder. Trustee Cyrus Bentley's outspoken criticisms were especially unnerving to Cooke, who believed Bentley would not criticize her without "very good evidence." To help, Mrs. Blaine hired an evaluator and assumed greater personal responsibility by becoming the assistant principal herself from 1906 to 1908 to focus on "the technical side of the school work." Miss Cooke thought this decision was "too good to be true."[27]

Twice Cooke was dismissed from her position as head of high school and twice reappointed. At this time she remained head of lower school and a lower school teacher. When trustees Cyrus Bentley and Owen Aldis mistakenly complained that Cooke let the school depart too far from Parker's principles and methods, they replaced her with a new high school principal from the East, Mr. R. B. Nason, whom Miss Cooke disliked on sight. She complained to Blaine that he had "the ideals and methods of a cheap political boss." Cooke forcefully told the trustees about Nason's poor relationship with the students and his incongenial attitude to the teachers. When the trustees dismissed Nason, Cooke resumed full principalship, but in 1909 these same trustees hired a second head of high school, whom they later dismissed due to what the trustees labeled "moral turpitude." Cooke was again reappointed to head the entire school in 1913 and remained principal until she retired in 1934.[28]

Perhaps it was Cooke's childhood fraught with hardship that caused her to be a self-reliant woman eager to accept challenge. Born the fourth of six siblings on Christmas Day in 1864 in Bainbridge, Ohio, Flora Juliette

Hannum's mother died when Flora was five years old, and her father died when she was thirteen. Described as an exceptionally active and unruly child, Flora Hannum was moved to six different homes within one year but at sixteen, she was finally adopted by her mother's close friends, Charles and Luella Cooke, whose name she took.[29]

Miss Cooke began her teaching career in a rural school house before becoming a teacher in Youngstown, Ohio, where she was appointed principal of the Hillman School between 1884 and 1889. Cooke's self-styled methods of teaching were readily approved by the Youngstown principal, Zonia Baber, a protégé of Francis Parker who had been trained at the Cook County Normal School. Miss Baber introduced Miss Cooke to Parker's philosophy and the new educational movement underway in Chicago. When Parker invited Baber to return to the Cook County Normal School to teach geography, Miss Baber prevailed upon Parker to invite "the gifted Miss Cooke" to train at the Normal School. Cooke enrolled for one year of training and remained to attend extension courses at the University of Chicago in education, science, and literature. She also worked for one year at the Armour Institute of Technology.[30]

When Cooke achieved the teaching standard of the Normal School, Parker assigned her a position as first grade teacher and supervisor of the practice work of other teachers. Cooke participated in reworking the curriculum for the kindergarten through the eight grades from separate and discrete subjects into an integrated whole. Her interest in beginning readers prompted her to edit a book on *Nature Myths and Stories for Little Children* (1895), which indicated to primary teachers the wealth of reading material within the students' reach. Cooke championed reading as something more than mere word getting while the child's reading habit was forming.[31] Her second publication, *First Primary Grade: One Year's Outline of Work in Science, History, Geography, and Music* (1897), articulated the first grade course of study. In the preface, Cooke wrote, "The guiding motive of the work was the cultivation of good taste and good habits of attention, industry, freedom of thought and expression, and the self-control in the exercise of power."[32] Cooke wrote numerous articles on education, but a recurrent subject was the life and contributions of Francis Parker.

Cooke slowly evolved into a public lecturer under Francis Parker's tutelage at the Normal School. When a new arrival at the Normal School, this shy woman said that she would die or resign before speaking at a faculty meeting. Parker told her to decide quickly which one it would be because if she stayed she must contribute to the discussion. "That is the only way you can learn and grow, and that's what we're all here for."[33] As national interest in Parker's educational philosophy intensified, Flora Cooke became one of his representative spokespersons. Cooke traveled to twenty-eight states and the territory of Hawaii to present lectures on progressive education.

To advance education, Cooke engaged in international and national activities. Following World War I, she was appointed a delegate to two international conferences on peace education in Lucarno, Switzerland, and Elsinore, Denmark, and served for eight years as president of the Association for Peace Education. In 1930, President Herbert Hoover invited Miss Cooke to attend the White House Conference on Childhood Health as a special delegate.[34] Cooke was also a member of the Board of Directors of the Progressive Education Association from 1923 to 1930. As a participant in the PEA symposium on "The Use of Tests and Measurements for Reading, Writing, and Arithmetic," Cooke supported the use of tests in progressive schools and established a Department of Measurement and Diagnosis at the Parker School in 1925. Through the Association, Cooke helped to launch the Study on the Relation of School and College, popularly known as the Eight-Year Study. Cooke asked the Parker School to contribute part of the $800 seed money for this significant educational research.[35]

Cooke's reputation as a prominent educator of a progressive school gave her recognition in the Chicago community. In 1930, she was appointed a director of Chicago's Teachers College, her former alma mater, previously the Cook County and then the Chicago Normal School. Lake Forest College of Illinois conferred on her an honorary degree in 1931 as a pioneer in progressive education, and later Columbia College of Chicago did likewise. In 1932, she was one of the three founders of the Graduate Teachers College of Winnetka, and between 1946 and 1953 she became a trustee of Roosevelt College (University) of Chicago. Upon retirement, Cooke continued to serve the Parker School as a member of the Parker Board of Trustees until 1948 and as a member of the Parker School Educational Council until her death in 1953.[36]

A humanitarian of keen intelligence, Cooke involved herself in more than twenty social and cultural organizations in the city. She was also a reformer and a defender of causes. At age eighty, as a member of the National Association for the Advancement of Colored People, she tangled publicly with the late Senator Bilbo of Mississippi, who filibustered against a fair hiring law. When, in their correspondence, Bilbo referred to her as a Negro, she replied that she was white but just as indignant about the filibuster as if she were Negro.[37]

Miss Cooke was an indefatigable person, insistent on high standards, and humble about her achievements. Among the many accolades and honors she received throughout her long and illustrious career, she considered the most meaningful tribute a remark by Francis Parker, who told a friend after observing her, "Today I visited a first grade room and saw a young woman really teaching a little child." [38]

Educational Principles Were the Basis for the School's Curriculum

When the Francis W. Parker School opened its doors in 1901, Francis Parker had been transforming American education for nearly three decades. Now, in the last year before his death, he transferred his experiment to the new school with Anita McCormick Blaine, Flora Cooke, and a corps of thirteen teachers.

Two sources captured the essence of the school's philosophical principles: Parker's *Talks on Pedagogics* (1894), and "The Origins and Aims of the Francis W. Parker School" (1912), an essay written by Anita McCormick Blaine, Flora Cooke, and the faculty delineating Blaine's reasons and expectations for funding an experimental school for new education. Blaine believed that much of the current education was "the waste of inner human values," and she asserted that "the Parker School is holding to educational principles as the basis of its existence." Blaine called the prime rock of the school's foundation "the freedom to carry out better educational policies." She envisioned an "educational superstructure" made up of five parts: the child's triple nature—body, mind, and spirit—and two great towers: "the development of the right attitude of the individual to self as related to others and the development of the individual's initiative in his own processes." Philosophically and religiously, Blaine placed great stock in what became known as the social motive in education, which ruled out competition, self-aggrandizement, and artificiality and favored cooperation, altruism, and reality. Blaine said little about the school's course of study or teaching methods except that children should be brought in touch with the riches of history and of nature. She believed in activity as an integral part of intellectual work because, as she wrote, "In the early years the hand contributes to the brain," and in later years the brain contributes constantly to the skill of the hand.[39]

The faculty built on the whole of Parker's text, but selected four specific quotations that captured the essence of the philosophy and printed them as epigrams at the front of each *Catalogue and Course of Study* published by the Francis W. Parker School for thirty years (see Figure 6.1).

The first epigram transformed the narrow definition of a traditional subject-centered school as solely an intellectual enterprise to a broader concentration on the whole child in which the curriculum was organized psychologically.

The second epigram on "community life" defined a school as "a model home, a complete community, and an embryonic democracy," which expanded the horizons of the school to incorporate more institutions to assist in developing citizens. The concentration on community differentiated the Parker School, whose goal was creating a more just, humane, and egalitarian society, from the Rousseauean child-centered school, whose goal was to develop the individual. The child had a responsibility to the community, where spontaneity was disciplined by and through the child's function in it. The community had a responsibility to the child to set and to hold high standards of moral and intellectual behavior and conduct.

The third epigram showed how education and community were interrelated to develop character. The Parker faculty equated character development with inner discipline, self-control, and the postponement of reward. Character development also meant that the self-centered behavior of the young child was transformed into society-centered behavior of a responsible adult for the betterment of the community, eventually the society, and ultimately the self. One rationale for using the community in the educational process was that "in his maturity the individual sustains to the complex society . . . . relations which are foreshadowed in his association to his school and playmates." The specific traits of character that the Parker School wished to develop—"truthfulness, fidelity, courage, forbearance,

Figure 6.1
The Philosophy of the Francis W. Parker School

These epigrams appeared at the front of each *Catalogue and Course of Study* published between 1901 and 1929.

Everything to help and nothing to hinder.

School motto.

"Education is the all-sided growth of the individual—physical mental and moral. Community life is the ideal of education, because it is the only ideal great enough to provide for this all-sided development of the individual."

"Community life is that state of society in which every individual member orders his conduct with reference to the good of the whole; the whole being so constituted as to necessitate the highest development of its members."

"Character constantly realizing itself in practical citizenship, in community life, in complete living, is the immediate, everlasting, and only purpose of the school."

—*Colonel Francis W. Parker.*

"The formation of character, and not the acquisition of knowledge as an end in itself, is one of the chief purposes of the school—a purpose which the home and the school should pursue together in close coöperation with each other. Neither can do separately all that should be done for the child since each has many opportunities peculiarly its own."

—*Cyrus Bentley.*

"Who is the great man? He who, among the multitude of feet passing on the highway, ready to follow where it goes, ready to be led, whithersoever,—is willing to break into the unbroken, to seek the light, in order to find a better way for the passing feet—a shorter, surer road to the dawn; he who would rather fail seeking that better way than succeed on the road he does not believe in—surely he is a great man."

—*Mrs. Emmons Blaine.*

Press of the
FRANCIS W. PARKER SCHOOL
330 WEBSTER AVENUE
CHICAGO

helpfulness, a spirit of cooperation, and considerate feeling—virtues of importance in practical life upon which democratic institutions rely"— were social virtues to be inculcated at home and in the school. Another facet of character was inner discipline. When pupils learned to balance freedom with responsibility, external rules imposed by the school could be minimized. As Principal Cooke explained, "Discipline will proceed through freedom as a voluntary effort to achieve self-control and power and not through compulsion and force." But she also added, "The school will not tolerate infraction of those rules established for orderly conduct of the work of the school." Reasonable rules, she believed, "will not be broken by normal children, whose attention and interest were aroused."[40]

Trustee Bentley's selection from Parker's book embodied three overlapping concepts: the formation of character, the acquisition of knowledge, and the role of the home in the educational process. Progressive education was not to be soft on knowledge or on intellectual life, but the acquisition of knowledge was aimed at constructive, thoughtful, and moral behavior and at action.

In Mrs. Blaine's quotation, she saw the development of education as synonymous with the development of the great man. The school motto, "Everything to help and nothing to hinder," synthesized the school's most important value, the social motive in education, which was also captured in the Parker word *responsibility*. At a Morning Exercise, students were often asked, "What is the Parker word?" In unison, they stood and responded, "responsibility!"

Francis Parker discovered many pedagogical principles, but he created only one theory of education, the theory of concentration and correlation (see Figure 1.1). The underlying principle of Parker's theory of concentration began with the child:

> The child stands in the center of a circle; around him is the environment
> of the universe, man, and nature. Everything in its elements touches the
> child's soul; the child's soul goes out toward everything, reacts upon
> everything.[41]

Parker reasoned that since the subjects and methods used in education depend on the original nature of the child, then geography, geology, mineralogy, physics, chemistry, botany, zoology, anthropology, ethnology, physiology, and history constitute the child's environment and are therefore the central subjects of study. The theory proposes that these subjects be continued as a child began to learn them until that period of the child's mental development when specialization of subjects can emerge from the foundation of related knowledge of all subjects. The teacher is to select the materials for worthwhile activities because the student is not intellectually qualified. Activities in observation, investigation, constructing and problem solving, and experimentation precede any logical consideration of an isolated subject by itself.

As Parker explained, "The entire purpose of education consists of training the child to work, to work systematically, to love work, and to put his brains and heart into the work."[42] The activities in the course of study should lead to the highest ethical behavior. The matter of interest was an additional feature that enhanced the value of activity-centered learning. Parker saw immediate gratification as a powerful motive for intense activity which increases a child's effort.

Lower School Course of Study: Central Subjects

During the thirty Pioneering Years, lower school teachers based the course of study on the theory of concentration. The disciplines were correlated according to the central subject, defined by Parker as "the main branches of one subject, creation." The aim of correlation was to enable the child to see "unity of knowledge." The teachers correlated subjects according to two centers—the sciences, which included geography, biology, physics, other sciences, and at times mathematics, and the humanities, which included skill classes, literature and dramatic arts, English, history, and foreign languages. The skill classes presented language study, speaking and listening, reading and writing, acting, and playing games in English and foreign languages. Additional time for English language training—writing, spelling, and reading—was taken from all subjects, and these skills were made an obligation for all teachers. The skills and most of the visual and performing arts classes were offered in separate classes before they were integrated with the central subject. When possible, both the sciences and the humanities concentrated on the same topic. Each of the first eight grades emphasized a different central subject.

The first grade course of study focused on the experiences of life at home. In the science cluster of classes, the pupils examined their own homes and the natural environment—the air, soil, water, and climate. The six-year-olds compared their homes with caves, wigwams, igloos, and other homes throughout the world. In geography, pupils learned how varying natural environments produced different materials, which caused people to build different kinds of houses. In clay modeling and manual training classes, they built models of these homes to mathematical specifications to learn measurement. The arts complemented the central subject. Domestic arts teachers taught the pupils to design wallpaper, sew curtains, weave rugs, and decorate houses. The music teacher taught folk songs and the drama teacher read myths and fairy tales from different nations and helped the six-year-olds write and perform original one-act plays. The first graders integrated national, religious, and school festivals—Christmas, Hanukkah, St. Patrick's Day, County Fair, and Maypole Day—and compared them with festivals of other cultures. They sewed national costumes in needlework classes to wear during the celebrations and planted crops in the school garden to prepare in cooking classes for festival meals.

For twenty-five years between 1907 and 1934, Miss Hattie Walker taught first graders about the Indian's wigwam, the Mexican's adobe village, the Eskimo's igloo, and the Aborigine's thatched hut. A pioneer of progressive education, Miss Walker studied at the Froebel School in Cleveland, where she became keenly aware that "learning by doing" sparked the children's imaginations and enhanced their curiosity about the surrounding world. An author, Miss Walker utilized the "children's natural interest in story to introduce them to people of another land and to give them material rich enough in content to serve as a stimulus for their own projects and activities." She wrote and used as classroom texts: *Shining Star*, a story about an Indian boy and *Snow Children,* a tale of Kooloo, the Eskimo.

Many adults have a difficult time remembering how a first-grade teacher affected them, but Ruth Linnell Byrnes '41 and Barr McCutcheon 'x44 recalled celebrating foreign holidays and learning how to make candles. Some first graders recalled the sun melting the igloo they built on the playground; others recollected the school year ending before their wigwam was completed and the vegetables from the garden were ripe. Most remembered that Miss Walker was almost as small as they were. The six-year-olds whispered to each other that Miss Walker wore her silver-gray hair swept on top of her head in order to appear taller. The gossip was that she was never going to retire.[43]

The second-grade teachers interpreted the central subject differently and examined four industrial activities that paralleled the story of human progress: farming, harvesting, milling, and cloth making. The activities varied from owning and caring for a dozen chickens to an excursion to observe wheat harvested in the fields of Central Illinois and baking bread with flour from the mills they had visited.

The third graders traced the growth of Chicago from the romantic days of the French explorers, trappers, and traders; through the rugged pioneer epoch; to the village period, when Chicago was called Fort Dearborn. They explored the North Side water tower and the remnants of the city that burned to the ground in 1871, and they visited the South Lake Shore Drive museums, products of the "White City" of the 1893 World's Fair. The eight-year-olds also investigated the growing metropolis, examining the underground tunnels and the elevated trains that made a "loop" and gave the central city its name. Their curiosity was whetted by lessons in engineering conducted during trips on the Chicago River and Lake Michigan to examine the reversal of the flow of the river and to watch the locks control water.

An exemplary pattern for the correlation of subjects was the fourth graders' focus on Athens. "The fourth grade inherited the study of the Greeks and Greek life and nothing could more wisely feed their demand for beauty [than] to dream, to paint, to write, to sing of the heroism of that old world." In science and geography, students explored the topography of the Greek coastline, the physiography of the landscape, the formation of limestone and marble, and introduced anatomy and physiology through the study of the body of the Greek athlete. Literature emphasized the life of Socrates, the story of Homer's *Odyssey*, and the tales of "four old Greeks." In history, the pupils researched and read about Greek customs and habits. Each nine-year-old studied a specific mythical character—Zeus, Androgeny, Persephone, and others—wrote monologues and dialogues and designed costumes to wear when they dramatized the mythical legend for students and parents. The fourth graders read and wrote Greek poems and dramas, and sang and danced to Greek music. In visual arts classes, they molded Greek vases from clay, studied and developed Greek landscapes, created Greek designs and decorations, and drew human figures.

The fourth graders gathered around their teacher Mary Davis to read passages from the *Odyssey* "without compromise for our vocabulary or ability to pronounce Agamemnon, Clytaemnestra, Menelaus, Zeus," remembered an alumna. Fourth-grade teacher for thirty years between 1924 and 1954, Mary Davis held a place in the memories of her students long after they graduated. "She is symbolic of all that we love and cherish in our school," wrote the Class of 1950 in its yearbook. She stimulated children to "reach out to improve what [they] had done, to strive for greater understanding, and in turn form questions for [themselves]." Miss Davis had traveled to Greece and her love and knowledge of Ancient Greece was infectious. "I dressed, thought, acted, created, and lived for myself Homeric times," revealed one of Miss Davis's students in 1942.

Miss Davis created her magic by converting the second-floor classroom into a stage, with "Ionic pillars supporting the balcony, the chariot, the cast of the Parthenon Equestrian group mounted on the walls, and continuous displays of our art and shop work." But Miss Davis's magic had a dose of pragmatism—students had to learn long division, decimals, fractions, improve their reading, and assume the care of white mice and turtles. Miss Davis possessed the capacity to bridge the study of Ancient Greece in fourth grade with the study of Greece in high school and college.[44]

The fifth-grade course of study changed from Greece to America. The Colonial Period correlated the sciences and the humanities. Fifth graders examined trade routes to India and learned about the discovery of America by the Viking, Spanish, French, and English explorers. They extended their study to the colonization of North America with a focus on Indian and pilgrim life, combining academic disciplines as they explored how settlers lived. The literary selections were primarily nature poetry by American authors and biographies about explorers. The class utilized the arts similarly to other central subjects, but the identifying mark was the geography map on the floor of the fifth grade room.

Fifth-grade teacher Herman Lukens believed that "mental imagery of even the most fundamental geographic concepts originated in maps and models and not merely in observation of the actual world about us." Dr. Lukens taught Parker ten-year-olds from 1907 to 1934 in the third-floor room filled with numerous visual learning devices. To teach geography, Lukens constructed a map of North America on the floor of his room—a giant, linoleum block print on a scale of twenty miles to the inch. Rivers were tooled into the linoleum, cities were brass shapes nailed to the floor, and mountains were constructed in metal. Pupils lived and walked on the map, learned directions and mathematics from it, used it as a theatre for representative warfare with toy soldiers, and traced the boundaries of states. John Holabird '38 remembered sitting over Cuba all year. A large Time Line of Western World Explorers covered the walls.

A trim man with a cropped white goatee and steel-rimmed glasses, Dr. Lukens always dressed primly in dark gray suits. The days were full and organized, and Lukens was strict and demanding, requiring one math paper and one composition in history or English each day. Dr. Lukens demanded "precision, clarity, and logical thinking." On Friday mornings, pupils had to exhibit ten correct or corrected papers on their desks. Once a week the class boarded the bus for an excursion. At Christmas, students began to "calculate the length of each school day from the listed sun up at 5:29:14 to listed sunset at 4:15:32." On Friday afternoons, Lukens scheduled the Literary Society as a period for students to recite poems, act out stories, read original compositions, and be read to by a stern Dr. Lukens, who was an author himself. "He broke my soul and still I never learned more in one year," remembered one student. "He dedicated his complete life to making us non-savage and more educated."[45]

The Colonial Period extended forward in history to the westward expansion of the United States, the sixth grade topic, and backward in history to the Medieval Period, the seventh grade topic and the last grade of the central subject. The students examined the Middle Ages through the study of chivalry, romance, high religious endeavor, medieval arts, and the industrial guild system. This evolution through six centuries laid the background for the eighth grade study of contemporary America, which examined such issues as taxation, money, immigration, slavery, the Declaration of Independence, the Constitution, and the Bill of Rights. To prepare eighth graders for high school, subjects were presented topically rather than organized centrally.

Francis Parker's philosophy and theory of concentration provided the foundation for the course of study, which the faculty developed and the pupils followed throughout the Pioneering Years. In this era, the teachers concentrated on the course of study for the first eight grades more than on the high school grades because secondary education did not gain momentum until World War I and again during the Eight-Year Study of the 1930s.

High School Course of Study: Traditional Courses

In this era, the high school course of study was more traditional than in the lower school. The theory of concentration and correlation among most disciplines was less aggressively sought. Courses were more subject centered than experience centered, and subjects were isolated rather than correlated. Except for the arts, little curriculum experimentation occurred during this period, mainly because secondary schools were dominated by college requirements and the 1892 subject guidelines of the Committee of Ten. Twenty-six years later the *Cardinal Principles* of 1918 replaced subject-centered goals with life-centered goals, but these seemed to have had little effect on the Parker high school course of study.[46]

The teachers divided the four years of English into five categories of learning: (1) reading non-dramatic classics to develop good literary taste and to become a leisure reader; (2) reading, performing, and staging dramatic works; (3) oral expression; (4) composition or writing in all genres; and (5) formal English or the study of the technical aspects of the language. At times English, drama, and history were combined for learning effectiveness and efficiency, and the subject matter was implemented by the natural method of instruction or "learning by doing" through individual and group projects.

The teachers of English interrelated the English courses and school activities. One organizational plan of integration between classes and activities was called "lines of writing." Teachers presented writing skills which the students applied to advance the quality of their publications, including the yearbook, the newspaper, and the literary magazine. Another was the teaching of speech in English class coordinated with an extemporaneous speaking team outside of class, with Morning Exercise, Student Government, and Forum, a student activity featuring the arts.[47] All students learned how to present a Morning Exercise and were required to do so.

A "close relationship between the library and the high school English department" helped the school emphasize reading. Pupils experiencing difficulties could take remedial reading while gifted readers could follow a supplemental reading list. Library work was required of all students, and

Librarian Isabel Clayton explained, "The purpose of the library is to stimulate and develop a taste for good reading and to serve, for all classes in the school, as a laboratory in which pupils may find effective help in specific subjects."[48] The librarian met with the English classes weekly to help to achieve these goals. The English teachers closely observed student progress in reading and created individual records of student accomplishments. While the content of the English courses was traditional, the teaching methods and the function of English in relationship to the whole school were not.

The course of study in history was traditional in content and approach, but the instructional method was progressive and the values inculcated were liberal if not radical. Although only one unit of history was required for graduation, four sequential history courses surveyed the progress of mankind from the days of ancient Egypt and Babylonia to the twentieth-century United States. One history teacher wrote, "For the cultivation of mental and moral character the proper study of history is perhaps the most direct and effectual means." The mission of the history department was to educate citizens for a democracy, and the goal of history was to teach tolerance, right thinking, and broad humanitarianism, as well as "the struggle between education and catastrophe"; "the folly of injustice, of selfish ambition, of national haughtiness, of racial animosity"; and "the interdependence of mankind."

Like history, science was taught as an isolated subject but emphasized learning through concrete experiences. All high school science courses were laboratory courses and brought "the pupil into direct contact with a great variety of material, experience, and observations. . . . This opportunity for experience with actual materials gives to the science courses a concreteness which distinguishes them sharply from other courses," where symbolic materials were used almost exclusively. The science course objectives distinguished themselves from traditional read and memorize courses: (1) to give an intelligent understanding of the significance of science in remaking the world, (2) to teach the interrelation of facts and phenomena and the slow and painstaking effort needed to make scientific progress, and (3) to teach appreciation of the scientific method and problem solving and transfer the techniques to personal life. Science played a major role in student life, and it was the most complimented department in the evaulation of the high school in 1922.

Three other disciplines completed the high school course of study: mathematics, foreign language, and physical education. The mathematics teachers wrote, "It follows that if the fundamental principle of 'learning to do by doing' is to be applied to the teaching of arithmetic, pupils must have opportunities of acquiring the ability to interpret and formulate their own problems from concrete situations by practicing work of this character in the school."[49] Once teachers had grounded students in the principles and processes of algebra, they gave them many opportunities to practice using algebra as a tool for solving real-world problems. The high school required two years of algebra and geometry for graduation and offered intermediate algebra, solid geometry, and trigonometry. Students could choose from four foreign languages—Latin, German, French, and Spanish, two of which had been introduced in the lower school. A daily meeting ranging from fifteen to sixty minutes was scheduled for the physical education or outdoor sports.

Unlike its traditional counterparts, the high school accented both cognitive or knowledge objectives and affective or behavioral objectives, student involvement in the school community through the interaction of curricular and extracurricular activities, and the use of projects in all disciplines. The high school teachers' methodology encouraged active student participation, individual projects, and critical thinking. The course of study built effectively on the students' habit of "learning by doing" deeply ingrained when the students were in lower school. As the Pioneering Years came to a close, the high school teachers began to reorganize the course of study in preparation for their involvement in the nationally renowned Eight-Year Study.

The Arts: Significant Role in the Course of Study

The fine and manual arts played a prominent role in the high and lower school course of study. Unlike traditional schools of the era, the Parker School firmly held that the arts completed the learning act or, in other words, that expression demonstrated comprehension. As Francis Parker explained:

> Attention and expression are the two modes or processes of human action which have most to do with the evolution of the human race . . . . [Expression] is the manifestation of thought and emotion through the body by means of physical agents . . . . Attention and expression together are

the action and reaction of the whole being in mental and bodily movements and are organically related by motive.

Expression was at the core of learning because it "is fundamentally the means of developing that which is noblest in a human being—the impelling power to action."[50]

The purpose of the arts for all grades was to unify "action, thought, and expression" in the learning process."[51] The first eight grades balanced the manual arts—manual training, clay modeling, molding, gardening and cookery, sewing and weaving, and pottery making—with the fine arts—drawing, painting, and music. The high school concentrated mainly on the fine arts and offered other opportunities like English classes on extemporaneous speaking and oral reading and elective manual arts courses.

In the high school, the visual art teachers taught techniques in separately scheduled classes. Teachers believed, "the acquisition of technique will not be forced, but each child will be assisted to overcome the difficulties of which he is conscious so that execution will keep pace with his power of criticism." After the students learned techniques, visual arts classes combined with central subjects in the lower school because "much of the stimulus to art expression comes from the work which the children are doing in geography, history, literature, science, and handwork." Throughout the twelve-year sequence, the goals of the visual arts were to acquaint students with a variety of materials and genre, to advance their techniques and skills, and to unify knowledge and expression. Students also learned to develop interpretation and criticism, to express themselves, and ultimately to see the interrelationship between art and life.

Music was the preeminent art during the Pioneering Years. A distinguished music faculty presented a serious, thoughtful, deliberate, and well organized program in choral music. The teachers believed that most children loved music and were capable of singing, but for those few who were "tone-deaf," special classes were designed to study the development of music, to heighten music appreciation, or to learn musical vocabulary. Pupils were trained from kindergarten through the senior year to sing increasingly difficult songs with greater independence of interpretation. In kindergarten, the aim was to attain a tonal sense and the ability to imitate musical tones. In the primary grades, children learned sight reading and imitative exercises, and in grammar school they learned two- and three-part songs, canons, and rounds, with an emphasis on individual voices. The aim in the lower grades was "to increase the love of music and to direct the pupil's taste to what is best." Between eighth and twelfth grades, the teachers joined freshmen with sophomores and juniors with seniors, dividing male and female voices. The music teachers were as interested as any English teacher to identify and develop talent in the music field.

To prepare for community singing, students learned the fundamental aspects of the songs in the classroom, rehearsed with the entire grade, and then met in full rehearsal in the auditorium with all students and the entire faculty. Typical songs for choral performances for five- to thirteen-year-olds might include: Rosetti, Brahms, and old English and German folk songs. The Parker Song Book for Morning Exercise included folk songs, Negro spirituals, Christian hymns, and selections that the music teachers considered good but less difficult. Music performance played a key role in uniting the community at Morning Exercises, holiday gatherings, and school celebrations.

Orchestral music played a small but significant part in the life of the school. In the "Twentieth Recital of the School Orchestra," the pupils played short pieces by Mozart, Mendelssohn, Weber, and Schubert. In 1910, the parents inaugurated a Fund for Artist Recitals, and by 1929 the Fund had supported forty-eight recitals. Additionally, groups of musicians from the Chicago Symphony performed for the school community intermittently.

The teachers believed that drama was the most integral and integrating discipline in the educative process. The teaching of drama was based on five main goals: to bring about freedom and expressiveness of voice and body; to hear clearness, distinctiveness, and beauty of speech by training the ear; to train the speech organs to form well-shaped vowels and distinct clear-cut consonants; to train the children to read intelligently and with a purpose, and to read aloud simply and naturally with clear perception of meaning, emotion, content, and form. Plays were performed in English, Latin, French, and German. Drama teachers called acting "the most educative act" because:

> [acting] embodies "the dramatist's creations, giving them flesh and blood . . . . requires sensitivity, intelligence, and judgment . . . [makes] intellect, emotions, and will cooperatively active in an attempt

to share thought and emotion with an audience, and requires great power of concentration and discipline of will."[52]

The visual and performing arts were integral to all areas of the curriculum—to central subjects, to the other arts, to the humanities, to school activities, and to the community. As an integral part of the activity-centered school, the arts gave the school a unique identity and aided the school in developing and/or illustrating new pedagogical principles.

Six Pedagogical Principles Proven by the Parker Teachers

As educational innovators, Parker School teachers were eager to identify and illustrate new pedagogical principles. In the Pioneering Years, the teachers collectively identified and illustrated six new teaching principles that validated the new education:

1. Social motive can be taught/learned to replace individual motive (1912)
2. The Morning Exercise is the socializing and active unifying influence in the community and the measure of the School's effectiveness in achieving its social goal (1913)
3. Expression trains motive and is necessary to complete the learning act (1914)
4. Concrete experiences are the most effective method of instruction (1915)
5. Teachers are able to adapt the curriculum to meet the needs of the individual (1920)
6. The community must require the cultivation of the habit of "creative effort" (1925).

The teachers explained these six pedagogical principles in six volumes entitled *Studies in Education* between 1912 and 1925.

The teachers explained social motive as a pedagogical principle in all types of work based on the assertion that work is socially motivated when the child feels deeply responsible for the thing undertaken. Teachers defined social motive as "the controlling principle in social organization . . . . the feeling that one does not and cannot work alone . . . but is a single unit of a large pattern." Francis Parker called the chief aim of education training in motive "because motive is the impelling power of all human action."[53] The higher the motive, the higher the action. Cooke too discovered that social motive in education was "the most ennobling of all true springs of action . . . . the feeling that one does not and cannot work alone; that whatever one does is a single unit of a large pattern that is being built by many contributors." The teachers observed that social motive as an impulse in school "makes of work there a real and worthy thing, converts school activities into earnest living . . . . [and] creates and trains for mature society . . . people of social conscience and social power." The advantage of the social motive in education was that "work is judged indisputably by being put to the proof of use. Reward and punishment alike come with no flavor of injustice or favoritism, but with a purifying and invigorating truthfulness. Thus to work under ennobling incentives, to be disciplined by hard tasks, to see one's results used with a high impersonality, gives to struggle a meaning, to success a joy, to failure a cleansing power, that no small motive can furnish."

Social motive was most apparent in community activities such as collecting food and clothing for a family at Thanksgiving or restoring toys at Christmas for distribution to the needy, and in grade-level activities like an eighth-grade project of building a playhouse on the playground for use by all young children. Social motive also dominated the visual arts. Building a model medieval cathedral taught seventh graders that "if you want beautiful things for yourself you must do your share toward bringing them to some one else." The results of the experience were several: pupils accepted their level of talent in different artistic endeavors, learning that "some pupils have the ordinary power to express but the extraordinary power to appreciate" and vice versa; they learned their limits and possibilities; they were able to contrast results of individual expression with group expression; and they came to recognize the pleasures and problems of working in a group versus working alone.

Similarly social motive was a powerful force in musical performance. The faculty set out deliberately to "cultivate the feeling for music as a necessary and valuable part of the life of the school community from the youngest to the oldest students." The school's unique approach to teaching choral music, which called for classroom instruction, grade-level rehearsals, and all-school rehearsals, let pupils experience smaller groups swelling into a larger group and vocal parts slowly and effectively becoming a musical whole. The rehearsal process itself taught self-control, patience, subordination of self, sharing with other ages, and propelling oneself to excellence. Music was called "the important social function in creating emotion and unity." It created a feeling of responsibility of the individual to the whole, provided the satisfaction of being useful, and enabled the pupils to throw themselves body and soul into the activity at some personal cost of strength, patience, and time. The students recognized music as "a great unifying social influence—people who sing together are moved by one impulse and one thought through which the spirit of the whole can be expressed in a single result."

Drama was also a powerful socializing force and a most satisfactory means of expression: the actor concentrates on audience and not on self, the actor and the audience learn that moral human actions result from motive and have consequences, and a character study can provide elementary psychology that can be a guide to personal behavior and to empathy. Teachers discovered the socializing influence of drama in the training of the voice and ear and language, the tools of communication for community conduct, the creation of group design, the production of costumes, and the construction of stage sets. They also recognized the shortcomings of dramatic expression—the over-stimulation of "self-appreciation," a disinclination for "less interesting work," and the encouragement of insincerity, artificiality, and extravagance. However, the social value of drama—to develop social consciousness, to overcome self-consciousness, to subordinate self to the group, to stimulate sympathy, to develop insight into self and others, to cultivate initiative, to train judgment, to establish moral ideals, and to develop concentration—far outweighed the shortcomings.

The printing press also held a central position in developing social motive. Students practiced printing with different degrees of involvement from seventh grade until graduation. Printing, considered "a distinctly social art," required group effort and was organized in an apprentice system of labor. The students assumed responsibility for printing *Reading Leaflets* for the primary grades, their *Weekly* newspaper, institutional forms for the office, and programs for concerts, recitals, and commencement. Because the school held a negative view of textbooks, faculty authors often wrote their own materials, which students printed and the school sold. Each year, the students printed the more than 100-page, faculty-developed *Catalogue and Course of Study* and some years a *Studies in Education* of even greater length.

From 1907 to 1940, Leonard Wahlstrom taught social motive through printing and toy shop. Wahlstrom headed the manual training and industrial arts department. His major project was the introduction of a Toy Shop in 1910 where students refurbished their broken and discarded toys to give to the needy. He encouraged participation by pupils and parents through posters printed in the shop that read "Wanted at Once: Forgotten or Broken Toys." Mr. Wahlstrom divided the pupils into divisions—the book department, the sewing department, and the wrapping and packaging department. Depending on the level of difficulty, the older pupils, teachers, and parents assisted the youngsters in sewing heads on teddy bears and dolls and soldering broken pieces together. Time cards were given to workers and cashed in at the school bank for "five happy days for each hour worked." The endeavor was informed by the social motive; the children's viewpoints gradually transformed from their individual pleasures to the greater pleasure of helping others. Various organizations throughout the country adopted Wahlstrom's toy shop model.[54]

The second pedagogical principle the teachers confirmed was the socializing influence of the Morning Exercise, considered "the active unifying influence in the community" and "essential to unity, harmony, and success." Every morning, all members of the school filed to assigned seats for a carefully prepared presentation that opened with a hymn and an inspirational reading. The twenty-minute presentation was most frequently the outcome of classroom work. Every class was assigned a certain number of Morning Exercises a year, and each pupil was required to participate in at least one Morning Exercise, called "the family altar of the school to which each pupil brings his offerings to contribute and to share in the intellectual and spiritual life of the community."

The faculty classified the 1901-1913 Morning Exercises in three categories to illustrate their socializing influences:

1. "Exercises That Have as Their Purpose the Awakening of a Social or Civic Consciousness": school projects, summer experiences, civics, current events, or exercises in the form of town meetings or special holidays

2. "Exercises Which Have as Their Underlying Motive the Development of the Aesthetic Sense": how to plan a play, sketch a nursery rhyme, decorate the kindergarten room, make a cartoon or block printing, design a Greek vase; including music rehearsals, performances, and recitals

3. "Exercises Which Have as Their Purpose the Reviewing, Intensifying, and Widening of Experiences": subject-centered presentations on domestic science, geography, mathematics, science, Latin and Modern Languages, and class excursions.

Pupils learned the power of expression—a child with something to tell and an audience to listen. The habit of meeting an audience every day gave students power, skill, and self-possession; eliminated the agony of self-consciousness; and cultivated an innate desire to do things in the company of others. Morning Exercise was also the natural place to meet teachers and students, a place where the individual child learned his role in the community, thus making the Morning Exercise "wholesome training in altruistic thinking and living." The aim in the training of social motive in the Morning Exercise was to put "the child into possession of himself and his material in order to establish the habit of using both of these freely with understanding and taste for the profit and pleasure of the community."[55]

The teachers verified a third pedagogical principle, "expression trains motive." Psychologically, attention and expression were organically related by motive. Expression was the organic part of the whole growth process and was called "the action part of the circuit: because thought that does not end in action dies." It was a means of developing the child's "impelling power to action" and unifying "the movement of the body and mind in the communication of meanings." "Motive that controls expression is the motive to make others feel, think, and act in accordance with personal ideal."

The faculty used expression to train motive in academic coursework by creating "strong mental imagery through vigorous self-actuated observation, by experiments using wide and varied sense impressions, and through early and continued contact with actual material." The performing arts teachers trained motive through seven different modes of expression: (1) gesture—changes in the body manifested in thought and feeling; (2) voice—talking and singing to communicate shades of meaning; (3) speech—oral reading, extemporaneous speaking, plays, dialogues, and language; (4) music—singing cultivated to enhance emotion; (5) making— training in manual arts for practical use; (6) painting, modeling, and drawing—for the idealization of thought; and (7) writing—communicating with those not present. The teachers also trained motive through expression with "the activity of play."[56]

The fourth principle the faculty discovered was that using concrete experience was the most effective method of instruction. As Miss Cooke explained:

> The absolute dependence of the imagination and the powers of apperception upon those concepts which come into the mind by observation is probably the best known and the most undeniable fact in psychology . . . . The strength of apperception depends mainly, if not wholly, upon the clear and visual concepts gained by observation . . . . The direct and continued experience with materials and the participation in constructive activities of an applied and practical character are an essential condition of the educative effort. Personal contact with the actual materials creates adequate mental images, obtained through individual experience, which provides the basis upon which future work is laid.

The teachers considered instruction complete only when "the application of facts learned was made by the student and their usefulness demonstrated by the solution to problems of a practical character, which developed out of the study itself." Again, the premise was that ideas died unless they were used.

For each grade, the teachers developed a set of concrete experiences as the basis for learning. One effective and common concrete learning experience was the excursion. From kindergarten through fourth grade, the students took an average of six excursions a year for nature study, history, and geography. Students went to Hull House to learn weaving and to the Lincoln Park Zoo to study an animal that they were asked to model from memory in clay. Another effective concrete experience was an observation, which was followed by a drawing and a written description or a story about the observation. The visual and performing arts and the laboratory science experiments provided concrete experiences with materials.[57]

A fifth pedagogical principle showed how the teachers adapted the curriculum from an emphasis on social motive to a focus on the individual. In the 1920s, the education emphasis turned away from social motive toward a focus on the individual, undermining a major unifying principle in the

Parker School. "After signing the armistice," Cooke explained, "we found ourselves looking at the war-time influences in school life with a critical eye and this fresh centering of our interest illustrated the general idea of adaptation of the curriculum to social and individual needs."[58] The adaptations were mainly in the direction suggested by new external trends like the child-centered school, Freud's influence on free expression, and William Heard Kilpatrick's famous Project Method. Whereas this shift to individual impulse and away from the social motive was contrary to the Parker School's general direction, the school was intent on developing the individual's talents as well.

Like principle five, the sixth principle, "the cultivation of the habit of creative effort," was also individual centered and diverted the emphasis away from the social motive. It should be remembered that Francis Parker did not believe in free expression without artistic and moral guidance, and the school had mainly been focused on reconstructing society. The Parker teachers did define the concept of creative effort broadly, giving three explicit interpretations. The first explained the school's contribution to a child's creativity: "The child has a great deal to express, probably more than adults realize, and the school built up rich backgrounds that fired the children's imagination." The second interpretation explained how the school offered innumerable opportunities for expression because it held that "every child has the right to try every avenue of expression to find how he can best and most happily express himself." The third described how the school provided a community where expression was not only welcomed but required. The creative effort was encouraged through different expressions and could be observed in the academics, the arts, and in student activities.[59]

These six pedagogical principles and their applications, which faculty and student experience validated in the classroom over the decades, were fully explained in *Studies in Education* written by different groups of teachers and edited by Flora Cooke. These *Studies* were "not records of perfection attained [but] accounts of attempts to improve on our own methods and to avoid some of our past failures and errors."[60] Of the ten *Studies in Education*, the four earliest pedagogical principles concentrated on the social motive in education: *The Social Motive in School Work* (1912), *Morning Exercise as a Socializing Influence* (1913), *Expression as a Means of Training Motive* (1914), and *Education through Concrete Experience*

(1915). The two volumes written in the 1920s emphasized the "individual impulse" in education: *The Individual and the Curriculum: Experiments in Adaptation* (1920), and *Creative Effort* (1925). National progressive trends altered the Parker School's experimental course of study, reflected in the final, subject-centered volumes: *The Course in Science* (1916), *Social Science Series: The Course in History* (1923), and two volumes on *Experiences in English Composition and Literature* for Grades I-VIII (1932) and for Grades IX-XII (1934).

In general, these studies answered Dewey's call for progressive schools to add to the current knowledge of curriculum by developing "organized subject matter" and studying "the conditions favorable to learning." Dewey believed that qualitative analysis, which explained the application of principles when quantitative measures were impossible, was an important first step to developing a science of education.[61] The twenty *Catalogues and Course of Study* and the ten *Studies in Education* met Dewey's definition and illustrated that Parker teachers attempted to contribute to developing a science of education.

Following the qualitative expositions of educational principles, the teachers attempted quantitative analysis, and Miss Cooke organized a Department of Measurement and Diagnosis in 1925 in response to the development of new "standardized tests which replace, rather than augment, the old forms of educational measurement and rating." Cooke explained that the school "recognizes the necessity of accurate measurements of results and adequate recording of individual abilities, attainment, and character traits." The three aims of the Department of Measurements and Diagnosis were to serve the needs of individual pupils, groups, and the whole school. To study "individual pupil adjustment," the school measured eight traits: (1) individual abilities and disabilities, (2) traits and interests, (3) experience, (4) attainments, (5) learning habits, (6) rate of progress, (7) causes of disability in school subjects, and (8) maladjustment. Some of these measurements were part of the admission process and others were implemented in academic classes. To diagnose group work, measurements included: tests on different methods of instruction, studies on learning, test construction, graphic presentation of test results, and continuous surveys of achievement or attainment. Measurements of the smaller group concentrated on psychological studies of mental processes, studies of group levels of efficiency, and diagnosis of special groupings of pupils in experimental studies. To measure the whole group, the teachers examined attendance, health, promotion, school records, reports to parents, and curriculum studies. Miss Cooke warned:

> It goes without saying in this day and age that the use of standard intelligence and achievement tests are a part of our program, for the sake of the insight and knowledge which they throw upon the ability of the children; but not for their classification into superior and inferior groups. More than ever we need to keep our vision clear to the value of those elements of life and education which cannot be measured and which give the highest aspiration and inspiration, which create in us standards of taste and attitudes toward life, which go far to protect us from the ugliness and sordidness in our environment.[62]

With the rise of the field of educational measurement, Cooke made small steps to formalize curriculum decision making with data.

Teachers: Must Be "Cultured, Educated, and Trained"

According to Francis Parker, "as is the teacher, so is the school." "A teacher skillful in drawing arouses, by the exercise of his art, a strong desire on the part of his pupils to do the same thing the same way." By the same token, "Failure in knowledge itself, failure to command subjects of thought, failure to understand relations, inability to present conditions for mental growth, lie at the root of most imperfect teaching."[63]

Parker held teachers and teacher training in the highest regard, believing that the development of professional training made the education revolution possible. He defined a good teacher as one who "has a profound appreciation of his responsibility and influence" and one who should think "that my influence over immortal minds is eternal, that whatsoever I am goes into the immortality of my pupils; [that] their true success depends, to a large extent, upon me—upon my knowledge, skill, and character." He named the highest qualifications of a teacher as: (1) a dominating love for children manifested by a strong desire to help them, (2) a love for the subjects of study, (3) power and skill in the manifestation of thought, and (4) the courage of his convictions.[64] Miss Cooke used Parker's words to establish the position of the teacher as pivotal and central to the success of the Parker School:

Parker considered that the teacher was the educational lever. At one end was the child with infinite possibilities to receive the weight of education. At the other end society, the power agent, made up ideally of socially useful and happy people. The teacher is responsible for moving the fulcrum, to have a balance, an equilibrium for complete and happy living. In order to do this [the teacher] must know what forces have moved society forward and what have held it back . . . must create a rich and stimulating environment for the child to grow in . . . keep the child in contact with beauty in all forms . . . cultivate the child's imagination to enable him or her to put himself in the place of other people and to have tolerance and understanding of them.[65]

The "cultured, educated, and trained" teachers that Francis Parker considered essential to produce an effective education characterized the original corps of teachers at the Parker School. Francis Parker trained this corps of teachers at the Cook County Normal School, and they collaborated with him in the evolution of the new education. This corps provided stability, continuity, and a confident professionalism that shaped the first experimental era. The school utilized several approaches to assure excellent teachers of the caliber that Parker and Cooke required. President Parker and Principal Cooke searched for the finest teachers with backgrounds in progressive education and training from Cook County or another Normal School. Cooke set a model for teaching that faculty observed and could adapt. In turn, she observed their teaching. To teachers new to the Parker School, Cooke taught progressive philosophy and methods and saw to it that novice teachers were also trained through assistantships. By 1930, Miss Cooke assigned an assistant for each of the first eight grades and for the fine arts. Weekly collaboration to write the course of study also let master teachers mentor novices. With the help of a critic teacher and other designated faculty, a new teacher would prepare a unit comprised of an outline of the subject matter and a list of teaching methods and teaching devices for adapting the material for age-appropriate attainment by students.[66] One month in advance of teaching, the new teacher presented the plan for criticism and suggestions for further development to several teachers chosen from a number of disciplines. Teachers were required to write elaborate "knowledge papers" to demonstrate their intellectual grasp of the subject. In at least these six ways the original

Parker teachers passed their pedagogical legacy to the next generation confidently and securely.

Miss Cooke also defined different kinds of faculty positions and assigned varying responsibilities. The lower school gradehead teacher concentrated on the central subject and correlated the teaching of geography with the sciences, history, literature, and mathematics; integrated skills with all of these subjects; and drilled in spelling, reading, and writing. The gradehead teacher was also responsible for the nonacademic needs at each of the first eight grades. The special teachers taught separate special subjects—manual, domestic, visual, performing, or physical arts.

Cooke also designated teachers for primary and secondary responsibilities. To stress that teachers taught children, not subjects, some teachers were assigned as assistants in other disciplines at different grade levels. An elementary grade teacher might assist in a high school history class and a high school teacher might teach in fifth grade. This cross-level teaching and exchange of master and assistant roles provided curriculum unity and knowledge of the students and resulted in equal status among the faculty. Outside the classroom, teachers were library assistants, Curator of the School Museum, or Officer of the Day, who observed and reported positive and negative activities to the principal and directed the numerous visitors in the school.

One-third of a Parker teacher's day was committed to classroom teaching, another third was dedicated to the preparation and planning of teaching techniques and materials, and the final third was scheduled to assist and supervise children or to attend professional meetings. The replacement of textbooks with experience-based curriculum necessitated that teachers develop their own teaching materials.

During the Pioneering Years, the faculty wrote more than a dozen books for classroom use on a variety of subjects. Flora Cooke wrote two books; Jennie Hall was the author of six history texts used in the primary and middle grades, including *Weavers and Other Workers, Four Old Greeks, Buried Cities, Viking Tales, Our Ancestors in Europe,* and *The Story of Chicago.* Gudrun Thorne-Thomsen's fairy tales and realistic stories for young children included the classic *East of the Sun and West of the Moon.* The foreign language teachers wrote three texts for German,

Spanish, and French students, and Herman Lukens's psychology book explained *The Connection Between Thought and Memory* . Teachers also wrote pamphlets, a source of inexpensive educational materials. The faculty adapted thirteen plays, ranging from *Robin Hood* to the *Return of Odysseus* and *Iphigenia* for use by teachers of fourth through eighth grades. For reading lessons in Grades 1-4, the teachers and students wrote Reading Leaflets in history, literature, handwork, nature study, and experimental science. Faculty also wrote educational pamphlets about the art and science of teaching such as the Study of Industry, First Grade Work on Trees, and Mental Imagery in Geography. The school printed, published, and sold most of the books and pamphlets.[67]

Committee work was central to school unity, and Cooke assigned teachers to different faculty committees—Library, Laboratory, Arts, Morning Exercise, and the Parent Committees—as well as to supervise one or more student committees. Pivotal was the Curriculum Committee of the whole, which constructed the course of study for all grades. The teachers met every Monday evening from 1901 to 1914 to plan, discuss, critique, and write a course of study based on a shared vision. The teachers thought their curriculum meetings so significant that they even complained when Cooke tried to move them to Wednesday evenings. The teachers produced nineteen *Catalogues* between 1901 and 1919 and ten *Supplements* between 1920 and 1930. Published by the school for distribution to parents and for purchase by educators in the nation, these *Catalogues* were often in short supply because the demand was great.[68]

The original *Catalogue*, consisting of fifty pages, doubled by 1910, and by its final year numbered 175 pages. Until World War I, the only changes in the course of study were minor, caused by experimentation and evaluation; but following the war, the *Catalogues* revealed more dramatic changes as the school shifted its focus from the social to the individual motive. In 1915, some faculty began to think that a "new and radically different Course of Study should be undertaken." For the first time, the faculty divided into subject-matter committees, and the 1919 *Catalogue and Course of Study* presented most subjects dually by grade levels and by departments rather than simply by grade level. These changes were not merely cosmetic but were reflective of the gradual trend toward a new emphasis on child-centered learning and an increased attention to subject-based curriculum. It seemed that the universal tendency for teachers was to return to the old rather than advance the new.

The faculty postponed a new *Catalogue* in 1920 because of the conflict over two issues: whether the social motive or the individual motive in education should be emphasized and whether the curriculum should be experience based or subject based. Instead, the school published *Supplements* that repeated the work of previous years. The 1929-1930 *Course of Study* was a variation on the original catalogue, and it was the last catalogue published. With its demise, an era of unified curriculum experimentation ended. The teachers were meeting less and less as a curriculum committee of the whole and more and more in departments. The strength of unified knowledge transferred by the original corps of teachers sustained through the Pioneering Years.

The major strength of the school depended on long-range teachers, who were knowledgeable about the history and practice of progressive education and who willingly and intentionally passed on the Parker legacy to the next generation. Four of the original corps of thirteen teachers transferred the Parker legacy directly throughout the Pioneering Years: music teacher Helen Goodrich laid the ground work for music education between 1901 and 1930, and drama teacher Jennie Hall established the foundation of the performing arts between 1901 and 1921. Kindergarten teacher Mary Topping and seventh grade teacher Elsa Miller mentored other faculty in the lower grades from 1901 until 1931 and 1922, respectively. Between 1907 and 1909, Miss Cooke hired fifteen new faculty, of which six outstanding members remained for an average of twenty-seven years. Fifth grade teacher Herman Lukens and first grade teacher Hattie Walker developed and sustained lower school faculty from 1907 to 1934. John Merrill was pivotal in the drama department between 1909 and 1939. Mainstays in the high school were foreign language teacher Jesse Barnes, who taught from 1907 to 1938, social studies teacher Arthur Dettmers, who taught from 1909 to 1930, and manual arts teacher Leonard Wahlstrom, who taught from 1909 to 1940.

Miss Cooke hired five other long-range contributing faculty members during the World War I era. Louella Cornish, who taught from 1913 to 1955, and Marie Claussenius, who taught from 1917 to 1948, helped to lay the foundations of visual arts education. Mary Davis, who taught fourth grade between 1924 and 1954, introduced the Greek tradition to the lower school; and Hazel Cornell, who taught history and headed the Eight-Year Study, taught from 1917 to 1941. Additionally, Miss Cooke invited three Parker graduates to join the faculty: Perry Dunlap Smith '06 and Katharine Taylor '06, who went on to head progressive schools, and Sarah Greenebaum '15, who taught eight grade from 1922 to 1963.

Sarah Greenebaum '15 learned about progressive education as a Parker student and joined the faculty as an apprentice to eighth grade teacher Irene Cleaves in 1922. Upon Miss Cleaves's death in 1930, Miss Greenebaum was appointed eighth grade head. With compassion and respect, she guided eighth graders through the transition from lower school to high school. She taught civics, the history and government of Chicago, and American History. She required students to study the Declaration of Independence, the administration of Jefferson and Jackson, and the slavery question from the Revolution to the Civil War. The students traced the development of the English constitution from Magna Carta. Her classes created knowledgeable and active citizens. In science, students mastered the geology of Lake Michigan, building models in plasticine and studying Miss Greenebaum's extensive rock collection.

Inspired by the social motive, she expected the eighth graders to present four Morning Exercises a year to share what they were learning. "For her, Colonel Parker's idea of responsibility was not a burden to be accepted but, rather, a personal commitment."[69]

A supporter of liberal causes, Miss Greenebaum was a consistent leader for an interracial school. "Her forthright comments in meetings kept the educational principles of the school in focus." When Miss Greenebaum retired in 1963, the school honored her fifty-five year association with the Parker School as student, alumna, and beloved teacher by establishing the Sarah Greenebaum Distinguished Visitors Program, which provided finances for educators to visit the school for a week in order to share their perspectives and to enrich the teachers' thinking about educational developments. Visitors of distinction were more than willing to devote a week to the school. Miss Greenebaum, who attended several meetings of the organizing committee, said the Visitors Program was the best gift she had ever received (see Chapter 8).[70]

From 1901 to 1932, the faculty increased four-fold to sixty-one full and part-time members. The well-planned and thoughtful process of enlarging the faculty ensured that each teacher was introduced to the history, the experimental ethos, and the practices of the institution. Just because teachers served an average of twenty-five years did not necessarily imply effective instruction. But teachers who were "cultured, educated, and trained," who understood and implemented progressive philosophy, and who contributed in their own right as well as transferred the legacy to new teachers with whom they worked collaboratively, assured excellence. Teachers new to the school entered into a community of scholars and readily assimilated its high standards. This dimension alone produced faculty growth.

During the Pioneering Years, the teacher was central, the administrative positions were few, and the school employed only a handful of nonteaching staff members, including a school hostess to greet parents and visitors, a switchboard operator, a registrar, and four secretaries. Like the faculty, the staff was asked to take a holistic approach to its work and place the welfare of the child as the prime goal.

Students: Their Needs Determine the Work of the School

Whether racing down the field with a football underarm, writing an editorial for the *Weekly*, debating at the Forum, completing a chemistry experiment, or gathering eggs from the school's chicken coop to sell at the County Fair, the students' lives were activity centered. Most activities were extensions of coursework and demonstrated the manner in which students advanced what they learned in classes by transforming ideas into action.[71]

The first graders built model houses as part of their study. The second graders ground wheat, used beets to dye fabrics red, made cornstarch pudding, and farmed a little plot of ground for their study of farm life. The study of Chicago led third graders to examine prehistoric swamps and birds of the Chicago area, to construct a diorama of the John Kinzie home, and to map out the city in the sand table. The fourth graders especially enjoyed reenacting the Greek assembly by scheduling classroom forums. During their study of Greek architecture, they cast models of the Acropolis. Performing plays and singing were the most popular activities that extended learning outside of the classroom. The schedules of lower school students were filled with class activities, but young students did not undertake separate activities as high school students did.

When high school classes ended at 3:15 p.m., the corridors came alive with activity. From freshmen to seniors, the arrangement between class and activity was reciprocal; each reinforced the other. For example, Morning Exercise provided a forum to debate current events first examined in an English class where debate was taught. The history teachers introduced democratic ideals that invigorated the student government. Several disciplines inspired student journalists to pen articles for the newspaper, which the English teachers advanced in composition classes. The students extended what they learned in visual and performing arts classrooms into after-school activities. Teachers were assigned to guide, supervise, and critique each activity and to provide strong positive leadership. Teachers measured the effectiveness of the classroom by the success of the related activities based on the premise that the learning was measured by the doing.

Activities and classes were given equal status and all academic disciplines were valued equally. Haydn and Picasso were no less valued than Thucydides or Shakespeare, Darwin or Einstein, Marx or Freud. The Parker way combined classes with activities, making knowledge not merely the accretion of inert ideas but a means for critical thought and action. Student projects were encouraged as long as pupils reached for excellence and developed their fullest potential. The activity-centered approach intensified learning and compelled students to remain at school long after classes ended. Activities made work like play.

The major all-school activity was the Morning Exercise, which brought social unity to the school, taught citizenship, and developed character. At Morning Exercise, pupils learned to understand and appreciate others, to think on their feet, and to make their point understood by an audience. As an audience, students were trained in courteous attention. Miss Cooke believed the habit of courtesy was rooted in kindness—putting oneself in the other's place. Cooke admonished, "Anyone unwilling to devote twenty minutes a day to the betterment of the Community either as speaker or audience is unworthy of School membership. Pupils who cannot respond positively are either weak people or selfish people."[72]

Morning Exercise taught character in the sense that it provided a forum for students to share diverse experiences. The Morning Exercise allowed individuals, classes, activities, and school traditions to be heard, recognized, and celebrated. Guests also shared their experiences with students—

operettas performed by the Chicago Civic Opera, Negro spirituals sung by the Hampton Institute Quartet, and a ten-year-old prodigy played the violin. They listened to Shakespearean interpretations of character presented by Ian Keith '31, who became a professional actor, and were exposed to distinguished intellectuals like Viennese psychologist and psychiatrist Dr. Alfred Adler, physicist Professor Albert Einstein, settlement leader Jane Addams of Hull House, and Leo Tolstoy's daughter Alexandra, who explained her father's works. Some Morning Exercise guests exposed students to different cultures, like Chief Oshkosh, who spoke about the condition of Native Americans, and Mr. Basu, who explained progressive education in India.

Character and citizenship were two sides of the same coin and Morning Exercise served both, as Flora Cooke explained in 1916:

> Each one will exert an influence, be it great or small; each will make the community better or worse because of his influence. To achieve, one must aim. There are times to follow; there are times to lead; but there is no time to selfishly drift. The aim of education is to make the highest motive a fixed habit. That accomplished, the results will take care of themselves.

Through Morning Exercise, students were made aware of social problems and learned to help others as they did. They collected and sent food to settlement houses, raised money for the City Unemployment Agency, repaired toys, and donated old clothes for the needy. Students helped Teddy Roosevelt in his fight to conserve the nation's natural resources, and they joined the American Civic Association to preserve Niagara Falls. As "ideal citizens" students devoted themselves to the war effort, adopting wheatless and meatless days, knitting clothes for the soldiers, and buying Liberty Bonds. Boys joined the working reserve to help with the nation's labor shortage, and girls joined the Junior Red Cross. They bought "Bonds to Save Life" to help Armenians who had been driven from their homes in 1915 by the Turks and Germans. In 1922, they organized a bazaar and raised money to send Russian relief after the brutal revolution and civil war. Morning Exercises taught students to be active citizens and critical thinkers who tackled moral issues, debating whether Parker should continue to teach the German language and study about German scientists while America was at war with Germany and raising questions about the League of Nations because they heard only arguments in its favor.

The cultivation of citizenship also played an integral role in the celebration of school traditions. For the County Fair, the first fall event of the year, each grade sold items they made, grew, or designed. There was plenty of candy and amusement for parents, children, and faculty who attended, and proceeds were designated for school needs. After Anita Blaine stopped contributing to the school, the students designated the proceeds for the scholarship fund. On Dig Day, the boys and male faculty undertook a project to maintain and beautify the building and surrounding grounds. The Big Brothers and Sisters program, instituted in 1917, created a caring spirit among high school students assigned as older siblings to students in the first eight grades.

Pleasure as well as responsibility motivated school traditions. On May Day, the class elected a senior girl and boy as Queen and Lord of the spring to preside over student poetry readings and a student procession. Field Day, held near the end of the year, engaged the student body in sports, dancing, music, singing, food, and general frolicking. Each grade held some special event in honor of the graduating class and presented the seniors with hand crafted creations.

Student government occupied many after school hours. Student interest in shaping a more democratic school surged with World War I. The juniors ran their class meetings according to parliamentary law; the freshmen adopted a point system that allowed them to allocate work more evenly; and students called conferences where the boys and girls met separately to discuss issues. These early attempts at asserting student self-rule were often chaotic but inspired many students to move forward in their quest. In 1919, student government was made official but was supported only by a small group of dedicated students. Issues arose over the lack of student interest, the amount of faculty power, and the inclusion of freshmen in government. After four years of struggle, student government had its first success in 1923 under the leadership of president Theodora Wagner '24, who arranged better order in the halls, a new system for tardies, and exciting and spirited assembly meetings. Students began writing a constitution to implement the following year and in 1925, they created subcommittees on deportment, Morning Exercise, study hall, and the lunchroom. The students introduced ballots and nomination speeches for student elections and by 1926 student government became a fixed part of the high school. In

1929, stumbling blocks caused many students to want to abandon student government, but Miss Cooke declared it a fixed institution in the school. Following her proclamation, students tried to advance their efforts at self-rule. But it took eleven years of struggle before president Arthur Galt '30 devised a student government booklet; the organization had still not matured.

Student publications flourished throughout the Pioneering Years. The earliest publication was the bi-monthly *Recorder*, a literary magazine and school newspaper introduced in 1903. By 1910, *The Recorder* preferred literary contributions over a record of school life, so students introduced a yearbook, *The Record*, in 1916. As its first editor in chief, Henry Channon '16 proposed that the *Parker Record* "commemorate what has been done, refresh memories, and record what may long since have been forgotten." From 1916 to 1932, *The Record* showcased a literate group of students with sophisticated tastes. Henry Channon wrote the class prophecy in four "cantos," each complete with numerous literary allusions. The leather-bound volumes featured formal photos and lengthy copy about the faculty, the graduates, and underclassmen. Each covered athletic events and student activities, giving team win/loss records and examples of accomplishments, and was dedicated to a teacher. These early issues were publications of great quality.

Student literary magazines rose and fell under a variety of names—*The Recorder* (1903-1911), the *Barnacle* (1921-1925), and the *Question Mark* (1934), but journalism and the newspaper took precedence over literary publications in these three decades. In 1911, the school introduced the first completely student-run newspaper in the country, the *Parker Weekly*, which gave students a powerful voice in the school. A student editorial explained, "The real and sincere manifestations of the Parker spirit may be found, written in printers' ink, amidst the *Weekly* files, untouched by subduing conventions."[73] The one-page *Weekly* quickly grew to a three-column, four-page newspaper, and its staff multiplied. By 1933, the *Weekly*'s regular features included a cover story, student editorials, an alumni news column, a "Who's Who" featuring new faculty, and mock student polls. *Weekly* editors Dorothy Heyn '29, Bernard Nachman '30, Nixon de Tarnowsky '31, and Richard Grauman '31 introduced the concept of training for the position of editor, purchased equipment, and advanced the newspaper's content and quality. As the *Weekly* staff gained experience, it could proudly proclaim that it had lived up to its name. Not a week passed without an issue, hot off the press. However, as of 1931, the staff had not yet met its other goal—"no technical or grammatical errors."

The students' exposure to the fine arts motivated one of Parker's most innovative organizations, the Forum, founded in 1915. High schoolers met monthly on a Friday night to share their talents in debates, extemporaneous speaking, oral interpretation, performance, and the visual arts. The Extemporaneous Speaking team had twelve male and only one female member, Ruth Kellogg '31. Programs varied but on a typical Friday night, students might play a jazz or a classical composition, present a debate, speak extemporaneously, or perform a short play. Raymond Immerwahr '30, Alfred Fisher '30, Shirley Greene '30, and Doris Lackritz '31 were great supporters of the Forum throughout their high school years. By 1934, the Forum included groups for drama, literature, music, debate, science, art, and advertising. The purpose was to create a showcase for students' talents and intellectual stimulation for the school.

Music and drama were most prominently showcased. In spite of the small high school enrollment, the high school introduced an orchestra in 1918 and a jazz band in 1920. Violinists Mol Greenspahn '30, Dorothy Dasch '30, and Joseph Rosenstein '30 entertained audiences as did pianists Irma Lyons '30 and Richard Gauman '31. The jazz band relied on drummer Alan Weiss '31.

Dramatic performances were directly related to English classes. The faculty and students held a special place in their hearts for performances of Shakespearean and Greek classics, perhaps due to the fourth grade central subject. Arnie Horween '16 played Claudius in the 1916 production of *Hamlet*, but by 1923 Shakespearean drama had given way to lighter fare— Barrie's *Quality Street* and Galsworthy's *The Little Man.*

Both male and female athletic teams were important to the Parker School, but students received a mixed message from their coaches and the school. The aim of the school was education of the whole child, which mandated that athletic programs nourish young bodies. The principle of cooperation encouraged sports teams to achieve excellence and all interested played in the games. The school was against competition, and as a result, Parker athletes were known not so much for their success at winning games as for their effort and undying spirit. *Weekly* articles often boasted of the previous week's football or hockey game as "a hard-fought victory" or "a hard-fought defeat." But over the decades, the principle of cooperation was overcome by competition. When the Parker School was allowed less practice time than their opponent schools, team captains like George Zehrlant '31 pleaded for more time in order to make a better showing and succeeded. The boys played football, basketball, baseball, tennis, and ice hockey against arch rival Chicago Latin and other Chicago area schools.

The girls competed intramurally—grade against grade or in two inter-class teams. In the late Twenties, when the girls challenged the absence of a girls' league, Parker held firm to its policy, which emulated women's colleges in the belief that competition created by interscholastic sports did not properly suit girls' needs. In response, the girls organized a Girls' Athletic Association in 1926 with the goal of involving every Parker girl in athletics. When girls' basketball was introduced in 1918 and led by Captain Virginia Martin '31, it became their major sport. Baseball was somewhat less popular, but Florence Goldsmith '31, Ethel Webster '31, and eight other girls earned letters. When an English coach led girls' field hockey for a term, Mary McKee '31 reported that they had a good season. The team was invited to the Chicago Latin School for a tea to celebrate.

Athletic uniforms for both girls and boys became more practical, graduating from baggy to form-fitting attire. Eventually, each male sport had a different uniform. The girls sported collared tee-shirts with vests and mid-thigh shorts for their sports. The girls' fencing team was impressively outfitted in its fencing armor.

Like athletic uniforms, school clothes also changed during these decades. At first, Parker students arrived at school in the fashions of the early 1900s. The girls wore dark long skirts, large collared white blouses, and laced boots. Their hair was shoulder length or cut just below the ear. Flappers were not seen in school because Miss Cooke implemented a uniform policy in 1919 to prevent over-dressing among high school girls. The girls accepted the uniform—a blue silk or wool dress with a choice of any collar or cuffs and oxford shoes—because it reduced dressing time in the mornings and eliminated competition. In the 1930s, the uniform was relaxed to a navy blue skirt and blouse and a navy blue sweater. The boys' apparel was proper—suits or slacks and jackets with vests and neckties. The younger boys wore knickerbocker pants. Eventually the boys replaced suits and jackets with sweaters, dress shirts, and neckties. The Code of Conduct in 1911 and the Uniform Code of 1919 added a certain propriety to the stimulating activity-centered atmosphere that prevailed in the corridors.

Students and teachers knew each other well. Students learned about the lives of teachers through faculty Morning Exercises at which teachers presented material about their field of study, a current event, or a summer vacation. The *Weekly* profiled new teachers at the beginning of the year, bid farewell to departing faculty at year's end, and offered brief faculty and administrative biographies in its "Who's Who" column. Each edition of the *Record* included a faculty section. Faculty developed relationships with students by supervising student activities, participating in Forum programs, and coaching athletic teams. The teachers hosted an annual party for the high school, and Flora Cooke befriended students by lunching with the seniors every Wednesday. Students and faculty could communicate well when controversies arose because they had established a rapport and learned to talk through their differences with a healthy respect for one another. Faculty were an integral part of community life and were respected, admired, befriended, and cared about by the student body.

The teachers wanted a school to be a place where the strengths, gifts, and natural interests of every child could develop to their fullest measure. The school provided the stage for performance, the classroom for knowledge, the auditorium for Morning Exercise, and the laboratory for experiments. The school was the studio for art and music, the library for research and reading, the shop for printing, and the playground and field for games and sports. The school was the quiet study hall for private reflection and study.

At the school's twenty-fifth anniversary, using the data from an Alumni Survey, Miss Cooke reflected, "A school cannot be judged by what its faculty thinks of it, but by the human output alone . . . . We can say with some certainty that the results of twenty-five years work of the school, judged by its graduates' achievement, is certainly encouraging." The creative opportunities of shop, laboratory, library, study, and classrooms, as well as contact with nature and life outside the school, seem basically right, judged by the tastes, attitudes, habits, and life activities of the graduates.[74]

Although progressive education sought to prepare students for life rather than college, ninety-five percent of Parker graduates attended higher institutions of learning during the Pioneering Years. Early matriculation records show that most Parker graduates attended the University of Chicago, Northwestern University, Swarthmore, Smith, Williams, and Yale; made the honor roll at Dartmouth and Princeton, were elected class presidents at Wisconsin and Vassar; and made All-American at Harvard. Students applied to and were accepted at first-rate colleges because the academic courses at Parker were intellectually rigorous, which colleges of that era demanded. For example, a survey of the Class of 1922 showed that several graduates named at least four subjects in which they were well prepared for college—science, mathematics, English, and foreign languages. Miss B. Topping, an honors graduate, named all subjects as strengths, as did Harvard student J. Greenberg. Lucy Smith at Vassar identified English and added music and drama. Louise Healy, who attended Smith College, named the arts and foreign languages. The excellence of chemistry preparation was pointed out by one-sixth of the class.

Although many students in the 1922 survey named academic subjects as the strengths of the Parker School, an equal number called "preparation outside the classroom" the most valuable preparation for college. Miss Montgomery designated "broad interests in subjects, the ability to study, growth of soul and character, ability to talk before a group, and responsibility." Lucille Hoerr identified "training in organization." Many pupils reiterated character development, responsibility, and a variety of positive results from the Morning Exercise experience. Others referred to the value of participation in specific activities and projects undertaken in and outside of class.[75]

Was the Parker School Progressive?

The Pioneering Years ended with the school's educational process at its apex, but its governance and the financial status at its nadir. Mrs. Blaine was the sole surviving trustee in 1930, and in 1934 Principal Cooke resigned, creating a vacuum in leadership. Not only was the school continually and increasingly hampered by a deficit, but the "old main building" was deteriorating, unsafe, and beyond repair. Blaine's three million dollar contribution had not ameliorated these financial problems, and now there was no new benefactor in the wings and no endowment. The teachers saved the school through their financial sacrifice, hard work, and expertise.

The philosophical foundations had proven valid. The principles of new education as enumerated by Francis Parker and repeated in each *Catalogue* sustained: (1) "education is the all-sided growth of the individual," (2) "community life . . . every individual orders his conduct with reference to the good of the whole," (3) "character constantly realizing itself in practical citizenship . . . is the only purpose of the school." The students grew intellectually, socially, and morally and developed as people of character and active citizens of the country.

The teachers worked to develop the science of education by effectively applying Francis Parker's theory of concentration through the process of central subjects, which they published in the *Catalogues* and *Supplements*. During these three decades, the faculty discovered and validated six pedagogical principles—that learning through experience deepens and broadens knowledge; that integrating the arts with academic subjects strengthens the grasp of ideas; that "learning by doing" or activity-centered schooling teaches life activities; that quality rather than quantity teaching increases long-term memory; that the whole child must be educated; that social motive, concrete materials, and expression are essential to the educational process to create educated citizens for a democracy; and that some measurement is necessary for the validation of a learning process. Some of these findings the teachers explored in several *Studies in Education*. The faculty also transferred the progressive legacy to new colleagues and assistant teachers. Five of the seven schools built in the Parker image were founded during this era (see Chapter 5).

The school was as progressive as it wanted to be with strong support from students, teachers, and parents. It matured and made its mark in the nation as an effective progressive institution, equal to and superior in many ways to traditional schools and to other progressive schools when measured by its alumni's performance. Miss Cooke and her teachers made Francis W. Parker School a national exemplar of progressive education by the mid-1930s.

Chapter 7

The Stabilizing Years
(1935-1965)

Historical Perspective: Poverty to Prosperity

In its Stabilizing Years, the school became the bastion of progressive education. The teachers continued the effective application of the original progressive principles—the education of the whole child for character, citizenry, and community—and by the end of World War II, they had developed a coherent kindergarten through twelfth grade course of study based upon progressive pedagogy. The highlight of the era was the school's participation in the experimental course of study for the high school, called the Eight-Year Study, which gave the school national prominence.

Between 1935 and 1965, the nation underwent major economic, demographic, political, cultural, and educational changes, which the Parker School reflected. Economically, America transformed from the poverty of the Great Depression to the prosperity of the postwar period. In the 1930s, the school struggled financially, almost closing its doors, but at the close of the era, the school managed to raise 2.5 million dollars to construct a new main building. The changing Chicago demography increased the school's enrollment and underscored its philosophy about the need for a diverse student body. The national political changes transformed the culture toward the progressive ideal of an open society. By 1935, progressive education implied all that was good about education, and its ideals and tenets were "the dominant American pedagogy," but as it grew more popular, it became the scapegoat for many of the problems in American education.[1]

Progressive education advanced nationally in the first decades of the Stabilizing Years. In the mid 1930s, seventy percent of American cities with populations greater than 25,000 were changing their school curriculum. In these cities, a 1937 survey of teachers revealed that their "curriculum thinking" converged around progressive principles.[2] Historians and professors of education arrived at a consensus and a common understanding about progressive education that was not apparent in earlier decades. At least three significant books presented a collective understanding of progressive education: Charles Beard's *The Unique Foundation of Education in American Democracy* (1934), William Carver's *The Purpose of Education in American Democracy* (1938), and B. L. Dodds's *That All May Learn* (1939).

As progressive education expanded and became more inclusive, it inspired different kinds of public and private, rural and urban, and child-centered schools. The expansion caused an indictment of the movement for losing its focus and goals. The criticism was led by none other than John Dewey, whose book *Experience and Education* (1938), criticized the new progressives for confusing progressive education with the absence of external controls in schools and admonished teachers, "The only freedom that is of enduring importance is freedom of intelligence," the result of "intelligent activity" not of "activity based on impulse."[3] "The variant of progressive education that had been established within the profession by the activities of the National Education Association . . . the schools of education, and the public education agenda had strayed far from the humane, pragmatic, open-minded approach advocated by John Dewey."[4]

Other academics joined in Dewey's criticism—Paul Woodring, a professor at Western Washington College, wrote *Let's Talk Sense about Our Schools* (1953), in which he complained that progressive educators avoided the criticism of their pedagogy.[5] Harold Alberty, a prominent progressive professor at Ohio State University and a member of the research team for the Eight-Year Study, believed that progressivism had an uphill battle against the traditionally entrenched logical organization of knowledge by disciplines. Throughout the fifties, what was called "the crisis in education" filled the popular press with attacks on progressive education. The Parker School, however, continued to build upon the original paradigm of progressive education: (1) a school to advance the science of education by utilizing new knowledge from the field of education and allied disciplines and (2) a school to act as a "lever of social change" to create a democratic society.

While the Parker School continued to bloom academically, national conditions between the Great Depression and the Vietnam War caused great turbulence in society, which affected education. Six American presidents charted a domestic policy that advanced the nation steadily toward the progressive social ideal that had begun to take shape in the 1890s. In the Depression years, banks closed their doors, farms and factories lay idle, and young and old were unemployed. President Hoover's sweeping large-scale measures were inadequate to resolve the crisis, but President Franklin Roosevelt introduced his New Deal in 1932, which was a deliberate effort to render the social system more just and humane. The New Deal introduced multiple programs—the Tennessee Valley Authority was a design to employ workers to remodel a river; the National Housing Act provided insurance for loans to repair and modernize houses, farms, and small plants; the Works Progress Administration was a plan to provide jobs to build roads, schools, and parks, and to finance projects for writers and artists. Roosevelt's Social Security Act provided insurance for the elderly, the unemployed, and the disabled. Of significance to schools was legislation that raised the compulsory schooling age to remove teenage workers from a depressed job market. This legislation caused high school enrollment to rise from forty-five percent of the age group in 1932 to sixty-five percent in 1950.

The effectiveness of New Deal legislation began to lose momentum in 1937 because attention was drawn to the foreign crises, which were deepened in 1939 by Hitler's absorption of Austria, his takeover of Czechoslovakia, his threats to Poland, and America's subsequent entry into World War II.[6] Upon Roosevelt's death, his vice president, Harry Truman, became president and extended the New Deal to the Fair Deal, slowed the pace of change, and pushed only at programs in areas of outstanding need.[7] Truman gave presidential support to civil rights, desegregated the armed forces, and introduced the Government Issue Bill of Rights in 1944, which subsidized tuition, books, and education fees for veterans, and provided a monthly subsistence allowance. In 1945, eighty thousand veterans obtained further training, and in the seven-year period when the G.I. benefits were available, four million veterans attended universities and colleges.[8] Their high academic achievements surprised college professors. The G.I. Bill changed the college student body and attitudes toward who could be educated and resulted in great economic progress in America.

President Dwight Eisenhower continued Truman's Fair Deal in a "middle course" between liberalism and conservatism. Fundamentally, his policies also meant greater economic and educational opportunity for the mass of people. During Eisenhower's term in office, several major books reflected the changing view of the relationship of the school to the society. The emphasis after the war was placed on educating all students. John Gardner's *Excellence* (1961) emphasized the development of human potential as a national goal and insisted that the nation could encourage both excellence and equality.[9] James Conant's *The American High School Today* (1959) explained how a high school of 1,000 students could educate all pupils by offering a combination of academic and elective courses for noncollege-bound students and advanced courses in mathematics, science, and foreign languages for the college bound. Conant encouraged innovative practices—team teaching, flexible scheduling, language laboratories, ungraded programs, school-university cooperation, independent study—as the way to school improvement and urged the schools to combine academic excellence and democratic values.[10] Harvard psychologist Jerome Bruner's *Process of Education* (1966) promoted quality teaching by placing emphasis on teaching the structure or the principles of a discipline through discovery or inquiry, which called for inductive reasoning, hands on learning, or "doing a subject."[11] These education texts became the teachers' bibles during the sixties, and Gardner's and Bruner's goals were compatible with the vision of the Parker teachers.

In 1960, when John F. Kennedy defeated Eisenhower's Vice President, Richard Nixon, he continued the Fair Deal in a liberal direction, pressured mainly by the effective strategies of minorities. Kennedy's Civil Rights Act, passed by his successor Lyndon Johnson in 1963, provided significant federal protection against racial discrimination in voting and guaranteed access to public accommodations, federally funded programs, education, and employment. Johnson's Great Society legislation of 1964-1965 included the Elementary and Secondary Education Act of 1965, which provided major government funding for poor school children. Consonant with the Civil Rights Act, the Great Society legislation shifted the focus of educational reform from the college-bound to the disadvantaged student.[12] In theory, at least, progressive philosophy supported civil rights and education for the disadvantaged.

Social historian Eric Goldman summed up the "crucial decade" following World War II as a period of "increased income . . . a break-through in status, a chance at schooling and occupations and ways of living that previously had been barricaded."[13] Although slum and suburban schools were vastly uneven in quality, by the end of the war, every youngster was able to attend an elementary and a secondary school. Legislation removed barriers and opened opportunity, causing educational participation to rise. Just as the 1930s increased secondary school enrollment, the late 1940s and the early 1950s increased enrollment in higher education. Higher education before World War II was not open on an equal basis to citizens, and participation was limited by accident of birth. The many students now completing secondary education were anticipating attending college, as did the returning veterans. College admission became more competitive and no longer the privilege of the few, although a quota system for minorities continued.

The Cold War between America and Russia following World War II threatened academic freedom. Challenged by coexistence with Russia, Americans experienced fear of communism, which resulted in attacks on university professors, the banning of books, the insistence on loyalty oaths, and the blacklisting of many teachers and artists. Many conservatives argued that communists in America were responsible for the New Deal, intended to inflict a labor dictatorship, and wanted to cause the destruction of initiative, profit, business, freedom, the individual, and the entire United States and should be gotten rid of. They perceived professors as communists, homosexuals, and New Dealers. The liberals countered that the free university was "the central mechanism of democracy."[14] Widespread suspicion of subversive persons in important high places found an outlet in 1949, when Wisconsin Senator Joseph McCarthy directed the national search for disloyal citizens. The national hysteria damaged many innocent lives and reputations and threatened democracy until 1954, when McCarthy clashed with the United States Army and was censured by the Senate in televised hearings that transfixed the country.

During the Stabilizing Years, the scientific and technological revolution also influenced American education. In 1939, Albert Einstein, Enrico Fermi, Leo Szilard, and other scientists warned that Germany was developing nuclear weapons. Three years later, under the west stand of Stagg

Field at the University of Chicago, Enrico Fermi began directing the first controlled nuclear experiments. In 1945, America tested its first atomic bomb over the New Mexico desert and then exploded the atomic bomb over Hiroshima and Nagasaki. To the surprise of American scientists, Soviet scientists exploded their first nuclear bomb in 1949. The Atomic Energy Commission was directed to continue its work on all forms of atomic weapons, including the hydrogen bomb, whose first explosion in 1954 revealed a great capacity for destruction. Russia's launch of Sputnik in 1957 pre-dated America's first satellite launch by one year, and a Russian cosmonaut was the first to orbit the earth.

Sputnik caused school change. Americans became convinced that American education was a failure, prompting the passage of the National Defense Education Act of 1958, which emphasized educational excellence, high academic standards, and improved teaching in mathematics and the sciences in secondary schools. At the same time, the action of the oppressed and their supporters, assisted by court decisions, opened educational opportunity. In May 1954, the Supreme Court decision of *Brown vs. Board of Education* held that school segregation was a violation of Fourteenth Amendment rights, striking down the "separate but equal" clause and introducing the concept of school desegregation. Several state governments resisted the ruling. In 1957, Governor Faubus defied the federal government by using the National Guard to block integration in Arkansas schools. In 1962, eight years after the Brown Decision, federal marshals were still needed to escort James Meredith into the University of Mississippi, and Governor Wallace tried the following year to bar black students trying to register at the University of Alabama.

World War II transformed society dramatically, and as a result family living patterns changed. Families became accustomed "to new conditions, new wage scales, and new ways of being treated."[15] By 1954, a female headed one in ten households, and women holding jobs outside of the home constituted one-third of the workforce. The mother who had been integrally involved in the school and provided volunteer help was less available. Home was becoming the place where the television set was located and where TV dinners, invented in 1954, were commonplace.

The cultural values shifted as did the demographics. Each year the white Anglo-Saxon Protestant majority diminished in percent of the population, and the minority population increased. Advances made by these minorities during World War II were challenged in its aftermath in race riots in the North, lynchings of Negroes in the South, violence against Negroes in Montgomery, Alabama, and vandalism directed at Japanese-American veterans. Jews were routinely excluded from housing, clubs, and schools. A columnist in the Cleveland *Plain Dealer* wrote, "We can't do it [be racists] as decent human beings and we can't do it as a nation trying to sell democracy to a world full of non-white people."[16] These complexities in city life prompted whites to begin moving to the suburbs.

During the Stabilizing Years, forces external to the school caused most of the educational changes. The legislation of the 1930s increased high school enrollment and in the 1940s increased college enrollment. The National Defense Act of 1958, the Civil Rights Act of 1964, and the Elementary and Secondary Education Act of 1965 were also turning points that climaxed in a national social and educational revolution. The Parker School integrated the changes without transforming the school radically.

Financially the school was in debt from 1930 to 1965 and unable to work itself out of its grave financial difficulties.

Board of Trustees: "Plain Living and High Thinking"

The Stabilizing Years of the school began in 1932 with Mrs. Blaine's establishment of the school as a not-for-profit corporation, her appointment of a new Board of Trustees, and her creation of an Educational Council. An Alumni Committee appointed by Mrs. Blaine and Miss Cooke recommended six new trustees—Richard Bentley '11, chairman; Perry Dunlap Smith '06, vice president; Elmer Wieboldt '08, treasurer; Katharine Taylor '06, Elliot Dunlap Smith '07, and Anita McCormick Blaine. Two of the five alumni were principals of schools.[17]

During this era, the Board of Trustees revised its by-laws on membership three times. In 1946, the by-laws allowed for eleven trustees, with seven at-large members, two parent trustees for a term of one year each, and two parents for two years each. The 1955 by-laws expanded the board to include alumni trustees and ex-officio representatives, including the president of the Educational Council, the head of the Women's Board, two faculty representatives, and honorary trustees. In May 1964 the by-laws again increased the number of trustees.

The trustees directed all business affairs of the corporation, elected Educational Council members, and on the recommendation of the Educational Council, appointed or removed the principal. The supervisory structure of the school was unusual if not unique, because the composition of the Board of Trustees was representative of the school community and the determining factor for board membership was interest in education rather than financial generosity. The by-laws provided that no one was eligible or could serve as a trustee who did not "believe strongly in the wisdom and righteousness of the principles laid down by Francis Parker."[18]

Two board chairmen served the school until it celebrated its fiftieth anniversary—Richard Bentley '11 from 1932 until 1938 and Clay Judson from 1939 to 1949. Chairman Bentley began his term with an address to the Parents Association at a meeting in May 1933, when he stated "four facts of significance" to the survival of the school: (1) school governance and management, (2) "a potential comprehensive plan for tuitions," (3) Miss Cooke's retirement and the search for her successor, and (4) the identification of the educational principles that the school was compelled to follow. President Bentley explained, "The educational principles of Colonel Parker must under our Charter at all times be upheld . . . this does not mean hidebound adherence to [his] doctrine," but it does mean adherence to "private schools acting as educational trail-blazers for public schools," "the accessibility [of the school] to children from homes of different financial means," and sufficient wages paid to teachers. Bentley assured parents that the school would not "countenance the paying of starvation wages to teachers."[19] Bentley's remarks were his attempt to shift the financial responsibility of the school from Mrs. Blaine, its guarantor for thirty years, to the parents and the alumni.

In the fall of 1933, Chairman Bentley appointed a Parent Committee to study the future of the school and to make a report and recommendations. Chaired by Clay Judson and composed of Parents Association President John Augur Holabird and six parents, the committee named four significant problem areas: (1) scholarships, (2) pensions, (3) land, and (4) the requirement of experimental and research activities. The committee completed its deliberations in 1934 and sent its report to parents, who were asked to "approve the proposed plan" by signing and returning it to the school. The parents approved the plan.

The first significant problem area was financing scholarships because financial aid to students was at the root of the persistent annual deficit. Low tuition and generous scholarships had helped Blaine and Francis Parker realize their "democratic ideals." Both considered scholarships of prime importance because "they permitted the most desirable children in the student body" and because they did not intend the Parker School to become a "rich child's school." Approximately one-third of the student body was on financial aid throughout this period. The Parent Committee reasoned that since the alumni "received far more than they paid for," they should "repay in some degree their indebtedness" by establishing a Scholarship Fund.[20] In the past, Blaine's contributions meant that in effect she paid approximately one-half the parents' cost of educating their children. From the onset of the Scholarship Campaign until the fiftieth anniversary, approximately 2,000 alumni raised an average of $19,800 per year for eight years, for a total of $158,551. While alumni donated throughout this period, they contributed less per capita than did graduates of other private schools.

The second "significant problem" the Parent Committee addressed for discussion by the trustees was a pension plan for teachers. Mrs. Blaine had made available $100,000 for a pension plan for all teachers who left or would leave the school by June 1934. She indicated that future pension accruals should become an ordinary operating expense of the school, and the trustees accepted the responsibility.

Land and buildings were the Committee's third major concern. The school owned the land under the main building and the entrance on Webster Avenue, but Blaine owned the remainder of the property. Between 1932 and 1934, Blaine donated the land north of the building along Grant Place and the land across Grant Place extending to Clark Street. She also offered to make a lease of the land east and west of the school for use as a playground. The problems of the "old main building" were apparent. For many years, enrollment had outstripped the building's capacity, forcing classes to be held in the twenty-year-old wartime portables and kindergarten classes to convene in the Webster Hotel across the street. The trustees set up a Buildings and Grounds Committee to identify the areas of greatest need. The Committee examined the vacating of Grant Place and the possible construction of a new Little School for the kindergarten. Because scholarship aid always seemed to take precedence over building needs, the trustees developed a contingency plan for closing the school permanently if funds for construction were not available.

The fourth consideration for the Parent Committee was that the school "remain experimental and undertake research activities." The trustees studied several experimental proposals. One proposal was to investigate the value of Parker as a city versus a country school. Trustees voted "that the school should look to having a country home of its own to supplement the city experience by field trips and periods of residence in the country." The proposal was unrealistic during the Depression years, and the country home never materialized for lack of funds.

The Depression presented chairman Bentley with other problems. As the economy suffered and the birth rates slowed, enrollment dropped from 451 pupils in the 1931-1932 school year to 338 pupils in 1939-1940. Parents sought to economize by keeping their older children at the Parker School and enrolling their younger children in public schools. When some parents fell behind on tuition payments, the trustees had to hire a collection agency to collect delinquent accounts, an odious act considering the school's ideals. Determined to keep the school alive, Bentley and his five board members gave their attention to increasing tuition income, to investigating ways to reconfigure space rather than investing in a new building, and to merging with the Girls' Chicago Latin School. Bentley was able to keep the school doors open without a merger, but the new main building was postponed until the early 1960s.

Richard Bentley '11 succeeded his father Cyrus as the second chairman of the Board of Trustees. He served a six-year term at a time when the school had to struggle with difficult financial problems and management concerns. Blaine's funding began to dwindle as she considered resigning from the board, and the principal of thirty years, Miss Cooke, resigned in 1934. A graduate of Yale University and Northwestern Law School, Bentley was a lawyer in his father's law firm, where after his father's death he managed Anita McCormick Blaine's legal affairs.[21]

Clay Judson, the third chairman of the board, served from 1938 to 1949. Previously chairman of the Parents Committee, Judson was deeply engaged in the Parker School and progressive education because of his two children, Alice '39 and Clay Jr. '44. Alice said that she learned about a school being an "embryonic democracy" from Morning Exercise and about the method of "learning by doing" from Miss Cooke, but it was from her father that she got the exciting feeling that she was part of a "great experiment." Mr. Judson pursued solutions to many of the same school problems as his predecessor.

In 1939, Judson authorized a fundraising committee to raise money for the new Little School building and to procure subscriptions to a yearly sustaining fund for additional scholarships. He hired Hauser Associates to make a population survey to decide whether the erection of a new school plant was justified. In 1941, the portables were wrecked, and by 1942 Judson and Principal Smith raised $150,000 to build the Little School, which was constructed for $87,768 debt-free because of Mrs. Blaine's contribution of $50,000. At that time, Blaine also transferred the title to her properties on the 2200 block to the school except those along Lincoln Park West. In 1944, the trustees authorized a War Nursery, which was operated by eight trained volunteers assisted by seventh grade students. One of eighteen in the city, the War Nursery served families with mothers who had entered the workforce during World War II.

Mrs. Blaine's funding ceased during Judson's term. To replace it was a special challenge in a school atmosphere which Judson thought marked by "plain living and high thinking." In one of the school's many attempts to explain that material things were unimportant, Miss Cooke asked one day at Morning Exercise, "Now what are the things you can do that don't cost money?" Seven-year-old Alice Judson responded, "Going places and doing things." Everyone but Miss Cooke laughed, Alice reported to her father that evening at dinner.[22] Alice expressed the school's belief in "plain living and high thinking," which excluded discussions of money.

Between 1950 and 1965, the end of the era, the trustees' agenda pivoted on the four "significant problems" identified by the Parents Committee in 1934. The pension plan for the teachers became accepted as a board obligation and was dropped from the agenda. Land became a lesser concern in the last decade of the era because Blaine had deeded most of the 2200 block to the school. In 1956 her New World Foundation deeded the east field to the school. In 1959, Grant Place was finally closed through the support of the Lincoln Park Conservation Association. The problem of enrollment, tuition, and scholarships was high on the board's agenda. Between 1950 and 1957 scholarship aid was estimated at $100,000 annually, while scholarship income averaged $22,000 annually.

To build the new building, fundraising had to become the board's top priority. The Executive Committee formed the nucleus of a Development Council, organized to raise funds for the new construction. The first donations were $100,000 from Blaine's New World Foundation and a $300 gift from the Class of 1955. The building fundraising extended over the decade of the 1950s. Marshall Holleb, a trustee for thirteen years, was one of the major fundraisers. Holleb originated a parents' bond plan, which allowed parents and others to purchase long-term Francis W. Parker bonds with interest deferred. Purchasers were encouraged to assign the bonds to the school as a charitable gift for which they could take a tax deduction. The participation provided equity for the construction of the new building. Beyond his contributions to the board, Marshall Holleb's activities at the Francis W. Parker School were extensive. His sons—Alan '64, Gordon '65, and Paul '66—were Parker students. His wife Doris, a strong proponent of progressive education, served as a member of the Educational Council and later became the chairperson. Mr. Holleb was the school's attorney *pro bono*, and when Dr. Thomas died, he was asked to give the eulogy at the memorial service.[23]

Although funds for the new building were as yet unavailable, the trustees argued about the architect. Trustee Greenwald favored Ludwig Mies van der Rohe, but the board chose the firm of Holabird and Root. Throughout the process, the Development Council had difficulty raising money, which meant compromises in the building design. At first it was thought that the building could be constructed in sections as the money was raised, but when that idea did not prove feasible, bids were let out in the summer of 1960, and the new building was constructed in school year 1961-1962 for $2.5 million. The Parker students moved into the new building in the fall of 1962.

From the school's fiftieth anniversary to the end of the Stabilizing Years, four men served as board chairmen, and their chief goal was to continue to raise funds for the new main building. David Wallerstein served between 1949 and 1953 as the fourth board chairman. The Wallersteins were a Parker family. His wife, Caroline Moos Rieser Rau Wallerstein; her brother, Leonard Rieser; two cousins, Alice and Bill Nachman; and three sons, John Rau '43, Michael Wallerstein '55, and David Wallerstein '57 attended the Parker School. Mrs. Rau Wallerstein was a Parker parent for twenty-eight years. This network of Parkerites provided Mr. Wallerstein with "exposure, loyalty, and belief in the school."

Chairman Wallerstein, recognized as a financial man, was a consensus builder. Called a "tiger" on knowing costs and controlling them, he helped the school establish fiscal controls. A "great people person," he also helped to bring collegiality and esprit to the board. A man of good judgment at a time when the trustees had hard decisions to make about the construction of the new main building, he applied his expertise. Wallerstein's main contribution to the school was the adoption of a fiftieth anniversary fundraising campaign. The campaign was launched in 1950 and continued for twelve years until the new building was completed in 1962.

Wallerstein's background prepared him well as a member of the Board of Trustees. Born in Richmond, Virginia, he earned an MBA at Harvard Business School in 1926. He moved to Chicago, where he joined Balaban & Katz, and became president of this major Chicago company that operated theaters. Mr. Wallerstein also served on nonprofit boards such as Michael Reese Hospital and the Jewish Community Center.[24]

James Weber followed Wallerstein as the fifth board chairman from 1953 to 1957. Chairman Weber, a vice president at the Leo Burnett advertising agency, continued the fundraising campaign. He created a sense of urgency by warning trustees of the rising costs of construction, reporting that construction would have cost $420,000 in 1937 and would cost $1,659,000 in 1956. Mr. Weber appointed a special fundraising committee to assist the executive committee and hired a fundraising firm to survey potential and needs for the new building. He investigated foundation grants and the plausibility of "perpetuation gifts." President Weber endorsed an Alumni Survey to use as part of the public relations plan for the new building. Weber interviewed candidates for a professional fundraising director and a General Chairman of the campaign, whom he believed should be of national or city-wide prominence.

Reuben Freeman, the sixth board chairman, was born in South Bend, Indiana, and moved to Chicago, where he attended public schools before enrolling at Northwestern University and graduating from its law school. His only son, Richard '50, was the source of his father's interest and commitment to the school. Mr. Freeman was appointed a Parker trustee in 1953, elected vice president of the board after serving for three years, and then became chairman from 1957 until 1958. His year was dramatically terminated with his sudden death at the early age of fifty-two.[25]

Freeman, a member of the Development Council, was slated to be "the chief fundraiser for the new building." A collector of modern art and a successful lawyer with many corporate clients, Freeman had close ties to the wealthy members of the Jewish community and because of his personal charm and interest in the new building, it was said by many, "Giving money to Rube was a pleasure." His death interrupted the fundraising campaign and further postponed the construction of the new building.[26]

David Silberman Jr. had been a parent trustee for a year when he was asked to take Mr. Freeman's place in November 1958 as the board's seventh chairman. His concern for his children motivated him to accept the position. "I wanted to make sure there would be a good school in the city for my children to attend." Silberman was a Parker parent for more than thirty years as father to Lore '64, Anna '67, David '70, Samuel '83, Mariann '86, and Kathy, who died while in high school.

As chairman of major gifts for the building campaign, Silberman knew well that large gifts were the key to financing the construction of a new building—but "those weren't such prosperous days and finding major gifts was difficult." A $25,000 donation was significant and scarce. Silberman believed that part of the problem lay with the composition of the board, which had been selected for its advice rather than its wealth and generosity. Silberman endeavored to transform the board from idealists to contributors.[27]

A Chicagoan, Silberman attended the Laboratory School at the University of Chicago before enrolling at Stanford University. He returned to Chicago and became a commodity dealer in furs. "A lifelong friend of the Parker School, generous, kindly, and interested," Silberman served as chairman until 1966 when he became financial vice president and secretary-treasurer, a position he retained until 1971 before becoming an honorary trustee in 1972(see Figure 7.1).[28]

Figure 7.1
Principals and Board Chairmen, 1935-1965

On average, each principal collaborated with three trustee chairmen to establish the continuity of the school. The educational governance was the domain of the principal, and the fiscal management was the domain of the Board of Trustees.

Principals	Board Chairmen
Raymond Osborne (1934-1937)	Richard Bentley (1932-1938)
Herbert Smith (1938-1956)	Clay Judson (1939-1949)
	David Wallerstein (1949-1953)
	James Weber (1953-1957)
Cleveland Thomas (1956-1967)	Reuben Freeman (1957-1958)
	David Silberman (1958-1966)
	Farwell Smith (1966-1971)

Educational Council: Maintains the Progressive Principles

The Educational Council grappled with a number of issues, but its main concern was the controversial issue of minority representation in the student body. The school philosophy stated that the composition of the student body was to be representative, but in 1936, Jewish children constituted thirty-five percent of enrollment, and the Council thought Jews were "over represented" in the school. That spring, the trustees passed a resolution to reduce admission of Jewish children to the first grade, and in November the principal reported a "reduction of the number of Jewish students by 4.2 percent." In 1941, the trustees confirmed that the school had "no hard and fast quota on Jewish students" but advised the Admissions Committee "to keep the group representative." The subject of Jewish enrollment was revisited in 1951 during a discussion about school finances—teacher salaries, tuition increases, reduction in scholarship aid, and the enrollment of more paying students. In order to achieve these goals, "the trustees would have to ignore the racial makeup of the school and allow more Jews." The matter was referred to the Executive Committee and not reported back to the trustees or the Council.[29]

In 1942, the Educational Council and the trustees reaffirmed "the principles stated by the founder of the school that there should be no color bar to enrollment." Before admitting Negro students, the school hired two "colored apprentice teachers" and asked that there be no publicity about the resolution because of "a possible misunderstanding" by the parent body about Negroes attending the Parker School. Principal Smith discussed methods for the enrollment of Negro students with Katharine Taylor '06 of Cambridge's Shady Hill School, which was also engaged in enrolling Negroes. Taylor suggested that Smith use a consultant for the families of possible applicants. "A Negro woman of distinction in the Chicago community" showed a real understanding of the problem and was extremely helpful. Negro students first enrolled in the lower school in 1944. The next year the board authorized $1,295 for a special fund for Negro students, and an anonymous donor contributed $8,000 for scholarships for Negro children. By 1945, ten Negro children were enrolled in the lower grades, and the principal established a faculty committee to advance Negro admissions and adjustments to the school. The faculty committee sought counsel and took steps to make these young people's experience satisfactory. The school's positive experience with enrolling Negro students was made the subject of a report by the National Preparatory School's Committee on Religious Education.

The Educational Council dealt with several other issues in this era—the difficulty of the teaching of opinions, the necessity of studying the Russian civilization, the Eight-Year Study, the evaluation of educational materials to determine the value of textbooks, and the use of audio visual aids. Foreign language and the introduction of the Gillingham Method in the lower school were other topics aired at Council meetings. Teacher training and the quality of student activities also occupied the Council agenda.[30] In this era, the Educational Council searched for and recommended three principals; invited and helped to organize the first Sarah Greenebaum Visitor, Ralph Tyler; and began to consider membership and reorganization of the Council in May 1964. The Educational Council was a potent force in stabilizing the school and maintaining progressive principles.

Administration: Two Principals Advance the Progressive Legacy

Two short-term principals, Raymond Osborne and Dorothy Blatter, and two long-term principals, Herbert Smith and Cleveland Thomas, headed the school throughout the Stabilizing Years. After serving as assistant principal to Miss Cooke from 1917 to 1934, Raymond Osborne was appointed principal from 1934 to 1937. During his term, he invited Dorothy Blatter to head the lower school, and later the trustees appointed her Acting Principal for school year 1937-1938. These principals governed the school when Richard Bentley and Clay Judson were board chairmen and Perry Dunlap Smith and Charlotte Kuh were Educational Council presidents.

After thirty-seven years of leadership by Flora Cooke, Raymond Osborne, and Dorothy Blatter, the school invited Herbert Smith to become the fourth principal of the Parker School. Mr. Smith became acquainted with the Parker School during the Eight-Year Study through his involvement on the Commission on Transfer to College.[31] A Harvard graduate, Smith had previously been the principal of New York's Ethical Culture School and was a knowledgeable and an experienced progressive educator.

During his administration from 1938 to 1956, he served with three board chairmen: Clay Judson, David Wallerstein, and James Weber and Educational Council presidents Helen Ross and Charlotte Kuh. Mr. Smith functioned in the Cooke tradition as the master teacher and educational leader of the school, placing greater emphasis on the pedagogical process than on the school's administrative and financial issues. Like Miss Cooke, he underscored the centrality of the teachers in the educational process. He praised the Parker faculty for its contribution and willingness to experiment in the Eight-Year Study and credited the teachers for the achievements of the students—"the intellectual curiosity of the Parker student comes in large part from the faculty . . . . The teachers do not fear to step outside the usual adult conformity in the exercise of their work."[32]

Smith's Ivy League tweed jackets and professorial appearance projected a seriousness of purpose reinforced by a certain aloofness. Tall, thin, fair-haired, and gentlemanly in demeanor, he was an available person who seemed to soften his expression only when he talked about sailing on Cape Cod or visiting some village in New England, which he loved to do. Smith was a man of integrity who handled his many responsibilities with ease and decorum.

Smith established high standards of performance for teachers and students, who considered him a rigorous and demanding teacher of the Senior Seminar on English literary classics. The seniors thought "he inspired a twelfth-grader's love for Thackeray and Frost," describing him as a person who spoke in "staccato, precise, and clear" language, covering a multiplicity of subjects with brevity. Smith's communication skills were impressive; his reports were well written and his oral presentations thorough, detailed, and documented. His high-quality preparation and presentation of ideas made him a positive role model for the students and the teachers alike.[33]

Not only was Smith an effective educational leader and teacher, but he also served as college counselor. He became principal at the close of the Eight-Year Study, when the course of study was unencumbered by college entrance requirements. As part of the experiment, the participating colleges expanded the admission requirements to include an assessment of the students' character, ability, and achievement as well as grades and test scores. With full knowledge, Smith was able to describe accurately these attributes of each student in prose statements to college admissions departments. College acceptance and performance of the graduating classes during his principalship were laudable.

In the late 1930s and the 1940s, the school was embattled by financial crises. The budget was stripped to bare essentials, but the debt mounted. The trustees reduced faculty salaries and postponed the serious repair required for the aging building. It was Principal Smith who was confronted with moving the school out of the city or affiliating it with the Girls' Chicago Latin School to remain solvent. He had to awaken the trustees, the alumni, and the parents to fundraising if they wanted the school to remain on its original site.

Smith was not prone to extend his talents to the administrative aspects of the school nor was he noted as a fundraiser, but he did effectively raise money for the first new construction since 1901—the Little School, which opened in 1942—and he did not leave a debt. The trustees then asked Mr. Smith "to take steps to free himself of daily school operation in order to concentrate on fundraising during the autumn term" to replace the old main building. His second fundraising endeavor was less satisfactory; Smith's request of $100,000 from the Ford Foundation was rejected because the foundation did not fund buildings.[34]

The Parker School recognized Mr. Smith as a successful educator, an effective college counselor, and a strong leader. Additionally, Smith provided national educational leadership. In 1942, he helped to establish the National Council of Independent Schools, which spoke for twenty-four constituent associations and represented nearly 1,000 independent schools. In 1944, Smith founded the National Registration Office to report on student performance in the thirty experimental high schools and 300 colleges that participated in the Eight-Year Study. He housed the registration office at the Parker School for almost a decade until 1953. He also established the Committee on General Composition for the College Entrance Examination in 1949 in order to supplement multiple choice questions with essay questions. He invited Parker English teacher Emily Whipple Ellison to participate with other English teachers in the country to correct the essay exams. Miss Whipple was appointed to a committee to design a new approach to correcting the essays. In 1957, Smith initiated the Ralph W. Tyler Commission Report on the Value to American Society of the Independent School, which publicized the positive results of the Eight-Year Study. Because of Smith's contributions to education an Award in Human Relations was granted to the Parker School by the Chicago Commission on Human Relations.[35]

Smith was a man with great educational authority among the independent schools in the nation and a principal who gave the progressive approach to education at the Parker School greater national status. Under Smith's leadership, the Parker School continued to be an effective progressive institution governed by the new science of education. Miss Cooke and Mrs. Blaine, who died in 1953 and 1954, respectively, saw the fruits of their experiment in educational progressivism realized during Smith's reign.

Following Smith, the Education Council recommended Cleveland Thomas to serve as the fifth principal of the Parker School. Called Gadge by his friends, Dr. Thomas was considered "a man of great promise in the educational world."[36] Between 1956 and 1966 Thomas governed with three board chairmen, Reuben Freeman, David Silberman, and Farwell

Smith, and presidents of the Educational Council Dr. Eldon Lindberg and Doris Holleb. When Thomas accepted the position, the trustees informed him that he would be the pivotal figure in fundraising for a building to replace the original old school, now fifty-five years old and a firetrap. Thomas felt optimistic about the undertaking and fully qualified to accept the challenge.

Immersed in the legacy of progressive education, Dr. Thomas had been the Dean of Faculty at North Shore Country Day School, Parker's suburban "sister school," and was therefore familiar with the school's philosophy, policies, and practices. Previously, he taught English at the Ethel Walker School for Girls and the New Canaan Day School, both in Connecticut. An English major at Antioch College, Thomas began his master's work at Harvard University and completed both his master's and doctoral degrees at Northwestern University.

Thomas was the first principal to break with the Cooke tradition of principal as headmaster. The trustees and Dr. Thomas expanded the principal's function to include educational, administrative, and financial management. The trustees charged him with the responsibility for the entire school operation from balancing the budget to fundraising. The school did not employ a business manager, but instead Margaret Lindsay, a gifted secretary, and Dr. Thomas capably managed the financial affairs of the school from Miss Lindsay's small one-desk office at the end of the administration wing. Additionally, Thomas was the admissions officer, the college counselor, an English teacher, planner of the new building, and the public relations officer.

When Dr. Thomas accepted the position, he was forty-two years old, energetic, and able to manage a broad range of responsibilities. His first goal was to improve the organizational structure of the school. He appointed one new position, a Dean of Faculty, to address personnel issues and faculty concerns, assist departments with curriculum planning, and generally to assume the educational leadership which was previously the charge of the principals. Jack Ellison, a Parker teacher since 1937, was well qualified for the position. Like Thomas, Ellison was immersed in the progressive education legacy through philosophy, education, and experience. To advance the course of study, Thomas departmentalized the high school teachers and appointed a chairperson for each department. To assist in school discipline, he organized a Committee of Four, made up of four respected, vintage gradehead teachers and the principal, responsible for student deportment. The head of lower school under Dr. Thomas was Fred Segner.

Thomas understood the importance of public relations and found the need to hire a consultant to raise the school's profile in order to attract the best candidates to fill the 200 additional places that would be made available to students by the new building. The enlarged enrollment enabled the school to increase diversity of the student body, which suggested trustee diversification. Thomas appointed the first black trustee, Mrs. Sadie Nesbitt, to the Parker Board, a long overdue decision that had a significant influence on other independent schools.

Thomas's second goal was to establish a ten-year plan for the school. The plan promoted teacher growth by establishing financial incentives for curriculum development and study, by clarifying responsibilities of the gradehead teacher versus the special teacher, and by encouraging Parker faculty to teach in university teacher-training programs in order to open the doors for more practice teachers at the school. Thomas's plan also expanded teacher in-service training and offered financial assistance for faculty publishing books and articles. Another part of the ten-year plan reconfigured the school schedule and created additional courses such as the ninth grade, team-taught media program, the eleventh grade sex education course, and the twelfth grade independent study.[37] He was also enthusiastic about the school's cooperation with public schools in joint educational programs.

Thomas kept the entire community informed through a progress report on his ten-year plan each September at the opening faculty meeting. "Determined and confident, he threw himself into the job without restraint."[38] He set a fast pace and high standards and many willing faculty followed in his footsteps. With all his other responsibilities, Thomas continued to teach. He was an English teacher with an avocation for the theater. For six months he had been a member of a Little Theater Group and when he arrived at Parker, he made drama the centerpiece of the Senior English Seminar Course, which he team-taught with drama teacher Lake Bobbitt and English teacher Marie Kirchner Stone. The senior play, as it was called, was the highlight of the senior seminar course, and all twelfth graders engaged in its production. Thomas and Stone read and analyzed the selected play with the students and then assisted the drama teacher with the rehearsal and performance. Thomas loved the Greeks and would recommend plays such as *The Orestia* or *Antigone.* The experienced drama team teacher often argued with Dr. Thomas over their different interpretations of the play, but Stone, new to the school, was quiet and learned to work hard under the demands and challenges of the principal. The seniors, bright critical thinkers with independent views, flourished in the confrontational environment.

The three teachers jointly developed an extensive course syllabus, which included Thomas's favorite *Hamlet* Project. Each year at an all-school Morning Exercise the seniors shared their interpretations of *Hamlet*, which they presented through a dramatic, musical, or artistic rendering. Linguistics was in vogue at the time, and Thomas insisted on including a unit in the syllabus. The Senior Seminar kept Thomas aware of the daily pleasures and problems of a high school teacher and acquainted him with the seniors he served as college counselor. Sharing his teaching with the school also placed Thomas on a level with other teachers, vulnerable to the same criticism or praise.

Thomas was a good decision maker. He consulted all constituencies before deciding an issue, but once he made a decision, it was not to be broken whimsically by teachers or students. Members of the community did not want to be confronted by him if they compromised his decisions. A passionate man who could be stubborn when angered, Thomas was capable of losing his temper. A short man with abundant silver hair, attractive features, and a generous smile, some compared him to Napoleon when he was angered. Thomas had a revealing face and his prominent jaw jutted out when provoked, but his eyes twinkled with joy when he was pleased. His colleagues called him "a man of passionate feeling and intellect, an idealist with a practical agenda." Dean Jack Ellison found him to be a "solemn person who knew how to laugh—life was fun." Trustees said he possessed "diplomacy, charm, and gracious patience." Parents thought that "he stood sturdily for what he believed but did not take the spotlight."[39] "He wanted his opinions and vote to carry no more weight than the newest teacher."[40]

Outside of school, Thomas became the leader of the Educational Practices Committee of the Association of Independent Schools. He was especially enthusiastic about the work of Allan Guttmacher, a sexologist who advocated a realistic and honest sex education program for the student population that appeared to be increasingly sophisticated in these decades. Thomas not only encouraged the creation of a sex education program at the Parker School, but he also brought sex education to the attention of the principals of other independent schools in the Chicago area. Thomas was a man with courage who tackled controversial issues.

Among Thomas's numerous accomplishments was his ability to raise money in order to build "a handsome new $2,500,000 building on the same North Side site" as the original building. According to Thomas, vital were the $750 loans from parents, which provided "the highest order of parent participation of any school I have ever known." When Harvard University's Dean John Monro spoke at the opening ceremony of the new building, he commented, "The parents could feel confident of a sound investment . . . I have never known a dull boy to come to us from Parker. They all care a lot about something that really matters."[41]

Thomas worked long hours but still managed time for his children— Tony '62, Jock '62, and Kim '68. Like their father, the Thomas children were engaged in the arts, especially drama and writing. Kim often wrote and published poems in *Prints*, the Parker literary magazine. The demands of Thomas's position were astronomical, and in 1967 he died suddenly, still a vibrant young man, while on a college counseling trip in the East. He had made the new building possible, expanded and strengthened the faculty, offered new and enriched curriculum, and enlarged the student body without losing the essential character of the school or diluting its tested principles. The 1962 building is testimony to only one of his many contributions to the school.

High School Experiment: The Eight-Year Study (1932-1940)

In the Pioneering Years, the high school course of study did not receive the same experimental attention as did the lower school because college requirements restricted the teachers' freedom to determine the curriculum. Then, in the spring of 1930, 200 teachers assembled in the nation's capital to consider how America's secondary schools might better serve young people. The Progressive Education Association, with financial support from the Carnegie Foundation, the federal government, the Parker School, and two other participating schools introduced an Eight-Year Study on the Relationship of School and College to find an answer.

The Eight-Year Study (1932-1940) was the largest study of secondary education in America. Its two major purposes were "to establish a relationship between the school and college that would permit and encourage reconstruction in the secondary school and to learn, through exploration and experimentation, how high schools in the United States could serve youth more effectively."[42] In the Study, 1,475 students from thirty experimental high schools were matched with their counterparts from traditional schools. The Study traced, measured, and compared student performances in college. The matched pairs of students were evaluated for different periods—the 1936 graduates were compared for four years of college, the 1937 graduates for three years, the 1938 graduates for two years, and the class entering in 1939 for one year.[43] For the duration of the Study, these colleges accepted students from the experimental schools without the usual entrance requirements.

The Eight-Year Study engaged about fifty nationally recognized professionals representing education, curriculum, and measurement. The founding twenty-eight commission members, including Parkerites Perry Dunlap Smith '06, Katharine Taylor '06, and Flora Cooke, helped to originate and organize the Study. In 1933, they gave full responsibility and authority for the supervision of it to a sixteen-member Directing Committee chaired by Wilford Aikin, the Director of the Study, and Ralph Tyler, Research Director. Participants included the Committee on Evaluation and Recording, the Evaluation Staff, the faculty of participating schools, and the authors and coauthors of the five volumes that reported the Study.

As Tyler was talking with Hilda Taba, an Eight-Year Study curriculum consultant, late one afternoon, he sketched a design for the Study on a napkin.[44] Tyler's diagram guided the experimenters through a four-step sequence. First, the faculty used the school philosophy combined with psychology and sociology as a filter for selecting and determining the society-, child-, and subject-centered objectives they wished to achieve; second, they established and implemented the learning experiences that would achieve these objectives; third, they organized the learning experiences so learning could be transferred both vertically and horizontally; and fourth, they evaluated the achievement of the objectives by pre- and post-testing. Tyler's four new questions became known as the Tyler Rationale, which made evaluation an integral part of developing a curriculum scientifically.

The Parker teachers wrote a philosophical statement and established goals and objectives. The statement began with the quotations from Francis Parker on education, community, character, and citizenry that were used as epigrams in the *Catalogue and Course of Study* (see Figure 6.1). The teachers adapted a philosophical statement which was appropriate for the 1930s:

> We of the Francis W. Parker School believe in the democratic way of life, holding that democracy gives each individual the maximum responsibility for the well-being of all. The functions of a school in a democracy are threefold: (1) it interprets the dominant characteristics of the world, (2) it transmits . . . the cultural heritage of this environment; (3) it points the way to further possibilities in this society for human development—physical, mental, economic, aesthetic, and ethical . . . We hold that the tradition of American democracy must be extended by new ideas and ideals . . . pointing the way to further possibilities for human development.[45]

Based on this philosophy, the faculty established eight overriding goals that the Parker School wanted to develop: (1) an improved living standard, (2) employment in productive work, (3) conservation of material and human resources, (4) cooperative planning, (5) training for leisure, (6) participation in the arts, (7) reason and arbitration to replace force in disputes, and (8) the application of scientific thinking for solutions to individual and social problems. The teachers identified society-, child-, and subject-centered objectives that would support the goals. The four societal objectives were cooperation, participation in community problems, involvement in democratic processes, and insurance of a diverse student body; the three child-centered goals were achieving a better understanding of each child, finding ways to discuss psychological problems, and providing a changing environment for different age levels; and the three overarching subject-centered objectives were creating critical thinkers, applying interdisciplinary organization of subjects, and using different forms of expression.

Each department assumed some or all of these objectives and additionally established its own subset that supported the overarching subject-centered goals.[46]

In this process, the history teachers abandoned the traditional history courses and required a six-year sequence in social studies for students from Grades 7-12. Seventh through ninth grades focused on world history, including the Orient; and tenth through twelfth grades used their world history background to analyze the development of political, economic, and international democracy.

The English teachers directed reading to what literature could contribute to a broader and deeper understanding of human behavior. Writing was taught for application in a variety of disciplines, and research techniques were taught for social studies, foreign language, and English. The most experimental English course was a motion picture project in which juniors and seniors between 1937 and 1939 produced fifty-seven short films on human relations and edited them to provoke discussion by church groups, labor unions, public schools, and colleges.[47] The analysis of propaganda was added as the basis for some units of study in English classes.

Although the physical sciences, modern languages, Latin, and the arts made changes to meet the eight new goals, mathematics and physical education did little to revamp their courses. Built on the eighth experimental goal, "the application of scientific thinking," science teachers chose an experimental approach that distinguished the department and made critical thinking the pervasive pedagogy in high school courses. The science teachers also framed the physical and biological sciences in a moral and social context by correlating science with social sciences long before it became fashionable. The science department added electives, designating two "leisure periods" a week to allow laboratory time and help sessions for students. Each general science and biology class took five to eight field trips per year and viewed six to ten films. Science made the most major changes, which resulted in a high-profile science department that had great influence on other subjects.[48] Changes in one department meant changes in other departments because an effective curriculum is a unified one.

The modern language teachers broadened their scope beyond language study and made every attempt to combine foreign language, English, the arts, and social sciences. The experimental work in modern languages was based on three aims: "(1) mastery of the language, (2) an introduction to a foreign country and its civilization, and (3) a better understanding and appreciation of English."[49] Some of the teachers were native speakers. Two native German speakers—Thea Scherz and the world-renowned psychologist Alfred Adler—offered German I, II, and III. Dr. Adler also offered Experimental Work in Latin. Lura Smith taught four years of Latin with the senior year considered "college preparatory." Barney Negronida offered Spanish I, II, and III and three years of French. French students learned to research and write in French and read their French long themes at Morning Exercises to an audience that sat quietly and listened, although fewer than fifty students understood the language. Each teacher adapted his course differently to meet the overarching subject-centered goals and the departmental objectives.

Always central to the Parker School curriculum, the performing and visual arts faculty was now free to experiment. Two of the eight experimental goals—training for leisure and participation in the arts—encouraged additions to and improvements in the arts department such as the construction of an art gallery, the creation of a corridor-wall timeline of the history of education from primitive man to Francis Parker, an introduction to movie making, and increased correlation between the arts and foreign languages and between the arts and social studies. The objective of the fine arts in foreign languages and social studies was to compare American and foreign cultures through drama, music, and the visual arts. The success of the new emphasis placed on the arts in the high school was validated when the Class of 1940 replaced the usual commencement speaker with a performance of Beethoven's *Appassionata* Piano Sonata, opus 57.[50]

On another level, new classes and programs helped to attain child-centered objectives. A new psychology class provided students with a theoretical perspective to discuss psychological problems. The invention of the graderoom and the advisory system allowed for the students to discuss group and personal problems respectively. The ninth through twelfth grade students met in separate graderooms daily to discuss community and specific grade issues such as ninth grade adjustment to high school or senior graduation. The high school advisory system addressed individual differences among students and offered individual pupils guidance and direction. To create an advisory group, one teacher was assigned a small group of students from all high school grades for four years.

The Eight-Year Study was the first authentic research designed for high schools by professional curriculum planners and an evaluation team. Many advantages accrued to the participating schools. The Study enabled an exchange about curriculum among the teachers of the thirty participating experimental schools. Within the school, it eliminated department barriers through the correlation of subjects and interdisciplinary teaching. The faculty captured their work in five lengthy and detailed annual *Reports of Experimental Work,* which the school published between 1936 and 1941.[51]

The results of the Study were manifold. New content was added in social studies, English, the arts, sciences, and foreign languages. The school introduced new strategies for pupil guidance—namely, the graderoom, the advisory system, and a psychology class. The teachers used new evaluation methods to check on the students' factual material, attitudes, beliefs, and scientific thinking. The main effect on the students was that "they automatically relate everything they see and hear to its effect on human beings."[52] Additionally, the graduates of the thirty progressive high schools fared well in college. When compared to graduates of traditional schools, students from progressive schools:

1. Earned slightly higher grades in all subjects
2. Received slightly more academic honors in each year
3. Were more often judged to possess a high degree of intellectual curiosity and drive as well as precise, systematic, and objective thinking
4. Demonstrated a high degree of resourcefulness
5. Participated somewhat more frequently in the arts and enjoyed them more
6. Participated more in all organized student groups except religious and "service" activities
7. Earned a higher percentage of non-academic honors (officership in organizations, roles in plays and musicals, etc.)
8. Demonstrated a more active concern for what was going on in the world.[53]

Parker graduates performed particularly well: (1) fewer participated in organized activities than in the larger group but when they did they achieved distinction, (2) most made superior adjustment to college life in contrast to their counterparts, (3) most described their school experiences as 'superior preparation for college,' and (4) sixty-three percent placed in the highest category in intellectual achievement versus thirty-nine percent of the comparison group. The performance of the Parker School graduates made a positive statement about progressive education.[54] About the Parker School and its role in the Eight-Year Study, Tyler wrote:

> The school was a leader in the study. It worked out educational proce-
> dures which served effectively to develop students who were devoted to
> democratic principles, who were able to think critically and who partic-
> ipated constructively in community life . . . and in the improvement of
> American education, both public and private.[55]

Ralph Tyler's background and training as a curricularist and statistician qualified him to be an excellent choice for the Research Director of the Eight-Year Study. After teaching high school, Tyler earned his doctoral degree in statistics at the University of Chicago in 1926. He was research assistant at the Bureau of Educational Research at Ohio State University when he was invited to serve as Research Director. This appointment earned him national prominence because of its focus on the controversy between progressive and traditional education and because of the first application of the Tyler Rationale. His Eight-Year Study design resulted in a course syllabus which Tyler then taught at the University of Chicago. Eventually his work became the book, *The Basic Principles of Curriculum and Instruction* (1949) which was published in nine editions and several languages. An authority in the field of education stated, "If for no other reason than establishing a scientific method of evaluation, Tyler's contribution to American education and to the field of curriculum must be considered significant and of lasting importance." After the Study, Tyler held several positions at the University of Chicago— University Examiner and Dean of the Division of Social Science between 1938 and 1953.[56] During this period, the Parker School remained one of his major interests, and Tyler made himself readily available to serve as a Distinguished Visitor to examine the school and to consult with the faculty and administration in 1963. As a member of the Educational Council from 1968 until 1990, he also engaged the middle school faculty in a national research project on experiential learning, which resulted in an effective community service program, the foundation of today's program.

Parker High School teachers contributed greatly to the Eight-Year Study. Miss Cooke invited history teacher Hazel Cornell to become the in-school chairperson because of her leadership qualities, her grasp of progressive principles, and her knowledge of the school's philosophy. Miss Cornell directed all departments in their development of curriculum, met annually with the Commission, and assisted in the preparation of the *Curriculum Reports* and in the evaluation of students. The task was a large one, but she met it with steadfast earnestness.

Miss Cornell, considered a "simply sensational" teacher by her eleventh and twelfth grade history students, possessed the talent of transforming history texts into life and making historical figures into flesh and blood. She was an intellectual with a broad and deep understanding of the nature of history and the way it functioned as a discipline. Her genius as a teacher was her ability to convey her grasp and appreciation of history to students whether in fourth, sixth, seventh grades or in high school. Her thematic approach to teaching history was a break from traditional chronology. For example, the seventh grade class "traced city government through the ages from Thebes and Rome to London and Chicago."

During her thirty-two years at the Parker School between 1917 and 1949, Cornell taught modern and ancient history and civics. Her definition of teaching was "seeing a mind awaken." Her ramrod-straight carriage symbolized her attitude toward discipline in class. A strong advocate of progressive education, Cornell joined several other Parker faculty as a member of the staff of the Graduate Teachers College of Winnetka to train progressive educators. With Miss Cooke, Cornell traveled in 1929 to attend international educational conferences. Characterized as "brilliant, witty, blithe, curious, and wise," Miss Cornell was a woman of great moral dignity who imparted her high sense of ethics to students and colleagues alike.[57]

Vintage Teachers: Transfer the Progressive Legacy

The end of the Great Depression, the destruction caused by World War II, and the cultural upheaval in society were events that dramatically changed the nation between 1935 and 1965. The school itself also underwent a transformation caused by the construction of two new buildings and the sharp rise in enrollment as the Stabilizing Years came to a close. The newly enlarged student body and the effectively developed high school curriculum caused the school to function in ways that began to differ from the smaller and more familiar school of the earlier era. In this era, the teachers slowly retreated from the vital principle of collaborating as a full faculty and began to develop curriculum in smaller groups. The results were deleterious to a cohesive progressive curriculum, and by 1950 the K-12 curriculum began to show weaknesses. The lower school teachers permitted the central subjects to stagnate. Their approach was to add new isolated courses that fragmented the curriculum in the lower grades. The high school teachers focused almost entirely on the Eight-Year Study from 1932 through the 1960s, when the Distinguished Visitors became available to consult with them (see Chapter 8).

The full faculty had not produced a new *Catalogue and Course of Study* since 1930. The old *Catalogue* had presented the course of study by grade level and by department. Instead of reinforcing each other as anticipated, the grade level horizontal and the department level vertical sequence created a reverse effect. Now lower school teachers worked independently and outside of departments while the high school teachers used the departmental approach solely. These fissures were the beginning of the great divide in curriculum development in the school as a whole. When developed in isolation, the curriculum slowly translated into curriculum divisions among lower, high, and eventually middle school. Students learned lessons when presented in a sequence spiraling to more and more levels of complexity. In the absence of curriculum coordination, the students themselves were put in the position of transferring learning from course to course. The increasing absence of full faculty meetings designated for curriculum development of the Grades K-12 Course of Study detracted from the first contribution that the Parker School made to curriculum in the Pioneering Years. The teachers neglected Comenius's advice in *The Great Didactic*. "Nature does not rush life, proceeds in order, does not take leaps but develops from within, completes all acts, and avoids all obstacles" (see Chapter 3).

The faculty learned several lessons. They learned that it was difficult to sustain strength across all areas of the school. As one division in the school gained strength, another division weakened. For example, an improved high school curriculum resulted in a less effective lower school curriculum. Additions to the lower school course of study were made only as new discoveries about learning indicated, such as the Gillingham Reading Program adopted in 1950 to assist the learning disabled. The faculty also learned that new and experimental courses were more successful than the repeated courses. A greater emphasis on administrative matters resulted in diminished attention to educational issues. Finally, the new focus on academic subjects diminished the role of student activities.

In spite of the national and school transformations, the faculty remained a stable cohesive group that relied on a shared vision of an acknowledged progressive philosophy, proven pedagogical principles, and the uninterrupted transfer of the school's legacy from the vintage teachers to new hires.

To train the "new guard" of teachers, the school continued to rely heavily on vintage Parker teachers. Fortunately, a sizable nucleus of experienced teachers was available to pass on the legacy. Although twenty-five teachers resigned or retired when Miss Cooke resigned in 1934, others who began between 1910 and 1930 remained to train teachers in the Stabilizing Years. By this time, the vintage teachers understood the ingredients of an effective faculty in a progressive school. The finest teacher candidates were what Francis Parker referred to as "cultured," and able to socialize with all types of students—lower and upper class, minority and majority, male and female. They were educated broadly in the arts and sciences and knowledgeable in at least one but preferably two disciplines. Teachers holding advanced degrees and conversant in the fields of education, psychology, and sociology could experiment, evaluate, and research. Those who were not qualified to lead in these areas needed to be able to interpret the findings of educational research.

The school sought candidates who could move beyond their conventional roles. Pivotal to a Parker teacher's effectiveness was thorough preparation of the course syllabus and the daily lesson plans so that students were aware of class objectives, that is, where they were going intellectually. Of equal importance was the teacher's knowledge of the student's background, attitude, achievement, interests, talents, and weaknesses—all necessary to arrange for flexibility in instruction. To achieve this goal, teacher candidates needed to commit to knowing the students and their parents by reading the records, supervising outside class activities, and being a presence in the school before, during, and after hours.

To help new teachers adjust to and advance in the school environment, the vintage teachers were appointed as critic teachers. Some conducted new teachers' meetings on school philosophy, principles, and policy, and all used classroom observations to demonstrate pedagogy. Vintage Parker teachers were respected and lauded for their accurate and reflected judgment and their willingness to admit teacher error. They were responsible and organized, followed through on promises, returned assignments promptly, and kept engagements with students and colleagues.

Teachers had to possess skills that enabled them to be a faculty of the whole. They had to communicate and collaborate, an essential for curriculum development, team teaching, and experimentation. They also had to be able to give and take criticism and to share their ideas. Experience proved that often teachers jealously guarded their ideas from colleagues. It seemed that a student's praise for one teacher was an unintended insult to another. Such misinterpretations had to be transcended by the younger faculty. Teachers also had to learn to compliment one another and to gain perspective. It was a rare teacher who did not think him or herself to be a good teacher.

The emotional investment of teachers in their students coupled with the students' burning desire to succeed produced a breathtaking chemistry. At its greatest, it brought out the best in both parties—the ability to initiate and guide and the ability to absorb and be shaped. The relationship raised the stakes and elevated the pupil's performances to levels the student might not have aspired to on his or her own. Inevitably this meant much was at stake for both parties. Success rebounded to the enduring credit of both mentor and pupil; failure was defeat and humiliation for both. The pleasure of the successes more than compensated for the occasional failure.

Ten vintage teachers spanned the Stabilizing Years and transmitted the Parker legacy to the teachers of the next era. Foreign language teacher Barney Negronida served from 1929 to 1970. Eggert Meyer's tenure spanned the Stabilizing Years from 1934 to 1967, during which time he taught biology, sex education, was the eleventh grade gradehead, and a member of the Disciplinary Committee of Four. Music teacher Chauncey Griffith carried on the legacy from 1935 to 1972. Karl Long '13 was remembered by students and teachers alike for teaching physical education for a quarter of a century from 1935 to 1959. In the lower school, Clare Lyden established the new kindergarten and taught five-year-olds at Parker from 1935 to 1966. Hope Hambright taught and trained kindergarten assistants from 1948 to 1974, and fourth grade teacher Lynn Martin taught and trained lower school assistants from 1946 to 1976. In 1945, Damon Barnes joined the staff to teach English and Latin and serve as sophomore gradehead until 1966. Mathematics teacher Barr McCutcheon x44 joined the faculty in 1949 and remained until 1998.

Between 1935 and 1972, Chauncey Griffith was Mr. Music at the Parker School. For thirty-five years, he taught hundreds of students to learn how to sing and more importantly from his perspective, how to listen to music. He formed his philosophy of teaching music based more "on what the music does to the students than what the students do to the music." He challenged the chorus to sing selections that most high school music teachers would consider beyond the students' abilities. Mr. Griffith defied his slogan, "never repeat any song," after a student performance of "The Messiah" for Christmas in 1947. "What the music did to the students" caused Mr. Griffith to permit its repetition once every three years to give everyone over seventh grade a chance to sing it twice. In school, he conducted special music classes and full chorus in the auditorium with the assistance of all of the faculty. He also served outside of Parker as the Music Director for the Fourth Presbyterian Church.[58]

Lynn Martin was hired in 1946 to teach junior kindergarten. Her thirty years at the Parker School earned her the reputation of being among the finest of the school's teachers. Following the legacy of Mary Davis, she began teaching fourth grade in 1953. She immersed twenty-three fourth grade classes in the study of ancient Greece. The nine-year-olds entered the classroom unable to locate Greece on the map and exited with a life-long knowledge, appreciation, and love for all things Greek. What the fourth graders learned about Greek government, arts, drama, and debate they carried with them a lifetime—to a ninth-grade literature class on the *Odyssey*, to a twelfth-grade performance of *The Orestia*, to a college Greek literature course, and on their travels to Greece.

Lynn Martin's image and style were unique—she could not be emulated. A tall thin woman with a knot of salt and pepper hair at the nape of her neck, she was learned, tough, accomplished, and unrelenting. Her demeanor was serene and stern, but her touch, her smile, and her deep caring were soft and belied that regal exterior. She would readily challenge the opposition in an educational debate when she was curriculum coordinator and later head of the lower school. In 1982, Mrs. Martin was invited to be president of the Educational Council, where one of her pithy well-thought-out statements on education, deftly delivered, could overwhelm its members. Her teaching assistants were awed by her performance as a teacher and grateful to her for sharing her talent. Her colleagues and students appreciated her commitment to the school and her friendship.[59]

A native of Marseilles, France, Barney Negronida was hired in 1929 to teach French and Spanish. A tall, dignified handsome man, Mr. Negronida was reserved, proper, and traditional in his tastes. In his sports jacket pocket, he always carried a three-by-five note card with a neat list of responsibilities for the day. As he completed the tasks, he would check each one off. No matter the hour, if the check list was incomplete, Mr. Negronida remained at school.

The school relied on him and assigned him a multiplicity of positions. Each morning he conducted the senior grade meeting, which placed him in charge of twelfth grade activities and graduation. After graderoom, he taught foreign language and mathematics, and in late afternoons he was the physical education teacher until it was time to coach football in the fall and basketball in the winter. As a member of the disciplinary Committee of Four, he signed students' notes with the letter "J," taken from his initials BJN, which he joked stood for "Jack of all trades." During the summers, Mr. Negronida ran the summer day camp.

Mr. Negronida had as many names as he had positions. The students affectionately referred to him as Barney, the athletes called him Coach, and he called himself a "Dutch uncle," perhaps because he was available to help, consoling teachers and students while giving advice. Several years before he retired, he served the school in yet another capacity, as the boy's college counselor and the Dean of Faculty. Throughout his forty-one years at Parker, he exuded a deep care and love of the school, where his wife Virginia Beard '31 taught and his four children graduated.[60]

Many faculty remained at the school for extended periods of time and sometimes at great personal expense. Teachers were inspired by the school's philosophy, the development of their own potential for growth in an experimental atmosphere, and the students' engagement in the life of the school. Francis Parker believed in high salaries for teachers and wanted to pay teachers whatever was required to attract them. As Parker stated, "There is not a coin small enough, ever stamped by the hand of man, to pay the salary of a poor teacher; there is not gold enough in the mines of the world to measure the value of a teacher who lifts the souls of children to the true dignity of life and living."[61] Although Board President Richard Bentley verbally reinforced this commitment in 1933, twice the trustees reduced teachers' salaries, once by ten percent, which forced the teachers to consider unionizing. Ironically, it was the faculty who subsidized the scholarship program by their low salaries, which counted for a greater percentage of the scholarship aid than the amount contributed collectively by the alumni, the parents, and trustees. Several teachers were willing to sacrifice their livelihoods, accept low wages, postpone retirement like Miss Cooke, or work until illness overcame them like Mr. Osborne.

During the Stabilizing Years, Principal Smith captured the Parker faculty in these words:

> The standards of the faculty were extremely high. They showed an unusual willingness to spend time and effort in order to produce quality. The intellectual curiosity which Parker students have traditionally shown existed in the faculty and doubtless came in large part from them . . . . They were firm supporters of academic freedom and did not fear to step outside the usual adult conformity in the exercise of their work.[62]

The two new buildings in 1941 and 1962 meant increased student enrollment, which resulted in an increased teaching staff. Twelve teacher assistants were added in the lower school. Two Negro apprentices were hired in 1943 to help newly enrolled Negro students adjust to the school community. The expanded faculty required more new teacher meetings, more observation, and more curriculum meetings.

The Parker teachers fulfilled the school's original purpose—"to educate children" and "to train teachers" by teaching progressive educators for the nation at Roosevelt University, Pestalozzi, and the Graduate Teachers College of Winnetka, where several teachers earned advanced degrees— Alfred Adler, Merlin Bowen, Ruth Byrnes, Eggert Meyers, Jack Ellison, Barr McCutcheon x44, and others.

Students: "The Quiet Struggle"

In the 1930s, the student body was joyfully oblivious to the financial difficulties that plagued the school and nearly closed its doors permanently. As far as the students knew, "the great experiment" was continuing unchallenged and meeting more and more of their expectations. Yet student life during the Stabilizing Years was a dimmer version of the Pioneering Years, as the activities surrounding the central subjects for lower school pupils decreased in number and intensity and the central subject diminished as an organizing "doctrine."[63]

In the lower school, "learning by doing" still dominated the noisy corridors filled with happy children and the activity-centered classrooms of productive students. Third graders chatted in small groups as they sat on the floor sewing beads on their originally designed Indian headbands. Fires, a theme in Chicago history since the Great Fire of 1871, became a topic of a physics study after the second graders notified city officials about a fire they saw from their classroom window. Field trips to the Bowman Dairy Farm, the Salerno Cookie Factory, Marshall Field's Department Store, the famous Wrigley Building, and the Water System Plant continued to be favored by lower school pupils. Theatrical performances were highlights. For example, in 1948, the eighth grade performed an original play about civil rights, a topic of rising interest in the nation and one studied in class. In 1957, the fourth graders performed their own version of *Antigone*. Life for these lower school youngsters had not changed appreciably except that their numbers had increased because of the new pupils enrolled in the wartime nursery school and the addition of a junior kindergarten now housed in a new "Little School."

The upper classmen, like the younger children, continued to live activity-centered school lives, but activities occupied less of their time. The irony of the Eight-Year Study was that instead of freeing students from the dominance of colleges, it increased the emphasis on college. The Eight-Year Study inadvertently shifted Parker's dual emphasis on classes and activities by elevating the classroom and making nonclassroom activities of lesser importance. The high school students were highly interested in the curricular experiment and in the new and increased courses and were now more motivated toward academic achievement than before the Eight-Year Study. The reasons were unclear. Perhaps it was the students' way of proving to colleges that progressive education at the Parker School was effective.

The *Weekly* labeled the high school students' struggle between activities and academics "the quiet struggle" because although college pressure was increasing, neither parents nor teachers seemed aware. College admission was no longer automatic, as it had been in their parents' era, and after the Eight-Year Study, college competition accelerated as more high school graduates and veterans applying with the G.I. Bill of Rights competed for places in college. The persistence of the "quiet struggle" became manifest as the high school students dropped old activities, changed activities, added a few new ones, and participated less and less.

The student government was a shadow of its predecessor. Student government presidents Carl Stern '33, Abbott Patterson '33, Ernest Jaffee '42, Tom Cottle '55, Rozell Nesbitt '62, and others struggled over the three and a half decades to organize an effective student government. Student government reorganized almost every other year and the constitution was completely rewritten time after time. Turmoil within the government and friction between students and faculty over the students' capability to self-govern made students apathetic. In 1941, a student expressed the general opinion when he said, "Ah heck, another student government. Well, I can do my homework." In 1942, student government had power struggles with the faculty disciplinary Committee of Four, which gradually usurped responsibilities of the student government by dispensing punishments for such infractions as smoking, theft, idleness, and lack of courtesy. The infractions became more serious in the 1960s, and the faculty challenged the students' capacity to deal with them. Only when the students gained control of student finances did they earn a somewhat stronger voice in deliberations with the faculty.

The students' frequent attempts at an honor system or self-government were a failure in practice if not in philosophy. In 1958, the faculty instigated deficiency slips called Blue Slips and Yellow Slips. Both indicated substandard performance, meant a loss of student privileges, and required attendance in study halls, which were monitored in the early decades by students and later by teachers. These changes tilted the balance of power toward the authority of the faculty and away from the democracy of the students, signifying failure in the implementation of Francis Parker's assertion that community life was "that state of society in which every individual member orders his conduct with reference to the good of the whole; the whole being constituted as to necessitate the highest development of the members." These agenda items remained unresolved until the end of the era: student- versus faculty-run study halls, the inefficiency of committees, and the penalization of students with excessive cuts and tardies. Lack of student accountability often reigned unchecked by the faculty supervisors. One question persisted among the student body—what was the reason for the continuance of student self-rule? Without addressing the problem, a major pedagogical principle was permitted to exist as a sham.

Student publications also became a shadow of their past and did not live up to the high standards of the Pioneering Years. At the onset of the era, funds were tight, and equipment was becoming dilapidated. For several years, the *Weekly* continued to meet the Monday deadline but with limited editions of two pages. As student interest dwindled, so did the *Weekly* staff. One editorial stated the case succinctly with the headline, "Fate of Parker *Weekly* Up to the School." Although the *Weekly* published its one-thousandth issue in 1950, it remained a touch-and-go operation until student apathy changed to engagement in societal issues and added articles on "*Brown versus the Board of Education*," "School Integration," "The Soviet Education System," and "The Danger of World Overpopulation." School issues always remained grist for the mill for editors Kathryn Kenley '62, Laurence Kirshbaum '62, James Schwartz '62, Karen Friedman '62, and photographer George Grossman '62. By 1967, the *Weekly* again seemed to be on the rise.

In the 1930s, *Record* editors Frank Rothschild '32 and Jane Dahl '33 found money scarce and student participation low. In 1939, the *Record* had its first deficit. During World War II, the *Record* staff kept its budget to a minimum. As a financial strategy, in 1952 the students separated the yearbook into three separate editions for fall, winter, and spring. Two years later, the *Record* and *Weekly* editors brainstormed for new ideas with other schools at the annual interschool conference. Throughout the late fifties and early sixties, the *Record*, led by George Basch '55, Margaret Abbott

'62, and Charles Heineman '62, continued to experience peaks and slumps. The quality of the *Record* depended on funding, the dedication of the student heads, and student involvement. As much as the editors tried, the *Record* during this period suffered from a lower standard in content, a reduced number of pages, blurred photography, and an unimaginative if not disorganized format.

Other publications were also doomed by the "quiet struggle." After a dormant period, a literary magazine called *Parker Prints* was revived by the tenth graders and edited by Parke Rhymer '55 and others. By the end of the era, the publication was functional because the junior English class was now accountable for its quality and survival. As in the Pioneering Years, the successful model for an activity-centered school was to place academics at the center and combine activities as the second concentric circle. Strong leadership and supervision by a teacher was a prerequisite for the success of the activity. Ironically, the students chose as supervisors teachers who had a hands-off policy.

Participation in the performing arts activities sustained, bolstered by an effective link between academics and activities. Play performance remained associated with the Senior English Seminar, a new Glee Club and the orchestra became extensions of the music appreciation classes, and the new Motion Picture Project offered by the English Department in the Eight-Year Study stimulated a Cinema Guild.

The students organized the school's annual traditions with their usual rigor. Staunch against changing any aspect of the County Fair, May Day, Field Day, Big Brothers and Sisters, students made it difficult for the faculty to propose even minor changes like combining May Day and Field Day into a Spring Class Day. To students, the traditions embodied the school of the past, which they wanted to remember.

In 1955 the tradition of the Morning Exercise changed for the first time in fifty-four years when assemblies were reduced from five twenty-minute periods to four twenty-five minute periods a week. Increasingly, Morning Exercises topics reflected concerns over world issues—a social studies teacher spoke about Los Alamos, where the atomic bomb had been tested, a guest speaker addressed his six-year experience teaching at a communist school in China, and Registrar Polly Root Collier described her travels in Korea. Morning Exercise continued to feature the arts—a Russian composer, Kabuki dancers, and the Chicago symphony entertained for the assembly. Studs Terkel presented the history of jazz, and movie cinematographer Haskell Wexler '40 talked about prejudice during his life in Europe. The difficult task of organizing the schedule and the production of Morning Exercise was effectively undertaken by Joan Makler '55, Ann Voynow '55, Steve Ungar '62, and others during the era. Throughout the second era, the Morning Exercise continued to be an important activity for the students because it provided a connection with the entire school.

Some activities were transformed during this period. When the Forum was an active organization, it was led by Robert Weisert '33 and Alexander MacAvinche '33. It later evolved into a drama showcase and a talent show and merged in the 1960s with the Drama Association. Students also joined committees outside of the school—the American Student Union began in 1938, the Liberal's Club became a popular organization in World War II, and after the war, the War Work Committee, the Relief Committee, and the Inter-School Relations League flourished. Some students revitalized a Social Service Committee for community service in 1955.

One activity that improved in this era was athletics. New sports were added and popularity increased. In the 1930s and early 1940s, the boys earned league championships in football and basketball, helped by Richard Mavis '33, Seymour Kalom '33, John Ashby '42, and Jerry Wexler '42. Boys' baseball and boys' softball teams also grew in importance. Between 1941 and 1943, the school introduced track, tennis, swim, and crew teams for the boys, but their sporadic existence depended upon the talent and interest of students in a given year. In 1945, a boys' golf team was begun but struggled from lack of interest and talent. Football, led by Joseph Haroutunian '62 and Robert Corkran '62, was made compulsory for all high school boys in 1967. Six Parker players made the all-league team, and the football team won the Independent School League title that year. In the late fifties, boys' basketball and boys' tennis met with great success. In 1959, a boys' soccer team was introduced. By 1968, the boys participated in varsity and junior varsity soccer, football, basketball, and baseball teams, and a very strong track team.

Girls' sports also advanced during the Stabilizing Years. While intramural play continued, a new and stronger Girls' Athletics League established interscholastic play. The girls successfully scheduled games with

North Shore School, Latin School, and University High School in basketball and field hockey, led in 1962 by Constance Shirakawa '62. Four
Parker girls made the all-Chicago hockey team in 1939. The girls elected
cheerleaders, agitated for increased gym time, and arranged their own
version of a stag dinner. Because of a dearth of funds, the school did not
purchase new athletic uniforms.

During this era, the dress code changed as students gradually gained
more freedom. In 1934, the uniform for girls from fifth to twelfth grade
was a navy blue skirt or jumper, a white blouse, and a navy blue cardigan
available at Marshall Field's Department Store. Conspicuous jewelry, cosmetics, colored belts, bandannas, shoes without socks, and high heels were
not allowed. By 1945, girls could wear red, light blue, or yellow sweaters.
The next year, make-up, colored socks, colored belts, and colored scarves
were allowed. By the end of the era, restrictions were so relaxed that it was
difficult to tell that there was a uniform. The boys had no official uniform,
but they tended to follow the clothing trends of the times. The sport coats,
ties, and jackets of the 1930s and 1940s became blue jeans and T-shirts in
the 1950s and 1960s.

Social life at the Parker School, unless related to school activities, was
considered a major weakness. Students complained about "the lack of
enthusiasm" for school events, about cliques, about the exclusion of non-
Parkerites in social life, and about the formality of social occasions.
Dances played a major role in the students' social life, and each high
school grade sponsored one. The dances were usually held in the lunchroom, sometimes decorated by the organizing committee. Some festivities
were held in the small gym. The students preferred the "get together" after
a team victory to an expensive prom.

The "quiet struggle" between academics and activities challenged the
philosophy of the school. The Educational Council discussed the problems
but provided no solutions. The faculty was oblivious to the shift away
from activities. The paradox was that inadvertently the Eight-Year Study
imposed college dominance on the Parker curriculum. When the student
body moved away from participation in the activities in which principles
from classes were implemented into action, it was the beginning of a sub-
tle first step back to a more traditional school. Activities no longer met the
philosophical criteria of the school—they did not encourage responsible

citizenship, the creation of the community, or social motive. Without classroom affiliation, teacher supervision, and school support, the activity-centered school could no longer claim that students were "learning by doing." Activities assumed a new and different meaning when colleges wanted student transcripts to indicate student participation in "extra-curricular activities." The students then enrolled in more activities, but their participation was often mere lip service.

A 1955 alumni questionnaire confirmed that students appreciated their years at Parker. Eighty percent of the 364 respondees answered "yes" to the question, "Would you prefer a Parker School type of education for your own children?" The reasons for their preference included: "gives attention to the individual's talents and abilities," "arouses intellectual interest and a questioning attitude," "encourages independent thought," "offers diverse activities," "provides good college preparation," "holds high academic standards," "liberal with freedom of expression," "friendly relationship with an excellent faculty," and "a sense of responsibility to self and community." When asked, "In what way was your Parker education significant?" Seventy percent answered their education in the arts and literature, sixty-six percent named their relationships with ethnic groups, and fifty-one percent identified their involvement in civic affairs. These alumni commented that "the school helped me develop the ability to face perplexity without dismay"; "the school associated freedom with obligation"; "taught me that it was more intelligent to understand than to scorn"; and "made me highly critical."[64]

College presidents and deans wrote in laudatory terms about the achievements and performances of the Parker graduates. The Dean of Admissions of the Massachusetts Institute of Technology wrote, "The most direct evidence I can address about the work of the [Parker] school has to do with students who have come to us. Over a period of eighteen years, we have had a group which, almost without exception, has been outstanding." Professor A.C. Hanford of Harvard University wrote, "A study of the records . . . from Francis W. Parker School shows that students have been eager, possessed of strong intellectual and artistic interest . . . an understanding of how to study . . . . are well prepared, and have participated in worthwhile pursuits."[65] At Parker, success was always measured by the students' success.

Although not a college prep school, more than ninety-five percent of the students earned four-year college degrees. Most began college upon graduation, but some postponed their studies for a year. The acceptance and achievement of African Americans, Asian Americans, and other minorities, matched those of the majority students. The professions pursued by 131 of 361 graduates between 1920 and 1929 included, in descending order, writing, medicine, law, journalistm, education, and business. The professions of 160 of 340 graduates between 1940 and 1949 changed somewhat; writing still led the list, education increased, medicine was similar, engineering increased, and law was similar.[66]

Was the Parker School Progressive?

Between 1935 and 1965, the progressive legacy extended within and beyond the school. Due to the contribution of the Parker vintage teachers, all faculty members had the benefit of training in progressive history, philosophy, and pedagogy. The Graduate Teachers College of Winnetka offered courses in progressive education to its graduate enrollees who practice taught on site at the Parker School. Several Parker faculty founded progressive schools. Parker teachers also accepted positions at colleges and universities, where they trained more faculty for progressive schools (see Chapter 5).

Not only did Parker train progressive teachers, but from a curriculum perspective, the school participated in the nationally famed Eight-Year Study, and made steps toward the development of a national progressive curriculum. The school was one of the few, if not the only, precollege school with a progressive curriculum for Grades K-12. It was true that as the high school course of study became more progressive, the lower school began to depart from the course of study founded on Francis Parker's theory of concentration.

Pedagogically, a decrease in emphasis on central subjects in the lower school was accompanied by a de-emphasis on activities, which began to erode slowly. In the lower school, fewer field trips, observations, Reading Leaflets, and other "learning by doing" strategies were used in the classroom. In the high school, a different kind of disconnection between classroom and school activities occurred, disrupting the goal of relating the class and activity to enable students to put ideas into action. The result of this disconnection was less student participation in activities. The teachers also lost momentum in the guidance and supervision they previously gave to activities. The visual and performing arts classes and activities remained interrelated, and drama took on greater prominence because it tied class with performance.

It is true that the students struggled with self-rule and democratic leadership, but too often authority outran student democracy. The Morning Exercises sustained their role in the development of character and citizenship through community, but little was done to restate the purpose of Morning Exercise and to reestablish its importance. The schedule was changed to four days, the prayer and recitation were eliminated, the responsibility of each class and individual to present a Morning Exercise was lost, and new assignments did not replace these omissions. What had been the essential bulwark of the school now continued as a symbol. Without the support of Morning Exercise, the school philosophy of "community, character, and citizenship" began to fall into neglect.

The school sustained its progressive philosophy in teacher training, curriculum, and pedagogy but not with the same intensity as in the earlier era. Some strong areas weakened. The activity-centered school diminished in importance, and a struggle between democratic and authoritarian rule ensued. Parker set a model for other independent schools by enrolling the first Negro students in 1943 and appointing the first black trustee in 1963. Parker graduates performed well in academic courses and in meaningful campus activities in college. The successful results of the students in the Eight-Year Study gained the school national prominence. In this era, the school effectively carried out and transmitted the progressive philosophy.

Chapter 8

Challenges to Progressive Education
(1965-1995)

Historical Perspective: Society Shaped the School

Between 1965 and 1995, societal unrest and educational reform and turmoil challenged progressive education and transformed the Francis W.
Parker School. The values the society held sacred for so many years were
under attack, and it looked as if the center of education in both traditional
and progressive schools would not hold.

The Parker School's spirit and mission were under tremendous pressure from within the school. Many of the legacies and programs that had
their genesis in the Pioneering Years and had given the school focus and
cohesiveness had lost their power. The last of the vintage faculty, the heart
and soul of the school who had carried on the spirit and mission of Flora
Cooke since the 1930s, had retired. The school had to hire new faculty,
tackle new societal problems, and engage all of the school's constituencies—the faculty, the students, and the parents—to succeed.

Beginning in the late 1960s, societal forces had a diluting and negative
impact on the Parker School. The many and varied effects of affluence ran
contrary to the social idealism of the progressives, and a culture of narcissism
and consumerism replaced the old progressive values of equality of opportunity and social justice for all. Additionally, the accompanying rise in meritocracy in high schools and universities obliterated the progressive goal of
"responsible citizenship" and replaced it with a new goal of financial success.
Christopher Lasch characterized the "Me-too" decade of the 1970s as an era
in which society discovered its enchantment with self-involvement. Lasch
explained the narcissism that shaped the goals of the young generation:

> In a society in which the dream of success has been drained of any mean-
> ing beyond itself, men have nothing against which to measure their
> achievement except the achievements of others. Self-approval depends
> on public recognition . . . Today men crave not fame but glamour and
> the excitement of celebrity . . . . what a man does matters less than the
> fact that he has 'made it.'[1]

The narcissism was accompanied by changing family patterns that influenced the school negatively. The basic belief that parental, family, and
individual civic responsibility was essential and rewarding was made foolish by the increasing cynicism. When the divorce rates rose dramatically,
especially among educated, middle-class young families, the school was
no longer perceived as a community in which the whole family participated and contributed. It came to be perceived as an expensive service that
one purchased if lucky enough to be accepted. For the large tuition, the
consumer was no longer a participant and a volunteer, but one who expected service and results.

Many Parker activities revealed significant signs of a change in parent values. The results were numerous and diverse. Those families loyal
to the school's values compensated for the "dropout" parents and
increased their innovative efforts toward fundraising. The investment of
new energy in fundraising and other activities by at least thirty percent of
the parent body resulted in a conflict between those parents who subsidized the school with their volunteer labor and cooperation and those who
did not. Never before was parental attendance at grade level meetings so
low. New were the disputes between parents and faculty over the curriculum. It now was no longer a given that "the curriculum was the
domain of the faculty," but the argument was waged over what was the
school's responsibility versus the parent's responsibility. For example,
should the school address drug education or was that a family responsibility? The argument pitted parents against parents, parents against faculty, and faculty against faculty.

Not only the transformation of the home but the changing community
had deleterious effects on the school. Just blocks west of the Parker
School, the community transformed within the decade. Single family
brownstones were carved into multiple low-rent apartments. Insurance
companies were denying insurance because of the danger of the neighbor-

hood. The decay was best symbolized in the once-proud apartment house on the north corner of Belden Avenue and Clark Street, directly across from the school. Built with a ballroom on the top floor, it was now a flop house. The deteriorating brownstone on the opposite corner became a haven for local streetwalkers and the homeless, who sat on the front steps drinking wine from bottles wrapped in brown paper packages. Stimulated by determined Parker parents, the tide gradually turned, and by the early 1980s the Parker neighborhood was again a prized place to live.

Many were the causes of these dramatic changes but chief among them was President Johnson's Civil Rights Act of 1964. The "color-blindness" mandated by the Civil Rights Act turned to "color-consciousness," and the interracial struggle for equality initiated in the South rapidly converted to a black movement that spread across the country.[2] Both leading Civil Rights organizations, the Congress of Racial Equality (CORE) and the Student Nonviolent Coordinating Committee (SNCC), became exponents of black nationalism. Black power consolidated at a conference in Newark, New Jersey, where rioting began and extended to Chicago, Cleveland, Detroit, Los Angeles, New York, and other major cities, where blacks were concentrated in poor and decaying inner-city neighborhoods. The black population in the central cities nearly doubled from 6.5 million to 12.1 million in the 1960s, and as it did, residential and school segregation increased.[3]

The 1968 assassinations of Martin Luther King Jr. and Senator Robert Kennedy seemed to scotch the hopes of young and old alike. The dissension over the Vietnam War increased as support for the war eroded and antiwar demonstrations surged. President Johnson, discouraged by the public criticism of his Vietnam policy, did not run for re-election in 1968. The citizens instead elected Richard Nixon because he pledged to end America's involvement in Vietnam. Antiwar demonstrations continued until Nixon signed the Indochina cease-fire agreement in 1973.

The combination of the black movement and the antiwar sentiment created a new radicalism on college campuses from Berkeley to Columbia University, which trickled down to American high schools across the country. The protesting college students were baby boomers, the first generation to grow up in an age of steadily expanding affluence. The "boomers" lived lives of comfort that were relatively unaffected by struggle.

"Affluence expanded the number [of students] who could afford to drop out and swell the ranks of the counterculture."[4] The protests of the left gave the baby boomers a "cause." Most held relaxed attitudes toward drugs and sex, and the ready availability of drugs became an important element in the developing counterculture. Harvard professor Timothy Leary, the leading guru, proclaimed that the drug LSD brought true insight and real education and all that schools had been doing and were doing was sham. Leary's *Psychedelic Reader* (1965) became a best seller.

Changes were transforming education as well. Elementary and secondary educators received contradictory messages from the nation. On the one hand, after Russia's launching of Sputnik in 1957, the nation called for the education of the gifted. The citizens indicted the elementary and secondary schools because they believed that "Sputnik had happened not because of what the Russians had done but because of what American schools had failed to do."[5] On the other hand, the 1960s were marked by massive federal legislation intended to improve education for the disadvantaged. The schools were unable to serve both groups of students, and they became the focus of criticism for those finding fault with American society. Citizens responded by demanding more federal aid to education, which created the "Curriculum Decade" between 1975 and 1985. The "Curriculum Decade" was marked by the proliferation of federally financed education programs.

For nearly 100 years, attempts to pass federal aid to education had failed, but following Sputnik the National Defense Education Act in 1958 provided federal education funds, and President Johnson was able to pass his Elementary and Secondary Education Act (ESEA) in 1965, which he aimed at improving schooling for poor children. While ESEA was constituted of several titles, almost five-sixths of all dollars were spent on Title I programs designed to meet "the special educational needs of educationally deprived children." Head Start was the Title I program designated for impoverished preschool-age children. It was considered one of the Great Society programs that allegedly really worked.[6] Over the years, about $100 billion was dispensed through the program. Later, however, researchers discovered that former Head Start students did not remain superior to those disadvantaged students who did not attend.[7] However, the push for earlier and earlier education in the form of nursery schools and daycare centers grew from a trickle to a flood. The Parker School, a promoter of preschool education, was positioned to ride the wave and offered a Head Start program for the preschool-age children of Chicago.

Many school districts offered the Title III ESEA programs, which sponsored "innovative projects" such as open classrooms, team teaching, multi-age grouping, and other innovations new to traditional schools but familiar pedagogy in progressive schools. Title VII, the Bilingual Education Act, passed in 1968, covered "children of limited English speaking ability." Bilingual education focused on low-income children and was initially offered for Hispanics, but the concept was intentionally defined vaguely so the programs could be adapted to meet the needs of any school district. The results were uneven and the overall effectiveness dubious. During the first year, the federal government spent $7.5 million for demonstration programs, and by 1977 the U.S. Office of Education allocated $115 million to more than 500 school districts. By 1980, thirteen states mandated bilingual education. Bilingual education became a new buzzword, and although federal funds were unavailable for private schools, the Parker School offered bilingual classes to determine its benefits for Hispanic students.

In 1970, the Nixon Administration announced funding for the Experimental Schools Program (ESP), a comprehensive approach encompassing all twelve grade levels and including curriculum development, staff development, and community involvement.[8] Five years later, Congress enacted the Education for All Handicapped Children Act of 1975, which required that every handicapped child receive, at public expense, an education "specifically designed to meet the child's unique educational needs . . . in the least restrictive environment . . . with non handicapped peers [whenever possible]."[9] Federal funding of education programs peaked in 1976 without fulfilling the objectives for the gifted or the disadvantaged. Federal aid declined over the next several years as Presidents Reagan and Bush turned their attention to the economy and deregulation. President Clinton revived educational spending but not at the same level as Presidents Johnson and Nixon. The public challenges to education were unmet, and the federal programs did not answer society's educational problems.

Other trends influenced the curriculum at the precollege level. The National Science Foundation played a large role in curriculum revision for mathematics, biology, chemistry, and social sciences. The result was new science, new math, and an entire new curriculum. In the humanities, the old reading lists were overwhelmed by a rush of new titles. George Eliot's *Silas Marner* disappeared from the curriculum, and teachers were encouraged and supported to teach about that which they felt strongly. An entire new literature was in the making.

Prior to the 1960s, the pantheon of American authors was predominately populated by white males. Now, as the black experience became the subject of black novelists, biographers, dramatists, and poets like James Baldwin, Toni Morrison, Lorraine Hansbury, and LeRoi Jones held positions of honor on classroom reading lists, as did ethnics and women. The study of grammar in secondary school collapsed under an assault from universities that derided the faulty linguistic base of traditional grammar and proposed linguistics instead. Such notables as Fred Stocking, Professor of English at Williams College, mocked the pedantic obsession of secondary school teachers with spelling and grammar. Art, drama, and music were newly emphasized to meet the levels that the Parker School had established at the turn of the century. The old requirements were replaced by a burgeoning number of electives. Before this period, most high schools were proud of their fifty- or sixty-course college prep syllabus; by the 1970s it was not unusual for a high school to publish a two- to three-hundred course syllabus.

Tests were aggressively debunked. Standardized testing, which at its inception in the 1910s and 1920s was part of the science of education and therefore a mainstay of progressive education, came to be seen as the master rather than the handmaiden of education for which it had been designed originally. The Scholastic Aptitude Test (S.A.T.), which for years had reported scores only to colleges, was now forced to report scores to high schools and eventually to students. Research showed that the S.A.T. was biased against minorities and women, but with all of its flaws it remained a powerful ingredient in college acceptance. Only a few colleges, most notably Bowdoin College, announced that they would no longer require the S.A.T.s for admissions.

Progressive educators had to ask themselves some hard questions. Should progressive schools introduce education for the gifted when they stood philosophically for developing the full potential of all students?

Should progressive schools replace their present science and math courses with new science and new math courses? Another challenge came from society's changing values. In a meritocracy guided by narcissistic goals, the progressive ideals of character, citizenship, and social motive were replaced by college admission, the parents' number one goal for their off-spring. Students from progressive schools were entering the colleges of their desire and doing well, but parents believed the pupils could do better and pushed for a more traditional course of study. Progressive education professed the ideal necessary for a society—critical thinkers with character to stand for what they believed—but these values were shunned for good grades that promised high salaries. The progressives could not make an impact because they were not an organized movement and did not have a public voice. The great percentage of public schools did, however, adapt progressive pedagogy because of the nature of the federal legislation as well as the changing approach to teacher training.

Administration: Six Principals Face the Challenge

For thirty years, one principal and one chairman of the Board of Trustees governed the school. In contrast, for the thirty years between 1965 and 1995, nine board chairpersons, six principals, and ten Educational Council presidents governed the school. This turnover reflected the changes in society, in the field of education, and at the Parker School itself. Nationally, new demands were placed on school principals, and at Parker compatibility between the school philosophy and the principal and between the chairman of the board and the principal were essential ingredients determining the principal's tenure. The increasing turnover of principals working with more board chairmen and Council presidents increased the potential for conflict.

Mr. Jack Ellison was the fifth principal of the school from 1967 to 1972. He governed first with chairman Farwell Smith and later Morris Kreeger, M.D.; presidents of the Educational Council, Doris Holleb and Haskell Bernstein, M.D.; and Business Manager, Gordon Muirhead. Ellison preferred to guide through scholarship and to motivate through ideas rather than to give directions. He understood learning as self-effort and wanted both the faculty and students to pursue ideas actively. To him learning was as natural as breathing. New faculty often felt intimidated by his intelligence, but Ellison was more nurturing than intimidating. An educated humanist, Ellison strongly supported human rights and advocated the arts, expanding the school's program to include dance and photography.

Dignified, confident, and stately in manner, Mr. Ellison was a tall lean man whose appearance changed little with age. His horn-rimmed glasses exaggerated his owl-like wisdom. His hair grayed during thirty years of teaching, but his mind was alert and active and his soft-spoken discourse enabled him to say a lot to many without being perceived as a take-charge person. Only when student behavior in the Morning Exercise did not meet his expectation did he raise his gentlemanly voice. Ellison revered Morning Exercise and was in attendance at all of them. At the close of each one, the audience sat quietly until he rose from his seat on the aisle in the middle of the auditorium and declared, "This concludes the Morning Ex."

Ellison was a proven teacher and a distinguished national educator. He began teaching English and social studies at Parker School in 1937 and became a gradehead for the freshman class. Ellison's main teaching interest was anthropology, and he introduced a course for seniors and initiated "Man, A Course of Study," an experimental anthropology course for sixth graders. Toward the end of his career, he was appointed chairman of the Wingspread Conference on Social Studies, sponsored by the National Association of Independent Schools.

In the classroom, "he held high quiet standards of excellence for himself and others around him." Students esteemed him for "his low-keyed but academically rigorous" ninth grade class, "the values he communicated," and "the different and engaging ways he taught the senior anthropology course." To some students, "his classes were heavy reading courses and intellectually exciting." To others, "his friendship in and out the class shaped their lives." To a few, "he was too demanding and too critical, but his ideas and the way he did things was always interesting." Ellison's goal as a teacher was "to maintain the humanistic tradition and a level of intellectual rigor in a context where the students recognized why they were learning."[10]

After twenty-six years of teaching, Ellison was appointed Dean of Faculty in 1963 and served in that position for four years, overseeing curriculum development, hiring new teachers, and meeting with parents and students. A strong advocate of teacher training, this position offered him the opportunity to observe and train teachers. He offered classes to new faculty in the history, philosophy, and pedagogy of progressive education.

When Mr. Ellison was appointed principal in 1967, he realized that the position had become too large to be a solo undertaking and he employed Business Manager Gordon Muirhead and expanded the administrative staff, adding Dean of Faculty Barney Negronida, Dean of Students Marie Kirchner Stone, and a coordinator of middle school, Delafield Griffith. Other administrators included head of lower school Betty Kays and head of high school Dr. James Bowditch. Ellison designated the two deans as college counselors and insisted that faculty appointed to administrative positions remain classroom teachers first and administrators second.

Ellison was a headmaster in the Cooke tradition, and as such, the educational process became the school's hallmark during his term. He elevated the classroom to the center of importance by insisting that "the curriculum was the domain of the faculty," rather than the purview of outside experts, trustees, or parents.[11] As he had done when Dean of Faculty, Ellison read and critiqued the teachers' curriculum reports to acquaint himself with changes in the course of study and in preparation for the numerous informal classroom observations he made to help teachers advance. During classroom observations he took copious notes that dealt with essential questions for the teachers. The follow-up conferences were explorations rather than criticisms of what he observed. He gave time generously to teachers, who eagerly anticipated the conferences because "the discussion and interpretations resulted in self-criticism, which created a teacher's growth."[12] These were truly teacher observations and not evaluations.

A believer in the deliberative body, Ellison utilized the expertise of faculty and parents and consulted with the Educational Council and outside experts about the national unrest resulting from the Civil Rights Movement, the Free Speech Movement on college campuses, and the Vietnam War. He addressed the tension between adolescent idealism and activism and called for decorum, discipline, and rigor in the school. Ellison sought to balance the expectations of those teachers and parents who thought the students had too much freedom and those who judged the school too conservative. In the spirit of a truly progressive school populated by critical thinkers and "responsible citizens," he weighed all sides of an issue, questioning and debating before deciding the course of action.

As principal, he was committed to constructing a relationship between the school and the community. For the seniors, as a culmination to the Parker educational experience, he initiated May Month, a month-long, off-campus work-study course taken under the guidance of an out-of-school expert. The May Month became an educational success and was replicated in schools throughout the country. He also invited Parker drama teacher Pauline Zanetakos to design an after-school program for neighborhood youngsters, using the Parker playground. For four summers, Mr. Ellison and the Parker School sponsored summer workshops on the Leicestershire Open Classroom, which was led by distinguished teachers from England for the Parker faculty and other teachers from the National Association of Independent Schools. In 1971, with parent leadership, he introduced a series of Parker Evening Courses taught by Parker faculty and parents for the community, a concept also duplicated by other schools. The Evening Courses improved community relations and raised money for the Scholarship Fund. Ellison also increased minority enrollment and secured a $25,000 grant from the James E. Merrill Foundation to assist in increasing the number of black students and in improving school and community relations.[13] Parker School was one of ten percent of schools that met the challenge of the National Association of Independent Schools for minority enrollment in the 1970s.

Mr. Ellison and the Parker School seemed a perfect match. Ellison had a firm grasp and a thorough comprehension of the psychology and philosophy of progressive education. He understood what Dewey intended for a science of education and what Comenius meant about a pedagogy based on "learn to do by doing it" (see Chapters 2 and 3). The values of progressive education "to educate the whole child to become a responsible citizen" were integral to Ellison's personal and professional philosophy. A social activist and political liberal whom some labeled a radical, he attempted to begin a teachers' union at the school and also went abroad to fight against Fascism in the Spanish Civil War.

Canadian-born Ellison was formally educated before coming to America, where he completed his graduate work at the experimental Graduate Teachers College of Winnetka, Illinois. There Ellison said that he learned, "Teachers need to be driven by a passion for teaching in order for students to gain an "intensity for learning."[14] His wife, Emily Whipple, was an English teacher whom he met at the Parker School. Their daughter Jane Ellison enrolled at Parker but left to avoid having her parents as teachers, and their son David Ellison '70 graduated from the Parker School before becoming a physician. Ellison was a member of the Sarah Greenebaum Distinguished Visitors Committee, and after he retired, he joined the Educational Council and became a member of the city-wide Board of Scholarship and Guidance, a program which Flora Cooke championed that assisted families with education needs.

During the Ellison era, the school heightened its resolve for an intellectual life and deepened its commitment to progressive education. Mr. Ellison was an egalitarian who did not believe in a hierarchy. His standards demanded the highest performance by a group that he considered his equals. Regarded highly by the Parker community, vintage teachers quoted Ellison frequently at meetings, and new administrators and teachers often consulted with him. To many affiliated with the school from the time of the Great Depression until 1972, when Mr. Ellison resigned, he was Mr. Parker.

Upon Ellison's retirement, an Administrative Committee directed the school until John Holden was appointed acting principal for school year 1972-1973. Although Mr. Holden came to the Parker School with a broad range of teaching, administrative, and consulting experience from the Putney School, the Woodstock County School in Vermont, the Boston public schools, the Colorado Rocky Mountain School, and Bowdoin College, his child-centered philosophy of progressive education was incompatible with the Dewey-Parker model of social reconstructionist progressive education. The school sustained the status quo for one year until the trustees appointed William Drennan Geer Jr. as principal.

Called Dren by most, William Drennan Geer Jr. served as the seventh principal of the school from 1973 to 1986. He governed with five successive board chairmen: Morris Kreeger, M.D., Charles Goodman, Irving Stenn, David Heller, and David Ruttenberg; and five Educational Council presidents: Haskell Bernstein, M.D., James Saft, M.D., Whitney Addington, M.D., Lynn Martin, and Lynn McCarthy.

Geer had been a teacher at a private school, a principal at a large public school, and a nationally renowned educational innovator when, in mid-career, he deliberately searched for a school with an enrollment of fewer than 1,000 students and an integrated program that served kindergartners through twelfth graders. At Parker, he found the school that met his expectations.

Like Francis Parker himself, Mr. Geer could not remember a time when he did not want to teach. A New Yorker and a Harvard University graduate, Geer began teaching at age twelve, giving swimming lessons to Harlem students who had been declared unteachable, and he became a volunteer teacher in social programs during his college years. In his first position as English teacher and coach at Lawrenceville Academy, a private school in New Jersey, he founded a summer program, funded by the Ford Foundation, for promising black students and teachers from the Trenton public schools. As principal of the large suburban Newton South High School in Newton, Massachusetts, he introduced a number of innovative curriculum projects and developed the concept of a small school within a larger school, again with Ford Foundation funding. A national educational leader, Geer was called upon to be the chairman of the Education Policies Committee of the Massachusetts Principals Association, when the role and authority of the high school principal were in flux. The Massachusetts governor appointed him a member of the Governor's Council for Vocational Education. He also served actively on the College Board, challenging many of its decisions about testing.

During this period controversial societal issues overwhelmed the school's educational process. The radical issues that had plagued college campuses in the 1960s became high school issues in the 1970s. The Vietnam War protest, the changing standards of personal appearance and manners, the sexual revolution, a new and freer style of expression, the introduction of drugs—all these issues and problems nearly split the school asunder. The progressive voices clashed more vociferously than before with the conservative voices. Geer, a methodical, inexhaustible, and tenacious man, was an educator with the breadth of experience and the energy to attempt to develop a common ground between the opposing perspectives.

Geer's administrative style was similar to Dr. Thomas's; both encompassed the totality of the school and not only the educational process. His first goal was to restructure the administration, changing Delafield Griffith from coordinator to head of upper school; retaining the head of lower school Betty Kays before hiring Marsha Millar, Lynn Martin, and Norma Nelson respectively. He appointed the first upper school Curriculum Coordinator, Marie Kirchner Stone, and several successive lower school coordinators—Dr. John Sherman, Lynn Martin, Annabelle Williams, and JoNell Bailey. He appointed Vince Threet and Catherine Chambers Haskins as middle school coordinators when Griffith became head of upper school. Geer also named two successive business managers, Bob Wulkowicz and Kay Burbidge.

Geer strengthened the academic environment by instituting a curriculum committee comprised of department chairpersons, placing academic subjects high on his list of priorities and emphasizing mathematics, science, and language arts skills. Geer supported the introduction of curriculum experiments like the middle school electives and the high school Intensive-Extensive Study. An athlete, a swimmer, and a biker, Geer also expanded the girls' athletics program.

During his tenure, the issues of society dominated the energy of the school because they were impinging on the education process. Geer applied progressive principles in a "democratization experiment." The process called for positioning a cross section of trustees, administrators, teachers, students, parents, and experts on a series of newly designed school committees. The purpose of these representative committees was to examine and seek solutions to specific societal problems that affected the school, such as drugs, new sexual behaviors, racial tension, and appropriate language and dress. The function of each democratized committee was to plan action for the resolution of an assigned problem and to implement solutions.

Participatory democracy engaged more people in the education process of the school than ever before. The democratization process solved some problems, prevented others, and created new ones. It solved the problems of language and dress by setting a standard called "audience appropriate." It solved part of the drug problem by the introduction of a comprehensive new school health program. Health classes provided information on problems and alternative, intergenerational drug-free activities like sports, games, and dances for teachers, students, and parents provided reinforcement. Another committee dealt with family concerns in a series of meetings and increased communication by letting students advise their friends' parents about societal issues rather than their own parents. These effective strategies had long lives in the school and lasted throughout and beyond the era.

New problems resulted from the involvement of all constituencies in committees. Responsibilities became blurred because it was difficult to define boundaries between "home and school" and "school and community." Many teachers, trustees, and parents could not accept testing democracy to its outer limits. It felt less safe than authoritarian rule. The questions were many—How much student freedom? What were the consequences of actions contrary to community life? When did the discussion end and implementation begin? Who was responsible for the final decisions? How would decisions be communicated? The undertaking was large and cumbersome. As a consequence, the experience in democratization died prematurely from uninformed participants, a discouraged leadership, and conservative opposition resistant to the democratic approach. Geer had positioned the school on the cutting edge for the discovery of new principles of community engagement, which extended the principle of "democracy and education," but the experiment suffered from structural disadvantages. More preparation, improved communication, and effective decision making were essential ingredients but were absent.[15]

Geer had an open office, eagerly shared his ideas, and insisted on faculty participation in educational issues not only in but out of the school. He encouraged teachers to serve on national, state, and local committees, and the Parker teachers were frequently invited to speak at educational conferences. Teachers chatted with Geer about education over coffee at the end of the day. Often the street lights were already on when Geer and a group of teachers left the school together. Geer held Saturday morning meetings in his office and evening meetings in his home, where he served his hot homemade bread. The dialogues were unending.

Another of Geer's goals was to encourage school diversity. Geer recruited minority teachers and insisted on the black teachers' active engagement in the community. He disapproved of the separatist Black Student Union, which emerged and died in this era, because it divided the community into factions. Against the opposition of many faculty, he supported the celebration of Martin Luther King Day to develop community awareness of diversity in the school. Geer also responded to women's issues, a topic dear to his heart as the father of four daughters—Leydie '76, Gretchen '78, Amanda Katherine (deceased), and Hilah, who graduated from another high school. His wife, Mussy Geer, rounded out the family's dedication to education. She taught fourth grade at the Parker School between 1982 and 1986 and was then appointed head of the lower school at North Shore Country Day School.

As principal, Geer reinforced progressive philosophies—placing the development of the whole child as central, reactivating the home in the educational process, engaging the community, and placing emphasis on Morning Exercise and other school traditions. He insisted that the teachers be a "presence" in the school and be educated about it. He asked the curriculum coordinators to develop the Parker School archives. With the expert assistance of Patricia Sundheim Winter '56 and Susan Stern Ettelson '46, Ms. Stone gathered materials from the past and present and filed them for perpetuity.

Tall, imposing, and physically fit, Geer possessed a great vitality and enthusiasm that energized the school; some wanted the status quo to remain, but he was willing to explore new ideas, to confront old problems, and to devise creative solutions. No problem was too small or too large. He could and did it all. Some thought he moved too slowly and others thought he progressed too rapidly, but most realized Geer propelled the school to a new height.

Geer's thirteen-year tenure was controversial. He was the first principal evaluated by an outside consultant. The consultant's report, called the Munitz Report of December 1981, described the principal as:

> a strong leader and effective manager of academic personnel . . . he is recognized within the school and across the country as a quality human being and a most concerned educational spokesman.[16]

During Geer's tenure, the school celebrated its seventy-fifth anniversary with the publication of *Between Home and Community* (1976). The school year closed earlier than usual on May 30, 1986, to facilitate the construction of the new middle school wing for the opening on September 5, 1986. The addition of the new wing paralleled the passage from Principal Geer to Acting Principal Fred Dust.

At that time, the trustees seemed unclear of their direction, and in the next decade appointed an acting principal, an acting principal who became principal, and an interim principal. The main problem seemed to be that the governing bodies were unsure whether to remain a progressive school or become a traditional school.

Fred Dust, who became the head of upper school following Delafield Griffith, was appointed the acting principal for school year 1986-1987. Mr. Dust governed with Chairman David Ruttenberg and Educational Council president Lynn McCarthy. His administrative staff included most of the same personnel as Mr. Geer's staff. A graduate of Purdue University who earned his Master's Degree in education at Harvard University, Mr. Dust began his teaching career as a sixth grade teacher at the Parker School, where he had more than ten years of teaching experience. He was able to implement the plans and programs initiated earlier by Mr. Geer. His two sons, Fred and Nathaniel, both attended Parker School.[17]

After Mr. Dust's year as acting principal, the trustees appointed John Cotton acting principal in 1987, and he became the ninth principal of the school from 1988 to 1993. Cotton governed with successive chairpersons: David Ruttenberg, King Harris, and Lynn Mills; with successive Educational Council presidents: Ted Oppenheimer, John Elson, and co-president Richard Press and Carol Ouimette; and with Business Manager Paula Haarvei. He also served with head of lower school Norma Nelson, head of upper school Dr. Daniel Frank '74, Lower School Curriculum Coordinator Joan Bradbury, Upper School Curriculum Coordinators Peter Barrett followed by Rebecca Rossof, and Middle School Coordinator Maryanne Kalin-Miller.

A graduate of Phillips Exeter Academy and Harvard University, Mr. Cotton earned a graduate degree in Asian Studies from the University of Colorado. Prior to accepting the principalship at the Parker School, he had been headmaster at three college preparatory schools and the vice president of the Episcopal Diocese of Southeast Florida for almost a decade. Cotton's education and orientation were traditional in nature, and his curriculum goals, mainly subject centered, were to enhance the mathematics and science programs, to place foreign languages in the middle school, to add advanced placement courses to the high school course of study, and to introduce the Internet. He worked effectively with the Educational Council, whose goals were similar to his. Mr. Cotton was involved in the "new governance plans" instigated by the Munitz Report in 1981, which required that he evaluate teachers for tenure and be evaluated himself.

An affable, well mannered, and pleasant gentleman, Cotton served during a relatively peaceful period in the society, but not in the school. When he resigned, the school had not yet resolved its traditional versus progressive identity crisis and therefore hired an interim principal, Dr. Timothy Burns. Dr. Burns served from 1993 to 1995 with two successive board chairpersons: Lynn Mills and Robert Krupka, and co-presidents of the Educational Council Richard Press and Maryanne Kalin-Miller. He was assisted by the same administrative staff as Principal Cotton. Dr. Burns earned degrees at John Carroll University and Georgetown University in English literature and his doctorate at Ohio State University in Early and Middle Childhood and Educational Administration. He possessed experience in both elementary and secondary education. For sixteen years he was an interim headmaster or a headmaster at various schools.[18]

During Burns' two years at the Parker School, he placed the greatest emphasis on the lower school, which seemed to be his first love. The grade schoolers were delighted when Principal Burns greeted them by name at the entrance door every morning. His primary accomplishment was the integration of computers into the curriculum throughout the school. He began the process with a visual presentation to illustrate his plan and a teach-in for all faculty. Conversant in progressive philosophy, he was willing to innovate, and he gave strong support to the introduction of new programs such as the video program in the high school.

The father of two daughters, Molly and Katie' 95, Burns subscribed to the philosophy of leadership described by Lao-Tse, "When his work is done/his aims fulfilled/they will say/we did it ourselves." After Burns completed his interim principalship in 1995, the challenge to progressive education at the Parker School remained unresolved. The school had moved to the right and now was known in the city of Chicago not as a progressive school but "the other good school down the block" from the Latin School.[19]

Board of Trustees:
Basic Changes in School Governance and Operations

In 1965, the Parker School was governed by the principal, the Educational Council, and the Board of Trustees. The principal then had almost unlimited authority to run the school. The Educational Council was in charge of the school's progressive mission, and the trustees managed the school's finances. Financial problems altered this delicate balance.[20]

Between 1965 and 1980, the school suffered from financial problems second in gravity only to its problems during the Great Depression. A mortgage acquired to finance the new main building in 1962 and a growing operating deficit nearly overwhelmed a school reluctant to raise tuition and cut financial aid. Compelled to make fundraising its centerpiece, the Board of Trustees turned to parents, alumni, and faculty. The self-perpetuating Board of Trustees established in 1932 but expanded by the bylaws of 1946 and 1955 had only nominal parent and alumni representation, but in 1967, the bylaws were amended to provide for eighteen trustees-at-large with six-year terms, two alumni trustees with four-year terms, and four parent trustees with two-year terms. The president of the Women's Board and the president of the Educational Council, the principal, the business manager, other administrative staff, and a faculty and a student representative attended meetings. The honorary trustees attended ex-officio. As these constituencies gained a larger voice on the board, they learned more about the school's problems, which helped lead to the transformation of the governance and operation of the school in the 1980s.

The groups that responded to the trustees' call for financial assistance were the Women's Board, the Development Council, and a number of parents not involved in either organization. In 1962, the Women's Board opened the Parker Bazaar at a storefront on Clark Street. A volunteer parent staff made the resale shop a financial success that generated between $50,000 and $75,000 annually. In 1973, the Women's Board established a bi-annual auction which first netted $60,000 and in the 1990s netted more than $150,000. A group of parents, teachers, and the principal planned, partially staffed, and implemented an annual series of Evening Courses beginning in 1971, which netted $30,000 and increased annually to more than twice that figure. Parent John Holabird Jr. introduced a tile program in 1961, which allowed a donor to purchase a tile for an honoree for a small fee. Fourth graders painted the tiles, and the art teachers adhered the decorated tiles to the walls of the school with the name of the designated honoree. The tile program continued throughout the era, earning $3,000 to $5,000 annually. House tours, book sales, theatrical productions, and other fundraisers contributed to the coffers. The new fundraising efforts not only worked for the Parker School but broke ground that was adopted by other schools and not-for-profits in the Chicago area.

Under the vigorous leadership of Edwin Eisendrath '47, the Development Council instituted innovative fundraising strategies such as a subordinate debenture program, which asked parents to lend the school an interest-free $150 annually. Edwin Eisendrath's commitment to the school emanated from his numerous family members who attended the school, including his two sons Edwin III '76 and John '77. The Development Council also initiated a Fair Share program, which asked parents to contribute one percent of their annual income to close the gap between tuition and the actual cost of the student's education. Head of the Fair Share Program for many years was Jerome Ettelson, the husband of Susan Stern Ettelson '46 and the father of four alumni—Lawrence '74, John '76, William '79, and Nancy Ettelson-Holceker '81, and grandfather of four grandchildren who now attend Parker. With the dedication of Messrs. Eisendrath and Ettelson, the Fair Share Program was a financial success.

The first to chair the larger, more representative Board of Trustees was Farwell Smith. Smith served as the eighth Chairman of the Board of Trustees between 1966 and 1971. Smith had a clear vision of the progressive direction that the school should take. The trustees were therefore able to accomplish their goals and move the school in a direction compatible with the progressive mission established by Anita McCormick Blaine.

The new composition of the Board of Trustees altered the nature of the board meetings. Meeting agendas were now comprised of reports from the Women's Board, the Development Council, and a number of fundraising committees like the Alumni Association, which was successfully raising money for an endowment fund; the Public Relations Committee, which intermittently paid a consultant but did most of its work as volunteers; and the Building and Grounds committee, which informed the trustees of the status of the building and the surrounding grounds. The agenda also included the reports by the principal and the president of the Educational Council, which discussed the education status of the school. Not only fundraising activities and the school's financial status but also school-community relationships, educational programs, and societal issues dominated the meeting agendas.

School and community activities included the implementation of workshops offered at the Parker School for students from the Cabrini Green Housing Project, funded by the Office of Economic Opportunity, a "great books" exchange with nearby public Waller High School, and other successes and failures. On its first day the Waller exchange was abandoned when a gun shooting by a Waller student took place, and Waller School personnel could not locate the Parker students in response to frantic Parker parent phone calls. Farwell Smith championed the school's commitment to society in spite of the potentially tragic consequences, but the English teacher would not be accountable for the Parker students. School safety had not yet risen as an issue, and the school's mission was to be a model for public schools.

Figure 8.1
Principals and Board Chairmen, 1965-1995

The turnover of principals became more rapid, and Geer governed with the most chairmen—five.

Principals	Board Chairmen
Jack Ellison (1967-1972)	Farwell Smith (1966-1971)
	Morris Kreeger Jr. (1972-1975)
John Holden (1972-1973)	Morris Kreeger Jr. (1972-1975)
William Geer (1973-1986)	Morris Kreeger Jr. (1972-1975)
	Charles Goodman (1976-1979)
	Irving Stenn (1979-1982)
	David Heller (1982-1985)
	David Ruttenberg (1985-1988)
Fred Dust (1986-1987)	David Ruttenberg (1985-1988)
John Cotton (1987-1993)	David Ruttenberg (1985-1988)
	King Harris (1988-1991)
	Lynn Mills (1991-1994)
Timothy Burns (1993-1999)	Lynn Mills (1991-1994)
	Robert Krupka (1994-1997)

Drug abuse and race relations were frequently on the agenda. The Educational Council reported on drug abuse by the students, and Farwell Smith and Jack Ellison established a faculty committee to interview each student confidentially in an attempt to assess the size and nature of the problem. In an interview, the psychologist and a group of high school teachers asked individual students a series of prepared questions and tabulated the information in an attempt to target specific groups and grade levels in need of help with drug-related issues.

Race relations came to the foreground in 1968 when two black students boycotted football. The Black Student Union was formed, but it was believed to divide the school. Not all blacks favored the Union and not all whites were against it. Teachers and students organized a committee on race, and the trustees increased black student enrollment in 1969. Trustee Edwin Eisendrath was invited by an *ad hoc* faculty committee to propose to the board that two minority students be added to each middle school grade. The trustees granted the group of teachers permission to recruit and interview candidates, and the teachers raised several thousand dollars for scholarships to implement the enrollment. With the advice and support of Chairman Smith, the school was able to endure the racial controversies and yet keep its mission intact.

Farwell Smith had strong philosophical and familial ties with the school, stemming from its origin. His two uncles, Perry Dunlap Smith '06 and Elliott Smith '07, served on the school's second Board of Trustees and its first Educational Council. His uncle Perry founded the North Shore Country Day School (see Chapter 5).

After graduating from Harvard College, Farwell Smith returned to Chicago, enabling his four offspring to become Parker students—Matthew '73, Temple '75, Loren '77, and Brendan '80. In small and large issues, Chairman Smith was confident, pleasant but stern, and understanding of the nature of the school. He had his hand on the rudder and knew where to steer.[21]

Morris Kreeger, M.D. was elected the ninth chairman of the board and served from 1972 to 1975. Dr. Kreeger's seasoned executive skills, diplomacy, and mature leadership helped the school advance in spite of its financial difficulties. Dr. Kreeger's background helped him to understand educational problems. Born in New Jersey, he attended Rutgers University and completed postgraduate work at New York's Mt. Sinai Hospital, where he became associate medical director. He moved to Chicago to become medical director of Michael Reese Hospital, where he spearheaded the urban renewal of the blighted environment surrounding the hospital. Dr. Kreeger's children, Charles and Lora, attended the Parker School for fourteen years, and when Anne, his daughter by a second marriage, enrolled in the Parker School, his interest was renewed.

The educational issues on Dr. Kreeger's agenda revealed a concern about the new progressivism touted in the country. For example, Kreeger asked trustee Chuck Olin, several faculty, and two students to attend a "Colloquium on Affective Education," which dealt with students' attitudes, interests, and habits, as opposed to cognitive education, which addressed academic subjects. Educational Council President Dr. Haskell Bernstein presented a comparison of the British and the Parker systems of education and introduced the teachers' plans for the Intensive-Extensive Study Experiment. The board discussed after-school electives for students, workshops for teachers, summer school for education and for profit, senior citizen attendance in Parker classes, the creation of special programs with ASPIRA, a Spanish-speaking settlement house, and a five-Saturday seminar series on an outdoor education program. In 1973, after two years of grappling with a myriad of unresolved issues and innovations, Dr. Kreeger established a Long Range Planning Committee to develop a new statement of the school goals and mission which was undertaken by Council president Haskell Bernstein.

The financial picture did not improve, but many new fundraising ideas were suggested. Patricia Sundheim Winter '56, the new director of the alumni association, helped establish an endowment fund. New events like Grandparent's Day were profitable. The trustees also considered selling the land now used for the play field to build an underground garage or purchase and develop adjacent land. Dr. Kreeger also considered sharing facilities with the Latin School for the second time in the school's history. Initiating a twelve-month school year was analyzed. Investigation proved that most of these ideas were not viable because educational and economic goals were incompatible.

When the proposed operating budget increased dramatically in 1974, Dr. Kreeger was forced to stop providing free tuition for children of faculty, who now had to apply for financial aid like other parents. The trustees also increased lower school tuition, but an operating deficit persisted. When Dr. Kreeger died suddenly, the board appointed his wife, Dr. Renee Kreeger Gelman, as a trustee. Dr. Gelman served on the board until their daughter Anne's sophomore year, when they moved to Boston.[22] In spite of the tragic event, the transition from one chairman to the next was smooth.

Charles Goodman had been the treasurer of the board before being elected its tenth chairman from 1976 to 1979. His affiliation with the school was through his wife, Susan Crown Goodman '51, one of the early co-chairpersons of the Parker fundraising auctions, his sons Richard '74 and Leonard '80, and his daughter Barbara Goodman Manilow '78, who went on to become a lower school teacher.

A graduate of Massachusetts Institute of Technology, Mr. Goodman was a businessman who helped solve the school's dire financial problems. He effectively met budget and operation costs as well as fundraising goals. In spring 1976, Goodman was instrumental in changing how students were charged tuition. Previously the tuition scale rose at an even rate, although the cost of education in the lower grades had been higher than the tuition charged. Goodman introduced a step-level tuition that reduced the disparity between junior kindergarten and twelfth grade. The tuition for earlier grades was raised by a greater percentage than for the upper grades, which resulted in a substantial increase in income. Reflecting on the status of the school at the seventy-fifth anniversary, Goodman reported:

> We have met or exceeded all of our goals before the year was out. The Fund raising committee under Edwin Eisendrath '47 and Margaret Skidmore had the best year in history. The Voluntary Gift Program under Jerry Ettelson and Elroy Sandquist met its goals. The Endowment Fund led by Patricia Winter '56, Carolyn Bergen, and Dr. Whitney Addington has provided the school with a nucleus of a fund. The school's fiscal operations under the extraordinarily able and dedicated leadership of Dren Geer will have operated at budgeted costs or lower.

The Seventy-Fifth Anniversary Fund was a success with $600,000 in pledges.

The accomplishments of the Goodman-Geer-Bernstein administration strengthened and advanced the principles and mission of the Parker School. Goodman freed the Parker School of an operating deficit, Geer advanced the school educationally, and Dr. Bernstein reaffirmed the positive role of the Educational Council. The future boards always credited Mr. Goodman as the school's economic savior.

When Irving Stenn served as the eleventh chairman of the Board of Trustees from 1979 to 1982, the school was on solid financial ground. Mr. Stenn was a lawyer whose main interest in the Parker School derived from his three children, David '79, Rachel '81, and Sarah '85. Stenn's board was comprised of thirteen at-large members, nine parent trustees, three alumni trustees, honorary trustees, and fifteen nonvoting representatives until the trustees dissolved the Women's Board and eliminated its president from the board in 1982. In 1980, Stenn asked committee chairmen to submit written reports before the meeting and to simply summarize them at the meetings. This enabled trustees to discuss ideas and to hear feedback from the nonvoting trustees.

With Stenn at the helm, the school went beyond "crisis management" and operated with a small surplus, for which Stenn, like other chairpersons, credited former chairman Charles Goodman. Under Stenn, the Board of Trustees' accomplishments were numerous and praiseworthy. The board reorganized fundraising, improved recordkeeping, broadened the base of potential giving programs, and moved the bazaar facility from Clark to Halsted Street. It also purchased the building at 2234 Clark Street to house the development offices, and it commissioned the Leggett Report to present schematics and options for expanding the 1962 building. Stenn also initiated an evaluation of the governance and operation of the board, the principal, and the Educational Council by hiring consultant Dr. Barry Munitz, Chancellor of the University of Texas at Houston. Because of the good will he created, Stenn was the only chairman in this era invited to serve a fourth year.[23]

In the early 1980s, power began shifting slowly away from the principal to the trustees. Three jobs formerly delegated to the principal were reassigned. Now the trustees and not the principal represented the school in teacher salary negotiations; the business manager, formerly an adjunct to the principal, became an adjunct to the board and became the financial manager of the school. The new Director of Development served several powerful and active board committees, spearheaded fundraising, and was responsible for thirty percent of the annual operating budget. The position of the principal was becoming powerless.

David Heller '49 served as the twelfth chairman of the Board of Trustees from 1982 to 1985. He had been an alumni trustee for nine years before being elected the second alumnus to serve as board chairman. After graduating from Harvard College, Heller earned his MBA from the University of Chicago and became president of Advisory Research, Inc. Elected because of his fiscal ability, Heller possessed a broad perspective and held greater expectations for the school as an alumnus. His vision for the Board of Trustees was "to cause the changes that would make Parker School into a more effective educational institution [than it was presently]," which meant "to give the children a better education, a more meaningful learning experience, and to help prepare them to exercise the options which they should have coming out of a school like Parker."[24]

When Heller took the helm, the school was fiscally sound and fundraising was in the hands of an all-star parent line-up—Irving Stenn, Jerome Wexler, King Harris, Caryl Susman '48, and Ted Oppenheimer. Heller was proactive and focused on an effective school operation. He employed an admissions director to streamline admissions, elevated faculty salaries, and implemented an intelligent pension plan and compensation package. Heller also defined a formula to dispense scholarship aid logically.

Chairman Heller considered the governance of the school as its main problem and saw evaluation of the governing bodies—the board, the Educational Council, and the principal—as an inroad to a solution.

The Munitz Report provided the road map. Although initiated in 1981 by Chairman Stenn, the final Munitz Report on "school governance and operation" was completed and presented to the trustees during Heller's tenure in June 1983.[25] The Munitz Report proposed a Governance Steering committee (GSC) made up of the principal, the chairman of the board, and the president of the Educational Council that would meet monthly to structure the agenda for the board and the Educational Council.

For the Board of Trustees, Munitz recommended: (1) the evaluation of each trustee's performance (2) a balance [among trustees] in expertise, education, and orientation to the school philosophy, (3) a commitment to the board rather than to the constituency that nominated the trustee, (4) a need for confidentiality, and (5) the assessment of views about the educational process of the school from all constituencies as well as the collection of opinions from other schools.

To improve the Educational Council, the Munitz Report clarified its five roles: (1), "the board nominates twelve voting members with at least three trustees, chosen primarily for their knowledge of educational policies and methods"; (2) "the key charge directs the group to advise and counsel the trustees regarding educational questions, and consult and advise the principal or his staff upon issues concerning teaching, educational policy, and personnel"; (3) the Council and the principal work together "to help the school achieve educational objectives"; (4) the Council submits one or more nominations for the principal; and (5) the Council "is not a court of appeals . . . it is a body where a general perspective can be provided . . . and a 'testing ground.'"[26] The Munitz Report recommended that the Educational Council work as a partner with the board and the principal and become well informed, active, and independent participants. In Munitz's view, the Council needed a budget, a full-time staff member to plan and to organize regularly scheduled meetings and to keep minutes, and a dedicated chairman ready to commit considerable time to the job.

The Munitz Report also recommended an evaluation of the principal every three years by an external consultant, in which the principal spells out goals, evaluates how they have been achieved, and sets forth his future goals for the board and the Council. Munitz also recommended that professionals conduct a series of annual interviews with the key constituencies about the principal's performance. The categories to investigate should include planning issues, administrative concerns, curriculum issues, student affairs, faculty development, physical plant, trustee affairs, financial management, fundraising, and external relations.[27]

Munitz introduced the preliminary report on governance with the caveat, "No radical surgery should be suggested for the current governance structure, since it is working relatively well." Munitz believed that "a more formal or tighter framework should not be adopted—although tempting—since it would tend to force a resolution of inevitably ambiguous issues or promise answers to irreconcilable dilemmas." Munitz warned against "sharpening the formal aspects of governance or revising the bylaws since it is the interaction of people rather than the formalization of structures that can improve the Parker School."[28]

Except for the evaluation of the principal and the introduction of a teacher evaluation process, few Munitz recommendations were implemented. The Governance Steering Committee was not formed nor were the recommendations for the Educational Council implemented.

The "governance and operation of the school" remained an open-ended question for David Ruttenberg '58, the thirteenth chairman of the Board of Trustees. Buzzie, as he was known to most, is father to Geoff '85, Ali '87, and Jacob, 2012. Mr. Ruttenberg graduated from Cornell University and attended the London School of Economics before returning to Chicago to attend Northwestern University. He was a trustee for eight years before being elected as chairman from 1985 to 1988, a time of changes in principals.

Ruttenberg implemented the Munitz Report recommendation to hire an educational consultant to undertake a second evaluation of the principal after three years. He selected Larry Cuban, a well-known educator, who prepared the Cuban Report (1984), which clarified the relationship between the principal and the trustees and defined the difficulty of the principalship:

> The principal of the Parker School is expected to be all things to all people—quickly and perfectly . . . . the size of the expectation is mammoth. The dilemma is irreconcilable . . . conditions need to be established that permit the principal to perform the primary leadership role.[29]

The Cuban Report spelled out the eight roles and responsibilities of the board, including appointing the principal, determining the budget, effecting compensation and position for faculty and staff, and managing the business affairs of the corporation. In contrast, the Cuban Report identified only two roles and responsibilities of the principal to the board: preparing a budget for trustee approval and supervising and controlling the educational process of the school, including hiring and firing and determining the course of study and admissions. Cuban's observations revealed that the shift of power away from the principal to the trustees was complete, and Principal Geer resigned in 1986.

Successful fundraising at all levels permitted Ruttenberg and the trustees to plan the construction of a new floor to the east wing of the school. To improve school operation, Ruttenberg continued the Long-Range Planning Committee under the assertive and organized leadership of William Singer. The Long-Range Plan streamlined the school administration, fundraising activities, and operation issues, and also improved communication among the constituencies. The projected long-range plan was well received by the parents, who met for discussion and feedback in small groups according to the grade level of their children.

Although the school was sound educationally and fiscally from 1975 to 1985—admissions were high, new construction proceeded, and the societal turmoil subsided—controversial issues relating to the governance of the school remained unresolved. As the board became stronger, it diverted the school's educational leadership by the principal and the Council away from the very education it was trying to improve. The trustees addressed education issues—"What is progressive?" and "What is excellence?"—but the discussions were less than fruitful and provided few new insights. These questions were more appropriately the domain of the Educational Council, the principal, and the faculty.

King Harris had been a trustee in 1982 and was aware of the conflict over governance. He became a first vice president of the board in 1986 and served as the fourteenth chairman between 1988 and 1991. Mr. Harris attended Phillips Academy in Andover, Massachusetts, earned a bachelor of arts degree at Harvard College and an MBA at the Harvard School of Business. He was president and Chief Executive Officer of Pittway Corporation, a manufacturing and publishing company in Chicago. His son John attended Parker School from junior kindergarten until ninth grade.

Chairman Harris was active on the Long-Range Planning Committee, but his major contribution was as a fundraiser. Harris began his involvement in the $4 million building campaign in the early 1980s with Irving Stenn and continued throughout his chairmanship. An altruistic and social-minded person, Harris explained his goal—"Money to do things was always an issue, but if we agreed on a common course, we could find the money." Harris's second goal was to make Parker the best possible school, which adhered to progressive education principles. He too, like his predecessor Ruttenberg, asked the Educational Council to study what progressive education at the Parker School meant. In a series of meetings entitled "Progressive Visions," the Council presented definitions of progressive education to different constituencies of the school. Harris also asked the Council to design a five-year educational plan for the school. To insure a strong student body, the trustees created an extensive five-page recruitment plan "to achieve full enrollment of the school at all grade levels with well-qualified students of diverse racial, social, and economic backgrounds."[30]

The principal, the faculty, and the Educational Council were declining in power. The "hiring and firing" of teachers was the principal's responsibility, but the trustees now provided the guidelines for the teacher evaluation and dismissal policy. Originally, teachers held a central position in the educational process, but they were slowly becoming pawns of the school. In response, the teachers created a Faculty Association in 1985 and affiliated with a National Teacher's Union at the end of the era. The Educational Council also lost its identity when it did not adhere to Munitz's five guidelines, and the trustees made few changes to improve the Educational Council. In spite of grave difficulties over issues in the school, the Harris board served the school well, making long-range plans and initiating a capital campaign for future building.

King Harris nominated the first and only woman, Lynn Mills, as chairperson of the Parker Board of Trustees. Mrs. Lynn Mills's interest in the school emanated from her broad interest in education and from her two daughters—Holly '93 and Sarah '96. Lynn Mills was chairman of the parents committee and therefore a trustee in 1987 and a trustee-at-large in 1988 before serving as the fifteenth chairperson of the Board of Trustees from 1991 to 1994. The rapid succession of principals necessitated the strengthening of the trustees' power over the totality of the operation and placed many decisions in her capable hands.

Prompted by a potential contribution from a parent, one theme of Mills's chairmanship was to investigate the nature of "academic excellence"—an elusive concept that was difficult to define. Did excellence mean developing the full potential of each student as progressives defined it and if so how could the variable be measured? Or was excellence measured traditionally with students achieving an "A" in all disciplines, passing all advanced placement tests with flying colors, becoming National Merit Scholars, achieving a perfect score on their Scholastic Achievement Tests, and matriculating to Ivy League Schools? The answer called for reflection and debate, which could not be forced, and discussion was significant because it introduced the old criticism that "progressive education was soft" and did not produce excellence. Neither the trustees nor the prospective donor could clarify what "excellence" meant, but the contribution inspired strong debate.

Another force shaping Mills's chairmanship was the continuing conflict about school governance. Extending the Munitz and Cuban Reports from a decade earlier, she placed emphasis on trying "to restructure and reconstitute the Educational Council to act in partnership with the principal and the trustees." Without the support suggested by the Munitz Report, the Council was dysfunctional. Women of the school were proud of Lynn Mills's accomplishments in this male-dominated position.

Robert Krupka served as a trustee for seven years before becoming the sixteenth chairman from 1994 to 1997. His two daughters, Kristin '96 and Kerry '98, were the source of his commitment to the school. Mr. Krupka earned a bachelor's degree in physics but was an attorney when he chaired the board. Four major issues dominated his board's agenda: (1) the employment of a new principal in the absence of an Educational Council, (2) the governance issue, (3) the continuing deterioration of the 1962 building, and (4) the development of a Capital Campaign to fund new construction.[31]

In this era, the chairmen and the trustees made the Parker School a financially sound institution. The board retired its mortgage for the 1962 main building in 1980 and operated without a deficit. Parental fundraising activities proliferated and accrued substantial sums. Enrollment increased by about 100 students from 695 in 1965 to 785 students in 1990. Financial aid for a diverse student body was always made available. Between 1965 and 1995, the trustees elected their chairpersons well, and each left his or her imprimatur on the school (see Figure 8.1).

Educational Council: Judges Educational Process

From 1932 until the mid 1980s, the Educational Council had provided the educational authority which enabled the principal and faculty to develop and implement programs that addressed and frequently solved the most challenging and perplexing educational issues of the day. Under its guidance, the faculty continued the ground-breaking work of the school's first thirty years and created an innovative and stimulating curricula and learning environment. The understanding was always that the principal and the faculty would present and defend what they were doing to the group of distinguished educators who made up the Educational Council. When the Council operated at its best, it considered the issues and concerns the principal and the teachers presented to it, reviewed and critiqued new programs and curricula, and addressed any questions that the board might have about the educational program. The board had little involvement in the educational program of the school.

The Educational Council's contribution was uneven throughout its sixty years of existence. For example, in the 1970s, the Educational Council became proactive and focused on general issues of the school rather than specific curriculum interests. Presidents Haskell Bernstein, M.D., James Saft, M.D., and later Whitney Addington, M.D., emphasized the school's progressive philosophy, underscoring twelve basic elements to which the school should adhere:

1. Diversity in student body and faculty
2. Deliberate experimentation
3. Interpersonal learning (students teaching each other)
4. Learning is a pleasure
5. Students should derive their own clear perception of reality and trust teachers' knowledge of the past
6. Right of each individual not to be manipulated (operative between teacher-student, teacher-teacher, and teacher-administrator)
7. Achievement of autonomy and establishment of values
8. Effective and responsive use of skills
9. Respect for individual child
10. School is a community of learners
11. Commitment to scholarship
12. Available help inside and outside of school.[32]

The major agenda items of the 1980s focused on class size, the computer program, the approach to mathematics teaching, the effectiveness of the science department, multicultural education, and the questions of governance and operations of the school raised by the Munitz Report (1983) and the Cuban Report (1984). The Munitz Report identified guidelines to refurbish the Council, but the trustees did not implement them. Questions arose concerning the Educational Council's function and necessity. In the spring of

1994, board chairman Lynn Mills established a subcommittee of the Long-Range Planning Committee with administrators, Daniel Frank and Maryanne Kalin-Miller; fifth grade teacher Harriett Cholden, and high school English teacher, Mary Dilg to examine the role of the Educational Council. The subcommittee failed to investigate the history and legality of the Council and proposed that it be abolished, although Blaine's 1932 charter of incorporation had charged the Council with preserving the school's progressive principles and nominating principals. The subcommittee presented its proposal at a faculty meeting, and it was rejected by more than 95 percent of the teachers, who interpreted the proposal as a rejection of the Parker School's progressive identity. The faculty suspected the subcommittee members of collusion, naiveté, or ignorance in supporting the trustees' move to uproot the school's progressive legacy.

The Educational Council's uncertain status arose in the 1994 search for a new principal. Traditionally the Council's responsibility, the nomination of a candidate for principal, fell to a search committee co-chaired by John Levi, vice president of the Board of Trustees, and Bill Duffy, English teacher. For the first time in the school's history, a search committee rather than the Educational Council nominated the principal. A suspended Educational Council was convened to approve the committee's choice on November 18, 1994. The Parker School was now one of the few, if not the only, school in the National Association of Independent Schools without an academic committee.

Nine Distinguished Visitors: Consult on Curriculum

A quarter of a century after the Eight-Year Study culminated in 1941, the school invited Distinguished Visitors to evaluate whether and how the progressive principles established by the school's philosophy and reaffirmed in the Eight-Year Study were implemented throughout the school.

The Distinguished Visitors fund, created to honor alumna and teacher Sarah Greenebaum '15, enabled curricular specialists to consult with teachers, students, and parents about a specific department or a school issue. The Distinguished Visitors interviewed community members, observed and analyzed classes, advised the faculty about curriculum development and revisions, and prepared a written report and an oral presentation for the community. Between 1964 and 1988, nine Distinguished

Visitors left their marks on an improved school. The first six visitors placed their emphasis on curriculum and the classroom and the final three focused on school relationships.

In 1964, Ralph Tyler, research director of the Eight-Year Study, returned to reexamine the curriculum of the high school, spending time in each grade to observe all variety of classes. He was favorably impressed that the school was living its progressive philosophy and found that the progressive pedagogic principles used by the teacher at all grade levels stimulated learning. He challenged teachers who were applying the principles of curriculum and instruction but neglecting the principles of evaluation. He also challenged the absence of vertical and horizontal organization of curriculum. His curriculum analysis was generally laudatory.

In 1965, Professor Hilda Taba, a pioneer in curriculum development in the field of social studies, presented her ideas with tremendous verve and provoked serious thinking among the faculty, the administration, and the parent body. Her ideas on the process and development of critical thinking and on the Grades 7-12 social studies curriculum organization designed in the Eight-Year Study prompted the Social Studies Department to reevaluate its goals, content, and pedagogy.

Psychologist Dr. Ernest Hilgard focused on the major trends in learning theory during his visit in 1966. After observing Parker's tightly scheduled classes, in which students went from class to class to class without a break, he recommended loosening the schedule in order to relieve student fatigue and faculty strain, improve interactive participation among students, and increase the opportunity for student-initiated activities. His criticism was the impetus for a complete overhauling of the high school schedule and for schedule changes in the middle school in the mid 1970s.

During his April 1968 visit, Dr. Robert Iglehart, chairman of the Department of Art at the University of Michigan, urged much greater use of all environmental opportunities in the educational process in order to help students find those things that would make their world more livable and to learn to implement their findings in their lives.

Dr. Paul Diederich, senior research associate at the Educational Testing Service, suggested an approach to obtaining consistency in the

English teachers' evaluation of writing during his December 1968 visit. The English teachers from Grades 7-12 implemented a writing trial to achieve the goal. All students in these six grades wrote a short essay on a given topic in their Friday morning English classes. To mask their identities and grade level, students selected any seven-digit number like 8273500, which was recorded on their essay and a master list so teachers could return essays. English teachers gathered in the seminar room to read and evaluate essays in a group until all essays were read. Two teachers marked each essay, and if they disagreed on its quality, a third reader was required. The department chairman tabulated these scores by grade level and counted the range of grades and percentages by matching scores with the master list. The teachers enjoyed working with each other, realizing how differently they graded the same work. They were surprised at the difficulty of differentiating a seventh from a twelfth grader's writing, and they decided to repeat the trial several times in order to obtain some consistency in evaluation.

On the third trial, the students coded all papers with π, 3141592. The joke was on the English teachers, who wasted the day because no one noticed that the numbers were identical until after the essays were evaluated. The students and the mathematics teacher were gleeful about their joke. The English chairperson refused to talk to the math chairman for the remainder of the year and would not repeat the trial.

Dr. David Hawkins, a member of the Mountain View Center for Environmental Education at the University of Colorado, again recommended changes in the schedule during his visit in 1972. A renowned environmentalist, scientist, and educator, Dr. Hawkins also proposed a scheme to bring specialized teachers into regular classrooms to help grade teachers recognize the connections between science and art and science and music. The goal was to help children assimilate and integrate "the specialties."

The final three Distinguished Visitors targeted school life rather than the classroom. Dr. Carl Fields, then Dean for minority students at Princeton University, visited the school in 1969 to focus on the problems of the black community at Parker. After his visit, enrollment of black students in the lower and high schools increased. Harvard sociologist Sarah Lawrence Lightfoot concentrated on interpersonal school relationships during her 1983 visit. She identified points of tension such as the relationship between the school and minority families as well as the expectations for the involvement of families. In 1988, Elise Boulding, professor of Sociology at University of Colorado and a member of its Institute of Behavioral Science, encouraged the school to teach skills of reflection, meditation, and conflict resolution that she felt would be required of world citizens.

Department by department analysis and the evaluation of the school as a whole showed that the curriculum had progressed in the forty years since the Eight-Year Study. The written reports of the Distinguished Visitors were insightful and extensive and had much to offer the teachers, the departments, the parents, and the administration.[33]

Lower School Course of Study

In this era, the principal divided the school into three rather than two divisions: lower school, Grades K-5; middle school, Grades 6-8; and high school, Grades 9-12. The significant curricular experiments were undertaken in the middle and high schools, but it was only the middle school that applied Ralph Tyler's "principles of curriculum and evaluation." After sixty years of experience, the central subjects had not been advanced but were replaced by English, history, mathematics, science, and the arts taught as separate disciplines. The new courses used a vertical organization by discipline, such as "The Lower School Science Perspective" for Grades 1-5, which was now taught by a lower school science teacher rather than the grade teacher.[34]

New research suggested additions to the lower school course of study. In 1970, the teachers replaced the Gillingham Reading Program, introduced in 1950, with a Learning Improvement Program that provided remedial services for learning disabled students who exhibited disorders in one or more of the psychological processes—attention, listening speaking, thinking, reading, spelling, written expression, and/or mathematics. Mrs. Jacqueline Rudman, who had no intention of becoming a teacher until informed that her son was reading disabled, was appointed the first Learning Improvement teacher in 1970. Little was known about learning disabilities or about how children learn to read or do math differently so Mrs. Rudman enrolled at Northwestern University to study the field. As Lower School

Learning Improvement Coordinator, she helped teachers diagnose and teach students with reading difficulties and worked with small groups of students to alleviate their problems. The program's effectiveness prompted the school to expand instructional help for learning disabled students throughout the middle and high school in the 1990s.

In the mid 1970s, the lower school transformed the physical education program in an approach that ran counter to the growing trend of isolated subjects. Specialist Lil Lowry Manning increased the physical education skills and the number of sessions scheduled per week by integrating physical education with other subjects—arts, geography, health and safety, history, and mathematical concepts.[35]

In the lower school, the course offerings and the instructional strategies could no longer be characterized as progressive, but in 1977 Dr. John Sherman, Lower School Curriculum Coordinator, identified four common progressive objectives which the teachers made part of the lower school ethos: (1) "to help the child become a citizen who can function effectively in a political democracy, which involves an understanding of voting, community membership and responsibility, the development of personal autonomy based upon reason, and an experiential understanding of democratic values"; (2) "to help children develop public roles and responsibilities and to expand individual interests as a citizen . . . [because] the children's interests are the stuff from which adult vocations, avocations, careers, hobbies, pleasures, pastimes, passions, and loves are made . . . the base upon which the deepest pleasures and joys in life are built"; (3) "to help children learn through doing and experiencing, based on Dewey's definition of intelligence as the ability to solve problems"; and (4) "to help each child develop an inquiry/critical approach to what he hears, reads, and observes."[36] Teachers used these four progressive tenets as overarching goals as the high school teachers had done in the Eight-Year Study and incorporated them in English, history, mathematics, physical education, the arts, the new experimental courses, Morning Exercises, and outside activities. These four themes running through all of the instruction in the courses was a second way to make a progressive course of study.

In 1980, Lower School Curriculum Coordinator JoNell Bailey experimented with a Lower School Experiential Program, a one-week activity-centered learning experience that used Lincoln Park as its classroom. The zoo and the park provided opportunities for pupils to work with animals and to study nature. The teachers replaced the regular classes with experiential electives, and parents helped to teach in the program. The lower school also introduced computers to students. A computer teacher placed computers throughout the school halls and classrooms and held separate computer classes and the gradehead teacher integrated computers into other courses.

Another lower school experiment was the Lorado Taft Outdoor Education course, designed by Science Department chairperson Ann Marie Fries. A group of teachers chaperoned the fifth grade class to the Lorado Taft Campus near Oregon, Illinois, where they experienced a three-day environmental education opportunity. The class members learned about outdoor education and about each other by developing interpersonal relationships with teachers and other students.

The lower school began with junior and senior kindergartens, whose teacher's main responsibility was to introduce the pupils to all disciplines in the school. Their classrooms were built to accomplish this goal. Each area represented a different discipline: a drama corner, a building block area, library shelves, a place for shelf games, a painting area, a listening center, an arts and crafts table, a wood work and clay table and a water play table. For science, living things like plants, guinea pigs, and fish were in the classroom. The students selected from among these activities, and teachers prepared units of study that emphasized "The Home Around the World" or "Awareness of Ourselves as Individuals and as Group Members."[37]

Beverly Verona Greenberg began teaching kindergarten in 1971. Clad in a pair of faded blue jeans, a sweatshirt that announced "100 percent Italian," and an elephant pin clamped on her right shoulder, "Greenie" led a classroom in a "state of creative disorder." Adopting the posture of teacher for one child, mother for another, and sister for the next, her main concern was to help each child become relaxed and confident, gain a sense of self-worth and pride and a feeling of security. Her students read and wrote, drew and painted, sang and counted. She taught them to attend Morning Exercises and participate in the school traditions. She was inventive and creative in ideas for projects, priding herself on being called "the life skills" teacher. She found a way to weave real life expectations into everything she taught.[38]

Beginning in 1972, Alison Abbott was assistant and then teacher in the senior kindergarten for eight years. She transferred to first grade in 1980 because of her interest in teaching reading. Abbott wanted to be a teacher at an early age. As a teenager she loved babysitting and working as a camp counselor. After earning a degree in education from Case Western Reserve University in Ohio, Abbott taught fourth grade in a troubled Chicago public school. The job discouraged Abbott, and she left to search for a position in a school that was compatible with her vision of education. She found it at the Parker School, where she taught throughout the 1990s while her two children attended the school.

Her first grade classroom had a distinctive arrangement: each region of the room dealt with a different area of the curriculum—reading, writing, mathematics, art, central subject, and computers. A posted schedule clarified which activities took place when and where, providing an effective organizational structure for six- and seven-year-olds. When Abbott became a first grade teacher, she and JoNell Bailey designed a successful curriculum experiment that used the central topic of Mexico to introduce the children to another culture through literature, music, crafts, cooking, games, and other activities.[39]

In the lower school, each grade had a topic focus—in senior kindergarten, the farm; in first grade, Mexico; in second grade, Japan; third grade, Chicago; fourth grade, Egypt and Greece; and fifth grade, the Middle Ages. The lower school culminated with the fifth grade, which was ably taught by Harriett Cholden during the entire era. A graduate of the University of Iowa, Harriett Cholden did not become acquainted with progressive education until she accepted the position as the gradehead of the fifth grade in 1963. She felt fortunate to be assigned fourth grade teacher Lynn Martin as her coordinating faculty member. Martin taught her about progressive education and more. Martin's unit on the Greeks suggested ideas for Cholden's central subject on the Medieval Fair, which also combined history, literature, and the visual and performing arts.

Each spring, the fifth graders, costumed as medieval ladies, knights, or peasants presented the Middle Ages to the school in a fair-like atmosphere. Crimson, blue, purple, and gold banners and flags adorned the corridors and the courtyard and welcomed curious young students, upper classmen, and proud parents to join in the festivities— a joust and a knighting ceremony, a parade of players on Carl Orff instruments, a morality play, juggling, and a demonstration of dye making and creating stained glass windows. The fifth graders' immersion in the Middle Ages was easily awakened when as seniors they studied medieval literature, history, and the Catholic religion.

Cholden achieved her main teaching goal— "to imbue in students a broader perspective of what they can accomplish"—and many students verified her effectiveness. At the end of her fifth grade year, student Julia Felsenthal explained, "Mrs. Cholden introduced the most new ideas, and opened up my mind to different kinds of learning . . . When you walk into Mrs. Cholden's classroom there is a sudden change in the atmosphere . . . a kind of zest for learning. Mrs. Cholden is almost always teaching something new. Even the kids who never liked school get used to learning and sometimes like it."

Cholden published articles on the Medieval Fair, education, and on several social studies themes. An expert on "the problem of homework," she and child psychologist, John Friedman, Ph.D., were invited to discuss the subject on radio and television, were featured in newspaper articles, and coauthored *The Homework Handbook* (1998) for students and parents.[40]

Middle School Course of Study

Principal Ellison created the middle school in 1970 and named Delafield Griffith its first coordinator. The absence of college requirements gave latitude to experiment in the middle grades. The teachers designed the course of study upon Tyler's "principles of curriculum and instruction," modeled from the Eight-Year Study. The faculty began curriculum development using the school philosophy, with psychology and sociology as a filter, formulating the objectives, selecting the learning experiences, organizing them so learning could be transferred vertically and horizontally, and evaluating their effectiveness.

The curriculum design focused on child-centered, subject-centered, and society-centered objectives based on the school's progressive goals. The subject-centered objectives, which included traditional disciplines like history, English, science, and others, already dominated the course of study when they were part of the lower school and were taught as isolated subjects. The middle school teachers employed progressive instructional strategy based on "learning by doing" in these disciplines. Although the available research showed few positive results about teaching foreign language in the middle grades, the faculty experimented with Spanish for Grades 7 and 8. Unfavorable results prompted teachers to change the course and experiment with teaching about language concepts like etymology, semantics, connotation, and rhetoric instead of learning a language. With a multilingual teacher from abroad, John McGuinness, the course fascinated the students and opened their minds to new discoveries about language; but when Mr. McGuinness had to return to England, hiring a second multilingual teacher was difficult, forcing the teachers to abandon the language class and shift to another variation on teaching language—a reading class. The central organizing principle for reading was to prepare students with both the habit of reading and the skill to read different kinds of materials differently. The teachers planned two approaches.

The first was a two-year trial that was a cross-graded, interdisciplinary activity-centered Group Reading project taught by all middle school faculty. In a pre-test, students were interviewed about their reading interests and each student completed a written reading inventory. The middle school teachers and the librarian prepared a list of appropriate titles that related to the various disciplines. The students selected one of the books from the list and in groups of twelve students and a teacher searched for a way to present the book through another medium to encourage others to read it. For example, the science teachers supervised science fiction reading; history paired with historical dramas; and literature combined poetry, choral readings, and novels. At the end of each month, five days were designated for groups to present their interpretations of the books to the other middle schoolers. Students could utilize any media for presentation—the arts, music, or drama.

The most evocative presentation was the visualization of the destruction of an environment based on a collection of science fiction stories. Students learned to love science fiction, a fairly new genre then, and teachers made it a permanent part of the seventh grade reading list. A postreading inventory in ninth grade confirmed that the experiment succeeded in creating readers. Both students and teachers found Group Reading interesting and meaningful.[41] The Group Reading program created readers but did not meet the second objective, students learning to read different materials differently.

In another trial, the teachers implemented a Developmental Reading approach. The faculty had to meet with an outside expert to improve the teaching of reading in their content areas—history, science, literature, and mathematics. The goal of a Developmental Reading class was to advance students' reading skills for all disciplines. First the course was taught separately by a reading specialist, and the next year the content teachers applied the reading assignment to their specific disciplines. The result was that students learned to read for major and minor points in history, learned that all points were of equal importance in science, and learned when and how to skim, scan, and peruse. Their adaptation to different ways to read improved speed and comprehension. Both trials in reading were effective, but Group Reading had to be eliminated from an over-burdened schedule and Developmental Reading was integrated into the subject-centered classes after a two-year trial. The teachers gained satisfaction from the courses devised for subject-centered curriculum.

For the child-centered approaches, the teachers designed two major experiments: mini courses to develop the middle school students' needs and interests, and a new middle school advisory system. For six weeks of the academic year, the teachers canceled regular classes while the students enrolled in two activity-centered, interdisciplinary cross-graded courses. The classes lasted two-and-half hours each, one in the morning and one in the afternoon. The students selected from a series of twenty-five courses inspired by different disciplines. The instruction was activity centered and included construction of projects and field trips. Artistic and manual expression dominated the classroom.[42]

The mini courses were met with great enthusiasm. Much to everyone's surprise, the evaluation results indicated that the trial was inappropriate for this age level because the learning was fragmented and students were not transferring learning from one mini course to the next. Many students, teachers, and parents were disappointed by the evaluation results since the students seemed engaged in learning, the knowledge segments in the courses were high, and the needs and interests of the students had been captured. Because the evaluation data revealed fragmentation of knowledge, the faculty reluctantly eliminated the program.

A second way the child-centered objectives were met was by the introduction of an advisory system modeled on the high school advisory. At first, the students organized across grades and met with their advisory teacher to discuss personal, academic, and social concerns for one session a week. Later the system changed to a small group of students from a single grade meeting at lunch hour. Like the high school advisory, the design achieved positive results with middle schoolers.

The society-centered objectives were achieved mainly through a Community Service program, which permitted the students to select an agency or project from a list prepared by the teachers, who used readings, films, and presentations given by members from different agencies to teach students about the goals and activities of the agencies. The students and the teachers planned sites where students were to participate and divided students into groups of twelve sixth, seventh, and eighth graders to work at the agencies. The students captured their experience in diaries, journals, or written interviews of a participant or a recipient in the agency. The student groups delivered a culminating presentation to the entire school. Originally, Community Service was part of a national research program under the auspices of Ralph Tyler. His national evaluation data demonstrated the value of experiential learning.

Coordinator of Middle School Delafield Griffith designed the mini courses. Mr. Griffith began as a teacher of seventh grade social studies in 1962. For five years he taught twelve- and thirteen-year-olds to love history by narrating stories of heroes, which the students reenacted; discussing current events; organizing field trips; and teaching them how to read and write history like little detectives. Griffith opened the youngsters' minds to what history was and how it worked.

The seventh graders were surprised when they entered the eighth grade English classroom in 1967 to see Mr. Griffith standing behind the desk. Versatile, gifted, and well read, Mr. Griffith taught the "little urchins," as he affectionately called them, to read the classics, write three-paragraph expository essays, and behave like ladies and gentlemen. He read and quoted from Dickens's *Tale of Two Cities* and soon the eighth graders were heard quipping, "It was the best of times and the worst of times." Not only the novel but the eighth grade play held a prominent role in the English course, and often Griffith cast the plays to advance the status of an exceptionally quiet or troubled student. In her autobiography, *Unafraid of the Dark*, Rosemary Bray '72 remembered Mr. Griffith as a milepost on her journey from "the projects" to a career as a writer and an editor of *The New York Times Book Review*. Bray wrote:

> He asked me how I liked school, and which subjects I liked best. I con-
> fessed to loving reading, of course, and told him how whenever I read,
> all the people came to life inside my head. 'It's like having a movie
> screen inside my forehead,' I told him. And then he looked me straight
> in my eyes. 'Do you know you're the kind of student that a teacher waits
> his whole life to teach?' . . . Nothing could have induced me to leave
> Parker after that . . . Mr. Griffith saw me, knew me for who I was and
> who I might be. It was enough.[43]

"A kid at heart," "a master of trivia," "respected by a most diverse group," Mr. Griffith acted like a "frustrated minister" when in the kindest and often humorous way, he would persuade students or teachers to do the right thing. He would sing when he walked down the halls wearing one of his checked sports jackets, a striped tie, and a white shirt. Born in West Virginia and a thorough southern gentleman, he addressed people as "child" or "girl." He added levity and a smile to a troubling day. His absence changed the tone of the school, and years later teachers still told Delafield stories. After five years of teaching social studies and two years of teaching English, "Grif" was appointed coordinator of middle school from 1967 to 1970 and head of upper school from 1970 to 1974.

Another history teacher, Vince Threet, a graduate of Roosevelt University, began teaching eighth grade history in 1970 and was appointed Middle School Coordinator in 1974. From a military family and a former marine, Threet's passionate commitment to America made him emphatic about teaching his students the U.S. Constitution and the Declaration of Independence. The focus of his course was American history, and Mr. Threet, a poet and a lover of poetry, often used the genre to teach history. Students said that lessons taught by Mr. Threet were lessons still remembered in their junior U.S. History course.

Middle school history teacher Catherine Chambers Haskins joined the faculty in 1974 and followed Mr. Threet as Middle School Coordinator from 1978 to 1979. Haskins also served as Middle School Community

Service Coordinator from 1982 to 1984. Effective in meeting middle schoolers' needs, she was both a nurturing mother and a demanding intellectual. In the Community Service program, Ms. Haskins utilized the Morning Exercise to its fullest advantage by presenting a slide show profiling the community program. She organized her students to collaborate with public school students in a "Kids Convention 1996" that focused on student issues and the presidential campaign. Ms. Haskins was invited to speak about the program at education conferences in New York and Atlanta, Georgia.[44]

Another middle school coordinator was Lee Dreuth, who said that his trumpet helped him to secure teaching positions. In 1959, at King Elementary Public School, he was hired because the principal wanted a middle school teacher who could teach instrumental music. When the principal transferred to the Montefiore School for delinquent boys, he wanted Dreuth and his trumpet. Again in 1962, when Parker School Spanish teacher Barney Negronida met Mr. Dreuth, Negronida told Dreuth that the Parker School was doubling enrollment and needed middle school teachers who could teach instrumental music.

At Parker, Dreuth chose to teach sixth grade. When teaching English, he introduced the *Parkerite*, a middle school student publication. Later, Dreuth joined the history department and centered his curriculum on the era between the Renaissance and the American Revolution. To this history course he added Voyageur's Night, when students dressed in voyageurs's clothing and spent all night in the lunchroom learning about canoes, hunting with a bow and arrow, getting lost in the woods, and making fur hats. He also introduced colonial Fete Week, when pupils dressed as colonists and lived vicariously. Its highlight was an appearance by "Minister Markwell," whose homily, based on Jonathan Edwards's "Sinners in the Hands of an Angry God," evoked fear in some students and questions in others about heaven, hell, and salvation.

Dreuth wore brightly colored golf shirts and a white golf cap when he left the building. His big smile covered his broad face and his neatly groomed mustache and gray hair held the memory of the red hair that once was there. Extraordinarily polite and friendly, a standard he set and held for his students, Dreuth held many positions—Middle School Coordinator for five years, safety officer for twenty-five years, a shop teacher, and the ninth grade head. He introduced a baseball clinic, and became the first soccer coach and the respected golf coach. Ironically, he did not teach music and only once was heard to play his trumpet magnificently at Morning Exercise.[45]

Maryanne Kalin-Miller was appointed Middle School Coordinator in 1992. In that position as in her other professional appointments, she applied her creative energy and problem solving skills. She joined the Science Department in 1969 and taught science at every grade by letting students "mess about in science," which encouraged both genders to engage in the discipline. A seventh grade girl reported, "This is the first time I liked science," and a boy admitted, "I finally understand what science means." Ms. Kalin-Miller introduced the popular high school course in Animal Behavior and taught ninth-grade Physical Science. Whatever the name of the course, it was characterized by stimulating content, organized plans, well-selected materials, fresh ideas, and stimulating and "chatty" discussions. Ms. Kalin-Miller was chairperson of the Science Department from 1971 to 1974 and trained lower school science teacher Anne Marie Fries to assume the chairmanship.

Appointed seventh grade head in 1980, Ms. Kalin-Miller took over the Middle School Community Service program and became the central voice in advancing community service as a high school requirement. She also introduced the middle school student portfolio, a file created by students containing two assignments from each subject area that students considered "special" but not necessarily their "best" work. The portfolio was shared with parents and teachers. In 1990, Ms. Kalin-Miller was selected as one of twelve educators to travel to Caracas, Venezuela, to teach residents of the area about wildlife conservation. A graduate in biology from Purdue University, Kalin-Miller was a part-time college professor at DePaul University.[46]

High School Course of Study

For high school students and teachers, time became the enemy of learning. Since 1940 the Eight-Year Study curriculum grew by accretion, as teachers added Independent Study, a May off-campus program, half-credit courses, and mini courses. The knowledge explosion and the fermentation in society called for new subjects in the course of study. To history was added eastern civilization, to literature was added new minority authors, and science now emphasized the discovery method. The schedule fragmented the day into four or five forty- to sixty-minute modules and became incompatible with progressive teaching methods such as field trips, class projects, viewing films, and play rehearsals. To accommodate the knowledge explosion and to use these progressive strategies, teachers were constantly exchanging class time with colleagues or asking them to excuse students from their classes for field trips. Departments were constantly competing for additional time, and overburdened students struggled to shoehorn sports, play rehearsals, and other school activities into their crowded schedules.

The school stopped the clock in spring 1974. Inspired by Distinguished Visitors Dr. Hilgard and Dr. Hawkins, who indicated that the schedule was too tight, the high school faculty held a two-week trial of immersion learning in preparation for a larger scale undertaking. These one- or two-week immersion classes offered for a full day on one subject freed students from the constraints and fragmentation imposed by the traditional schedule and permitted a richer use of resources, the development of important skills, new approaches to teaching, and a closer interaction between teachers and students. Students selected one or two of thirty-two courses ranging from "Concert Consciousness Raising" to "Art and Propaganda," "Shakespeare's Characters Alive," and "Cross Country Skiing." Learning by doing was the prevalent instructional strategy.

The effectiveness of the Immersion experiment led teachers to develop the Intensive-Extensive schedule, which was introduced in 1975, lasted until 1986, and lingered until 1996. Intensive courses followed the immersion pattern of longer periods of time per class, and extensive courses continued the traditional forty- to sixty-minute pattern. The teachers could offer courses for a semester or a year, and eventually settled on the semester as the dominant time frame. A twenty-minute module allowed classes to range from forty-minute classes held five times a week to 140-minute sessions held three times a week. Some courses were offered for a single grade, and a few were cross-graded for all high school students. Many courses were interdisciplinary and/or team taught. Some were required and others were elective.

Intensive departments were English, history, science, the visual arts, and drama. Typical intensive courses were cross-graded for two grade levels and offered in 140-minute sessions three times a week for a semester. Mathematics, foreign language, music, and physical education followed the extensive model, which offered courses five times a week for forty minutes a day.

The experiment transformed the curriculum by altering course content, course selection, the sequence of courses, and diploma requirements. The schedule converted course content from general required subjects to specific required courses from which the student could select. For example, instead of English I, II, III, IV, students enrolled in Bible, Myth and Epic, Dramatic Literature, Prose Fiction, Poetry, American Literature, Shakespeare, World Literature, and British Literature. Journalism and other English electives were added. History changed from History I, II, III, IV to Library Research, Economic Theory, European Cultural and Intellectual History, and a series of other requirements and electives. Science became a sequence of required and elective courses—physics, biology, chemistry, were offered in sequence like Physics A and Physics B, Animal Behavior, Earth Sciences, and other science selections were also offered. Instead of Art I, II, III, and IV, students selected sculpture, painting, drawing, photography, or other fine arts. Drama also divided courses into specific areas. Physical education transformed from grade level courses to cross-graded courses in specific life skills. The extensive courses in foreign language, music, and mathematics remained grade level courses.

English teachers' intensive courses were frequently oversubscribed. Dr. William Duffy, a consummate teacher dedicated to the students, came to Parker in 1975. "Duffmaster" taught the required sophomore intensive in Dramatic Literature, exposing students to European and American theater. For his upper division elective courses in Twentieth Century British Literature and Political Literature, juniors and seniors went to great lengths to obtain one of the twenty available seats. For more than a quarter century, Duffy taught W.B. Yeats, whom he was praised for presenting masterfully. One alumna who went on to complete her doctorate at Oxford on Yeats thanked Duffy for changing her life. Another commented that her classes at Yale were "less intellectually stimulating than the classes I had with you." More recently, a Harvard graduate called Mr. Duffy "the best teacher I ever had."

Recognized by students and parents alike as a "special teacher, who matters to the kids," Duffy proceeded quietly through the day in a low-profile fashion, taking satisfaction from a class well taught, a student essay well written, or a senior achieving an "A" on "the mother of all tests," the final exam given in the Twentieth Century British Literature course. He earned his doctorate in English at the University of Chicago before coming to the Parker School. His primary interest is in psychoanalysis and literature.[47]

The school's concept of the teacher as artist sustained English teacher Bonnie Seebold throughout her Parker career, where she taught Shakespeare, Fiction and Poetry Writing, Chamber Theater, and a freshman required writing course. When Miss Seebold came to Parker School in 1977, she adapted the existing freshman class on Bible, Myth and Epic to coincide with her interests in psychology through storytelling, fiction, and poetry writing. She also taught a Fiction and Poetry class for which she developed and coordinated the publication of *The Fiction and Poetry Reader*, a collection of student writing used as the course textbook. Miss Seebold was advisor to the school literary publication, *Phaedrus*.

Her work in speech, theater, and oral interpretation was reflected in her freshman writing course, where students performed readings and in her Chamber Theatre course, where students scripted, directed, and enacted stories on the stage. Her course in Shakespeare also incorporated performance; students acted scenes or presented an edited version of a full play at Morning Exercise. Seebold codirected Aphra Behn's Restoration comedy, *The Rover*, and William Inge's *Dark at the Top of the Stairs*, and she directed the senior play production of Tina Howe's *Approaching Zanzibar*. Her teaching methods were perfectly suited for the Intensive schedule. Her students said that she "inspired some of the school's finest creative efforts through her sensitive and patient guidance."[48]

The Intensive schedule invigorated the high school students and offered many excellent educational opportunities. Most of the courses were well taught and used progressive instructional principles; courses were activity centered and used expression as a learning technique. Over the decade, however, the Intensive schedule eroded, and by 1986 it dwindled to a few team-taught courses and eighty-minute classes. The curriculum committee monitored all of the schedule and course changes by a vote; however, the tendency of many teachers was to "regress to the norm," to return to the safety of the past rather than to explore the possibilities of the new schedule and the ideas it evoked. Only history, English, and science remained intensive, and the science department was discussing a return to the extensive schedule in 1986.

Several problems plagued the experiment. New teachers had to be trained in progressive pedagogy in order to sustain student interest for an extended class period. The administrators seemed to favor a more traditional schedule because it was easier to control the student body when schedules were similar and predictable. The weaknesses of the Intensive Schedule were curriculum fragmentation, time inequities among departments, lack of transfer of training, and inability to chart student progress because students constantly moved from one teacher to the next. But the Intensive experiment was dropped without an evaluation.

The Intensive schedule was popular with the students, and the effects were positive. Students learned to arrange a four-year plan over which they could exercise control instead of a dictated plan. Students liked the fact that all days were not identical, that they could pair the more rigorous classes with the less demanding ones. The schedule catered to student interests and intensified their involvement in classes, and most students thrived on the variety and the intensity.

The experiment was unscientific. In the original design no pre- and post-evaluation tools were set in place; therefore, there was a lack of empirical or qualitative data to measure the ten-year experiment. Tyler explained that evaluation was essential to develop a science of education but the teachers were busy developing new courses and no one was assigned the task. The teacher debates in the curriculum committee were based not on collected data but on opinions, passions, and personal wishes, which carried the day to the regret of many students and teachers. For most participants, both teachers and students, the experiment had great value, but from an educator's perspective, little was learned about the educational process or student achievement.

The Intensive-Extensive program had the strength of utilizing the library because the approach individualized group instruction. For example, one group of students was studying and reading about Russian authors while another was researching a science project. The library was effective in this way because the librarian could order specific categories of books to meet curriculum needs like a collection of black writers or women authors. Throughout the school's history, the library shared the school philosophy: "a responsibility to provide the student with the opportunity to master skills and basic knowledge, to develop disciplined exploratory intuitive thinking and imagination and the spirit of inquiry and to experience the joy of learning."[49] During the Intensive experiment, the faculty found a way to use it, but until 1984, the library had been a "weak and neglected link in the chain of school resources." The budget was increased significantly after the 1984 Self-Study of the Illinois School Association of Central States reported severely inadequate space, staff, and funding.[50] From 1985 to 1995, the librarians made considerable progress in correcting these problems. The librarian increased the print collection to about 38,000 volumes, 122 periodical subscriptions, and a growing vertical file. The fiction collection became substantial and able to serve students of all levels. The nonfiction collection helped teachers and students research specific subjects such as eastern and western religions, culture and history, African American literature, and other topics. The collections were not used in the same way after the Intensive experiment ended.

Not only did the library serve the Intensive-Extensive program well, but the librarians introduced lower and middle school activities such as a read-aloud program for third graders, an after-school story hour for kindergartners and their parents, a book club for middle school students, and library outreach with other libraries. The friends of the library, a parent group, also sponsored two book fairs each year.

In this era, four librarians served the school—Mrs. Silverton began in 1965, followed by Mary Stollman and Mary Sue Voth. The backbone of the library was Anne Duncan, who came to Parker School in 1983 and was praised by students and teachers as literate, well informed, competent, resourceful, and knowledgeable about sources and available to share her time and expertise. She and her assistant Margaret Threet were generous in their services to the students and the community. When a third grader filled in the library survey asking, "Who is your best friend?" she answered, "Mrs. Duncan."

Teachers: The Classroom Is Central

Most vintage faculty who taught in the years before World War II had retired by the early 1970s. Principal Geer replaced this old guard with a corps of new teachers hired to carry forth the progressive legacy. Geer placed the educational process as central and established curriculum development as a priority. He placed the responsibility for curriculum development on two Curriculum Coordinators and the department chairmen, who constituted a newly organized curriculum committee. For curriculum coordination, Geer established three goals: (1) experimentation with and the advancement of the course of study, (2) vertical and horizontal articulation of learning experiences, and (3) the evaluation of the course of study.

The Curriculum Coordinators for the lower and upper schools were given identical goals but functioned differently. The lower school did not utilize a curriculum committee *per se* because the upper school curriculum committee was formed by department chairpersons, many responsible for all grades. All of the lower school teachers considered themselves members of their curriculum committee. Kindergarten teacher Dr. John Sherman was appointed the Lower School Curriculum Coordinator for Grades K-5 and English teacher Dr. Marie Kirchner Stone was appointed the Upper School Curriculum Coordinator for Grades 7-12. In collaboration with the appropriate chairpersons, both coordinators assisted teachers in developing course syllabi. Both also arranged these syllabi by grade level or by department and year to create a curriculum library from which all teachers could draw. They distilled the syllabi into course descriptions and constructed three Course Description Booklets for the lower, middle, and high schools. Each coordinator made an overview of the course of study, diagnosed weaknesses, and then arranged small teams of teachers to work with them on resolution. For example, the Lower School Coordinator examined the choice of the central topic, the instructional strategies used, and the vertical and horizontal organization of curriculum. The Upper School Coordinator planned the development of the middle school program, designed a health program for Grades 6-12, introduced Developmental Reading, and organized a team-taught ninth grade class entitled "Writing Across the Curriculum." The coordinators introduced the Parent Open House, where parents attended mini classes to become acquainted with the course of study. The Parent Open House became an annual event. The coordinators also created curriculum libraries, which housed syllabi for use by other teachers.

Five successive Lower School Curriculum Coordinators followed Dr. John Sherman's leadership: Lynn Martin, Annabel Williams, JoNell Bailey, Joan Bradbury, and Ann Breed. When third grade teacher Joan Bradbury served as Curriculum Coordinator between 1988 and 1996, she drew on her strong knowledge of progressive education. A graduate of Swarthmore College and the University of Chicago, she was a founding member of the North Dakota Study Group on progressive education and attended Institute II, a small group of teachers who studied progressive education each summer in Bennington, Vermont.

Marie Kirchner Stone was appointed the first Upper School Curriculum Coordinator in 1975 and served until 1985. She was a challenging and demanding upper-division English teacher who began teaching at the Parker School mid-year 1966 as team teacher of the Senior Seminar with Principal Thomas. To a new teacher, this experience was an ordeal by fire. Students especially liked her American Literature course, and she favored the team-taught interdisciplinary courses like Richard III or Literature and Religion. Dr. Stone taught every kind of writing—the expository essay, journalism, nonfiction, and scriptwriting. Her students' essays and articles were always promptly returned but with abundant and often illegible criticism and either a "No" or "A" or the comment "Revise." Students complained about the work, but all twenty places in the writing classes were occupied each semester.

Dr. Stone was said to be "a dynamic presence in the school." "When she walked down the halls with her purposeful stride, arms full of books, briefcase in hand, blazer thrown over her shoulders, it was like Moses parting the Red Sea. Some students shrunk to the side lines to avoid her; others flocked around her to talk."

She was an "instrument of positive change who brought prestige to the positions she held"—the first Dean of Students, the first college counselor, the chairman of the English Department, a part-time professor at Loyola University, and the author of several books and many papers. The National Association of Independent Schools appointed her to its twelve-member Academic Committee, which studied national educational issues and presented conferences for the 1,000 member schools.

In spite of her numerous activities, Stone cared about her students and opened her home to them. Advisory was the coveted period of her day.

She had a rule. A student in trouble could call her at any hour of the day or night and she would help, providing the student let her call another person for assistance if needed. When one student ran away to Kansas City, Stone called Mr. McCutcheon.[51]

Mathematics teacher Peter Barrett served as the second Upper School Curriculum Coordinator from 1986 until 1991. After arriving at the Parker School in 1977, Mr. Barrett taught every mathematics course from Grades 6 through 12 and served as the chairman of the Mathematics Department. He was also the Middle School Coordinator in the early 1980s. Although he insisted on a low profile, the students discovered his value and dedicated the 1984 Yearbook to him because "he took on responsibility beyond eight to five" and "made the school a pleasant place to come each day."[52] The seniors frequently invited him to present commencement addresses. Mr. Barrett resigned his position as Upper School Curriculum Coordinator to return to full-time teaching, and he was followed in the position by Rebecca Rossof.

Besides performing the traditional functions of the position, the well organized and thorough Ms. Rossof supervised the growing number of Independent Studies selected by half of the senior class. She also examined student transcripts and introduced the concept of "a student in good standing," which matched credits, requirements, and grade averages according to a set of standards. She made teacher self-evaluation a part of the course syllabi and helped students promote student evaluation of courses. She also encouraged student evaluation of teachers in the fashion of colleges that evaluate professors and post the appraisals. Rossof was instrumental in advancing computer technology for teachers and departments.

In 1977, Ms. Rossof joined the science department and taught science as a process of inquiry whether it was Science 9, physics, chemistry, or biology. "Rossof challenged students to develop critical thinking skills as they researched current understandings, investigated problems, and analyzed data." She was experimental in her instructions and applied progressive methodology. Ms. Rossof insisted that students develop reading and writing skills and extend their knowledge beyond the classroom. An advocate of individualizing instruction, she adjusted the science class materials to the needs of the students. As Science Department chairman, Rossof treated department members respectfully and kept communication confidential, making her a trustworthy colleague. Her advice was sought by teachers not only on departmental matters but also on personal matters.

Ms. Rossof was also the gradehead for the juniors for three years, and as such the class sought her advice, which was calmly and coolly delivered. Deliberate, determined, and hard working, Rossof enriched the lives of the eleventh graders as gradehead, but it was her advisory that stood out as her major contribution to the life of the school. Always properly attired, a ready smile, a twinkle in her brown eyes, Ms. Rossof could be counted on to fulfill all obligations in a timely fashion and with excellence.[53] Ms. Rossof was the last faculty curriculum coordinator.

An Upper School Curriculum Coordinator served as a member of the curriculum committee, which chose its chairman from among the department chairpersons. In this era, the Intensive-Extensive experiment was the main focus of curriculum committee meetings. Conflict over scheduling evoked considerable hostility and great controversy among department chairpersons and too frequently resulted in fatuous compromises.

Dr. Bernard Kent Markwell was the perfect choice as chairman of the curriculum committee. A diplomat, he was able to motivate the most adamant department chairpersons to collaborate. Colleagues noted that "fresh and original ideas for courses flowed naturally from him." A gifted scholar and a gentleman, he was always willing to work out a balance between those who wanted to change little and those who wanted to adapt the subject matter to the current demands of society. Dr. Markwell was also chairman of the History Department, and he taught a remarkable variety of electives, including Psychoanalysis and History, History of Economic Systems, American Politics and Government, Newberry Library, The Renaissance in Italy, and perhaps the most famous, Richard III, a team-taught course involving three faculty members and a parent volunteer.

Broadly and well educated and erudite, Markwell earned degrees at Wesleyan University, when its history department enjoyed a golden age in the late 1950s and early 1960s, and at the University of Chicago, where Martin Marty was his dissertation adviser. Markwell really believed what he taught. He thought history to be the most important means for understanding the human animal and based on that understanding, he worked for a better future. He did not separate act and thought. He studied Christian

Socialism and professed it. As his morals insisted, he worked for a better here and now at the Parker School, sponsoring Amnesty International, marching for peace, and actively advocating equality and dignity for African Americans, Hispanics, Asians, and gays and lesbians. These qualities plus the fact that his ideas were well suited to the progressive "climate of opinion" of his time enabled Markwell to become an outstanding Parker teacher. Markwell had a "pied piper effect" and maintained close relations with large numbers of students. Author and journalist Andrea Gabor '75 wrote in the *Parker Magazine*, "For a whole generation of us Bernie was Parker, the best of Parker."[54]

Including Dr. Markwell, nine department chairpersons were curriculum committee members. Debating and deciding on most issues that affected the educational process, this collective body held most of the power in the upper school, and many teachers complained that departments were "fiefdoms." At times department chairpersons failed, but when they wielded their power positively, the results were an excellent faculty, effective teacher training, and a successful course of study.

Marsha Brumleve Wagner joined the faculty as an upper school Spanish instructor in 1977 and became chairperson of the Foreign Language Department for Grades 9-12 the next year. She studied at several universities in America and abroad and supplemented her formal education with extensive travel to Spanish-speaking countries. Mrs. Wagner also frequently arranged travels for students, beginning with a trip to Spain in 1978.

She tried several experimental approaches to teaching foreign language. For example, she mapped out a two-year sequence in Spanish in which she enrolled analytically bright language students with slightly younger students from bilingual homes. The experimental question was: would they learn more or less than in a conventional class? The results of the experiment were positive and extended beyond graduation when the older students remained in communication with the younger students through e-mail in Spanish. Her experiments extended to middle and lower school language classes and bilingual high school Spanish classes.

Clad in peasant-like blouses, long Spanish earrings, and Spanish beads, Mrs. Wagner's casual appearance belied her demeanor. In the classroom she could be unrelenting in her demands on students. She insisted that everyone learn a foreign language, even the learning disabled. Whether she was decorating the Spanish room, making a teaching video, chatting with students, or greeting colleagues in hall, she spoke Spanish. Each year, she presented a Morning Exercise with hundreds of students congregated from her Spanish classes. The students were sure to sing off key but with perfect Spanish pronunciation.[55]

Unlike the Foreign Language Department, which covered Grades 9-12, the Physical Education Department was organized for K-12 by chairperson Lillian Lowry Manning. Ms. Lowry began at the Parker School in 1963 by teaching social dancing to well-attired middle schoolers who met in the lunch room every Friday afternoon. Lowry taught more than dancing; she insisted upon good etiquette and proper social manners. The boys had to learn how to invite the girls to dance and how to thank them afterwards whether they wanted to or not. In 1974, Ms. Lowry advanced to a full-time physical education teacher and was appointed chairperson of the physical education department four years later.

As department chairperson, she converted the dreaded required physical education courses into a series of sought-after elective courses ranging from fencing to gymnastics and from jogging to aerobics. The program met with great success and transformed numerous student class cuts to full attendance and increased participation in sports. Ms. Lowry, who considered her greatest contribution to be the transformation of the physical education program, ended her Parker career as Dean of Students for nine years. As Dean, she was an academic and social counselor to students and parents and head of the disciplinary Committee of Four. An African American, Ms. Lowry also recruited minority students and at times helped direct Martin Luther King Day. A woman of diverse talents, she designed and produced greeting cards, wrote poetry, and raised a family. Her first husband, Bill Lowry '52, graduated from Parker and her children attended the lower school. After she resigned, she studied to become a minister.[56]

Like the physical education courses, the visual arts courses were abundant and permitted students to develop their specific area of interest or talent. Roger Gleason began teaching at the Parker School in 1970 and was chairman of the Visual Arts Department from 1971 until 1993. Gleason always dressed as if he stepped out of an Eddie Bauer or Lands' End catalog, and he never seemed to age. When meeting someone in the hall, he waved his hand and smiled to cheer the day. Gleason was a Vietnam War veteran and a graduate of the School of the Art Institute. In his first position at Parker, he taught an interarts program called Media, introduced by ninth grade English teacher William Idol, and throughout his career at Parker, he also taught courses in painting, design, sculpture, and photography. A perfectionist, Gleason's demanding criteria for assignments were quietly given and quietly explained. He preferred one-on-one teaching through explaining and critiquing a pupil's work, convinced that "talking doesn't get the teacher or the student far. Superior results emanate from the students producing work and the teacher explaining the work in a number of different ways."

Gleason assigned art teachers to present classes to all grades from kindergarten to twelfth grade rather than to a single grade. He also introduced the first use of computer programs in the art department. He contributed to the aesthetics of the school, serving as advisor to the *Parker Yearbook,* helping teachers prepare visuals for Morning Exercise, assisting in designing sets for plays, and putting up art exhibits to improve the appearance of the school. He was invited by his former student Cindy Gordon '84, an editorial assistant to a publisher, to write *Seeing for Yourself: Techniques and Projects for Beginning Photographers* (1992).[57]

The curriculum committee divided the performing arts between music and drama. While the Drama Department chairmen changed often, Bart Wolgamot served as Music Department chairman for Grades K-12 from 1974 throughout this era. When Mr. Wolgamot came to Parker in 1967, instrumental music was an extracurricular activity. Students studied an instrument privately outside of school and met weekly in school to play ensemble with teachers, alumni, and parents. Wolgamot's major goal as chairman was to offer both choral and instrumental music classes. After two years, he achieved the goal and the lower school had an instrumental music program. To begin, the fifth graders produced "remarkably sophisticated percussion" from glass, metal, plastic, and other materials. After a short period, the lower school pupils learned to play Orff instruments—xylophones, vibraphones, marimbas—and to play the recorder with the mentoring of art teacher James Mesplay, an accomplished woodwind player. The Suzuki method was then introduced, and after several years all lower school pupils had the opportunity to participate and advance in the expanding instrumental program. The orchestra produced world class violinist Isabella Lippi '86, cellist Doris Heinrich '75, jazz pianist Ric Jans '67, and other noteworthy musicians.

Wolgamot's music classes were fast paced, demanding, and exciting. He transferred his passion for understanding music to his students, while reminding pupils of the discipline and perseverance needed for music appreciation and performance. Mr. Wolgamot possessed many other talents. He had a replete grasp of literary classics, knew history with an exactitude, was bilingual in Italian, was a talented actor, and could tell when a painting or a piece of sculpture featured in a setting for an opera was an anachronism.

As music director for Parker's dramatic productions, Mr. Wolgamot created a special sort of excitement. On the night of a musical performance, the lights in the auditorium dimmed, the orchestra tuned up, a silence descended, and Mr. Wolgamot stepped to the podium, picked up his baton, and took an almost magical command of the evening. He radiated an energy and vibrant intelligence that inspired the performers and enchanted the audience.

Mr. Wolgamot loved the grand and the grandiose and auditioned huge casts for musicals. His biggest undertaking incorporated a cast of eighty-five lower and upper school students who performed Benjamin Britten's *Noah's Flood* in 1981. Wolgamot had runways constructed from the back of the auditorium to the stage and two by two, lower school children dressed like leopards, bears, giraffes, elephants, cats, snakes, and birds crawled along the runway until they stepped into the ark on stage and sang the story until the dove returned with the olive branch. Jason Wulkowicz '82 and Chip Kestnbaum '87 participated, John Eley '81 played God, and James Hallett '81 played Noah. The magnificence of the performance could only be surpassed by its repetition. The response to Mr. Wolgamot's production was, "Only at Parker!"

Barr McCutcheon x44 attended the Parker School until the eighth grade, earned a bachelor's degree from Harvard College, and later became an intern at the Graduate Teachers College in Winnetka. In 1949 he returned to visit the school, was hired the next day as a teacher of mathematics, and remained until the end of a long and distinguished teaching career. He became chairman of the Mathematics Department and senior gradehead. Mr.

McCutcheon was a mathematics genius who developed unique and original mathematical methods which he called "McCutcheonisms." As the students of 1977 explained in the dedication to him in the yearbook:

> He has his own language,
> we all call them clubs,
> Dinglehoofers and Whoosies,
> and Ozos and tubs.

McCutcheon's goals were to emphasize understanding concepts over memorization and to entertain and instruct students simultaneously by bringing mathematics to life. Kathy Koretz Abeles '63, who taught mathematics when McCutcheon was department chairman, captured his pedagogy in these words: "He could take sophisticated mathematical concepts and extract their essences, simplifying the ideas for consumption by young learners." Mr. McCutcheon believed a teacher should never answer a question if it was one that the students should be able to think through themselves. Thomas Campbell '78, who also taught in the department, explained, "He simply hinted that there was something there we might want to know and left it to us."

Throughout his career, George Barr McCutcheon retained an independent spirit that many might label eccentric. A humorist and rebel, he once brought his dog to school to protest an all-day faculty workshop. The dog slept throughout the meeting and made McCutcheon's point. He delighted in the management of the seniors' production of "The Twelve Days of Christmas," sang with a barbershop quartet, and often accompanied Parker vocalists on the piano. A poet, he was frequently in search of the perfect word and despised jargon, especially the word *skills*. His trademark was to use humor as a device to treat everyone and everything.

McCutcheon never raised his voice and was never in a hurry. He seemed able to accomplish many tasks without stress. His best times were spent with students—before school, during lunch, after school in his office and at his home, doing math or playing chess. If an advisee was having a problem with math, the advisor could telephone Mr. McCutcheon at any hour to ask for his help, and he would return to school to provide it. His unique combination of mathematical brilliance, educational innovation, and humor made his classroom exciting to students and to other teachers. To many students, McCutcheon was the best teacher they ever had, and to many math teachers he was the "guru."[58]

Although the interests of the English Department were also lodged in the lower school, Dr. Andrew Kaplan was the chairman of the upper school English Department. As chairman of the largest and most influential department in the school, he provided faculty leadership. Since his arrival at the school in 1975, he taught most courses in the department. His mainstays were Bible, Myth, and Epic, a required course for freshmen, and World Literature, an elective course for juniors and seniors. Throughout his career, he designed and taught diverse new courses such as Public Life, Rhetoric, Philosophy, and Gender and Character. The most experimental and effective course he designed was a ninth grade interdisciplinary course on the life and works of Galileo Galilei, which combined the teaching of English and science.

Kaplan's scholarship was extensive. His research in the iconography of biblical and mythical traditions earned him an award for Independent Studies in the Humanities from the Council for Basic Education. He published articles on diverse subjects including such progressive education topics as "Education and Character" and "Education and Democracy."

As advisor to the student government, beginning in 1979, he helped high school students to shape the government's role in the school. He effectively worked with more than a dozen student government presidents—Max Rovner '80, Raymond Harth '87, Deborah Wexler, '91, Justin Oberman '92 and others—providing helpful direction with "level headed composure." The class of '89 called Andy Kaplan "someone who transcends the bounds of what a contract requires by infusing his instruction with supportive guidance." Students considered him a "focused, organized, and efficient" teacher who effectively imparted his love of literature and the English language. He does not limit his insightful counsel strictly to the classroom. This teacher of many talents began his education as a Parker School student, earned his doctorate in English at the University of Chicago, and was a professor at Northwestern University while still having time to play his guitar at Morning Exercises.[59]

In 1976, Anne Marie Fries became a lower school science teacher, and with Maryanne Kalin-Miller, she developed the first sequential lower school science program to which she later added junior and senior kindergartens and then sixth grade science. By 1984, Mrs. Fries completed the sequence and in 1986 became the first lower school teacher appointed department chairman. A year later she became the eighth grade teacher of Physical Science at a time when the department was making changes in personnel and course offerings and was attempting to integrate science with mathematics. By 1990, when she added teaching eleventh and twelfth grade science electives to her eighth grade responsibilities, Mrs. Fries had taught the entire spectrum of science courses from Grades K-12.

Mrs. Fries's science curriculum included classes as well as science activities and projects. She introduced an Outdoor Education program for Grade 5 and a Science Fair for Grades 1-5, both of which were flourishing twenty years later. The 130 students who participated each year in the one-day Science Fair were motivated by their interest in science rather than their desire for a prize, as projects were not judged. Mrs. Fries became an adjunct professor at National-Louis University in Evanston, where she had earned a Bachelor's Degree in science and a Master's Degree in education. Her colleagues and students were impressed with her high level of energy, her passion for learning, and her ability to excite their curiosity. The students said that Mrs. Fries made science fun and meaningful.[60]

Each of these eleven vintage teachers taught for twenty-five or more years at the Parker School and was a department chairperson for at least ten years, serving as a member of the curriculum committee between 1974 and 1992, when its new format was introduced by the principal. Most of this corps of teachers applied and some advanced progressive education at the Parker School.

Staff: The Second Guard

A second guard of nonteaching professionals participated in the life of the school: secretaries, administrative assistants, building maintenance personnel, the registrar, the telephone operator, the school receptionist, the nurse, playground and development office staff, lunchroom staff, and other significant people who assisted the teachers informally in nonacademic matters and provided nurture or discipline to students.

Mrs. Jane McGwinn, who served longer than any other staff member, knew all eleven principals from Miss Cooke to Dr. Monroe. A Parker School student from 1918 to 1922, she returned as a parent in 1942 and during the next decade, volunteered to help where needed—receptionist, doctor's assistant, bus driver, and school nurse. She helped to set up for the County Fair, acted as liaison with settlement houses for school projects, helped with the Toy Shop, worked with students in the Civil Defense effort during the War, and was the faculty organizer for the Field Day, now called Class Day. Her numerous volunteer activities tell the early history of the Parker School.

Principal Thomas first hired McGwinn in 1956 to be the school receptionist. In 1962, when the new school was built, Mrs. McGwinn donned a hard hat and became the faculty liaison with the construction workers.

She knew and loved every nook and cranny in the old school. Although the building was a firetrap, there wasn't a scrap of paper messing the floors or books strewn in the corridors. Students worried about insufficient funds and tended the old school well. Soon after the new building was completed, McGwinn began to observe sloppy halls and slovenly behavior. The new building seemed to have a reverse effect on students, and Mrs. McGwinn was constantly picking up after them or organizing clean-up committees. She declared that the new messiness was contrary to the Parker values she and other teachers held so dear.

Mrs. McGwinn retired to her farm in 1970 only to be invited back to Parker in 1988 to order and distribute classroom texts. In her spare time at the school, she sewed costumes for Vespers and dramatic productions, attached commemorative tiles to the Parker walls, and arranged the "Blue Bulletin," a list of the daily events. After an eighty-year affiliation with the Parker School, there were few tasks she had not undertaken and few student lives she had not touched.[61]

Staff members were at times invited to chaperone field trips, as was receptionist Fae Webster, who joined an English teacher and student journalists Chet Wallenstein '94, Sara Berliner '94, Gabriel McHale '94, and others at a journalism conference at Columbia University in New York. The teacher arranged for the budding journalists to stay at the Algonquin Hotel to get a feel for Dorothy Parker and the Round Table. The group toured the *New York Times* with writer David Dunlap '69, visited the MTV studio, and saw other literary sights. Sure that even these robust eighteen-year-olds would be exhausted, the teacher called for lights out at 10:00 p.m. Filled with vigor and stimulated by Manhattan, the class asked Ms.

Webster to negotiate later night hours, promising to return to the hotel at the specific time. The teacher was opposed, but everyone kept the promise because a promise to Fae was a promise to be honored.

Fae Webster's position between 1975 and 1991 was school reception-ist, which located her centrally at the switchboard near the main entrance to the school. From her "oval office," Ms. Webster served as "the eyes and ears of the school." Like a second mother, she helped a frustrated junior kindergartner fasten her coat, listened to a teenage girl's tale of woe about an encounter with her older sister, or mollify a distressed parent or teacher on the phone. A hard worker with a passionate nature, she was "sharp, quick, and ready to help in a myriad of ways." For example, she would help collate a student's handouts for class if the student was running late or assist in folding *The Weekly* for distribution. On her glass booth in the front hall she posted messages—serious or foolish, like "meet Erika for coffee" or "you took your mother's car keys, return at once." She also corrected the behavior of thoughtless students, who responded without rancor because Fae was queen of the front hall. The students enjoyed joking with her and showed her special kindnesses and gratitude for her many favors. Some days she received flowers, other days a mystery or detective novel, which she read in her spare time between classes. Students constantly urged her to attend their Morning Exercises and dramatic performances. The Class of 1991 dedicated the yearbook to her as a final tribute before she retired.[62]

Students: Life after School Changes

The school began as an activity-centered school, but in this era, as in the Stabilizing Years, activities continued to be less important again because they were no longer affiliated with classes. A progressive school can be measured by whether it fulfills student needs, develops student interests, realizes student potential, and inculcates a lifelong love of learning. Learning through activities met these four goals and was therefore a vital part of the curriculum. In the lower school, fewer activities were offered. In the new middle school of the 1970s, activity-centered learning took on a special importance, and in the high school, except for the Intensive-Extensive courses of the 1970s, activities lost their momentum.[63]

Lower school activities still remained integral to the course of study. Beginning in junior kindergarten, students loved being weathermen, making potato prints, and joining in the Junior Kindergarten Olympics. The fifth graders were excited by their trip to the Lorado Taft campus on the Rock River, and the seventh graders anticipated Voyageur Night. Like most city kids, seventh graders appreciated their outdoor education trip to Spring Green, Wisconsin.

Middle school students thrived on the activities affiliated with the elective program introduced in 1973. The mini elective program integrated courses with activities, and the students immersed themselves in building three-dimensional sculpture, writing articles for their newspaper, playing softball, and doing science projects. Among the most popular activities were the production of stained glass windows and the "Environmental Awareness" course in which students learned to tie knots, climb up and down the sides of buildings and cliffs, and practice first aid. One middle school student who expressed the general sentiment about the mini courses commented, "I liked electives because they gave a student the chance to pick a course he enjoyed."[64]

The middle schoolers also participated in activities by serving others through their Community Service Program. Beginning in 1975, sixth, seventh, and eighth graders joined in the activities of specific social service agencies. They read to the elderly, tutored students, worked at the Anti-Cruelty Society, or babysat at a daycare center. The young teens took their community service seriously and found ways to raise money for their causes. Maryanne Kalin-Miller's advisory had an original approach. The advisory used a Morning Exercise to share its concern about animal care. Students showed a film and slide show about adopting animals, and for the finale, seventh grader Marcy Berkowitz '86 brought a barking hyperactive mutt onto the stage and petted it until the dog began to lick from her hand. While the audience swooned over the puppy, the seventh grade participants moved through the auditorium with collection cups to get donations for the Anti-Cruelty Society. Overlooking the school rule against dogs in school, even Principal Geer reached into his pocket and dropped his change in the cup.

With few exceptions, the teachers in the high school separated courses from extracurricular activities in the fashion of a traditional school. The gap between activities and courses broadened, and both suffered. When activities and courses separated, the scheduling of free-standing activities pitted students against parents, who mistakenly believed that college admissions placed more weight on grades and academic courses than activities. When student participation in projects was no longer part of the class grade evaluation, teachers reduced their vigilance over activities and the faculty, "the organizers of community life," provided less help to students in balancing their schedules between activities and academics. Teachers were also less willing to offer supervisory support for free-standing activities. In the absence of full participation in activities, the school could not achieve its overarching goals—"the development of character and citizenship." Nowhere was it more apparent than in the deteriorating quality of Morning Exercise presentations.

Morning Exercise was the product of all classes. Thanks to the strong Morning Exercise legacy, Parker students of earlier eras began learning in junior kindergarten how to present class projects and ask and answer questions with aplomb in front of hundreds. Now, instead of developing most presentations from class work, Morning Exercises too frequently relied on entertainment from outside the school, and many were canceled for lack of preparation. Additionally the deportment of student audiences grew restless and immature, as students arrived late, slouched in their chairs, chewed gum, and chatted with their neighbors. The taboo against applause, instituted by Francis Parker to prevent self-consciousness among presenters, was violated and now the audience clapped for individual students before the Exercises concluded.

Those activities still integrated with courses flourished. Drama and music classes continued to correlate with performance activities. The training and experience in drama and music classes and performances attracted a disproportionate number of students to participate in theater and film like David Mamet '65, Darryl Hannah '78, Jennifer Beales '78, Lisa Zane '79, Peter Jacobson '83, Anne Heche '87, Billy Zane '84, who distinguished themselves in these fields.

Interest in writing was high, but disassociated with classes, the quality of student publications diminished during this era. Although the *Weekly* newspaper grew in size and circulation in the 1970s by covering major national and world issues and mastering more efficient ways of printing and editing, the expansion made the publication more difficult for students to manage on their own. Lack of editorial supervision resulted in grammatical errors and uneven and sometimes incorrect news. As the *Weekly* expanded, the *Record* cut back on copy and relied more heavily on photos, largely because its budget was reduced when students felt that the *Record* drained too much money from the student-managed "sinking fund," which paid for all student activities. The *Record* turned to advertisements for income, doubling the size of the yearbook but not enhancing its quality. Many student photos were unidentified and copy was reduced, making the yearbook no longer a record of the activities of the year. The literary magazine *Prints*, managed by eleventh graders since 1959, was replaced in the early 1980s by *Phaedrus*, whose board was open to all high school students. Severed from an accountable class and teacher, the magazine drew fewer and weaker submissions, and deadlines were often not respected by students.

Writing, nonetheless, continued to spur great interest and student talent was developed by several teachers. Seth Kaplan '95 and Andrew Goldberg '95 wrote scripts for videos. A dozen students wrote extended interviews of twenty-year teachers. Writing in all genres was undertaken. The school graduated many writers who became prominent journalists: David Dunlap '69 of the *New York Times*; Jonathan Alter '75 of *Newsweek*; Jacob Weisberg '82, contributing editor to the *Washington Monthly* and the *New Republic;* Gardner Stern '71, a scriptwriter for "NYPD Blue"; and others. Writing in classes and for school publications inspired authors of nonfiction and fiction like Jean Holabird '64, Joseph Flynn '69, Rosemary Bray '72, Andrea Gabor '75, David Stenn '79, Colin Hall '89, Ronald Lieber '89, poet Elise Paschen '77, and other students throughout these three decades.

The relationship between courses and athletics was idiosyncratic. The students chose to enroll in physical education classes, participate in sports, or do both. Boys' athletics changed. Interest in football waned, and the team was abolished after the 1973 season and replaced by soccer. The soccer team finished second in the Independent School League in 1976 and held the title from 1981 to 1985. The boys also played golf in the fall; basketball in the winter; tennis, baseball, and track in spring; and joined volleyball and swim teams. Track, coached by math teacher Donald Cass, captured Parker students' interest and talent. The track team won the conference championships in 1972 and 1975. Parker boys won Independent School League titles in tennis and baseball in 1973. Parker boys showed an increased competitive spirit, which was contrary to the espoused school value of cooperation. Editorials like one that appeared in a 1970s *Weekly* favored playing only the best players. Before, the philosophy dictated that everyone played. The values of athletics were in transition and remained unresolved.

A gap between boys and girls sports continued, although the girls' teams increased in popularity. The Dean of Students argued that the girls should pay less tuition if the opportunities with male athletes were not equalized. The school heard the message, and the girls' sports increased. The girls played field hockey in the fall, and in 1975 the team broke a four-year losing streak, winning two games and tying for second in the Independent School League in 1985. During the winter, girls played basketball and by 1973 also had the option of volleyball and gymnastics. At times, girls were able to put together a small swim team. In the spring, female athletes played softball and ran track. Physical education teacher Chris Griffith and members of the faculty supported girls' athletics by organizing father-daughter banquets and instituting an athletic program in the 1970s for middle school girls. In 1974, Parker was the first school in the league to allow girls to join the boys' soccer team. Despite the increased attendance at athletic events, girls often wrote *Weekly* editorials about how girls' athletics lacked support from the student body in contrast to boys' sports.

Student government, central to a progressive democratic school, was never affiliated with a specific course. Although era after era students struggled with its structure and challenged its value. Each year they voted to keep student government as an integral institution in their school lives. During the major portion of this era, student government meetings were scheduled at midday to follow the Morning Exercise period, which permitted extended sessions to address complex issues, ranging from discussions of the Intensive-Extensive schedule, to school and parental authority over activities, and to race relations. The student government presidents were a committed group of leaders with exemplary supervision provided by English teacher Andrew Kaplan.

New activities were introduced in this era. In the late 1960s, the Black Student Union was an extremely important organization for black students. At weekly meetings they discussed racism at Parker and in

America and organized Morning Exercises and other events that dealt with the African American culture. When the Union began to fade in 1974, many students were discouraged because they felt that black students were losing their unity. Others saw it as a positive sign that race relations at Parker had improved, and the Union was no longer needed. Another group, the Seminar on Human Relations, dealt with racial issues that arose in the mid-1970s. The student-faculty group discussed diversity issues at Parker and researched the school's race relations and level of integration.

Some old but other new committees demonstrated that students had learned the importance of associating committees with courses such as the Ecology Club and science headed by Rick Michod '96 and Students Against Drinking and Driving (S.A.D.D.) affiliated with the Health Course and organized by Sara Field '96 and Jeff Earnhardt '96. By the end of the era, about a dozen free standing committees were in existence—Sarah Haskins '96 and Shelby Kohn '96 chaired the Student Senate, Rowen Balagot '96 and Casey Morris '96 organized American Field Service (A.F.S.), and Adam Smoler '96 and Philipp Conrad '96 introduced an Internet committee.

The majority of students appreciated the connection between activity-centered learning and classes in the decade of the Intensive-Extensive Schedule. Expression and the project method were two of the main instructional strategies used in the ninety intensives offered by six departments from which students could choose. These included such diverse courses as Advanced Scene Study, Astrology, the Study of Chicago, Journalism, and Video Production. The students enjoyed the Intensive Course of Study, and as one senior remarked, "School life for students is like a double-shift work day. . . after the last class we don't have to be students anymore; we can be athletes or actors, socialites or authors." [65] As the Intensive Schedule dwindled, students pleaded in articles in the *Weekly* to return to "learning for the sake of enriching themselves." In 1987, a small group of high school students struggled to keep "the well-rounded Parker education alive because they saw it as one of the most valuable assets of Parker." Seniors — Tim Marks '86, Richard Marks '86, John Rosofsky '86, and Max Rovner '86 — were happy to have been part of the experiment.

The Intensive schedule introduced new freedoms. Study halls disappeared never to return. Unscheduled time increased, which students often misused by socializing in the halls, chatting in small groups, or lying on the corridor carpet. Previously quiet and orderly, the corridors became an embarrassment: noisy, messy, and teeming with students who behaved without decorum. Despite the problem, juniors Carita Gardiner '87 and Liz Cicchelli '87 regretted the passing of the Intensive schedule. In 1994, Erica Simmons '94 established the first Curriculum Committee which again examined Intensive Study.

"Free time" extended to off-campus privileges. At the beginning of the era, students remained on campus. In 1968, the more radical students left the school without permission and joined the political demonstrations in Grant Park. The school granted off-campus privileges first to the seniors and eventually to all high school students. By the 1970s, groups of students left school and took the bus to the Loop to participate in Vietnam protests or peace rallies. By the 1980s, the answer to the question, "Do you know where your children are?" was "all over the city." Neither the parents nor the school could keep track.

Abuses changed in kind and increased in number, and the disciplinary Committee of Four increased its membership. Punishable abuses included tardies and excessive absences, theft in school, drug and alcohol abuse, promiscuity in school, security issues, littering and vandalism, cheating, and many previously unheard-of infractions. The school developed disciplinary policies relating to these issues. Ironically, from 1965 to 1985, the students called the disciplinary Committee of Four "one of the strongest and most productive bodies" in the school.

As societal forces modified the school and greater freedoms and responsibilities were granted, students introduced new traditions but remained committed to time-honored traditions, some nearly a century old like County Fair, Class Day, the Twelve Days of Christmas, and Big Brothers and Sisters. Students found the legacy reassuring and cohesive in contrast to the flux in society. In 1976, the seniors introduced Senior Day in their honor, later the parents introduced a Faculty Dinner so seniors could honor their teachers. In the next decade, the seniors introduced the spring Balloon Day, when 700 students gathered on the field to release blue balloons containing a student's name and the name of a favorite book. Letters and e-mail messages showed many respondents. Less frivolous than 700 blue balloons was college admission.

As in the past, at least ninety-five percent of the graduates completed four-year college degrees. Both majority students and students of color succeeded at the "natural homes" like Yale, Brown, Amherst, Princeton, and Harvard.

That Parker had encouraged them to develop multiple talents only made them more desirable to colleges. For example, Yale admitted a black student, Michelle Skaprow '99 for her academic record and for her musical talent. Adam Colestock '97, who arrived at Parker in his junior year, was accomplished and motivated in mathematics and science but also enrolled in many humanities courses. Accepted by several eastern colleges, he decided to attend Williams. After his sophomore year, he brought several Williams students to Parker to attend mini courses to learn about teaching strategy. The group went to India to teach for two years before returning to Williams to complete their degrees. Many avenues were opened to the seniors, and they had become equipped for interesting life-long learning.

Was the Parker School Progressive?

Although in this era the school met some of the biggest challenges to progressive education, it responded with many innovative solutions. One major challenge to progressive education was caused by the societal turmoil of the 1960s and 1970s, which caused students to change their in- and out-of-school behaviors and styles. A need to manage new student behaviors divided the school into two camps—the more conservative parents, who believed that by becoming more traditional the school would solve the problems, and the more liberal parents, who supported progressive education because it had solutions for just this kind of disturbance. Principal Jack Ellison strengthened the progressive approach and balanced student idealism with democracy and discipline. Principal Geer, who headed the school at the height of the societal turmoil, pushed the school to the cutting edge with his experiment in democratization, organizing representative committees composed of a cross section of students, teachers, and parents to join together in small groups to address these school issues. The newly formed committees resolved many issues, but Geer's experiment was aborted before it could advance or come to closure. Both principals were successful in their progressive approaches to a new kind of student life at school.

Student-parent-teacher relationships were familiar and trusting in spite of the societal challenges of the late 1960s and 1970s—teachers knew their advisory parents and families and were frequently invited to help solve problems and to join in the families' celebrations. The teachers' office doors were open so students and parents could easily schedule appointments or stop in after class to chat about student and parental concerns. The parents were at school so often that the students quipped, "Whose school is this anyway?" The maintaining of the school-home relationship also supported the progressive philosophy.

A second challenge originated with the Board of Trustees, who hired two consultants to examine the governance and the operation of the school by the board and the principal. In the process, the Educational Council, whose role since 1932 had been to support progressive education, was abolished at a 1994 faculty meeting. The carefully constructed balance of power and responsibility crafted by Anita McCormick Blaine was destroyed. Later, however, the Educational Council was restored, and again progressive education was supported. In the meantime, the trustees also democratized the board by transforming its membership from self-perpetuating to representative trustees to ensure that the direction remained progressive.

The most progressive aspect of the school was the course of study. Beginning in the 1960s, the curriculum was advanced through the Distinguished Visitor's program, and in 1975 curriculum experimentation hit a peak. Both the middle and the high school undertook large-scale experiments to meet the challenges and changing needs of the students and of the knowledge explosion. The newly organized middle school introduced effective mini courses, a successful and long-lasting community service program, and an advisory system. The high school undertook a successful two-week trial in Immersion Education that led to an Intensive-Extensive Study experiment for Grades 9 through 12 that lasted for more than a decade. The Intensive-Extensive experiment transformed the schedule, the courses, and the graduation requirements. In lower school, the introduction of a Learning Improvement Program and computers helped meet the needs of students in Grades 1-5 and eventually the whole school. This high and middle school curriculum development was as rigorous as the lower school's earlier experiment with central subjects in the

Pioneering Years and more extensive than the Eight-Year Study in the Stabilizing Years.

Educationally, instruction remained progressive. In the mini courses and the Intensive-Extensive schedule, the activity-centered approach was used, as was interdisciplinary education, team teaching, project methods, and other progressive strategies conducive to the extended blocks of time that the new schedule permitted.

The faculty also remained progressive. Several faculty spanned the era, and these vintage teachers provided leadership and training for young colleagues. Most teachers had been on the staff for at least a decade and were well grounded in progressive practice and policy, which they passed on to new teachers in specially arranged meetings. The Parker teachers also became part-time professors of education at local universities and also trained an increased number of student teachers at the school.

There was one notable exception to the school's ability to meet the progressive challenges of the era. The teachers, "the organizers of the community," did not make the Morning Exercise work effectively. Until World War II, the faculty had developed the school as a community, using the Morning Exercise as the philosophical nexus of the main progressive goals—the development of character, citizenship, and social motive. In the early decades, the teachers quoted these progressive goals in each school *Catalogue* (1901-1930) as reminders to the teachers and students of their meaning and purpose. Those teachers judged Morning Exercise as a form of community development of sufficient importance that they produced two Studies in Education on the subject—*The Social Motive in School Work* (1912) and *Morning Exercise as a Socializing Influence* (1913). After World War II the faculty let the overarching goals burn to ashes during a time of societal discord. The new enlarged student body remained ill informed about the function of the community in Morning Exercises, in student government, and wherever the school members congregated as a whole. The Morning Exercise itself changed—reading and reflections were eliminated, teachers were no longer required to present a Morning Exercise annually, and at times, students canceled Morning Exercises or scheduled outside entertainment like cartoons and films to replace classroom presentations. Students' behavior deteriorated, and their appetites slowly converted to the vulgar instead of to the enlightened as in the past. In the development of the community, the faculty accomplished little in achieving responsibility, character, citizenry, and social motive. The flaw became a central one in the school's philosophy.

The school was having a difficult time balancing freedom and responsibility in school life and cooperation and competition in athletics. Whereas the institution accented citizenship, it neglected to emphasize character. It maintained its progressive ideal of social reconstruction, but it neglected to develop education as a science. It retreated from experimentation, which was not well managed as in the Intensive experiment. Too few new people were made aware of Parker's historical roots, and many concepts and traditions were mere words without substance. Anita McCormick Blaine's ghost haunted the school with much to say if anyone would listen.

In spite of this, the "period of challenge" was second only to the Pioneering Years in its pursuit of the progressive direction of a society-centered orientation—the democratization of the school by Geer, the representative membership on the board, the introduction of community services, and the sustaining of a diverse student body.

Chapter 9

Toward the New Millennium
(1995-2001)

Principal Donald Monroe, Ed. D.

Historical Perspective: Community Supports School

The period from 1995 to 2001 offered real challenge to America's public and private schools. Public schools faced issues of accountability and diminished public confidence and became an important political issue at the local, state, and national levels, challenged from the religious right as well as more moderate or liberal interests. Issues of curriculum content and student performance were raised to a national level reminiscent of the focus on education in the 1950s. This time issues grew out of an interest in maintaining a competitive role in a global and technologically driven economy and from a continuing concern for the viability of urban schools to educate a new immigrant population and the urban and rural poor.

With educational issues shifting to the national level, curriculum associations such as the National Council of Teachers of Math created standards for curriculum at each grade level from K-12. State departments of education similarly created systems of accountability in which each school district was required to adopt standards, document performance, and describe programs of improvement based on results. In many ways, control of local schools and curriculum and accountability issues moved from the community and school district to the state and national levels. The pressure that resulted from published test scores moved schools to more standardized and prescriptive curriculum and more mechanical methods of teaching.

The push for school improvement and reform came at a time when the American family was in a state of flux. Patterns of work and parenting took on many faces, and schools struggled to forge a new and mutually beneficial relationship to the families they served. Matters related to health, nutrition, sexuality, character development, citizenship, and socialization shifted noticeably from families to schools out of both a sense of necessity as well as out of state mandates.

Playing against this background of social, political, economic, and school governance issues were a number of exciting initiatives that affected the understanding of learning and teaching. The field was presented with new understandings of multiple intelligence, emotional intelligence, brain research, and genetic research. The importance of interdisciplinary learning, project learning, student engagement, problem solving, and analytical thinking were given renewed stress. The availability of new electronic technology brought a powerful but yet not fully understood or incorporated new tool to teaching and learning.

The issues of local, state, and national accountability, standard setting, and performance testing did not offer a comfortable setting in which new and exciting educational understanding and possibility could be tested and implemented. The presence of public mistrust and the need to perform do not encourage experimentation or boldness. At the end of the twentieth century, teaching had still not arrived as a respected and well-defined profession. In *Education Week*, Ann Bradley described teaching as "The Not Quite Profession" and indicated that it had a long way to go to earn full professional status.

In the past several years, there has been a flurry of school reform efforts. In addition to the development, promulgation, and enforcement of national standards that have already been identified, there has been a reassertion of the importance of small schools as places in which students can be better known, better served, and can better learn the lessons of community living, citizenship, and character. In small schools teachers can gain a greater sense of the value of this work and can create a sense of collegiality and common purpose. Parents, too, can play a more central role in the school lives of their children. This movement toward smaller schools can be seen as local public schools take the initiative to form new combinations and in the creation of charter schools and specialty schools.

Parents, private interests, and teachers have come together to form new charter schools. Specialty schools identify themes such as the arts or foreign language around which their schools are organized. These specialty schools are a magnet for interested students and parents.

The high interest in education, the increasing population of school age children, the strong economy, and the recommitment to life in the city made this period a good but challenging time for the Parker School. Local public and other private schools offered strong competition, but the number of families willing to commit to a Parker education was high. Philanthropic activity permitted the Parker School to maintain and enhance its programs, facilities, and a diverse student body.

New Leadership Plans New Building

The succession of principals and interim principals between 1987 and 1993 disrupted the educational leadership, and the Board of Trustees felt the responsibility to assert itself in maintaining the administrative and economic viability of the school. An independent faculty became the bearers of the torch as the board sought new educational leadership that would stabilize and rejuvenate the school. The board's dominance and the faculty's independence were reinforced by the absence of an Educational Council between 1994 and 1997.[1] This period was characterized more by a need to maintain the school than by the development of a distinguished progressive school.

In July 1995, the board appointed Dr. Donald Monroe, who had previously served as superintendent of the Winnetka Public Schools from 1977 to 1994, to be principal of the school. In the 1930s and 1940s, the Winnetka Schools had been actively engaged with the Parker School in a number of progressive initiatives. Carleton Washburne, the former superintendent of the Winnetka Schools, was a cofounder of the Graduate Teachers College of Winnetka with Flora Cooke, the first principal of the Parker School. Dr. Monroe had also served as an external member of the Educational Council prior to coming to the Parker School.

Don Monroe governed the school with John Levi, the seventeenth chairman of the Board of Trustees, who served a four-year term from 1997 to 2001 and with Associate Principal Dr. Daniel Frank '74, who was appointed president of the Educational Council when it was reinstated in 1997. The trustees appointed Business Manager Dhiren Shah. In addition to Dan Frank, the academic administrative staff included Head of Upper School Eugene Gross, Middle School Coordinator Maryanne Kalin-Miller, Head of Lower School Ann Breed, and two successive Deans of Students, Prexy Nesbitt '62 and Joan Pippin.

At the beginning of Monroe's principalship, in the fall of 1995, the trustees appointed a Long-Range Planning Committee composed of teachers, parents, and board members. The committee identified facility expansion and improvement, class size, and diversity as the high-level priorities. The committee concluded that the amount of space in the school was limiting, and the quality of space was not conducive to good learning and teaching. Built in 1962, the main building's mechanical systems, space allocation, and appearance were inadequate to serve a growing student body or to house the school's programs. High school space was cramped, unattractive, and poorly maintained. The undersized library did not permit the incorporation of technology as well as areas for the student study. The cafeteria needed expansion in order to accommodate a growing student body, and with one gymnasium it was difficult to accommodate physical education classes and athletic team practices. The lower school faculty was concerned with the size of the classrooms; twenty-five students were being served in rooms intended for sixteen to eighteen students.[2]

The trustees accepted the recommendation of the Planning Committee and employed the architectural firm of Nagle, Hartray, Danker, Kagan, McKay to begin plans and estimate costs. A construction committee was named to oversee the remodeling and construction of the cafeteria, the high school, the library, administrative space, lower school classrooms, a new full-size gymnasium, and a conference center. A $24 million campaign was established, and the board employed a development firm to plan and oversee the campaign in conjunction with a board-appointed Campaign Steering Committee. In the winter of 1995, the Campaign for Parker was kicked off by a generous $3.5 million gift from a Parker family. The construction project presented a tremendous challenge to the board and the Parker community. Fortunately, this challenge came at a time when there was a general recognition of the need to invest in the school and to undertake a commitment to renewal.

The school opened in the fall of 1996 with a remodeled and expanded cafeteria, an indication of the school's commitment to renewal. A year later the remodeled high school space and the newly constructed fourth floor were completed. Many teachers who had shared classrooms for ten to twenty years now had their own rooms. The new space, which offered a vastly improved learning environment, included a computer lab, a room for faculty meetings, a learning resource room, and space on the high school floor for the head of the upper school and the Dean of Students. New windows and air-conditioning muffled the noise from Clark Street. In the administrative wing, remodeling offered new space for offices for the principal, the admissions director, the college counselor, and the registrar.

In September 1996, the board approved spending $6.2 million to create a new building at the south end of the courtyard with a new library that would include a children's room, five new math classrooms, a new full-sized gymnasium with an adjacent fitness center, and a new 100-seat multi-purpose conference center. Significant gifts supported these two projects. One Parker family donated a million dollars for the construction of the library, and another contributed a million dollars for the construction of the conference center. The purpose of the conference center was to host faculty meetings as well as small- to medium-size conferences for educators. The center would extend the school's outreach to exercise leadership in the promotion of knowledge related to teaching and learning.

When the building opened in September 1998, it provided second- and third-floor walkways that connected the formerly unconnected east and west wings. With these new hallways, the middle school and the lower and high schools were joined on the south side, and all divisions were connected to the library and gymnasium. This design purposely promoted a sense of community and access.

In January 1998, the project focused on lower school space. The Board of Trustees approved the teacher proposal to reduce lower school class size by enrolling fifty-four students per grade level and dividing each grade into three sections of eighteen students each. This proposal increased the lower school enrollment by thirty-two students and required seven additional classrooms plus new rooms for music, art, science, drama, learning resources, and lower school offices. It was felt that this would better enable the school to keep integrity with its commitment to individual and personalized teaching.

The second stage of this phase was to remodel the existing middle school and to add new space in order to bring all sixth through eighth grade classrooms together to create a distinct space for a better defined program and division. To accomplish these plans, the Little School, built in 1942, was demolished and replaced by a three-story 30,000 square foot building. The renovated east wing and the newly constructed addition allowed the first floor to house the junior and senior kindergartens and the first and second grades; the second floor to accommodate third, fourth, and fifth grades and the lower school art, music, and science classrooms. The third floor provided additional middle school space and a lower school classroom for drama. A bridge linked the Kupcinet Gallery to the new second floor, which connected the third floor gallery to the new middle school floor.

The final phase of the project, implemented in 2001, called for the front entry to be remodeled. Plans for the auditorium, the arts areas, and the science wing were put on a back burner but were a high priority in fulfilling the goals of the school's philosophy.

The cost of this new lower and middle school construction exceeded projections, increasing the fund-raising goal to $28 million. In January 1999, the trustees accepted the recommendation of a specially appointed committee to issue bonds in the amount of $23.7 million to help finance the building program. This was the first time the school had taken on debt since the construction of the 1962 main building. The bonds were issued in a context of a robust economy, healthy school finances, and demographic trends favorable for future enrollment. By spring of 2000, the campaign had raised $21 million because of the strong leadership of Board President John Levi and trustees Lori Kaufman and Jerry Meyer. Mr. Meyer was also chairman of the construction committee. Volunteerism was strong, and numerous generous parents and alumni participated. Because every attempt was made to cover construction costs without significantly affecting the operating budget of the school, programs were maintained or strengthened with only nominal increases in tuition.[3]

Curriculum: New Priorities

A committee of department chairpersons provided the curriculum leadership for the school. The chairs in science, mathematics, visual arts, music, history, physical education, and foreign language were filled respectively by Anne Marie Fries, Peter Barrett, Mark Matteson, Bart Wolgamot, Robert Merrick, Jan Steffens-Carone, and Marsha Wagner, who served in the last era. Mary Dilg was a new appointment to the English chair, and Leslie Holland was a new appointment to the drama chair.

The first areas of curriculum to be examined were science and mathematics. For many years, the arts and humanities programs flourished, creating a perception that they eclipsed the importance of science and mathematics. In 1995, the faculty addressed this perceived imbalance and reemphasized and redesigned a science and mathematics curriculum that was implemented in 1997.

The second area of curriculum was technology. Between 1995 and 2000, the school invested approximately $1.5 million in the equipment, staff development, and software needed to support technology. The building was equipped with a T-1 line and computers were networked. An online list serve, Burnham Square, to discuss school/community issues was created. By 1999, the school had lower, middle, and high school computer labs and a fully automated library. Classrooms were equipped with computers, and a technology department was formed to oversee the computer labs, to coordinate technology usage, and to facilitate and encourage the integration of computer technology in the curriculum. All academic departments integrated technology into their curriculum, and tech labs were made available for art and music. Although most homes were equipped with computers, the school provided a home computer for students who could not purchase one.

The English and History Departments reevaluated the departmental structure and offerings and focused on the value of examining our lives, broadening our knowledge and understanding of others, and expanding our capacity for empathy. With these values in mind, the English Department set out to offer year-long courses in ninth, tenth, and eleventh grades and a variety of elective courses in twelfth grade. With a view toward interdisciplinary learning, courses offered in the freshman and sophomore years, when coupled with World History, would enable students to understand patterns of human experience as they have emerged across continents and across centuries. Eleventh grade English, when coupled with American History, would enable students to immerse themselves in a year-long exploration of the history and literature of the nation.

Placing an emphasis on interdisciplinary teaching, Dan Frank introduced the Dewey Seminars, named in honor of John Dewey's contribution to progressive education. These high school electives shared a core set of concepts: the connection of subjects of study and methods of inquiry with issues of citizenship, the promotion of collaborative and independent inquiry that facilitates reflective thinking, personal responsibility, and social action. Aimed at promoting the study of the contemporary social world, the Dewey Seminars examined such topics as Adolescence in America, Twentieth Century Africa and Film, The Literature of World Religions, Studies in Ethics and Contemporary Social Issues, and Issues of Race, Culture, and Class. The High School Community Service Program now changed its emphasis. A new Coordinator of Community Service and Diversity, Prexy Nesbitt '62, transformed community service from an eighty-hour high school requirement to a longer-term association with a community service agency to enable students to address, understand, and consider solutions to problems that faced Chicago.

The middle school's reorganization into four sections per grade facilitated personalized and individualized instruction and developed closer and more consistent relationships with families. Middle school teachers played a key role in defining the new division, and the newly developed middle school teams and team leaders were creatively engaged. The effective middle school Community Service Program, introduced in the 1970s, continued on a weekly basis and expanded to include a curriculum on poverty. The middle school advisory program was strengthened and given more time. Time was also scheduled for tutorial assistance and student activities. These child-centered strategies improved the connection between home and school that is central to progressive education.

Lower school teachers were active in designing new classroom space and in the formation and conduct of new grade level teams. The lower school's reduced class size and inclusion of teacher assistants facilitated personalized instruction. This reorganization advanced other decisions. Parker, like most schools, was experiencing an increased number of students who required learning assistance. Classroom teachers felt stretched in their ability to diagnose individual learning needs and to provide the appropriate response. Therefore, in 1996, the school hired two additional learning resource teachers for the lower and middle school and one for the high school, totaling four full-time learning resource teachers. The school also increased the counseling staff and placed a new emphasis on healthy living and responsible action, focusing primarily on issues of nutrition, drug and alcohol use, and sexual activity. Counseling was provided to students who experienced disruptive personal or family circumstances.

To restore faculty leadership in curriculum and staff development, Dan Frank introduced the Corinthian Council, a series of bi-monthly meetings attended by teachers in leadership positions and by elected representatives. The intent was to create a more visible and direct forum for the faculty voice. He also introduced Grand Rounds, another new format for full faculty meetings. With a steering committee of teachers, topics of school and faculty interest were identified and planned.

Faculty and Students: Respond to Changes

What was exciting about this era was also problematic. New buildings and facilities, new programs, new teachers and colleagues, and a new administration evoked new issues and challenges. Between 1995 and 2000, a number of changes took place in the composition of the faculty. First, because of new and expanded programs such as computers and learning services and because of the creation of a third section in the lower school, seventeen new positions were added. During this period, the school hired thirteen new faculty of color and seven new staff of color. A second factor was that a number of senior teachers retired, diminishing the influence of the senior faculty. Retirements, normal attrition, and new teachers attached to new programs created a changed set of demographics among teachers and a new set of dynamics. In 1995, about one-half of the faculty was at the top of the salary schedule, and by 1999, about one-third was at the top. The average age and tenure of faculty members was noticeably lower. About eighty percent of the present faculty held advanced degrees, and many were actively involved in a variety of professional activities. Master teachers were engaged in training assistants, in presenting at regional and national conferences, and in writing and publishing.

Rapid change was difficult for teachers and students to assimilate, resulting in a sense of displacement and alienation, which evolved into mistrust about whether the school was going to remain progressive. The expansion of the building and the division of the school into three discrete sections, each with its own area, seemed contrary to the philosophy of the unity of the whole. In this milieu of rapid change, the Francis W. Parker

Faculty Association approved a proposal to affiliate with the American Federation of Teachers in 1999. For the two sets of negotiations that established the 1996-2000 and 2000-2003 contracts, the faculty sought to establish salaries and benefits competitive with independent schools and Chicago area salaries to ensure that senior faculty continued to receive fair pay increases and to request competitive extra-duty stipends. Considerable attention was paid to the definition of a full-time teaching position and to issues of equity between and within divisions.

With new facilities, new teachers, and new administration—a new principal in 1995, a new head of the upper school in 1996, a new dean of students in 1996 and another in 1999—the students felt that they had little control over their changing school environment. The school the students knew so well and where they felt at ease was less familiar. Students felt dispossessed and believed the changes to be an imposition. Along with changes in school personnel came a new schedule that was more traditional and confining. This schedule changed the patterns of class attendance and the pace of homework in a way that was unacceptable to many students. The school's increased interest in healthy student decision-making also met resistance from the students, who felt the school was imposing itself on the private preserve of student social life, especially on the weekends. When the school and parents worked cooperatively on this issue, the students felt distanced once again. Students felt removed from their familiar comfortable school and often equated changes and their impact with anti-progressivism. Conscious of the independence that the school offered, students felt that a good portion of their school life had been changed or infringed. This period served as an example of the way in which the importance and centrality of the individual rubs against the importance and centrality of the community. The school was asserting itself and acting on its need, and the students were trained to assert themselves rather than to succumb to the pressures of authority.

In the winter and spring of 2000, student government, discouraged by these changes, exercised its leadership to ascertain the status of progressive education at the Parker School. The student government identified Morning Exercise, Independent Study, the Dewey Seminars, art classes, and the student/teacher relationships as positive signs of Parker's continuing commitment to progressive education. Students expressed concern that more competition, hostile relations with administrators, lack of connections among classes, a loss of hominess, and new teachers uninitiated in progressive strategies led the school away from progressive education. For solutions, the student government suggested promoting an increased sense of community, mentoring and training for new teachers, a more integrated curriculum, a return to a more intensive schedule, a de-emphasis on grades, better communication, and the provision of space where students and teachers could naturally congregate. The student government also initiated several week-long experimental high school courses, which they called Cookies in honor of the first principal Flora Cooke. They modeled Cookies after the two-week immersion experiment of 1974. These elective courses responded to interests of students and faculty, were well conceived and conducted, and received a positive evaluation through a student survey.

As in the past, students implemented old school traditions like County Fair and Big Brothers and Sisters, served on the Board of Trustees, and were represented on the Educational Council and the Committee of Four. *The Record, The Weekly, Phaedrus,* and Morning Exercises continued with student leadership. Participation in athletics was high in both the middle school and high school. Sports included field hockey, soccer, golf, track and cross country, basketball, baseball, and softball.

Students also introduced several new organizations. Many activities were initiated to support diversity. The students formed Unity, a group to promote the value of multiculturalism, and a Gay/Straight Alliance. The student government created and facilitated a series of well-organized racial dialogues among high school students. Some students traveled to Philadelphia to protest the death penalty for Mumia Abu-Jamal.

The Parker School's commitment to a diverse student body was a founding principle, and between 1995 and 2000, the principle was challenged by two central issues: the extent of the diversity of the student body and faculty and the ability of the school's culture to accommodate diversity effectively. The alumni of color created a pilot mentoring program for students of color. Faculty included in their meetings discussion related to diversity. Interested parents formed the group AWARE to advocate for diversity at the Parker School and Gender Matters, a group in which parents, faculty, and students participated. Parents also supported speakers and activities that promoted a better climate for diversity. Issues related to the importance of economic diversity were widely voiced. The school also addressed equity issues, providing in-school S.A.T. preparation and tutoring for those who could not afford it privately. Beginning in 1997, Parker sent one of the largest contingents of students, faculty, and parents to attend the Students and Faculty of Color Conferences sponsored by the National Association of Independent Schools. In 1997, the school created the position of Coordinator of Community Service and Diversity. The school sought to stretch its programming to meet the needs of diverse students with a variety of learning styles and needs.

During this period, the admissions office adopted a more aggressive recruitment and outreach program and from 1998 to 2000 between thirty and thirty-five percent of students admitted were students of color. Economic diversity also became a central issue as tuition climbed toward $15,000. Even though $1.5 million budget for financial assistance was at an all-time high and parents and alumni contributed willingly to maintain a significant program of financial assistance, middle income families who were not eligible struggled to stay in school. Considerable thought was given to ways in which Parker's commitment to a diverse population of students could be increased and stabilized through an endowed fund. These student, faculty, parent, and school initiatives were effective diversity strategies that remain ongoing.

The Future: A Progressive Direction

Parker stands on firm ground. It is economically sound and has a new and excellent facility. In its community, there is a strong and positive effort to enhance Parker's place as a distinguished progressive school. With this infrastructure in place, Parker turns its attention increasingly to issues of curriculum, student activity, sense of community, and diversity. The trustees are closely tied to the school's mission and carry it out with commitment.

The Centennial provides an opportunity for the school to celebrate its accomplishments, to create closer ties with its graduates, and to recommit to its historic mission. In its hundredth year, the moral and financial support of alumni and parents is important. Moral support helps to enlarge the vision and provides the encouragement for the school to keep carving out its distinctive role. Financial support enables the school to complete the important reconstruction of the auditorium and of the music, art, and science wing. The school's commitment to a program of financial assistance to promote economic diversity is of sufficient historic and current importance to create an endowment that will expand and solidify it. Similarly, Parker's commitment to recruiting, developing, and rewarding an outstanding faculty and staff needs to be addressed.

The school's ability to stabilize a strong program of financial assistance can significantly affect the school's future. While the school and the city are currently experiencing favorable economic and enrollment circumstances, it is possible that demographic, economic, and neighborhood shifts could significantly affect the school. The school's ability to increase and stabilize the amount of financial assistance available will permit a greater presence beyond the neighborhood and a greater ability to attract a talented and diverse student body. The future offers a continuing challenge to forge functional partnerships with families that reflect the changing realities of home and school life.

The school's focus on developing character, citizenship, and a sense of responsibility needs careful consideration in a world increasingly dependent on technology. Ways in which the school promotes itself as a learning community as well as a social community will become increasingly important. When a student can receive a high school diploma online from a distinguished university, what role does a school play?

The future for the Parker School is particularly rosy if it does well what it purports to do well. There will be an increased need for a sense of personal attachment and a focus on issues of character and an increased value placed on the ability to relate to the world in a confident, resourceful, and creative manner. The ability to understand the world and to navigate it thoughtfully is at a premium. Responsibility, character, citizenship, artfulness, tolerance, and a sense of one's own possibilities will be crucial.

Parker's sense of purpose and identity will abide, and Parker will continue to struggle with its capacity to live up to its possibilities. With a sense that the school has a long future, it is important to keep the past alive and to apply enduring principles in ways that powerfully connect the school and its graduates to a new and changing world. At the center of this challenge is people. As always for the Parker School, the way in which this school carries out its mission depends on the quality of commitment, action, and care taken by its faculty, students, parents, and trustees.

Afterword

This history of Chicago's Francis W. Parker School traces a progressive, coeducational day school from its experimental roots in the pedagogy of Francis Wayland Parker, the philosophy of John Dewey, and the values of the Progressive Movement of the 1900s. Over the century, a corps of faculty has tried to clarify, develop, and implement this progressive social reconstructionist philosophy. At times, the experience with progressive education met with more success than others; however, progressive education was always supported by the students, the alumni, the trustees, the Educational Council, and a majority of parents, who frequently challenged but wanted and expected a progressive school.

It was Francis Parker who set forth the overarching goals that became the measuring stick for the quality of progressive education at the Parker School. To ensure that his goals served as guidelines for the school, Flora Cooke and her faculty included his philosophical principles at the beginning of each *Catalogue and Course of Study* from 1901 to 1930 (see Chapter 6). To achieve these five goals—"the education of the whole child," "the creation of community life," "practical citizenship," "the formation of character," and "the acquisition of knowledge"—the faculty defined each concept, implemented instructional strategies, and attempted to weave these goals into a fabric for all courses and activities and for instruction in the school. For example, music was also a class in character development just as science was a class in practical citizenship and history was a class in community participation. These threads had no beginnings, no endings, no priorities, but were all a part of each other. Every teacher was responsible for the child, the goals and values, the community, the subject matter, and making the whole greater than the sum of its parts. Francis Parker's main contribution provided the foundation for curriculum and instruction.

John Dewey and to a lesser degree Francis Parker recognized a more difficult major goal for the teachers—to make education a science through the application of knowledge from psychology and sociology. Education was to be developed as an applied science in a manner similar to medicine (see Chapter 1). With this goal in mind, the Parker faculty made attempts to contribute to the development of a science of education by using the new tests and measurements introduced before World War I and by experimenting with classroom trials between 1901 and 1930. The teachers also applied the principles of evaluation introduced by Ralph Tyler in his work at the Parker School during the Eight-Year Study and throughout the 1970s (see Chapter 7). The Parker faculty made fleeting and prolonged but often unsuccessful scientific trials. The faculty contributed to the science of education with these noteworthy pedagogical principles, which remain applicable today:

Principle 1:   Social motive can be taught to replace individual motive
Principle 2:   Morning Exercise is a socializing and unifying experience
Principle 3:   Expression trains motive and completes the learning act
Principle 4:   Concrete experiences are the most effective method of instruction
Principle 5:   Teachers are able to adopt curriculum to meet individual needs
Principle 6:   The community requires the cultivation of the habit of "creative effort."

Groups of teachers explained these principles in six of the ten *Studies in Education* published between 1912 and 1925 (see Chapter 6).

When, in the Progressive Era, the social reconstructionists envisioned the school as a fundamental lever of social and political change, the third major philosophical goal emerged (see Chapter 1). This society-centered goal differentiated the Parker School from the child-centered schools that became so popular in the 1920s. Historically, the school achieved considerable success with this goal through diversity and community service. From 1901 to the end of World War II, Anita McCormick Blaine funded a financial aid program in order to enroll a diverse student body rather than create "a rich child's school." The diverse enrollment continued to expand. The trustees kept tuition low to facilitate diversity and in the 1930s even considered closing the school doors rather than eliminating financial aid. In the 1940s, twenty years before the passage of President Johnson's Civil Rights legislation, the school admitted the first Negro students. The school was guided by Francis Parker's words in *Talks on Pedagogics* (1894):

> In their early life of children of all classes, of all nationalities, of all sects, of rich and poor alike, children of both sexes, shall work together under the highest and best conditions in one community for from eight to twelve years . . . before prejudice has entered their childish souls, before hate has become fixed, before mistrust has become a habit.

Now, in the twenty-first century, diversity continues to be one of the school's prime goals, underscored by admissions policies, hiring practices, parent and student activities and programs, educational assistance initiatives, and financial aid. The results are the alumni's exceptional involvement in a disproportionately large number of educational, cultural, and social agencies and boards, which provide help for those who are working to achieve the American Dream. The Francis W. Parker School thrived for one hundred years on Francis Parker's principles of community, character, and citizenship; on Dewey's directive to develop a science of education; and on the values of the Progressive Movement.

Throughout the school's struggles and successes, the faculty learned several lessons worthy of sharing with other educators:

Lesson 1: The teachers must know the students intellectually, socially, morally, and spiritually to be able to develop the full potential of all students.

Good teachers learn students, and students learn teachers, which results in effective classroom discourse. Personalization is an imperative that makes students confident learners. Formally, teachers accomplish this goal by reading student records, interviewing students enrolled in their classes, and asking students to create "portfolios" of their best work or the work they like best. Informally, teachers are a presence in the school, participating with students in projects and activities. They join them at cultural events, and are invited to students' homes. Students learn when the teachers tell stories about themselves to make a point significant to life. Student-teacher relationships are a distinguishing characteristic of the school that originated with Francis Parker's directives stated in the 1890s.

Lesson 2: The school and the home must develop a constructive relationship because parents are partners in the educational equation.

Francis Parker was the father of the first Parent-Teacher Association in the mid 1880s. At the Parker School, parent involvement extends through advisors, who schedule parents for individual meetings specifically focused on their child's needs and interests. The school also invites parents to grade level meetings and Open Houses to introduce them to the curriculum. Parents are given opportunities to discuss home-school issues with other students and parents who can provide insights and advice. Besides engaging in school activities, programs, and performances, parents introduce many socially conscious activities like "Gender Matters." As the first chairman of the Board of Trustees stated, the school and the home "pursue together" because "neither can do separately all that should be done."

Lesson 3: The teachers must be "cultured, educated, and trained."

Not the trustees nor the administration but the teachers are central to the educational process of the school because they are in daily communication with students and because the classroom is the source of the school's reputation. From his first years in education, Francis Parker held high expectations for his corps of teachers. He devised a practice teaching method called "illustrative teaching" that enabled young teachers to learn progressive philosophy and pedagogy under the tutelage of master teachers. (see Chapter 4.) Teachers must feel that the school is important and that they have to work hard and to earn a place. Many teachers remain at the Parker School for more than thirty years because the school offers exceptional opportunities for growth through curriculum experimentation, collaboration with talented colleagues, a provocative philosophy, and exciting and excited students. The high expectations, expert tutelage, hard work, and access to great opportunities presented by the city and the school for growth transform the lives of teachers and help ordinary teachers become extraordinary.

Lesson 4: The curriculum of the school should be developed collaboratively by the faculty of the whole.

At Parker, the teachers worked collaboratively to develop a unified curriculum of the whole. In departments, at the grade level, in divisions, and as the faculty of the whole, they designed an integrated course of study unified vertically from Grades K-12 and horizontally at the grade level. Teachers cannot teach their "own thing" but have to adapt their courses to the curriculum in order to create synergy in the education of the children. Preparing and writing the course of study together is another way Parker teachers grow. A well-written course report supervised by a master teacher strengthens weak teachers and makes good teachers great.

Lesson 5: Experiments should be introduced on a small scale with constant data collection, correction, and adjustment before being implemented on a full-scale basis to provide the option of stopping or advancing the experiment.

Successive experiments at the Parker School proved that focusing resources and attention on an experiment in one division of the school is more effective than undertaking experimentation in several areas at one time. A confined experiment better allocates resources. Experimentation also creates student excitement and interest that result in higher student achievement than in areas that remain unchanged. The division of the school that has large-scale experimentation becomes the strongest because it commands student and faculty attention. During the Pioneering Years, the lower school's experiment with central subjects made it the strongest in the school. The high school commanded the most attention during the Eight-Year Study. More recently, middle school mini courses and the high school Intensive-Extensive experiment strengthened those divisions. Nonetheless, each experiment was part of the larger experiment in progressive education.

Lesson 6: The school must have standards of achievement and standards of deportment.

Standards of achievement are difficult to derive in a student body chosen for its diversity, but teachers working collaboratively can establish a system made up of a variety of measures. Standards of deportment are equally difficult to identify, but moral education insists that infractions have consequences. The individual impulse and the needs of the community often conflict, but the school's philosophy dictates the preference for the community and communicates it to all students.

Lesson 7: The school's philosophy and educational goals must be presented clearly, consistently, and frequently.

Unless there is a radical change in the philosophy, the school's original statements should not be cluttered by new versions and restatements. Anita McCormick Blaine and Flora Cooke organized the Parker School to express Francis Parker's philosophy in every course and activity. Frequent new mission statements should be avoided because they make primary documents more complex rather than clarify what must be understood by all in common. The philosophy is the blueprint for life in the school. The more philosophy, the less philosophy.

Routinely, the main philosophical statements should be read, defended, and discussed with the body of the whole and applied when conflicts arise requiring clarification and resolution. The philosophy is not only the written statement, it is organic. The reading of Corinthians at each year's opening Morning Exercise, the repetition of the Parker word, "Responsibility," the school motto, "Everything to help, nothing to hinder," and school celebrations and traditions embody the philosophy for the students of the school and continue to reinforce Parker's tenets on community, character, and citizenship. The philosophy is as effective as the number of members in the community who know it, embody it, and uphold it.

Lesson 8: "Community life is the ideal of education because it is the only ideal great enough to provide for the all-sided development of the individual."

The Parker School continues to be an embryonic democracy. Critical thinking, the challenging of authority, the introduction of new ideas and new experiments often incite controversy, which is and should be the norm at the Parker School. Education for democracy is not peaceful.

After a century, progressive education remains ambiguously defined except for the theories stated in John Dewey's *Democracy and Education*

(1916). The concept invented in the 1890s is elusive, dynamic, and does not lend itself to certainty. The different variables seem to defy definition. For example, practitioners are uncertain what is meant by character, citizenship, and community and therefore unsure about the initiatives and strategies that will achieve these educational goals. Educators continue to try to define the science of education, but few can offer more than John Dewey, who explained how a definition of progressive education might emerge: "Man did not know the art of bridge building until he built the bridges." Similarly, more progressive schools need to be built in order to define progressive education and to develop a science of education.

Endnotes

Note: When a footnote cites several passages from the same book, page numbers are listed in the order in which the quotations appear in this text (see Chapter 1, note 26).

Chapter 1: Evolution of Progressive Education

1. Francis Parker, *Talks on Pedagogics* (New York, A.S. Barnes & Company, 1909), 439.
2. Lawrence A. Cremin, *The Transformation of the School: Progressivism in American Education, 1876-1957* (New York: Vintage Books, 1964), 91.
3. Parker, *Pedagogics* 4, 24.
4. Parker, *Pedagogics*, 27, 34.
5. Parker, *Pedagogics,* 205, 206.
6. Martin S. Dworkin, *Dewey on Education* (New York: Teachers College, Columbia University, 1959), 19-32.
7. Parker, *Pedagogics,* 337, 450, 349.
8. Dewey, *My Pedagogical Creed,* in Dworkin, *Dewey on Education,* 19-32.
9. Parker, *Pedagogics*, 254.
10. Parker, *Pedagogics*, v, 451.
11. Parker, *Pedagogics,* 418-420.
12. Parker, *Pedagogics*, 419, 420-421, 346, 423.
13. John Dewey, *School & Society* (Chicago: University of Chicago Press, 1900), 15, 3.
14. John Dewey, *Democracy and Education* (New York: The Macmillan Company, 1916), 99.
15. Dewey, *Democracy*, 136, 98.
16. Merle Curti, *The Social Ideas of American Educators* (Totowa, New Jersey: Littlefield, Adams & Co., 1966), 409.
17. Cremin, *Transformation,* viii
18. Cremin, *Transformation,* 22, viii-ix.
19. Parker, *Pedagogics*, 424, 427.
20. Mayer, *A History of Educational Thought* (Columbus, Ohio: Charles E. Merrill Books, 1963), 345.

21   Horace Mann, *Twelfth Annual Report of the Board of Education, Together with the Twelfth Annual Report of the Secretary of the Board* (Boston, 1849).

22   Parker, *Pedagogics,* 424.

23   Mann, *Twelfth Report.*

24   Dewey, *The Education Situation,* 158.

25   Dewey, *Democracy,* iii, 87.

26   Boyd Bode, *Modern Educational Theories* (New York: Macmillan Company, 1927), 39, 5, 9.

27   Parker, *Pedagogics,* v.

28   Parker, *Pedagogics,* 440.

29   John Dewey, *The Sources of a Science of Education* (New York: Liveright Publishing Corporation, 1929), 13.

30   Dworkin, *Dewey on Education,* 115-117.

31   Dewey, *Sources,* 22.

32   Dewey, *Sources,* 8, 9.

33   Dewey, *Sources,* 56.

34   Dewey, *Sources,* 60-64.

35   Raymond Corsini, *Encyclopedia of Psychology* (New York: Wiley, 1994) 531-532.

36   Bird T. Baldwin, "William James' Contributions to Education," *Journal of Educational Psychology,* September 1911, 373-374.

37   Cremin, *Transformation,* 108.

38   Charles Darwin, *On the Origin of Species by Means of Natural Selection: The Preservation of Favored Races in the Struggle for Life* (New York: A.L. Fowle, 1859), 97-98, 107.

39   Cremin, *Transformation,* 92.

40   Elsa Perverly Kimball, *Sociology and Education: An Analysis of the Theories of Spencer and Ward* (New York: Columbia University Press, 1932), 14-16.

41   Kimball, *Sociology and Education,* 14-15.

42   Cremin, *Transformation,* 97.

43   Lester F. Ward, *Dynamic Sociology* (New York: Appleton and Company, 1883), 21-22.

44   *The School Journal, Vol. IV* (1897), 3-4.

45   *The School Journal,* 18-19, 22.

46 Dworkin, *Dewey on Education,* 118.

47 Dworkin, *Dewey on Education,* 113.

48 Diane Ravitch, *The Troubled Crusade* (New York: Basic Books, 1983), 47-48.

49 Bode, 234.

50 Dewey, *Educational Situation*, 58.

51 Cremin, *Transformation,* 88.

52 Ravitch, *Troubled Crusade*, 46.

53 Ravitch, *Troubled Crusade*, 47- 48.

54 Harold Rugg and Ann Schumaker, *The Child-Centered School* (Yonkers-on-Hudson, New York: World Book, 1928), 324-325, vii, 2-5.

55 Ravitch, *Troubled Crusade,* 50-51.

56 Cremin, *Transformation,* 217.

57 John Dewey, "Progressive Education and the Science of Education," *Progressive Education,* Vol. V, 1928: 197-204.

58 George S. Counts, *Dare the School Build a New Social Order?* (New York: Arno Press, 1969), 9-10.

59 Harold Rugg, "The American Mind and the 'Class' Problem," *Social Frontier 2* (February 1936): 139.

60 William Heard Kilpatrick, "High Marxism Defined and Rejected," *Social Frontier 2* (June 1936): 272-274.

61 Dewey, "Class Struggle and the Democratic Way," *Social Frontier 2* (May 1936): 241-42.

62 Ravitch, *Troubled Crusade,* 43, 45.

63 Carleton Washburne, *What Is Progressive Education?* (New York: The John Day Company, 1952), 34, 16.

64 Washburne, 40, 41.

65 Ravitch, *Troubled Crusade,* 44-45.

66 Drawn from Washburne, *What Is Progressive Education?*

Chapter 2: Pedagogue, Philanthropist, and Philosopher

1 William M. Giffin, *School Days in the Fifties: A True Story with Some Untrue Names of Persons and Places, with an Appendix Containing an Autobiographical Sketch of Francis Wayland Parker* (Chicago: A. Flanagan Company, 1906), 110-111.

2 Giffin, *School Days*, 112.

3   Ida Cassa Heffron, *Francis Wayland Parker: An Interpretive Biography* (Los Angeles: Ivan Beach, Jr.), 20.

4   Giffin, *School Days*, 114.

5   Heffron, *Parker: An Interpretive Biography*, 20.

6   Giffin, *School Days,* 117.

7   Edward Dangler, "The Educational Philosophy of Francis Wayland Parker: Its Origins, Contents, and Consequences" (Ph.D. dissertation, New York University, 1939), 13.

8   Heffron, *Parker: An Interpretive Biography*, 21.

9   Willard S. Bass, "Colonel Parker the Soldier," unpublished manuscript, 1908, Chicago Historical Society.

10   Jack Campbell, *The Children's Crusader* (New York: Teachers College Press, 1967), 28.

11   Campbell, *Children's Crusader*, 43.

12   Campbell, *Children's Crusader*, 45, 53.

13   Campbell, *Children's Crusader,* 61.

14   Giffin, *School Days*, 128-129.

15   Giffin, *School Days*, 130.

16   Campbell, *Children's Crusader,* 84-85.

17   Parker, *Pedagogics*, 350.

18   *Studies in Education, Vol. 1: The Social Motive in School Work* (Chicago: Francis W. Parker School, June 1912), 11.

19   Dangler, *Educational Philosophy,* 32, 60.

20   Campbell, *Children's Crusader,* 42.

21   Parker, *Pedagogics*, 359.

22   Campbell, *Children's Crusader,* 98, 106.

23   Dangler, *Educational Philosophy*, 25.

24   Campbell, *Children's Crusader,* 106.

25   Campbell, *Children's Crusader*, 121.

26   Katherine M. Stilwell, "Colonel Parker as I Knew Him," unpublished paper, 1902, in Chicago Historical Society, 4.

27   Flora J. Cooke, "Socialized Creative Education," in *Independent Education*, March 1929, 13.

28   Parker, "The School of the Future," N.E.A. *Proceedings*, 1891, 89; cited in Dangler, *Educational Philosophy*, 105.

29   "Colonel Parker's Fad Factory," *Chicago Tribune*, January 30, 1899.

30 Heffron, *An Interpretive Biography*, 28.

31 Campbell, *Children's Crusader,* 80, 121.

32 Heffron, *An Interpretive Biography,* 107.

33 Campbell, *Children's Crusader*, 122.

34 Harrison, *A Timeless Affair*, 89.

35 Francis W. Parker, letter to Anita McCormick Blaine, December 15, 1898, Papers of Anita McCormick Blaine, McCormick Collection, Wisconsin Historical Society, Madison.

36 Heffron, *An Interpretive Biography,* 38.

37 Flora J. Cooke, "Socialized Creative Education," *Independent Education*, March 1929, 13.

38 Unless otherwise noted, information in this section was drawn from Gilbert A. Harrison, *A Timeless Affair: The Life of Anita McCormick Blaine* (Chicago: The University of Chicago Press, 1979), with the permission of the publisher.

39 Katharine Taylor, "Mrs. Blaine—Citizen of the World," speaking at a program in memory of Anita McCormick Blaine at the Francis W. Parker School on April 22, 1955, 14.

40 Blaine, handwritten theme dated March 26, 1881. Wisconsin Historical Society, Madison.

41 Nancy Blaine Harrison, "My Grandmother," speaking at a program in memory of Anita McCormick Blaine at the Francis W. Parker School on April 22, 1955, 11-12.

42 Robert Tostberg, "Educational Ferment in Chicago, 1883-1904," (Ph.D. dissertation, University of Wisconsin, Madison, 1960), 143.

43 John Dewey, *Experience and Education* (New York: Collier Macmillan, 1938), 25.

44 John Dewey, *Pedagogic Creed*, cited in Martin S. Dworkin, *Dewey on Education* (New York: Teachers College, Columbia University, 1959), 24.

45 Dewey, "Ethics and Physical Science," Andover *Review* 7 (June 1887):573-91.

46 Parker, *Pedagogics*, 450.

47 Merle Curti, *The Social Ideas of American Educators* (Totowa, New Jersey: Littlefield, Adams & Co., 1966), 500.

48 Some sources state that Dewey taught high school for two years; other sources state three years.

49   Harrison, *A Timeless Affair*, 96.

50   Melvin Baker, *Foundation of Dewey's Educational Theory* (New York: King's Crow Press, 1955), 80.

51   Dangler, *Educational Philosophy*, 195-196.

52   Curti, *Social Ideas*, 502.

53   Dangler, *Educational Philosophy,* 196-97.

54   Curti, *Social Ideas,* 514.

55   Tostberg, "Educational Ferment," 155-156, citing George Mead, *Mind, Self & Society,* ed. Charles W. Morris (Chicago: The University of Chicago Press, 1934).

56   Mead, "The Philosophies of Royce, James, and Dewey in Their American Settings" in Lawrence Sears, *The Development of American Philosophy* (Cambridge: Houghton Mifflin Co., 1940), 327.

57   Mayhew and Edwards, *The Dewey School*, 24-30.

58   Robert McCaul, "Dewey and the University of Chicago, Part I: July, 1894-March, 1902," *School and Society* 89 (March 25, 1961): 155.

59   McCaul, 155.

60   McCaul, 153.

61   McCaul, 153, 154, 153.

62   McCaul, 154.

63   McCaul, 152.

64   Curti, *Social Ideas,* 379.

Chapter 3: The European Intellectual Genealogy of Francis Parker

1   Jack Campbell, *Colonel Francis W. Parker: The Children's Crusader* (New York: Teachers College Press, 1967), 100.

2   Edward Dangler, "The Educational Philosophy of Francis Wayland Parker: Its Origins, Contents, and Consequences" (Ph.D. dissertation, New York University, 1939), 40.

3   M. W. Keatings (translator), *The Great Didactic*, cited in Dangler, *Educational Philosophy*, 39.

4   Francis W. Parker, *Talks on Pedagogics* (New York: A. S. Barnes and Company, 1909), 359.

5   Francis W. Parker, *Talks on Teaching* (New York: A. S. Barnes and Company, 1883), 180-81, 29, 160-161; Parker, *Pedagogics*, 12, 18, 292; Parker, "The Training of Teachers," N.E. A. *Proceedings*, 1895, 972.

6   Dangler, *Educational Philosophy,* 42.
7   Frederick Mayer, *Foundations of Education* (Columbus, OH: Charles E. Merrill Books, 1960), 34.
8   James Bowen, *A History of Educational Thought*, 3rd ed. (Columbus, Ohio: Charles E. Merrill Publishing, 1973), 197, 186-187.
9   Jean-Jacques Rousseau, *Émile, or On Education* (New York: Basic Books, 1979), 37-45.
10   Parker, "Outlines of Pedagogics," *School Journal*, 31, May 22, 1886: 325.
11   Lawrence A. Cremin, *The Transformation of the School* (New York: Vintage Books, 1964), 134; Parker, *Talks on Pedagogics*, 23-24.
12   Robert Ulich, *Three Thousand Years of Educational Wisdom* (Cambridge: Harvard University Press,1954), 481.
13   Dangler, *Educational Philosophy,* 42.
14   Parker, *Pedagogics*, 411.
15   Parker, "European Correspondence," *Dayton Journal*, Dayton, Ohio, October 14, 1872.
16   Friedrich Froebel, *The Education of Man* (New York: Appleton, Century, 1885), 238, 67.
17   Parker, *Pedagogics*, 251.
18   Parker, *Pedagogics,* v.
19   Froebel, *Education,* 48-49.
20   John Dewey, *School and Society* (Chicago: The University of Chicago Press, 1956), 117-18.
21   Bowen, *History of Educational Thought,* 236.
22   Charles McMurry, *The Elements of General Method Based on the Principles of Herbart*, 2nd ed. (Bloomington, IL: Public School Publishing, 1903), 236-237.
23   Campbell, *Children's Crusader*, 137.
24   Parker, *Pedagogics*, v.
25   McMurry, *Elements of General Method*, 237.

Chapter 4: Francis Parker Introduces New Education in American Schools

1   Horace Mann, Twelfth Report.
2   "Mann, Horace," *Encyclopedia of American Education* (New York: Facts on File, 1996), 570-571.

3   Jack Campbell, *Colonel Francis W. Parker: The Children's Crusader* (New York: Teachers College Press, 1967), 75.

4   Adams, Henry, *The Education of Henry Adams: An Autobiography* (Boston: Houghton Mifflin Company, 1918), 26.

5   Campbell, *The Children's Crusader,* 76.

6   Charles Francis Adams, Jr. *The New Departure in the Common Schools of Quincy* (Boston: Estes and Lauriat, 1879), 32-33.

7   Adams, *New Departure,* 34.

8   Adams, *New Departure,* 34, 31; Ida Cassa Heffron, *Francis Wayland Parker: An Interpretive Biography* (Los Angeles: Ivan Deach, Jr., 1934), 24.

9   Adams, *New Departure,* 35, 40.

10 Francis Parker, *Talks on Teaching* (New York: A. E. Barnes and Co., 1883),17; Heffron, *An Interpretive Biography*, 28, 23, 24.

11 Campbell, *The Children's Crusader*, 80-81.

12 Lelia E. Patridge, *The Quincy Methods Illustrated* (New York: E.L. Kellogg & Company, 1885), xi-xv, xviii.

13 Campbell, *Children's Crusader*, 81-82.

14 Patridge, *Quincy Method*, 573-582.

15 Patridge, *Quincy Method*, xiii, 3.

16 Adams, *New Departure,* 37, 40-41, 43.

17 Patridge, *Quincy Method*, xiii.

18 Patridge, *Quincy Method,* xiii, 1.

19 Heffron, *An Interpretive Biography,* 23.

20 *Annual Report, School Committee, Town of Quincy, 1875-1876,* 128-129.

21 Adams, *New Departure,* 42-43.

22 Patridge, *Quincy Method,* xiv.

23 Heffron, *An Interpretive Biography,* 23.

24 Patridge, *Quincy Method,* 6, 7-8, 2.

25 Annual Report, School Committee, Town of Quincy, 1877-1878, 130.

26 Patridge, *Quincy Method,* xii-xiii.

27 Patridge, *Quincy Method,* 8-9, xiii.

28 Campbell, *Children's Crusader*, 88.

29 Francis Wayland Parker Centennial Booklet (Chicago: Francis W. Parker School, 1937), 4.

30 "Elementary School Teacher," Vol. II, 744-745, June, 1902.

31 Campbell, *Children's Crusader*, 90-91, 92.

32 Campbell, *Children's Crusader,* 92-93.

33 Adams, *New Departure,* 37.

34 Dangler, *Educational Philosophy*, 217; Heffron, *An Interpretive Biography*, 25.

35 Campbell, *Children's Crusader*, 87.

36 Unless otherwise indicated, information for this section is drawn from Campbell, *Children's Crusader*, 107-124.

37 Wilbur S. Jackman, "Francis Wayland Parker," *Educational Report* 1901-02 (U.S. Office of Education, Report of the Commissioner of Education for the year 1902), 232-233.

38 Heffron, *Interpretive Biography,* 24.

39 Parker, F. W., "An Account of the Work of the Cook County and Chicago Normal School from 1883 to 1899," *The Elementary School Teacher*, June 1902, 761.

40 Parker, *Talks on Pedagogics* (New York: A.S. Barnes and Company, 1909), 284.

41 Parker, "Normal School," 770, 772.

42 Parker, "Principles of Correlation," *Course of Study, I,* February, 1901, 506.

43 Parker, *Pedagogics*, 450, 337-338.

44 Heffron, *An Interpretive Biography,* 50.

45 Parker, *Pedagogics*, 421.

46 Parker, "An Account of the Work," 761.

47 Faculty member Clara Isabel Mitchell (Millspaugh), "Textile Arts as a Social Occupation," *Elementary School Teacher*, Vol. VII, 142.

48 Parker, "An Account of the Work," 15-16.

49 Heffron, *An Interpretive Biography,* 56.

50 Heffron, *An Interpretive Biography,* 52.

51 Parker, "Normal School," 776.

52 Parker, "Normal School," 761.

53 Parker, "Normal School," 752.

54 Campbell, *Children's Crusader,* 117-118.

55 Tyler, Ralph, *Basic Principles of Curriculum and Instruction* (Chicago: The University of Chicago Press, 1949), 83.

56 Heffron, *An Interpretive Biography,* 40-41.

57 Parker, "Normal School," 778.

58 Heffron, *An Interpretive Biography,* 31-32, 38-39.

59 Parker, *Pedagogics*, 450.

60 Parker, F. W., letter to Anita McCormick Blaine, December 15, 1898.

61 Campbell, *Children's Crusader,* 214.

62 Harrison, *A Timeless Affair,* 90-91.

63 F. W. Parker, letter to Mrs. Blaine, September 14, 1899.

64 Harrison, *A Timeless Affair,* 93.

65 Campbell, *Children's Crusader,* 218.

66 Harrison, *A Timeless Affair,* 93-94.

67 Francis W. Parker, "Morning Exercises," *The Course of Study, 1* (July 1, 1900-June 1, 1901), 599.

68 Harrison, *A Timeless Affair,* 94, 220.

69 Minutes of the Board of Trustees, February 26, 1900; F. W. Parker, letter to Zonia Baber, January 3, 1900.

70 "Trustees Name Faculty," *Chicago Tribune* (Chicago, Ill.), June 19, 1899; "Blaine Faculty Is Chosen by Trustees," *Chicago Evening Journal* (Chicago, Ill.), June 19, 1899.

71 Harrison, *A Timeless Affair,* 93.

72 Campbell, *Children's Crusader,* 220-221.

73 Harrison, *A Timeless Affair,* 95, 90-91.

74 "To the Patrons and Friends of the Chicago Institute," June 1, 1901, signed by Blaine and Trustees Aldis, Favill, and Bentley; McCormick Papers, Wisconsin Historical Society.

75 Heffron, *An Interpretive Biography*, 33.

76 Robert L. McCaul, "Dewey and the University of Chicago, Part I," *School and Society,* March 25, 1961, 155.

77 Harrison, *A Timeless Affair,* 96.

78 Harrison, *A Timeless Affair,* 96-97.

79 Campbell, *Children's Crusader,* 222.

80 Campbell, *Children's Crusader,* 222.

81 Harrison, *A Timeless Affair,* 97, 101.

82 Campbell, *Children's Crusader,* 224.

83 DePencier, Ida B., *The History of the Laboratory Schools: The University of Chicago, 1896-1965* (Chicago: Quadrangle Books, 1967), 36.

84 McCaul, "Dewey," 155.

85 McCaul, "Dewey," 206.

86 Campbell, *Children's Crusader,* 224.

87 McCaul, "Dewey", 179.

88 McCaul, "Dewey," 181.

89 Harrison, *Children's Crusader,* 100.

Chapter 5: The Parker School Heritage: Second-Generation Schools

1 Information in this section is drawn from Ethel Mintzer Lichtman, *The Francis Parker School Heritage* (San Diego, CA: The Francis Parker School, 1985).

2 *The Handbook of Private Schools*, 76th edition (Boston: Porter, Sargent Publishers, Inc., 1995), 689.

3 Information in this section is drawn from Edward Yeomans, *The Shady Hill School: The First Fifty Years* (Cambridge, MA: Wildflower Press, 1979) and Edward Yeomans, "The Francis Parker Legacy to Shady Hill School, Cambridge," in *Between Home and Community: Chronicle of the Francis W. Parker School, 1901-1976,* Marie Kirchner Stone, ed. (Chicago: Francis W. Parker School, 1976), 288-289.

4 Stone, *Between Home and Community*, 290.

5 Information in this section is drawn from Nancy Geyer, *The Vision of Perry Dunlap Smith* (Winnetka, IL: North Shore Country Day School, undated), and Nancy Geyer Christopher, *The North Shore Country Day School: Seventy Years as a Community of Learning* (Winnetka, IL: North Shore Country Day School, 1993), iii-v, 17-32, 71.

6 *Handbook of Private Schools*, 574-575.

7 All quotes in this section are from Patricia L. Fry, *A Thread to Hold: The Story of Ojai Valley School* (Santa Barbara, CA: Fithian Press, 1996), 29, 75, 77-78, 145-149, 211-212.

8 Charles Haas, letter to author, February 15, 1999.

9 Information in this section is drawn from Chris Holabird, letter to author, March 20, 1999.

10 Information in this section is drawn from Chris Holabird, "Los Encinos Booklet" (Encino, California, 1980).

11 Francis W. Parker, *Talks on Pedagogics* (New York: A.S. Barnes & Co., 1909), 451, 446, 447.

12 Jack Ellison, "A New Approach to Teacher Education," in Stone, *Between Home and Community,* 286.

13   Carleton Washburne and Sidney P. Marland, Jr., *Winnetka: The History and Significance of an Educational Experiment*, cited in Christopher, *North Shore Country Day School*, 87-88.

14   John Leighton Tewksbury, "An Historical Study of the Winnetka Public Schools from 1919 to 1946," Ph.D. dissertation, Northwestern University, 1962, cited in Christopher, *North Shore Country Day*, 88-89.

15   Ellison, "A New Approach," in Stone, *Between Home and Community*, 286.

16   Tewksbury, "An Historical Study," in Christopher, *North Shore Country Day*, 89.

17   Ellison, "A New Approach," in Stone, *Between Home and Community*, 287.

18   Christopher, *North Shore Country Day*, 89-91.

Chapter 6: The Pioneering Years (1901-1935)

1   Larzer Ziff, *The American 1890s: Life and Times of a Lost Generation* (New York: Viking Press: 1966), 3.

2   Ziff, *The American 1890s*, 2, cover copy.

3   Henry Steele Commager, *The American Mind* (New Haven: Yale University Press, 1950), 41.

4   Charles Sellers and Henry May, *A Synopsis of American History* (Chicago: Rand McNally, 1963), 284.

5   Sellers and May, *Synopsis*, 255.

6   Sellers and May, *Synopsis*, 285, 308.

7   F. Scott Fitzgerald, *This Side of Paradise* (New York: Charles Scribner's Sons, 1920), 255.

8   Frederick Lewis Allen, *Only Yesterday: An Informal History of the Nineteen-Twenties* (New York: Harper & Row, 1931), 88,100.

9   "Subscription Agreement to Make up Deficit in Income of Proposed School, 1901," in Marie Kirchner Stone, *Between Home and Community* (Chicago: Francis W. Parker School, 1976),15.

10   Harrison, *Timeless Affair, 121.*

11   Parker School Trustees, "A Plan for Increasing Income from Tuition, 1924."

12   Minutes of the Francis W. Parker Board of Trustees, November 1930.

13   "Suggestions of Miss Cooke in Connection with Report of Special Committee on Buildings and Grounds," Minutes, January 4, 1936.

14 1930 Parker *Record,* 21-22.

15 Harrison, *Timeless Affair*, 119.

16 Minutes, January 10, 1906.

17 Harrison, *Timeless Affair*, 111.

18 Bentley, "Remarks," in Stone, *Between Home and Community*, 62-63.

19 Carol Lynn Gilmer, "Flora Cooke: Grand Old Lady of Education," in Stone, *Between Home and Community*, 43.

20 "Reflections, 1927," Flora J. Cooke; Cooke Collection, Chicago Historical Society.

21 "Reflections," 1927.

22 Gilmer, "Grand Old Lady," 44.

23 Woodrow Wilson, letter to Anita McCormick Blaine, April 22, 1918. McCormick Collection, Wisconsin Historical Society, Madison, Wisconsin.

24 Frances Levy Angel, "I Remember . . ." in Stone, *Between Home and Community*, 138.

25 Katharine Taylor, "Character," in Stone, *Between Home and Community*, 309, 312.

26 Flora J. Cooke, "History of Certain Past Policies and Traditions, 1938" in Stone, *Between Home and Community*, 138.

27 Harrison, *A Timeless Affair*, 118.

28 Harrison, *A Timeless Affair*, 119, 120.

29 Campbell, *Colonel Parker: The Children's Crusader* (New York: Teachers College Press, 1967),121.

30 Campbell, *The Children's Crusader*, 121.

31 Flora J. Cooke, *Nature Myths and Stories for Little Children* (Chicago: A. Flanagan Publishing, 1895), iii.

32 Flora J. Cooke, *First Primary Grade: One Year's Outline of Work in Science, History, Geography, and Music* (Chicago: Cook County Normal School, 1897).

33 Campbell, *Children's Crusader*, 121.

34 Stone, *Between Home and Community*, timetable.

35 Patricia Albjerg Graham, *Progressive Education: From Arcady to Academe* (New York: Teachers College Press, 1967), 89.

36 Flora J. Cooke, curriculum vitae, Cooke Collection, Chicago Historical Society.

37　*Chicago Daily News*, March 17, 1953.

38　Gilmer, "Grand Old Lady of Education," in Stone, *Between Home and Community*, 45.

39　Anita McCormick Blaine, "The Origins and Aims of the Francis W. Parker School" in Stone, *Between Home and Community,* 4-6.

40　Francis W. Parker School *Catalogue and Course of Study*, 1901, 5-7.

41　Francis W. Parker, *Talks on Pedagogics* (New York: A. S. Barnes and Company, 1909), 387.

42　Francis W. Parker, *Talks on Teaching* (New York: A. S. Barnes and Company, 1883), 161.

43　Catherine Chambers, "And Furthermore, Hattie, You're Retiring Too," in Stone, *Between Home and Community,* 96.

44　Joan Kearns, "Mary C. Davis: A Distinguished Teacher," in Stone, *Between Home and Community,* 95.

45　John Holabird, "Educating Incoming Angels to Behave Properly for Infinity," in Stone, *Between Home and Community,* 100-101.

46　Unless otherwise indicated, information in this section is drawn from the 1929 Parker *Catalogue and Course of Study.*

47　*Experience in English Composition and Literature, Vol. II: Grades IX-XII* (Chicago: Francis W. Parker School, 1934), 407-422.

48　*Experience in English , Vol. II.*, 456-457.

49　The Faculty of the Francis W. Parker School, "The Pupil's Experience in Arithmetic," in Stone, *Between Home and Community*, 180.

50　Parker, *Pedagogics,* 223-224, 27.

51　Unless otherwise indicated, information in this section is drawn from the 1906 and 1929 Parker *Catalogue and Course of Study*.

52　*Experience in English Composition ,* 209.

53　Parker, *Pedagogics,* 227.

54　*Studies in Education, Vol. I: The Social Motive in School Work* (Chicago: Francis W. Parker School, June 1912), 11, 53, 77-96, 74, 97-103.

55　*Studies in Education, Vol. II: The Morning Exercise as a Socializing Influence* (Chicago: Francis W. Parker School, 1913), 1, 4, 199-207, 189-197.

56　*Studies in Education, Vol. III: Expression as a Means of Training Motive* (Chicago: Francis W. Parker School, 1914), 11-14, 19.

57　*Studies in Education, Vol. IV: Education Through Concrete Expression* (Chicago: Francis W. Parker School, 1915), introduction, 1-3.

58 *Studies in Education, Vol. VI: The Individual and the Curriculum* (Chicago, Francis W. Parker School, 1920), 3.

59 *Studies in Education, Vol. VIII: Creative Effort* (Chicago, Francis W. Parker School, 1925), 166-176, 161.

60 *Studies in Education: The Course in History* (Chicago: Francis W. Parker School, 1923), 3.

61 John Dewey, "Progressive Education and the Science of Education," in Martin S. Dworkin, *Dewey on Education* (New York: Bureau of Publications, Teachers College, Columbia University, 1959), 125.

62 1929 *Catalogue*, 66,12.

63 Parker, *Pedagogics*, 284-285.

64 Parker, *Pedagogics,* 285.

65 Flora Cooke, address to seniors, 1927, Cooke Collection, Chicago Historical Society, Box 5, folder 36.

66 Campbell, *Children's Crusade,* 117.

67 1929 Parker *Catalogue*, 174.

68 Unless otherwise indicated, information for this section is drawn from the 1901, 1906, and 1929 Parker *Catalogue and Course of Study.*

69 Jack Ellison, "The Strength and Grace of a Clearly Held Position," Stone, *Between Home and Community*, 94.

70 Ellison, "Strength and Grace," Stone, *Between*, 93-94, 293; *Parker Magazine*, Winter 1992.

71 Unless otherwise indicated, information in this section is drawn from the Parker *Recorder*, Vol. 3 and 5; the Parker *Weekly*, Vol. 5-24; and the Parker *Record*, 1916-1934.

72 Cooke, "Morning Exercise," January 18, 1922, Cooke Collection, Chicago Historical Society, Box 5, Folder 30.

73 *Weekly,* volumes 14, 22; *Parker Record* 1925, 1930.

74 1927 *Parker Record,* 14-15.

75 Survey of Alumni, October 24, 1922; Cooke Collection, Chicago Historical Society.

Chapter 7: The Stabilizing Years (1935-1965)

1 Diane Ravitch, *The Troubled Crusade: American Education 1945-1980* (New York: Basic Books, 1983), 43, 78.

2 Ravitch, *Troubled Crusade*, 52.

3   John Dewey, *Experience and Education* (New York: Collier, 1963), 21-30, 64-65, 69.

4   Ravitch, *Troubled Crusade,* 79.

5   Paul Woodring, *Let's Talk Sense About Our Schools* (New York: McGraw-Hill, 1953).

6   Charles Sellers and Henry May, *A Synopsis of American History* (Chicago: Rand McNally & Company, 1963), 345-349, 359.

7   Eric Goldman, *The Crucial Decade: America, 1945-1955* (Alfred Knopf, New York, 1959), 66.

8   Ravitch, *Troubled Crusade,* 13-14.

9   John Gardner, *Excellence: Can We Be Equal and Excellent Too?* (New York: Harper, 1961).

10 James Conant, *The American High School Today: A First Report to Interested Citizens* (New York: McGraw-Hill, 1959).

11 Jerome Bruner, *The Process of Education* (Cambridge, MA: Harvard University Press, 1966).

12 Ravitch, *Troubled Crusade,* 148-149.

13 Goldman, *Crucial Decade,* 12.

14 Goldman, *Crucial Decade,* 7.

15 Goldman, *Crucial Decade,* 13.

16 Goldman, *Crucial Decade,* 183.

17 Unless otherwise indicated, information in this section is drawn from the Minutes of the Francis W. Parker School Board of Trustees from 1935 to 1965.

18 Richard Bentley, "Remarks to the Annual Meeting of the Parents Association," May 22, 1933; in Marie Kirchner Stone, *Between Home and Community* (Chicago: Francis W. Parker School, 1976), 62.

19 Bentley, "Remarks," 64-65.

20 "The Future of the Francis W. Parker School: Report and Recommendations of Parents' Committee," February 6, 1934, 17, 5.

21 *American Bar Association Journal,* July, 1961, 693; *Chicago Sun Times,* Wednesday, June 10, 1970.

22 Alice Judson Ryerson Hayes, letter to author, October 5, 1999.

23 Marshall Holleb, letter to author, December 8, 1999.

24 Board minutes; John M. Rau, letter to author, October 1, 1999.

25 Richard Freeman, interview by author, September 29, 1999.

26 John A. Holabird, Jr., letter to author, September 22, 1999.

27 David Silberman, interview by author, October 19, 1999.

28 Holabird, letter to author.

29 Board Minutes, March 7, 1936, November 21, 1936, February 3, 1939, January 4, 1936, May 9, 1941, June 9, 1951.

30 Report of the Francis W. Parker School Educational Committee, 1932-1957.

31 Wilford M. Aikin, *The Story of the Eight-Year Study, with Conclusions and Recommendations* (New York: Harper & Brothers, 1942), viii.

32 Herbert Smith, "The Francis W. Parker School Historical Statement," 1957-1958, 12.

33 Nancy Miller Wynne, "Dear Grandchild," in Stone, *Between Home and Community*, 47.

34 Board minutes, October 3, 1942, June 30, 1943, June 3, 1950.

35 Smith, *Historical Statement,* 8.

36 Marshal Holleb, in *Memorial Booklet* (Chicago: Francis W. Parker School, 1967), Chicago Historical Society.

37 Cleveland Thomas, Opening Faculty Meeting Speech, Francis W. Parker School, 1966, 1-5.

38 *Memorial Booklet.*

39 Jack Ellison, Marshall Holleb, and Helen LaCroix, Registrar, in *Memorial Booklet.*

40 Helen LaCroix, "Dr. Cleveland A. Thomas," in Stone, *Between Home and Community*, 49.

41 *Time* Magazine, "Progressively Progressive," June 8, 1962.

42 Ida B. DePencier, *The History of the Laboratory Schools* (Chicago: Quadrangle Books, 1967),127.

43 Aikin, *The Story of the Eight-Year Study*, 110.

44 Author interviews with Ralph W. Tyler, February-June 1994.

45 *Adventure in American Education, Vol. V: Thirty Schools Tell Their Story,* 296.

46 *Thirty Schools,* 296-299.

47 James Mitchell, "The Discussion of Human Relations through Films," Progressive Education Association 1939, 309.

48 *Thirty Schools,* 313.

49 Duane Barnes, "Experimental Work in Modern Language," *Reports*, 1937.

50   *Thirty Schools*, 311.
51   *Reports of Experimental Work,* 1936-1937, 1937-1938, 1938-1939, 1939-1940, 1940-1941 (Chicago: Francis W. Parker School).
52   *Thirty Schools,* 317-319.
53   Aikin, *Eight-Year Study,* 111-112.
54   Dean Chamberlin, Enid Chamberlin, Neal E. Drought, William E. Scott, *Adventure in American Education, Vol. Four: Did They Succeed in College?* (New York: Harper & Brothers, 1942), 177-182.
55   Smith, *Historical Statement,* 27.
56   Marie Kirchner Stone, *Ralph W. Tyler's Principles of Curriculum, Instruction and Evaluation: Past Influences and Present Effects* (Ph.D. dissertation, Loyola University, Chicago, 1985), 70, 47.
57   Kate Holliday, "If You Are a Teacher, You Can't Be Anything Else," in Stone, *Between Home and Community*, 90-91.
58   Chauncey Griffith, "Recollections of Music at Parker 1935-1972"; Robert Ashenhurst, "Parker Reminiscence—Chauncey Griffith," in Stone, *Between Home and Community*, 256-260.
59   Mark Martin, remarks at Lynn Martin Memorial Service; Lynn Martin, "Fourth Grade," in Stone, *Between Home and Community*, 167.
60   Jan Wolff Bensdorf '65, "Barney Negronida," in Stone, *Between Home and Community*, 152-153.
61   Parker, *Pedagogics,* 447-448.
62   Smith, *Historical Statement,* 12.
63   Unless otherwise indicated, information in this section is drawn from *The Weekly* Vol. 24 to 57 and the 1937, 1942, 1948, 1951, and 1955 Parker *Record.*
64   Smith, *Historical Record,* 18, 21-26.
65   Smith, *Historical Record,* 30, 29.
66   Stone, *Between Home and Community*, 110-111.

Chapter 8: Challenges to Progressive Education (1965-1995)

1   Christopher Lasch, *The Culture of Narcissism* (New York: W.W. Norton, 1979), 116-117.
2   Diane Ravitch, *The Troubled Crusade* (New York: Basic Books, Inc., 1983), 165.

3   Bernard Grun, *The Timetables of History: A Horizontal Linkage of People and Events* (New York: Simon and Schuster, 1975), 560.

4   Ravitch, *Crusade*, 227.

5   Ravitch, *Crusade*, 229.

6   Ravitch, *Crusade,* 149, 159.

7   James Traub, "Schools Are Not the Answer," *New York Times Magazine*, January 16, 2000, 55.

8   Ravitch, *Crusade,* 258.

9   Susan Hasazi, Paul D. Rice, Robert York, *Mainstreaming: Merging Regular and Special Education* (Bloomington, IN: Phi Delta Kappa Education Foundation, 1979), 6.

10 Michael Myers, "I Missed Mr. Ellison," in Stone, *Between Home and Community*, 50; Alumni interviews by author, April 1996.

11 Jack Ellison, interview by author, April 1996.

12 Faculty interviews by author, April 1996.

13 Minutes of the Francis W. Parker Board of Trustees, November 1969.

14 Ellison, interview by author, April 1996.

15 William D. Geer, interview by author, January 1997.

16 Barry Munitz, Ph.D., Munitz Report, Final Draft, December 1982, 15.

17 Board Minutes, 1986-1987.

18 John Cotton, Personal Statement to Francis W. Parker School, 1993.

19 A college admissions officer to Dr. Bernard Markwell, Spring 1995.

20 Unless otherwise indicated, information in this section is drawn from the Minutes of the Francis W. Parker School Board of Trustees, 1965-1995.

21 Farwell Smith, letter to author, March 13, 1999.

22 Renee Kreeger Gelman, letter to author, December 8, 1999.

23 Irving Stenn, letter to author, January 15, 2000.

24 David Heller, interview by Sally Eley, October, 1985.

25 Heller, letter to Parker School community, January 21, 1983.

26 Munitz Report, 7-9.

27 Munitz Report, 1-23.

28 Barry Munitz, Ph.D., Munitz Report, introductory observations, Preliminary Report, August 1981.

29 Larry Cuban, "Roles and Responsibilities: Report of Larry Cuban to the Educational Council," May 1984, 6.

30 King Harris, letter to author, March 17, 1999.

31 Robert G. Krupka, letter to author, March 1999.

32 Minutes of the Francis W. Parker Educational Council, October 27, 1970.

33 Information in this section is drawn from written reports submitted by the nine visitors, collected in "Reports on Parker School," Parker School Archives.

34 Maryanne Kalin-Miller, "The Lower School Science Perspective," Francis W. Parker School Curriculum Reports, 1976-1977.

35 Lil Lowry, "Physical Education and Integration with Other Activities," Curriculum Reports, 1976-77.

36 John Sherman, Curriculum Reports, 1976-1977.

37 Susan Anderson and Allison Abbott, "Awareness," Curriculum Reports 1976-1977.

38 Ayana Pressley, "Interview with Mrs. Greenberg," student paper, January 1992; Beverly Greenberg, letter to Stone, February 22, 2000.

39 Matthew Olins and Jonathan Singer, "Interview with Allison Abbott," student paper, March 1992.

40 Josh Koppel and Jason Berlin, "The Many Hats of Harriet Cholden," student paper, 1991; Harriet Cholden, letter to author, August 1999.

41 Marie Kirchner Stone, "Group Reading Project at the Francis W. Parker School," Curriculum Report, 1972.

42 Terri Schroeder, "Middle School Electives," in Stone, *Between Home and Community*, 204-206.

43 Rosemary L. Bray, *Unafraid of the Dark* (New York: Random House, 1998).

44 Catherine Chambers Haskins, letter to author, February 12, 2000.

45 Michael Feiertag and Joseph Brody, "Lee Dreuth, Man of the 90s, 80s, 70s, and So On," student paper, December 1991.

46 Tony Frenzel and Nash Furhman, "Reading Underwater," student paper, January 1992; interview by author, August 15, 1999.

47 William Duffy, letter to author, October 1, 1999.

48 Bonnie Seebold, letter to author, September 5, 1999.

49 "Library," ISACS/North Central Evaluation Self-Study, 1998, 98.

50 "Library," ISACS/North Central Evaluation Self-Study, 1984.

51 Emily Shelton and Wendy Rubin, "Stone's Office Is Grand Central Station," student paper, 1990; Caitlin Hunt and Stephanie Spencer, "The Jack of All Trades," student paper, 1991; 1969 Parker *Record*.

52 1984 Parker *Record.*

53 Rebecca Rossof, letter to author, September 2, 1999.

54 Andrea Gabor, *Parker* magazine, Fall 1996, 57; Bernard Markwell, letter to author August 23, 1999.

55 Marsha Brumleve Wagner, letter to author, November 12, 1999.

56 Lyndee Yamsbon and Regan Coin, "The Lily of this Valley," school project videotape, January 16, 1991; Lil Lowry Manning, letter to author, September 3, 1999.

57 Jenny Sorkin, "To Stay in an Old Movie for Over Two Decades," student paper, 1991; Roger Gleason, letter to author, January 2000.

58 Thomas Campbell, "George Barr McCutcheon," *Parker* magazine, Winter 1992, 20.

59 J.C. Moylen "Kaplan interview," student paper, 1993; 1989 Parker *Record.*

60 Anne Marie Fries, interview with author, June 29, 2000.

61 Jane McGwinn, letter to author, April 26, 2000.

62 Ericka Kons and Megan Pussilano, "The Mother of Francis W. Parker School," student paper, June 1991.

63 Unless otherwise indicated, information in this section is drawn from *The Weekly* Vol. 58-75 and the Parker *Record,* 1965-1995.

64 Nancy Ettelson, "A Change of Pace," in Stone, *Between Home and Community*, 207.

65 Katie Fox, "Parker after Hours," in Stone, *Between Home and Community*, 343.

Chapter 9: Toward the New Millennium (1995-2001)

1 Minutes of the Francis W. Parker School Educational Council, November 18, 1994; Daniel Frank, interview by author, May 2000.

2 Minutes of the Long-Range Planning Committee, 1995.

3 Minutes of the Francis W. Parker School Board of Trustees, 1995-2000.

Index

History of Schools and Schooling

THIS SERIES EXPLORES THE HISTORY OF SCHOOLS AND SCHOOLING in the United States and other countries. Books in this series examine the historical development of schools and educational processes, with special emphasis on issues of educational policy, curriculum and pedagogy, as well as issues relating to race, class, gender, and ethnicity. Special emphasis will be placed on the lessons to be learned from the past for contemporary educational reform and policy. Although the series will publish books related to education in the broadest societal and cultural context, it especially seeks books on the history of specific schools and on the lives of educational leaders and school founders.

For additional information about this series or for the submission of manuscripts, please contact the general editors:

Alan R. Sadovnik
Rutgers University-Newark
Education Dept.
155 Conklin Hall
175 University Avenue
Newark, NJ 07102

Susan F. Semel
Curriculum and Teaching Dept.
243 Gallon Wing
Hofstra University
Hempstead, NY 11550

To order other books in this series, please contact our Customer Service Department:

800-770-LANG (within the U.S.)
212-647-7706 (outside the U.S.)
212-647-7707 FAX

Or browse online by series at:

www.peterlangusa.com